Foundations of Primary Teaching

Third edition

Foundations of Primary Teaching

Third edition

Denis Hayes

 David Fulton Publishers

David Fulton Publishers Ltd
The Chiswick Centre, 414 Chiswick High Road, London W4 5TF

www.fultonpublishers.co.uk

First edition published in Great Britain in 1996 by David Fulton Publishers
Second edition published 1999
Third edition published 2004

10 9 8 7 6 5 4 3 2 1

Note: The right of the Denis Hayes to be identified as the author of this work has been asserted by him in accordance with the Copyright, Designs and Patents Act 1988.

David Fulton Publishers is a division of Granada Learning Limited, part of ITV plc.

British Library Cataloguing in Publication Data
A catalogue record for this book is available from the British Library.

ISBN 1-84312-131-X

Typeset by FiSH Books, London
Printed and bound in Great Britain

Contents

Preface

The content of a book about education and classroom life relies on many sources, including the author's thoughts and ideas, the effect of countless experiences and the combined wisdom and influence of colleagues, past and present. The content of *Foundations of Primary Teaching* is no exception. While the responsibility for what is contained in the book is entirely my own, I want to acknowledge the help and assistance of teachers, students and tutors associated with the Faculty of Education (Rolle), University of Plymouth, whose insights and practical advice have been of immense value. I have tried very hard to give credit to all the direct sources of information that I have used and quoted. If there are instances where this has not been explicit, I will do my best to ensure that it is remedied in any reprinted edition. In particular, I want to thank my colleagues Jeff Lewis for writing on Inclusion and Peter Noon for contributing the section on ICT. Thanks are also due to Gareth Parry of the University of Ulster for writing the chapter on Working Within the Law. The expert contributions of all three have been a major factor in enhancing the quality of the third edition of the book.

It is my earnest hope that *Foundations* will prove to be of some assistance to everyone who reads it. In this way, I shall feel that I am repaying in part something of the many benefits that I have accrued from the knowledge and guidance of others throughout my professional life.

I dedicate this third edition to my son Stephen, my daughter Kerensa and to the memory of my late son, Richard, whose death in the Democratic Republic of Congo at the age of nineteen was so influential in helping me to get life and eternity in perspective.

Introduction

Schools are about people

People matter. They matter because regardless of the quality of the education system, the level of training, the height of test achievements and the accolades that follow academic success, prosperity in its richest sense ultimately depends upon the way that people relate, respond and use the knowledge they possess. People matter because education is not principally about helping governments to meet targets or fulfil their political aspirations or even about guaranteeing a job and an income or to satisfy parents and other stakeholders. These goals are worthy ones but they pale in comparison with the main aim of education, which is to create a civilised, moral and contented society. Most teachers are in the job because they want to make the world a better place. Such sentiments may sit uneasily within the materialistic, statistics-driven and competitive emphasis that dominates present thinking, but they need to be reactivated if children are to fulfil their true potential as human beings.

Foundations of Primary Teaching is based on a belief that the role of the teacher is complex and that the job of teaching cannot be compressed into a set of standards or statements, however carefully presented or convincingly portrayed. Rather, real-life issues associated with confidence, self-assurance, sensitivity and empathy must be seen to be of fundamental significance for a full and comprehensive education. The book deals with many practical and pragmatic elements with which every teacher needs to be familiar. However, it also seeks to promote a fuller understanding and appreciation of the ways in which concerns for the people involved and the strategies for planning and implementing a curriculum are mutually dependent. *Foundations* is posited on a belief that a full education consists of considerably more than a set of grades and exam passes, however laudable they may be. Care, compassion, understanding, informed tolerance and a deep appreciation of the beauty that surrounds us are just as much part of the educative process as the formal curriculum. The barren philosophy of 'anything goes' and 'me first' has been exposed as a dangerous illusion. Sensitivity, creativity and liberation to fulfil our destinies and help others to fulfil their own are back on the agenda as the hallmark of a truly educated person.

The content of this book will not surprise anyone associated with primary schools. Part One considers the role and significance of the many different persons associated with school: children, teachers, parents, support staff. Part Two examines the strategies necessary for successful teaching and learning: learning styles, teaching skills, classroom management, assessment, recording and reporting, behaviour management and inclusion issues. Part Three discusses the induction year, working within the law, and career development. The main themes for each chapter are summarised in an introduction and there are a number of 'Activate your thinking' and 'Good Practice' boxes to stimulate further consideration of key issues and their implementation. To assist with the task of monitoring progress through the Standards for qualified teacher status (QTS) as described in DfES/TTA 2002, the relevant standards are listed at the end of each chapter, together with a case study and suggestions for further reading. Details of specific curriculum subjects do not form a major part of *Foundations*. All names used are fictitious and some details have been altered to protect identity.

The book has been written in the belief that teaching and learning is only possible in a school climate where everyone's rights are respected, responsibility for oneself and others is encouraged, and the promotion of positive images of self-worth, potential and belonging are central to the process. Although it is important to develop systems and plans for the curriculum, present them in the classroom, monitor and assess them and use the results to improve achievement, the real world of teaching and learning is far messier, less linear and more unpredictable than a simple action plan implies. Structure in teaching and learning is preferable to chaos, of course, but account must also be taken of the school context, the personalities of those involved and the need for emotional safeguards, especially for vulnerable children and busy teachers (whose welfare is also important). No amount of strategy or managerial system will be effective if emotional wellbeing is neglected, as frightened, insecure or disillusioned people, whether adults or children, have little hope of achieving their potential, fulfilling their goals or responding to the opportunities presented to them. Whether pupil, teacher, assistant, parent or head teacher, everyone needs encouragement, affirmation and the belief that they are valued. Learning resides as much in the heart as it does in the head. It is not uniform in character, but like the waves of the sea creeping up a beach, ebbs and flows in unexpected ways with times of calm and moments of unexpected and thrilling progress. And you are now a part of this exciting world.

Terminology used in the book

Trainee teacher:	Someone following a recognised route into teaching. In a one-year PCGE course in the United Kingdom, students spend 18 weeks in the classroom. In a four-year BEd course, they spend 32 weeks.
Newly qualified teacher (NQT):	Someone in the first year of qualified teaching.
Inexperienced teacher:	Someone with limited classroom experience.
Experienced teacher:	Someone with several years purposeful teaching experience who has been willing to continue learning about the job.

Supervising teacher:	An experienced teacher in whose classroom trainee teachers are based for their school placement.
Host teacher:	A teacher who works in the placement school.
Tutor:	Someone with direct responsibility for guiding trainees.
Mentor:	The teacher with responsibility for a trainee teacher's school experience, including regular assessment of their teaching ability.
Teaching Assistant:	A paid employee who supports the work of teachers

The best job in the world

Trainee teachers come from different backgrounds and are motivated in different ways. However, the following quotations are typical of many:

> In truth, I never had any life long ambition about teaching (except in childhood games when I almost always played the part). My mum is a teacher and I would often go into school to help her out whenever I was at home from college. I got on really well with the children. They were so lively and enthusiastic, made me laugh and were a source of joy. I've never felt the kind of exhaustion I felt after coming back from a day spent with 5–7 year olds. It was quite alarming but also felt like a reward for a job well done. Then suddenly the penny dropped that I could be a teacher too if I wanted to be. And I did!
>
> *Shima*

> Initially I worked in advertising and worked my way up to the position of manager by opening up a lot of business with large organisations. However, I wasn't happy in the job and had to make the very hard decision of giving up this very well paid employment to pursue a career that would be more rewarding. At this point I started to think about the possibility of teaching. After talking the matter through with many teachers, including my mum, two aunts and many friends, I decided to do three weeks as a voluntary classroom assistant in two schools with very different catchment areas. Nothing could have reinforced my decision to leave the advertising industry more! I loved my time in the schools and decided that teaching was the only job for me.
>
> *Archie*

Studies of the dominant motivating factors that influence people to select primary teaching as a career point to the importance of altruistic and romantic notions of the job, but with a stern realism threaded between. People often choose to train as teachers because they like children and have enjoyed working with them in a voluntary capacity. Factors such as salary, holidays, job security and status in society are also attractions, but the principal motivator is the opportunity to exercise a positive influence over children's lives through contributing positively to their education. When asked why they had selected teaching as a career, responses included:

I needed to find a career that would give me the chance to make a positive difference to children's lives.

You can make a real difference. It is a very challenging yet rewarding career.

What other job is more important? Without teachers you would not have any other professions.

I am motivated by knowing I can give the children opportunity, fun and success in the classroom and outside world.

Trainee primary teachers are also interested in the self-satisfaction that they extract from the job. They want a career that offers variety and fulfilment, opens up avenues for learning and is engrossing, not tedious. In a wide-ranging survey, Spear *et al.* (2000) found that those associated with job satisfaction were (in order of priority) the chance to work with children, relating to colleagues, and developing warm personal relationships with pupils. The second selection of students' comments listed below provides a reminder of how powerful these motivating factors are:

I love the sense of achievement you get from working with the children and teaching them.

I feel I just know this is what I want to do and my decision to teach was my own from the heart.

Children offer enthusiasm that adults cannot!

Being a teacher is one of the most rewarding and satisfying jobs that you can do, and I can't think of anything I want to do more than to teach.

People decide to train as teachers because they are passionate about doing the job (Day 2004). The description offered by the Teacher Training Agency (TTA) in England summarises the position well:

Teaching is like no other job. It is as inspiring, challenging and unique as each child you teach. It's a career that genuinely does make a difference.

No two children are the same. No two days are the same. You have the privilege of opening doors to learning, to turning children on to lifelong interests.

(TTA website 2003 http://www.useyourheadteach.gov.uk)

Your development as a teacher should start from day one and continue until the end of your career. The more that you can engage with issues and think through their practical implications, the more likely that over time they will have an impact upon your working practice. The journey will not always be a smooth one. Some trainee teachers find that it is not until they have their own class that they can begin to implement their personal priorities, and even then the situation is not always straightforward, for school policies may not accommodate their aspirations. Nevertheless, the principle of interacting with teaching and learning issues rather than being a passive recipient of other people's wisdom (however helpful this may be) should characterise your approach. There are four elements to effective development as you train for teaching:

- To learn from every situation
- To commit to memory key principles
- To ask probing questions about the things you are told and observe
- To transform your thinking into action.

On the understanding that it is important to be clear about our own beliefs and values in education, it is essential to interrogate why things happen the way that they do in school and what principles underpin them.

When they first go into school, it is a source of amazement for many trainee teachers that experienced teachers seem to cope with classroom life so effortlessly, to respond spontaneously to the constant demands upon their time and to always make the best use of learning opportunities with the children. Resources seem to be in the right place at the right time, children do as they are told (usually) and the working atmosphere is purposeful and calm. Inexperienced teachers find it hard to believe that they will eventually become like their experienced colleagues and fear that they face many years of trial-and-error, setbacks and mistakes before they can achieve similar success. The belief that 'there's no gain without pain' can be a daunting thought for all but the most highly committed.

On the other hand, the path to fulfilment in teaching does not have to be tortuous. Although mistakes are part of the learning process and confidence levels may pitch from one extreme to another, it is important to acknowledge that there are strategies available to shorten the time needed to reach competence. While it is true that there is no substitute for hard-earned experience, this book is written to help trainee and newly qualified teachers to enjoy success in the job as quickly and completely as possible.

Further reading

Arthur, J., Davison, J. and Lewis, M. (2004) *Professional Values and Practice: Achieving the Standards for QTS*, London: RoutledgeFalmer.
The authors use the eight standards from the General Teaching Council as the basis for their book.
Hayes, D. (2003) *Planning, Teaching and Class Management in Primary Schools*, London: David Fulton.
The book contains a systematic but flexible description of how to meet the standards for QTS, with numerous practical examples and suggestions.
O'Hara, M. (2004) *Teaching 3–8: Meeting the Standards for initial teacher training and induction*, London: Continuum.
The book provides an overview of the professional and practical requirements needed for work with children in the early years.

People in School

1

The Children

Introduction

This chapter is about the way in which children experience school and the important adult–child and child–child relationships that constitute such an important element of their lives. It also addresses the realities of school for children, especially the impact of friendships, behaviour and success and failure on their emotional and educational wellbeing.

A child's view of the world

School is an important element of children's lives and although they may not know or understand everything that happens in it, they are aware of a great deal more than some adults give them credit for. Children may not express their views openly to teachers but they do have insights about school life that affect their attitude to work as they interpret (and misinterpret) situations and circumstances (Pollard and Filer, 1996; Alderson 1999). As an evaluation of school effectiveness is enhanced by asking those most intimately involved in the process, teachers who make a habit of inviting children to express their views are often surprised by the perceptiveness and certainty of their comments. One teacher asked the nine- and ten-year-old children in his class to comment on the most significant event that happened during the past term. Several children referred to the class outings, another to the sports' day, but Yvette, a bright girl with a mischievous smile was happy to share her most vivid memory:

> I remember when you came into the room carrying a pile of books and looking angry. You slammed the books down on the desk, went red in the face and told us that you were ashamed of what another teacher had told you about our behaviour in the playground.

Oh dear! Hopefully there were more positive events that Yvette stored in her memory, too. Nevertheless, teachers need to be sensitive to the varied experiences of being a pupil in school and the things that they remember and relish. There are many aspects of school that children enjoy. They like to have access to friends, to learn interesting things, and to feel part of a community. They like to enjoy the work they do and have some fun. Children are very happy when they have opportunity to do something practical or go outside to study. All children get excited when adults share ideas with them, take an interest in their life beyond the school fence and celebrate their smallest achievements. Children like to get praise from adults they respect (but not from ones they resent) and receive external reward for their efforts (such as certificates and merit cards). Children like teachers who have a sense of humour but are not cynical, and are fascinated when they watch grown-ups behaving in a slightly frivolous way. Nearly all children enjoy games, competitions and puzzles. They love to draw, paint, create things from materials and work with others to produce models and murals. Children are happiest when they feel secure and are clear about what is permissible and what is proscribed. They respond best when they feel that they are being treated like important individuals and not as 'articles' to be taught, tested and processed through the school system.

There are also many things in school that children dislike intensely. They hate to be unfairly accused of something, especially when the adult concerned has jumped to an unwarranted conclusion or refused to give them time to explain the situation. Children also get irritated if they ask the teacher a question and are scolded for doing so or told that they should have listened in the first place. Teachers who show favouritism are particularly disliked by children, who become resentful if they perceive that one child gets away with something that another child is punished for doing. This perception is difficult to avoid when the adult takes account of a child's past history and temperament when making a decision about appropriate action, and modifies the sanction as a result. Consequently, two children may be treated rather differently for the same misdemeanour or one may be given a privilege ahead of the other. Unsurprisingly, children are not impressed when they are moaned at by a teacher for working slowly when they are doing their best to be conscientious. Children have little time for teachers who are always serious and those who use an artificial or unnatural voice, especially if it comes across as patronising. While schools do not exist for the sole purpose of keeping its pupils happy, it is a long established principle that children who have a positive view of the situation are more likely to learn effectively than those who have negative ones. Fortunately, studies show that the vast majority of children are contented with their experiences of primary school.

Salo (2002) carried out research into adult's memories of their time in school and discovered that they recalled incidents that probably seemed trivial to the teacher at the time, but burned deeply into the child's consciousness. Respondents remembered these critical moments in detail, including the teacher's clothes, the expression on their faces and the teacher's scent. In particular, moments of humiliation and guilt were powerfully engraved into the mind, as were times of delight and shared pleasures. Teachers bear a heavy responsibility to ensure that we offer children a secure learning climate and, in cases where they have to be disciplined or admonished, to do so with forbearance and in moderation.

Children need to be allowed to behave like children and not like mini-adults. The opportunity to mix with their friends, have the occasional giggle and feel good about themselves is a means of promoting a purposeful learning environment, enhancing creativity and generating a sense of enjoyment (Jones and Wyse 2004). Adults working with children need to remember that young lives are directly affected by their experiences outside the school as well as in it. Children who arrive at school in an emotionally or physically distressed condition are unlikely to make the most of their opportunities in school and deserve sensitive treatment, even when they are unco-operative. Similarly, a child who has a birthday or a special event is bound to be more excitable than usual and may behave out of character. Illness and disappointment can also take its toll, as children struggle to concentrate and apply themselves to their work. Sudden dips in performance may be due to children failing to work hard enough but can also be due to extrinsic factors over which they have little control. Wise teachers are alert to such possibilities.

In a very small number of cases, children may be aware of a conflict between home and school over learning priorities, allocation to a particular ability group, amounts of homework, lost or damaged clothing, personal possessions, and so forth. Children can feel trapped between their loyalty for a parent and a teacher, especially if negative things are attributed to the school by the parent with which a child is uneasy. As a trainee teacher in the school it is important to refer to the class teacher any adverse comments that a parent might make to you about an aspect of school life but, as far as possible, not to take it personally. Similarly, it is important to pass on any commending comments that parents make. Being told that their efforts are recognised and appreciated can uplift struggling and weary colleagues.

Finally, all children have moments of anxiety about things that may appear trivial to adults, who have a much fuller grasp of what is going on. Factors such as friendship patterns, anxieties about rougher children, fear of humiliation in front of the rest of the class, embarrassment about getting changed for PE, dread of the water in swimming and being labelled as slow, can all disturb and worry a child. Older children are anxious not to lose face and desperately want to be included with the majority group. This desire to be included explains in part the 'gang' culture that pertains among those of junior age. Younger children nearly always want someone to play with, though occasionally an aloof child may be insistent about being left alone. Regardless of age, all children want to be valued, respected and treated fairly. Whether you are training to be a teacher or have a class of your own, the same principles apply:

- To avoid favouring one group of children over others on the basis of background, ethnicity or home circumstances
- To help children assimilate and understand school conventions
- To understand that one measure that parents use to judge a school's success is their child's happiness
- To make allowance for lively, assertive children as much as for passive, compliant ones
- To reassure parents that the school and the teachers are working in the children's interests

Many schools work hard to include the children in decision-making and give them a 'voice' through the use of school councils and the like. Opportunities also exist each day to ask children what they think, canvass their views and demonstrate an interest in their opinions. The thinking behind this kind of approach is that if pupils are invited to contribute to the decision-making process, then certain advantages accrue, namely that they will:

- have a sense of ownership about decisions that affect them;
- behave more responsibly;
- offer a fresh perspective on situations; and
- provide suggestions about improving the school that are of genuine value.

Children do not always understand what is happening to them at school or why it is necessary. They will not feel pleased or agree with every decision. Their opinions will sometimes be distorted because of their own prejudices or those of adults at home. Nevertheless, part of the great privilege of being a teacher is to delve into the 'secret world of the child' and discover its hidden treasures.

Activate your thinking!

Consider the following questions that a child might be asking:

- Will I make friends?
- Is the teacher strict?
- Will the work be hard?
- Will I get bored?
- Can I sit where I want to?
- Will we do fun things?
- Will we go on trips?
- Can I bring toys to school?

All sorts of children

Effective teachers are professional observers of children (Sharman *et al.* 2000). See Monica, smartly dressed, climbing out of the family car. Her quality clothes and relaxed manner bear testimony to the secure and consistent life that she enjoys. Watch as she runs into school, confident that whatever the day holds for her, there is the safety of home and family awaiting her return. Then see Charley as she wanders alone through the school gate shortly after eight o'clock, still bewildered by the experiences of the previous night: the strange adult behaviour, the responsibility for younger brothers and sisters, the disturbed sleep, the early morning wakening and the temporary lodgings. How will Charley view school life today? As a haven, perhaps, and a chance to escape from the grimness of life in the outside world. Perhaps the harsh words that greeted her when she was scarcely awake will fade from her mind and heart as she now experiences kindness and patience. In school Charley will find sensitive and caring adults who will provide security through clearly explained rules, interesting and relevant work and the authority to protect her from the playground bully. Charley can relax now.

Both Monica and Charley enter the school. Both remove their coats, chat to friends, walk towards the classroom door. They notice teachers, parents, pictures on walls. Their noses tingle at the mixed smells of floor polish, plasticine, damp clothing, and toilets. They sit down on a carpet or line up at a door, answer to their names, respond to a request or command. The familiar sounds of teachers' voices issue instructions; the children are sensitive to tonal patterns and intonation. They recognise when teachers are cross, sad, bored or pretending, and modify their behaviour accordingly.

The day begins and the bum-numbing effects of assembly are replaced by work sessions and activities. Playtimes and mealtimes provide relief from classroom work. The children disappear into the frantic world of games, chasing, arguments, intensive relationships, erratic behaviours and unpredictable weather. They wonder about the paradoxes of school life: why teachers insist that they wear a coat when it isn't cold or enthuse that going outside is good for them when it is obviously miserable and damp. They see the teachers disappearing into the warmth and security of the staffroom and catch the odd snippet of conversation, wave of laughter, smell of coffee.

As each playtime ends, a few children hanker for a turn to knock on the staffroom door, return a teacup and inform the disappointed teachers that Miss Jenkins says that it's in-time (an expression used only in primary schools). The day continues. A hall-time offers chance for some fun ... if teacher allows. The end-of-afternoon story draws children and teacher together, and soon home-time heralds the end of another school day. Coats are pulled off pegs or scrambled for on the floor; odd gloves mysteriously disappear and reappear; accusations over property and other disputes reverberate down the corridors. Mothers, fathers and grandparents are there to pick up the children, ask brightly about the day, exchange a word with the teacher, flash a smiling 'thank you' and head for home. Monica skips off happily, keen to tell mum about her successes and show off her new reading book. Charley edges out of the room, casting a hopeful glance at the teacher, before moving away to pick up her younger brothers and sisters, and usher them along the pavements to the local shop to buy them a snack for tea. The teacher gives Charley a reassuring smile and wink: *Take care, Charley. See you tomorrow*. Charley can hardly wait for tomorrow to come: *Goodbye Miss*.

A few minutes later the welter of bodies has subsided. Children melt into the anonymity of their own lives, although a few linger, savouring the last moments of the school atmosphere, swinging their bags around their heads in joyful abandon before racing to the entrance with a whoop and a yell. In the distance, a few others are heard excitedly anticipating the after-school football or netball practice, impatiently waiting for the teacher. Children leave but the teachers remain, engaged in a variety of planning, administrative and organisational tasks that parents and pupils know little about.

Classrooms are mainly about teaching and learning, but effectiveness depends upon pupils being in the right frame of mind to participate in their education, well motivated and convinced that the effort is worthwhile. Classroom activity can be a mirage. Busy children may or may not be engaged in learning; for no amount of coercion can match a child's genuine desire to succeed. Every adult associated with school has a vital role to play in the process of motivating and encouraging children to engage enthusiastically with the curriculum and, perhaps more importantly, to learn how to learn. Schools, therefore, are about people, both small and large.

Activate your thinking!

Brown (1999) writing from the perspective of children who are coming to terms with life's challenges, emphasises the role of adults being 'supportive-carers'. Thus:
Through the supportive care of an adult, children are helped to make sense of their life experiences (page 89).

Induction into school life

It is difficult for adults to remember the excitement generated by a special school event, the tingling associated with particular smells or the first cut of a birthday cake. As we grow older, the imaginings of childhood are replaced by more pragmatic considerations and vain efforts to cram too much into too little time. Yet if teachers want to create a purposeful classroom environment, it is worth recalling some of the emotions, ideals and uncertainties which characterise childhood. Jackson (1987) argues that, to make sense of school, children draw on their past experiences and their own understandings. She reminds us that these perceptions 'may not necessarily match the perceptions of the teacher, for learning in school can be a very different thing from learning at home' (page 86).

Children are gradually inducted, both by peers and teachers, into patterns of behaviour and understanding that reflect and maintain school life. It is hard to come to a school for the very first time and have to learn unfamiliar and sometimes baffling procedures, routines and rituals. After all, where else but in school do you need to stick your arm up in the air before being allowed to speak or to sit for half an hour on an uncomfortable wooden floor listening to a grown-up reading stories? Only in a classroom do you have to ask for permission to leave the room, get dressed and undressed with lots of other children before going to clamber over large apparatus in a hall or endure the windy conditions of an exposed tarmac playground. Contrast the freedom of a park, typified by laughter, yells and screams, with the controlled atmosphere of a gym lesson and the scolding from teachers if the noise level rises. Compare the expectations of school and playgroup, babysitter or home. Little wonder that children who are new to school take time to settle, sometimes become confused, make mistakes, and find the experience unsettling.

Thankfully, over the weeks and months, the unfamiliarity fades and is normally replaced by a healthy adjustment to the vagaries of school life (Brooker 2002). Indeed, a reluctance to conform sometimes evolves into a zealous eagerness to defend the *status quo*. Older infants and younger juniors often vie with one another to see who can most vigorously uphold justice. We all recognise these comments as typical:

'You're not allowed...'

'Miss says you can't...'

'A-ah, I'm *tellin'*!'

All are examples of crossly disputed versions of the truth, accusations and counter-accusations. Imagine, too, the plight of the insecure younger child, unable to trust herself to place confidence in the teacher, yet shyly longing to hold an adult's hand at playtimes. See her in the classroom, holding back when there's a scramble for the best equipment or place in the queue, passively accepting her lowly position in the pecking order and storing up a growing belief that she will never be able to compete with her stronger, more assertive peers.

As they witness classroom and school encounters, children gain a view of what is important and what is trivial, of adult status and tolerance (Cullingford 1991, Charlton *et al.*, 1996). As they become more experienced in school, their intuition and familiarity with school routines and relationships alert them to the teacher's apprehension when certain adults (such as people in smart suits) enter the room. In the playground they are keenly aware of who dominates and who submits; which children are most popular and which are the target of derisive comment; who are the rough and noisy ones and who always get told off. They make a mental note that such-and-such a child can usually be blamed for misdemeanours, regardless of the truth. Some children discover how to approach the teacher in such a way as to gain sympathy or favour. Some children are expert at handling adults, others don't care enough to try. A few take delight in finding every opportunity to take advantage of grown-ups and luxuriate in the excitement of undetected misdemeanours.

Children rarely comment at the time but they soon know if different teachers are at odds with one another or if there is tension in the air. Some teachers wonder why the standard of children's behaviour deteriorates when life is most stressful in school. In fact, it is easily explained. Children are extremely sensitive to mood and atmosphere, so as teachers become stressed and less able to cope, the edginess is picked up by the children, who respond accordingly. Every adult working in school therefore contributes to the sense of ease or tension. There are no neutral zones!

Every school has its own culture and traditions which children gradually absorb and make their own as they become familiar with them. School life passes through many phases in a year (Brandling, 1982; Sedgwick, 1989, Smith and Lynch 2005) the conker season, marbles, swopping the latest card collections, paper aeroplanes, skipping, dances, songs, hairstyles, humour. Playtimes are characterised by waves of chasing games or children clutching the coat-tails of another as they imitate horses, charioteers or steam engines. Older children imitate their favourite pop stars or imagine themselves to be a football hero. Many schools employ a variety of strategies to foster positive play: boxes of dressing-up clothes and toys, brightly coloured motifs to stimulate imagination, the promotion of traditional co-operative games.

School life falls into categories for children and they sometimes confuse them. The energetic playtime behaviour can be brought into the classroom; the anticipation of going home can result in premature excitement. Teachers have to adjust their teaching and temperament to allow for these vagaries without losing the smooth flow of classroom routines or neglecting basic standards and attitudes by being unnecessarily strict or grumpy. The best teachers act decisively but refuse to be rattled by behaviour that is typical of most children the world over. Some inexperienced teachers over-react to these situations and become nervy or edgy, cross or agitated. Wiser ones learn to take circumstances in their stride, to discriminate between sabotage and exuberance, between insolence and informality, between hostility and high spirits.

Schools take some getting used to for children and, ironically, the more comfortable and relaxed they feel in the classroom, the more likely the boundaries between home and school will become blurred. The teacher who admonishes a child, 'Don't do that, you're not at home now', may be failing to recognise that such behaviour is often a sign of a positive and relaxed attitude towards school.

The vast majority of children love being at school. It gives them opportunity to meet their friends, experience challenges, handle stimulating equipment, contribute to collaborative ventures and work closely with a range of different adults, all of whom have a concern for them. Little wonder that one little boy commented:

> I like school because the teachers care about us and help us to learn good things.
>
> Wally, aged 6 years

Enough said!

Adults helping children

We noted earlier that most children have moments of anxiety about school. Some are concerned with their work and whether they can keep up with their peers; others worry about friendships or how to please the teacher. Even children who seem bold can harbour doubts about their ability to cope. The early days of a new school year can be a particularly troubling time for some children as they try to discover exactly what new teachers expect of them.

Part of the teachers' role is to provide reassurance for children, giving a clear message to them that everything is under control and that adults can be relied upon to be fair, supportive and firm. This may not be every child's experience of adults outside school and it may be a little time before some of them settle. Occasionally, older children seem to feel that certain adults, particularly those whom they perceive as powerless (notably mealtime assistants, cleaners and even trainee teachers) can be treated casually and mischievous youngsters find great pleasure in pushing their patience to the limit. Thankfully, the majority of primary-age children are willing to trust adults, enthusiastically enjoy school and do their best. For the adults concerned, this is a privilege and a joy.

It is important for children to know that their teachers and helpers want the best for them and will do all they can to assist them in achieving it. This is different from mollycoddling children or preventing them from gaining independence and the ability to make decisions for themselves. There is often a fine line between supporting children and smothering them with kindness. To assist a child at a moment in time has the ultimate purpose of fostering independence. Smothering makes the adult feel good but does not help children to become self-sufficient.

The importance of enjoying a good working relationship with children is rightly stressed as being important for learning, though this should not be confused with intimacy. Nias (1997) argues that 'There are dangers in placing too much emphasis upon the help and support which teachers can give to one another or to children' (page 18). She suggests that although adults in school gain great personal satisfaction in helping children, it is possible to care *too* much and lose sight of the children's academic needs. Nevertheless, MacGrath (2000) reminds us of the child's perspective:

> Remembering to make everyone feel special can make a difference. It may be simply a brief word, a warm look, but it can be powerful. It is often paying attention to things which may seem trivial to an adult but are very big in the life of a child, which help children feel you are on their side, you do notice and care. One of the most important things is to listen (page 74).

Where all teachers actively demonstrate their commitment to children, a framework of mutual support and encouragement is constructed that results in a happy school. Clark (1995), in considering significant factors when studying children, refers to the humbling experience of working with 'flesh-and-blood children in their need and vulnerability, in their optimism and eagerness . . . For these children – all children – are subjects, not objects' (page 21). Teachers need to remember that however frustrating a pupil may be, he or she is somebody's precious child.

Against this, every adult has observed the strategies used by a minority of children to gain attention, cause disruption or avoid responsibility. After all, it is easier to fool about and gain the admiration of your peers than to acknowledge that you don't understand, cannot remember instructions, or are confused by the teacher's comments. Some of these circumstances are discussed later in the chapter. The teacher's position will be examined more fully in Chapter 2.

McNess *et al.* (2003) provide an important reminder that teachers should be deeply committed to the affective dimension of teaching and learning. They argue that in the complex and difficult task that teachers undertake, there are many dimensions of their role for teachers to consider and negotiate. Thus, mastery of a curriculum area, organisational and pedagogic skills needed to plan and assess children's learning, and also social and emotional factors. McNess *et al.* quote evidence from the Primary Assessment, Curriculum and Experience (PACE) Project that suggests that this last factor has great significance for teachers as the affective dimension of teaching 'relied heavily upon joint negotiation and a close personal relationship between the teacher and the learner' (page 248). In other words, part of the skill of good teaching is not only to possess subject knowledge, or even to be able to put things across systematically and clearly, but also to empathise with the learner and build effective working relationships. To put it simply, consideration of the affective is necessary if you are to be effective!

Activate your thinking!

- Do you believe that every child has the potential to lead a purposeful and useful life, regardless of his or her academic qualities?
- Do you agree that every child is capable of being exceptional in some area of his or her life?
- How much and when do you trust children to make decisions for themselves?

- Do you agree that children flourish in a *risk-free* environment? If so, what are the implications for the way that you approach teaching?
- What attitudes to learning do you want children to possess when they leave your class?
- What do you want children to say to their friends and relatives about you as a teacher?
- How is a pupil in your class likely to answer if asked by a younger child what it is like being in your class?

In the hurly-burly of daily life in school it is possible to lose sight of the fact that influencing children is not only important for their sakes but for the welfare of the community and, ultimately, the nation and world as a whole. The seven-year-old with the paint-spattered shirt and flapping shoelaces today is the potential shop assistant, business executive, builder, social worker or dentist of tomorrow. Everyone in society benefits from a good academic and social education that adults in schools help to provide.

Good practice

Get into the habit of commending children as much for their kindness and the effort that they make to succeed as for the quality of their academic work.

Commitment to pupils

All teachers need to demonstrate that they are committed to ensuring that pupils are given the opportunity to achieve their potential and meet the high expectations set for them. This priority must also apply to trainee teachers when they enter school on teaching placement. From start to finish you must not only want to benefit children's learning but strongly demonstrate that this is so by your words and actions. See Chapter 11 for important details about the legal aspects of teachers' commitment. When children meet a new teacher, they want to know whether she or he is going to be fair with them, keep control and provide interesting lessons. Part of your task is to convince them that you will do all of the above, but it will take time to overcome their understandable reluctance to entrust themselves wholeheartedly to someone before being certain that the person is fully reliable. A small number of trainee teachers have lots of commitment to the job but little understanding of the way that children learn. Others have an intellectual grasp of teaching but lack the personality to inspire children in the classroom, while others have understanding and enthusiasm, but cannot provide the orderly framework for effective learning and therefore struggle with class order. The best teachers are characterised by exhibiting all of these attributes.

It is one thing to say that you are enthusiastic about teaching the children; it is quite another to demonstrate it. Commitment is a professional as well as a moral choice and means that you ensure that your lessons are well prepared, that you are clear about your teaching approach and, in presenting lessons, will take full account of children's learning needs and preferences. Important elements of the process include the following:

- Stating clearly to children that you want to help them do well
- Insisting of them that second best is not an option
- Explaining how they can improve their standard of work by offering them strategies for doing so
- Showing children examples of good quality work and clarifying your expectations.

In providing this support, remember that enthusing about high standards, improvements, expectations, aiming high or any other superlative will have little impact upon your pupils unless you can succeed in convincing them that these things are worthwhile. Your commitment needs to be transformed into pupil *self-commitment* as they catch your enthusiasm and zest for learning. It is quite common for the same set of children to underachieve with one teacher and excel with another. There is no secret attached to this anomaly. It is simply that the first teacher has engaged with the children and transmitted a 'can do' message, whereas the second teacher has not. The best teachers tend to:

- Take a keen interest in the standard of a pupil's work and make constructive comments about its quality and, where appropriate, how it can be improved
- Use discipline strategies that avoid humiliation or repression yet maintain consistent control, producing a healthy respect in the children for the teacher as leader
- Answer children's questions helpfully, in which case the child is more likely to venture other questions and see the teacher as an ally, and not as an assessor.

Whereas weaker teachers tend to:

- Tolerate low standards of work, with the result that the child gains the impression that 'good enough' is all that is expected or required
- Use harsh control methods, producing fear or resentment in the children
- Ignore or fail to answer questions clearly, in which case the child is likely to feel that it isn't worth making the effort and avoids asking questions in future

Children like teachers who are fair-minded, interested in them as people, transparent in their dealings, clear about their intentions, helpful in their explanations, non-judgemental in their words and unflinching in confronting situations when it is necessary. Charlton (1996) argues that pupils benefit enormously from teachers who are prepared to listen carefully to what children say to them. Thus:

> Children stand to derive much from being listened to: their academic success can be improved, their personal problems can be reduced, their self-esteem and motivation can be enhanced (page 63).

Children are not looking for 'pals' but for approachable, dependable adults who can be relied upon to give and take, provide a relevant learning environment, give credit where it is due, act swiftly to combat unacceptable behaviour and show that they value each child. Furthermore, children are drawn towards teachers who are interesting and interested people. The more that you can use your talents, gifts, experience and knowledge of the wider world in your teaching, the more likely that the children will come to view you as an adult who deserves their loyalty and best endeavour. It is a mistake to think that maintaining a suitable 'distance' from the class necessitates becoming detached and insipid; in fact, nothing could be further from the truth.

Non-conformist children

Regardless of the care with which teachers handle their day-to-day encounters, there will always be some children who find it difficult to conform or (more seriously) deliberately resist all attempts to help them do so. It is important to bear a number of considerations in mind as we examine what matters to children.

Misbehaviour

Classroom misbehaviour is many teachers' secret fear. Losing control of a class is a trainee teacher's worst nightmare! The prospect of indiscipline affects both teachers and children: teachers, because they want to avoid being humiliated; children, because they do not always possess the life-skills or strategies to avoid confrontation, steer clear of trouble or helpfully influence the behaviour of their peers. This last point is particularly important, for although a teacher may speak of a class of children as being 'difficult', it is often the case that the problems are confined to a very small number whose influence in the classroom gradually becomes pervasive. While it is true that a minority of children are reluctant to obey, won't listen to adults and prefer to antagonise other children rather than conform to the rhythm of classroom life, the vast majority of children are desperate for the security that comes through effective teacher control.

We need to be realistic here. Some children are born wanderers; some seem unable (perhaps, *are* unable) to sit and concentrate for long; others will delight in making life difficult for the teacher, regarding it as a personal challenge to see what they can get away with. It is also true that despite a teacher's efforts to make lessons relevant and interesting and to create a positive environment, there may still be children who persist in inappropriate behaviour. For this troublesome minority, there are usually sanctions that can be applied, varying from school to school, but such procedures can be time-consuming and wearisome (though sometimes necessary). In truth, most teachers have no desire to impose a strict regime upon the class if it is possible to avoid it, and would prefer to coax, persuade, encourage and set targets for achievement as a means of keeping children on the straight and narrow. Such action nearly always pays dividends with most children and increases the likelihood that the environment will be relaxed and purposeful, though the rewards are not usually immediate and you will need to persevere.

Ah, yes, but you haven't had to teach Harry. If you had, you wouldn't be so relaxed about discipline!

This is an understandable response from teachers when issues of control are discussed from the child's perspective and it is true that even one disruptive child can make life extremely tough for a teacher and the rest of the class (see Chapter 8). However, it is worth reflecting upon the fact that the child may be used to different codes of behaviour outside school – the degree of strictness, use of threats, loudness of exchanges. The accumulation of these emotions, experiences and expectations are brought into school and, if a pattern of misbehaviour at home is well established, this group of children may find it genuinely difficult to adjust to different expectations and the need for conformity. Such tensions are common and teachers require time and perseverance as they attempt to explain the rules to confused children or to insist upon them with unco-operative individuals. This is not to argue for a weak and passive approach to children's misdirected energies but rather to look behind the action and acknowledge the factors contributing to the behaviour before deciding upon appropriate steps. Despite the temptation to become gloomy about the attitude and behaviour of a minority, it is far better to stress positive aspects of children's actions whenever possible. In particular, it is worth remembering that as well as academic achievements, social successes and responsible behaviour are an important part of a child's full education. As James and Brownsword (1994) rightly remind us, not all children know how to behave; positive reinforcement of the appropriate behaviour of pupils by brief, sincere words of praise can spur other children to adjust and improve their own behaviour. Thus:

> If these acts or types of behaviour are recorded and praised, it will increase the likelihood that they will occur again and will inform the children what is expected of them (page 10).

Behaviour management and discipline are dealt with more fully in Chapter 8.

Success and failure

> I like going to school because my teacher tells us to have a go and do our best, then she helps us when we are stuck.
>
> *Clarissa, aged eight years*

Success in learning is the ultimate goal for everyone involved in children's education, but defining success is difficult. In its simplest terms, children are successful when they achieve measurably good results in their academic work. Most children are willing to persevere with their work for three principal reasons: (a) to achieve something worthwhile for their own satisfaction, (b) to compete with their classmates, (c) to please the teacher. Children will be motivated to a different extent by each of these three factors. Some children are strongly self-motivated and gain enormous pleasure at achieving something for themselves. They show a relentless determination to do well and, while sharing their joy with others, relish the opportunity to demonstrate their competence. Some children are highly competitive and view every task as a challenge to outperform everyone else. It is not possible to prevent children from being competitive and it can act as a spur to achievement, but if it becomes the dominating factor it can lead to an unhealthy situation in which individuals are vying with each other to complete work quickest or gain the best mark. The majority of children want to please their teachers, in the majority of cases this is because they like them, in a minority of cases because they fear them. While it is obviously desirable for children to want to seek a teacher's approval, it is more important for a child to seek *self-satisfaction* than to hanker after adult approval. You have an important role in encouraging children to feel proud of their achievements, however modest, to allow a degree of competitiveness without tolerating rancour and to acknowledge their successes warmly and wholeheartedly. (See also Gilbert 2002.)

At its deepest level, judging success should lie *within* each child and relates not only to how well the individual has done with respect to fellow pupils or stated criteria but how satisfied she or he feels after completing the task. Teachers have to exercise fine judgement when offering feedback to children about their work and effort. At one level there is a need to explain to the child how the work can be improved. At another level there is a pressing need, especially with children who have experienced limited academic success in the past, to encourage, praise and celebrate achievement, however modest it may be compared with others in the class. McNamara (1997) rightly reminds us that if academic attainment is influenced by self-worth, then 'it is possible that a focus on raising self-esteem . . . could provide an increase in academic achievement' (page 73). Katz (1995) suggests that parents and teachers can strengthen and support a healthy sense of self-esteem in children in at least seven ways:

- Help them to build healthy relationships with peers
- Clarify your own values to them and those of others that may differ
- Offer them reassurance that your support is unconditional
- Appreciate, rather than merely praise, their interests, and avoid flattery
- Offer them opportunities to face challenges as well as to have fun
- Treat them respectfully, take their views seriously and offer meaningful feedback
- Help them to cope with setbacks and use the knowledge they gain to advantage in the future

   (Based on Katz, 1995; further details from www.kidsource.com/kidsource)

Most primary children are optimistic about being part of an establishment that caters for their needs, spends time and effort in helping them to learn and gives them opportunities to do exciting things. However, we have already noted that not all children feel equally comfortable in school and this sometimes leads to problems in attention span and conforming to expectations. If they have come from home backgrounds in which schooling is not considered to be a priority, it is possible that their brothers and sisters will exhibit similar nonconformist tendencies and the whole family may (not always fairly) be referred to by staff as 'one of those families'. Many of these unsettled children, though enjoying the companionship and informal opportunities which school provides, are more likely to fight shy of the formal learning process.

To understand the tension between the formal and informal elements of school life, it is important to appreciate what is involved in a child's reaction to failure. It doesn't take too much imagination to grasp what it is like to be constantly at the bottom of the pile: always coming last, unable to compete with more able classmates, hearing little but criticism from exasperated adults, struggling to make an impression. Is it any wonder that a child, after a few years of this type of experience, decides that it simply isn't worth making the effort to conform to these demands any longer? Better, surely, to put his or her efforts into other more interesting and rewarding activities like disrupting the class, spoiling someone else's work or finishing the set task in rapid time with minimum effort in order to move on to an interesting activity.

If adults find failure hard to cope with, it is not surprising if children need help if they are to avoid spiralling into an attitude of negativity towards schoolwork and teachers (see, for example, Pye, 1987; Varma, 1993; Roffey and O'Reirdan 2003; Lloyd 2004). Perceptive and caring teachers, by their attention to the children's individual needs, can play a major role in preventing this from happening. Houghton and McColgan (1995) suggest that adults can help alleviate children's anxieties by being calm when dealing with their fears, trying to avoid giving the impression that the child is somehow to blame and sensitively encouraging them to 'approach what they fear' (page 41).

> ## Good practice
>
> Speak informally over a period of time to a small group of sensible children who are willing to talk naturally about their views of school and other aspects of life. As the conversations unfold, listen carefully to the comments they make that give clues to the insights they possess and the things that matter to them. Reflect upon the impact that such awareness might make on your attitude to the children in your class.

Friendships and conflicts

From the most immature nursery child to the boldest adolescent, friendships are a significant element of school life. Some children rely heavily upon their friends for companionship and assistance with work. Young children often feel more secure when sitting by their best friend; older ones like to be accepted as one of the gang. Although these patterns of relationship are evident in the classroom, it is often during activities which take place outside the classroom that we see the most obvious examples of relationship failures, such as when choosing partners or team members. While some children are sought for and cheered enthusiastically when chosen, others are regularly ignored, chosen last or grudgingly accepted.

The intensity of friendship patterns and preferences is evident from an early age but intensifies across the primary phase. As alliances and rivalries develop over the years, older children can become entrenched in their views of individuals and sometimes the animosity spills over into aggression. Whereas most reception class children will accept their allocated partner, the emergence of prejudice towards children who are 'different' from the majority needs firm, sensitive handling as children move through the school. Negative racial stereotypes are relatively rare during infant days but can become rampant during the upper stages if left unchecked. Most schools have policies to ensure equal opportunities but the teachers' attitudes are an essential factor as they seek to engender a caring and positive environment.

Common challenges for Foundation Stage and Key Stage 1 teachers include children who:

■ Become distressed if separated from a friend on whom they rely

■ Physically cling to a friend

■ Become upset when someone they want to be their friend chooses not to be

■ Do not appear to have a close friend and use the teacher or classroom assistant as a substitute.

Teachers of older children face other challenges with children who:

■ Opt to work alone and resist collaborating with others

■ Will only select an activity preferred by their friends

■ Become over-reliant on a friend for academic support

■ Try to enter a friendship group and are rejected

■ Become separated from friends when classes move up at the start of a new academic year.

And the problem which faces teachers of all ages – children who behave out of character when sitting with a particular friend and need to be separated, yet get upset when this happens. A friendless child is one of the saddest sights in school. You can help the situation by fostering a climate of 'united we stand', of which friendliness and helping each other is an integral element. Children will always have special friends, of course, but a classroom in which everyone is respected helps to create an *inclusive* environment in which no child is excluded or marginalised (see also Chapter 9).

Despite your best efforts, there are bound to be times when children fall out with one another, disagree and get upset. Adults have an important role on such occasions to provide a calm and reassuring presence and encourage harmony. This process is not always straightforward, especially when children have become over-excited or intensely angry, but there is little point in adding to the conflict by becoming fierce yourself. A calm presence pours oil on troubled waters.

Bullying

The word 'bullying' is used to describe a range of circumstances in which the child's welfare is at risk (Olweus 1993; Sharp *et al.* 2002). It is sometimes difficult to discriminate between high spirits and bullying and all children have squabbles that to adult eyes look more serious than they are. Within a short time, the animosity is forgotten and the two opponents are the closest of friends! On the other hand, there are situations that can cause long-term distress and unhappiness for children. Rigby (2001) argues that it is important to deal with bullying because it has three potential adverse effects. First, it lowers mental health. Second, it induces social maladjustment. Third, it creates physical illness. The circumstances which define bullying are usefully described below (OFSTED 1993):

> Bullying is a form of disruptive behaviour whose effects can be long term and deep-rooted, even on occasions leading to suicide. It takes various forms, from name-calling, teasing and physical abuse, to intimidation, extortion and serious physical assault (page 16).

The DfES website (www.parentcentre.gov.uk October 2003) refers to bullying as one of the most difficult experiences of a child's life. It defines bullying as being deliberately hurtful behaviour, repeated over a period of time, where it is difficult for those being bullied to defend themselves. Three main types of bullying are described: (a) Physical bullying, including hitting, kicking and theft, (b) Verbal bullying, including name-calling and racist remarks, (c) Indirect bullying, such as spreading rumours. Parents and adults in school should be alert to common signs that children are victims of bullying: regular headaches, stomach-aches, anxiety and irritability. Parents who suspect that their children are suffering are encouraged to contact the school immediately. Lawson (1994) suggests that there are three types of bullies: aggressive bullies, anxious bullies and passive bullies.

- The aggressive bully is the most serious, as weaker children may be injured. Aggressive bullies are often badly behaved in school and require close supervision and monitoring throughout the day. Controlling aggressive bullying must involve the whole staff to ensure that the malefactors are made to adhere to a strictly enforced set of rules governing their behaviour. Parental involvement is also essential in setting targets for improvement.

- Anxious bullies see themselves as failures and vent their frustrations on other children by saying unkind things and undermining their achievements. It is often younger, vulnerable children (unlikely to retaliate) who are subjected to their taunts. This type of bully needs to be helped to gain self-esteem by placing them in a position where they can succeed. Paradoxically, these pupils often relate well to younger children in a structured environment, supervised by an adult who can monitor the situation and offer encouragement and direction.

- Passive bullies are the 'support' members of bullying groups but not the principal perpetrators. The term 'passive bully' is not wholly satisfactory as it implies that such types are less guilty than their leaders. Nevertheless, it is probably true to say that many passive bullies do not particularly relish their role and would prefer to spend their time in other ways. Their fear of losing credibility with the aggressors and perhaps becoming victims themselves if they don't go along with the more assertive partner deters them from breaking free. Teachers and assistants need to help them to develop new friendships by providing them with positive alternatives and ensuring that they have a busy, interesting schedule, especially during break times. Needless to say, the principal characters in any gang need to be dealt with firmly.

Thankfully, aggressive bullying is rare in primary schools, but it is important to remember that the types of behaviour which emerge during primary school are likely to be continued once pupils transfer to secondary education and create a climate of fear and uncertainty for the victims (Balding, 1996). All adults are keen to promote not only a bully-free classroom (Beane 1999) but a safe school environment (Varnava 2002). Teachers can make a considerable difference by modelling behaviour which shows that they value individual children and by actively confronting any unsatisfactory situation using strategies such as:

- Listening carefully to explanations, especially from the victim
- Offering opportunities for children who have been bullying others to become involved in positive, supportive activities
- Clarifying expectations about mutual respect and tolerance
- Monitoring the bullied children to ensure that they do not, in turn, bully others. (See Byre, 1993.)

Although there are some children who always seem to be in scrapes, it may not always be helpful to refer to them as 'bullies' as this can become a label or stigma which hinders them from throwing off their bad reputation and establishing a more positive image. It is better to speak about 'bullying behaviour' with reference to a particular circumstance. Child 1 may bully child 2 who then bullies child 3. In these particular cases, some children are victims, some are bullies and some are both. The situation is made more difficult in that bullying tends to be selective and the pupil who causes grief to one child may be delightful with another.

One of the problems facing teachers in knowing how to deal with aggressive acts (physical or verbal) is that bullying becomes a learned behaviour that eventually acts like a stimulant; in short, bullying becomes enjoyable for the perpetrator. If bullying is not dealt with sooner rather than later, it becomes habit-forming and intervention to stop it being repeated becomes more difficult. Although pernicious bullying and frequent unsatisfactory behaviour which brings distress to others cannot be tolerated, the children concerned must also be shown that there are benefits attached to kindness, consideration and self-sacrifice that cannot be experienced by tormenting someone weaker than themselves. For some bullies this is a hard lesson to learn. Racist bullying is an unpleasant area of school life that has received a great deal of attention in recent years. All schools have to demonstrate that they not only have a policy to combat such behaviour but they are active in ensuring that it is implemented and monitored.

As teachers become aware of the power of friendships and the fears, frustrations and joys of complex child–child relationships, they discover that it is essential to pay attention to its consequences. Children do not attend school solely for developing friendships but attention to the implications arising from relationships is important in the quest for a good teaching and learning environment (Pollard and Filer, 1996). Bullied children, whatever the cause, will underachieve and be miserable not only in school but in life generally. They deserve and expect protection from adults.

Activate your thinking!

Which children tend to be marginalised in the playground? What practical steps can be taken to help?

Children's curriculum entitlement

Every child in a maintained school is entitled to receive an appropriate education as prescribed by the National Curriculum (NC) and associated statutory requirements (see Figure 1.1 for common acronyms). The curriculum experienced by the children must reflect the agreed whole-school plans and offer a properly weighted content that reflects the NC and the requirements of the National Literacy Strategy (NLS, DfEE 1998a) and the National Numeracy Strategy (NNS, DfEE 1999a). Schools must be able to show that every subject area is receiving an appropriate amount of time and that they are accommodating the needs of each child within the teaching and learning programme, with additional adult support where deemed necessary (see also Chapter 3).

ACRONYMS

DfEE	Department for Education and Employment (now DfES)
DfES	Department for Education and Skills
ITE	Initial Teacher Education
ITT	Initial Teacher Training
LEA	Local Education Authority
NC	National Curriculum
NC2000	National Curriculum 2000 (first published 1999)
NLS	National Literacy Strategy
NNS	National Numeracy Strategy
QCA	Qualifications and Curriculum Authority
SENCO	Special Educational Needs Co-ordinator
TA	Teaching Assistant
TTA	Teacher Training Agency

FIGURE 1.1 Common acronyms

The word 'curriculum' may be thought of as a specified course of study (Collins Dictionary) but its interpretation and implementation is far more complex. Indeed, there is not even a consistent view about how curriculum translates into practice. For example, contrast the following:

The curriculum should be thought out in terms of activity and experience rather than knowledge to be acquired or facts to be stored.

Consultative Committee 1931

The term curriculum is used to describe everything children do, see, hear or feel in their setting, both planned and unplanned.

Curriculum Guidance for the Foundation Stage (QCA/DfES 2000)

The school curriculum . . . should equip (pupils) with the essential learning skills of literacy, numeracy and information and communication technology, and promote an enquiring mind and capacity to think rationally.

NC2000, page 11

And the concept of a national curriculum that has to apply across all schools offers yet another interpretation of the word:

An effective National Curriculum . . . gives teachers, pupils, parents, employers and their wider community a clear and shared understanding of the skills and knowledge that young people will gain at school.

NC2000, page 3.

Although at one level the curriculum can be thought about as everything that a child encounters that might affect learning, the *formal* curriculum for schools consists of the Foundation Stage for children aged three to five years and a National Curriculum, separated into Key Stages (1, 2, 3 and 4) for children after the age of five years. Arrangements for statutory assessment at the end of each Key Stage are set out in detail in Qualifications and Curriculum Authority's (QCA) annual booklets about assessment and reporting arrangements. The relevant stages are summarised thus:

Foundation Stage from three to five years
The Reception year is the last year of the Foundation Stage in which the children reach statutory school age (five years).

National Curriculum

- Key Stage 1 (KS1) from 5 to 7 years (Year 1 and Year 2)
- Key Stage 2 (KS2) from 7 to 11 years (Years 3, 4 , 5 and 6)

And in the secondary phase:

- Key Stage 3 (KS3) from 11 to 14 years
- Key Stage 4 (KS4) from 14 to 16 years

Subject areas in the NC consist of core and non-core subjects as follows:

Core subjects
English
Mathematics
Science

Non-core subjects (formerly referred to as 'foundation subjects')

Design & Technology	Art & Design
ICT	Music
History	Physical Education
Geography	

In addition there is Religious Education, which varies depending upon the status of the school. Schools with a religious foundation have more flexibility in determining the RE curriculum than secular ones. A Modern Foreign Language (MFL) and Citizenship are only statutory in Key Stages 3 and 4 but both areas are receiving considerably more attention in primary schools and detailed non-statutory guidance is available. (See later in this chapter about citizenship.)

The NC is broadly organised into three parts: programmes of study, attainment targets and six key skills:

Programmes of Study (PoS)

- PoS set out what content pupils should be taught in each subject at each Key Stage
- They also provide the basis for planning schemes of work.

Attainment targets (AT)

- ATs set out the knowledge, skills and understanding which pupils of different abilities and maturities are expected to have by the end of each Key Stage
- They consist of eight level descriptions of increasing difficulty to assess pupils' attainment at the end of a Key Stage (including national tests that are commonly referred to as SATs).

Key skills across the curriculum
Communication

- Including speaking, listening, reading and writing.

Application of number

- Developing a range of mental calculation skills and the ability to apply them within a variety of contexts.

Information technology

■ Using a range of information sources and ICT tools to find, analyse, interpret, evaluate and present information for a range of purposes.

Working with others

■ Contributing to small-group and whole-class discussions.

Improving own learning and performance

■ Reflecting on and critically evaluating their work and what they have learned.

Problem solving

■ Identifying and understanding a problem, and planning ways to solve it.

The NC also states that 'Pupils should be given opportunities to apply and develop their ICT capability through the use of ICT tools to support their learning in all subjects, with the exception of physical education in Key Stages 1 and 2' (page 39).

In addition to the NC, the introduction of national numeracy and literacy strategies has had a major impact on the primary curriculum. The framework provided in the National Literacy Strategy (NLS) is intended to cover the statutory requirements for reading and writing in the NC, and also contribute substantially to the development of speaking and listening and have relevance across the whole of the NC. Consequently, skills in reading and writing non-fiction texts are intended to be relevant to every subject area. In practice, the 'literacy hour' has tended to be a self-contained lesson, incorporated into the daily teaching timetable as a distinctive learning episode, though less commonly at KS1. The suggested framework for the 'literacy hour' consists of the following:

■ About 15 minutes of shared reading and writing with the whole class
■ About 15 minutes with the whole class on 'word level work' (word recognition, phonics, spelling, vocabulary; also grammar and punctuation in KS2)
■ About 20 minutes group and independent work (including guided reading and writing)
■ About ten minutes plenary (whole class brought together to share and critically reflect).

Some areas of English have received less attention as a result of the highly structured nature of the literacy hour, including the opportunity for children to experience extended writing opportunities and the development of speaking and listening skills. However, the importance of speaking and listening has received closer attention in schools and there has been a re-emergence of the 'showing and sharing time' (where children bring, and talk about, things of interest to them) that was commonplace in most primary schools before the introduction of the NLS. Although the framework has helped to concentrate teachers' minds on the fundamental skills that children need to be literate, some practitioners have found the highly structured and objectives-driven nature of the hour has not allowed for spontaneity and exploration of unanticipated areas of learning. Consequently, some schools have tried to modify the teaching programme while remaining within the 'legal' requirements.

The National Numeracy Strategy (NNS) was developed to be used alongside the NC so that their contents would be compatible. Thus, the principles underpinning NC2000: 'Mathematics equips pupils with a uniquely powerful set of tools to understand and change the world. These tools include logical reasoning, problem-solving skills and the ability to think in abstract ways' (page 60) also apply to the NNS. The NNS framework contains yearly teaching programmes for Reception to Year 6 and consists of five strands, the first three of which link directly to the NC. Thus:

- Numbers and the number system
- Calculations
- Solving problems
- Measures, shape and space
- Handling data

The NNS framework has a heavy emphasis on the assessment of children's work and their progress. It is recommended that a typical lesson will consist of about five to ten minutes of oral work and mental calculation (often referred to as the 'mental-oral' phase), about 30 to 40 minutes of the main teaching activity and about ten to 15 minutes of a plenary at the end. Although teachers are given flexibility in the way they teach, the NNS nevertheless prescribes that 'each lesson should include direct teaching and interaction with the pupils, and activities or exercises that pupils do' (page 15).

Citizenship

Another important dimension of children's education is covered through *Citizenship*, which in Key Stages 1 and 2 is non-statutory but, in reality, is pursued by all primary schools. The QCA provide a scheme based on twelve individual units, including topics as diverse as 'Choices', 'People who help us' and 'Local democracy for young citizens'. Under the banner of PSHE (Personal, Social and Health Education) and Citizenship, the NC non-statutory guidelines provide a framework for KS1 and for KS2 under two main headings:

1 Knowledge, skills and understanding
2 Breadth of study

Knowledge, skills and understanding incorporates four sub-areas:

- Developing confidence and responsibility and making the most of their abilities
- Preparing to play an active role as citizens
- Developing a healthy, safer lifestyle
- Developing good relationships and respecting the differences between people.

For each sub-area, there are details about what pupils need to be taught. For instance, under *developing confidence and responsibility*, younger primary children should be taught to recognise what they like and dislike, what is fair and unfair, and what is right and wrong. They are also to be taught ways of sharing their opinions, to deal with feelings positively, to recognise what they are good at, and to set themselves simple goals. Older primary children are to be taught how to express their opinions and explain their views in writing, identify positive things about themselves, to make responsible choices and be responsible about the use of money.

In *preparing to play an active role as citizens*, younger primary pupils should be taught how to take part in discussions, debates about topical issues, recognise choices and follow group decisions. They also have to realise their responsibilities to others, to be alert to environmental effects, to contribute to class and school life, and to understand the place and purpose of money. Older primary children have to be taught how to discuss and debate topical issues based on research evidence, to understand rule-making, to realise the consequences of antisocial behaviour and to recognise their responsibilities to the community. They should also reflect on spiritual, moral, social and cultural issues, to make informed decisions, to understand the meaning of democracy, to recognise the place of voluntary and pressure groups and to appreciate ethnic and religious diversity. Finally, older primary children should have a grasp of economic realities and explore how the media present information.

Under *developing a healthy, safer lifestyle*, younger pupils should be taught how to make simple choices that improve health and wellbeing, maintain personal hygiene and to understand how diseases spread and can be controlled. They also have to be taught about the ageing process, names and parts of the body, harmful household products and rules for keeping safe (including road safety). Older primary pupils should be taught about the benefits of exercise and healthy eating, safe routines for minimising the spread of disease, changes to the body as puberty approaches and the availability and effects of common drugs. They also have to be taught about risk assessment, appropriate physical contacts, resisting pressure to do wrong and where to get help.

Under *developing good relationships and respecting differences*, younger primary pupils should be taught to recognise how their behaviour impacts upon others, to listen, play and work co-operatively, to identify and respect differences and similarities. They should also be taught about the importance of caring for friends and families, that all forms of bullying are wrong and how to get help to deal with bullying. Older pupils should be taught about the impact of their actions, to think about the lives of people in other places and times, to be aware of different kinds of relationships and to realise the effect of racism, teasing, bullying and aggressive behaviours. They should also be taught to recognise and challenge stereotypes, understand differences between people groups and where individuals, families and groups can get help and support. Full details of the curriculum programme are available through the NC web site (www.nc.uk.net).

Finally, for KS1 and KS2, there is information about the opportunities that pupils should experience to be taught the Knowledge, Skills and Understanding under the heading *Breadth of Study*. Thus, younger primary pupils should have opportunities to:

- Take and share responsibility
- Feel positive about themselves
- Take part in discussions
- Make real choices
- Meet and talk with people
- Develop relationships through work and play
- Consider social and moral dilemmas
- Ask for help.

Older primary pupils should have opportunities to:

- Take responsibility
- Feel positive about themselves
- Participate
- Make real choices and decisions
- Meet and talk with people
- Develop relationships through work and play
- Consider social and moral dilemmas
- Find information and advice
- Prepare for change.

For some parts of the knowledge, skills and understanding, there are recommended cross-curricular links with other areas, such as science, DT, ICT, PE and history. *Assessment* of children's progression in Citizenship is in terms of what knowledge and understanding most children should have to become informed citizens. Thus, KS1 children should be able to talk about and consider topics and issues, to begin to show understanding of simple citizenship (e.g. fairness and rules) and begin to show understanding of values (e.g. concern for others). Children in KS2 should be able to investigate topical issues, show understanding of some citizenship concepts (e.g. rights and responsibilities) and show an understanding of values. In respect of demonstrating skills of enquiry and communication, KS1 children should be able to respond to simple questions and explain their views and to listen to the views of others. KS2 children should be able to take part in discussions and debates, talk and write about their opinions, ask and respond to questions and understand different viewpoints. Finally, assessment of progress can be made by demonstrating skills of participation and responsible action.

You could be forgiven for thinking that if the non-statutory guidelines were followed thoroughly, there would be little time for anything else to be included in the curriculum! In practice, a number of elements of Citizenship are incorporated into assembly times, special projects (such as those dealing with neighbourhood issues, see Hicks 2001) and the warp and weave of daily school life governed, for instance, by behaviour policy and inter-personal relationships. See Alderson (1999) for further insights into issues concerning children's rights.

The teacher's role

Whatever the nature of the curriculum, the teacher's own role is critical to the process. During a single session, teachers can play a variety of different roles which closely relate to the need for children to learn in particular ways. They may act as informer, demonstrator, facilitator or interpreter. Each role carries with it a particular emphasis (Figure 1.2). As these teaching techniques are refined, the children's learning will also be enhanced in different ways (Figure 1.3).

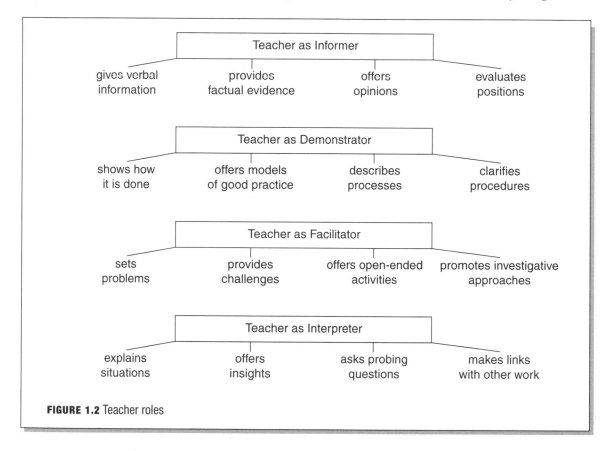

FIGURE 1.2 Teacher roles

These stages are not in watertight compartments, for during a single lesson there will be opportunities for many of them to be woven into the fabric of the learning process. For instance, if the teacher's role is principally that of *informer*, the children's understanding will be limited by the information that the teacher provides. As a *demonstrator*, the teacher not only tells but provides evidence. In the role of *facilitator*, the teacher provides the circumstances for children to explore and experiment and investigate processes for themselves. If the role is extended to incorporate *interpreter*, then children's understanding can be enriched as the teacher helps them to make sense of all their learning opportunities. All four roles may be evident during a single session, though one will normally predominate (Dean, 1992; 1998). Sometimes, a child will only be ready to receive direct information and not be ready for more challenging situations. On other occasions, after apparently grasping the concept, a child will

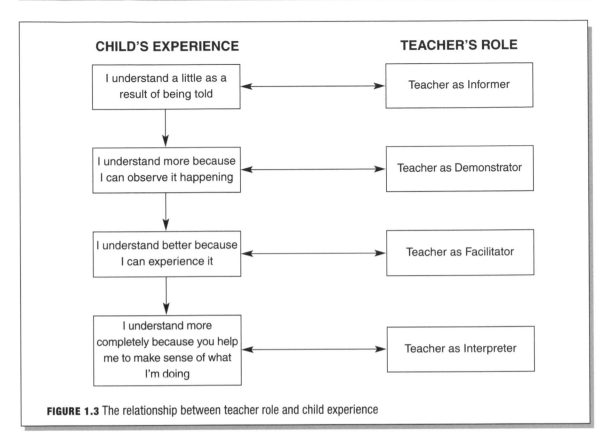

CHILD'S EXPERIENCE

| I understand a little as a result of being told |
| I understand more because I can observe it happening |
| I understand better because I can experience it |
| I understand more completely because you help me to make sense of what I'm doing |

TEACHER'S ROLE

| Teacher as Informer |
| Teacher as Demonstrator |
| Teacher as Facilitator |
| Teacher as Interpreter |

FIGURE 1.3 The relationship between teacher role and child experience

unexpectedly require reassurance through (say) teacher-demonstration or further hands-on experience. Judging which role should be adopted with which children requires sensitivity and care, and is one of the more important strategy decisions teachers have to make.

Promoting play

All children love to play, such that if a child does not appear to want to play, adults become anxious about the situation. Playing is a natural part of child development and wherever children are found: in every home, park, pre-school, nursery, play of some sort is evident. Most teachers of young children use play as a means of enquiry-based learning; teachers of juniors tend to encourage play only within the confines of a controlled learning environment such as drama.

In school, the importance of play has sometimes caused disagreements between teachers and parents. Expressions such as 'She went to school but only played' and 'We didn't do any work, we only played', indicate the way in which play is perceived by some children and parents: that is, as a time-filling activity without educational value. Teachers, on the other hand, view play as an essential part of the educative process and a powerful learning agent. Chapter 4 contains further details.

One of the challenges facing teachers of younger children in particular is the extent to which play should be directed. Left to their own devices, children play spontaneously and create imaginative situations from what is, for adults, mundane or lifeless (Duffy, 1998). Some teachers argue that play is not play unless it is free of adult contrivance, arguing that even if they try to intervene in a play situation, they receive short shrift from assertive five-year-olds. For these teachers, manipulating play situations undermines its purpose and produces an artificial learning environment. 'Children,' they argue, 'should be liberated to explore and come to terms with ideas without hindrance.' In such classrooms, young children are found busily involved in a variety of activities: sand and water play, construction kits and toys, dressing-up. Noise levels sometimes become high and the teacher, frequently involved in hearing a child read or working with a group on basic skills, may choose to ignore the free play activity. Permission for children to play is used as a reward for task completion or good behaviour.

Other teachers argue that the extent of the play should be more controlled and monitored by the teacher. For example, specific games are provided and activities are deliberately restricted by the provision of certain resources and the exclusion of others. Play outcomes are targeted in terms of measurable learning outcomes which are not necessarily academic but relate to social harmony, respect for property, tolerance and so forth. Play is seen as an opportunity for children to work through situations, solve problems, employ their imaginative powers to come to terms with new or exciting situations and exercise authority over confusing circumstances, bewildering paradoxes or worrying uncertainties. For these teachers, children use play to confirm ideas, create solutions and extend their thinking. Teachers use the opportunity to interact with the children, listen to their language and questions, and determine the extent of their understanding. Play thereby becomes a teacher-influenced strategy for learning rather than a completely child-directed one. See Drake (2003) for implications about the Foundation Stage.

The place of play in the school day will depend upon the age of the children and the teacher's philosophy. Very young children enjoy the freedom which comes from playing and a teacher may decide that this is justification in itself, in which case the children will be offered the opportunity to play whenever it is practicable. Younger children, who are familiar with school routines and able to cope with more structure, may be allocated play opportunities on a rota basis or as a reward for working hard. Sometimes a teacher needs the space to concentrate on the academic learning needs of a particular group and allows the others to play as a 'holding task'. Older children, too, need a chance to play, and although this is often reserved for break-times, the skilful use of improvisation and role-play in drama offers them the chance to relax while performing a purposeful activity. Whatever form of organisation appears most appropriate, the chance for children to take control over their learning with minimal adult intervention is an essential element of young children's development. This is probably truer for play than any other experiential learning.

Making decisions about children

Children are not mini-adults. Sometimes as children they get confused, bewildered, overwhelmed, elated; sometimes they excel; sometimes they struggle with work and their emotions; sometimes the world is a confusing, contradictory place. As the responsible adult, you often have to make decisions about taking appropriate action in their best interests. The following list is typical of the experiences and situations that require such decisions:

- *An infant loses her dinner money on the way to school.*
  Check with an older brother or sister; make sure that the dinner money really is lost; ensure that the child receives a dinner; ask the school secretary or administrator to contact the parent.

- *A seven-year-old complains that a 'funny man' shouted at her outside the school gate.*
  Ask gentle questions about the circumstances; find out if any other children saw the incident; if uneasy about matters, report the incident to the head teacher immediately; if reassured, mention it later.

- *Money goes missing and one boy is accused by several classmates of the crime.*
  Inform the class teacher immediately; avoid making accusations. Treat all instances of theft seriously, including those of children's snacks.

- *A top junior boy is sulky and refuses to work because he is not in the football team.*
  Talk the matter through with the boy; ask the games teacher concerned to speak to him; allow him time to get over the disappointment; at a later time speak to him again; monitor any further reaction. If you are in a position to do so, offer some guidance about how he might improve his skills. Suggest that the best way to be noticed is to be encouraging towards those who are selected. It won't be easy for him. Such matters are of major significance in some children's lives.

- *A reception age child continually cries because he wants to go into his older sister's class.*
  This phase usually passes quite soon. An arrangement can normally be made with the other class teacher to allow occasional access for the purpose of reassurance. Playtime offers further opportunities for interaction.

- *A girl who is weak academically produces a wonderful clay model.*
  Contact parents as soon as possible through a congratulatory note, telephone call or personal encounter; take a photograph of the girl holding her finished model. It is important not to miss the opportunity that these critical incidents afford.

- *A boy who was formerly well behaved suddenly begins to behave erratically.*
  Seek advice from senior colleagues immediately. It is more than likely that the cause lies outside school and the head teacher may decide that contact with the parent is needed. Children sometimes exhibit erratic behaviour if they are victims of bullying, though a more common reaction is withdrawal and sullenness.

- *A five-year-old starts to soil himself.*
  Make contact with the parent the same day; ascertain from colleagues whether there have been previous incidents; inform the head teacher. Soiling is a humiliating and frightening experience for a child. An isolated incident is probably not significant but repeated instances may indicate that there is a more serious issue as the root cause.

- *A ten-year-old boy with a good voice won't join the school choir.*
  Mention it to the parents next time you see them. Many older boys lose interest in

singing, much preferring sport. The more that singing is a fun element of classroom life, the more likely that boys will retain their enthusiasm for it. Teachers responsible for choirs do well to consider the choir's image and give serious thought to its repertoire and the way it is perceived by all children throughout the school.

- *A nine-year-old girl is crying because (she claims) her mother won't let her have a birthday party.*
Listen carefully to the child; explain that you are sure there is a good reason; if you are on good terms with the parent, quietly mention the matter to her. It is not worth becoming embroiled in domestic matters of this kind unless you have a concern over the child's welfare or conduct. Perhaps you can mark the occasion in class, though be careful not to exceed what would normally be done for other children or it might trigger ill-feeling or set a precedent that cannot be maintained.

- *An 11-year-old boy is heard describing a video 'nasty' in graphic detail to his friends.*
Ask the child directly whether he saw the video; ask whether he had permission from a parent to see it; discuss the issue with the head teacher before taking any further action. The head teacher will know the family and, if relevant, be in a position to gain informal advice from social services. Unless you suspect that there is abuse, it is difficult to do much more other than tackle it indirectly through the personal, social and health education curriculum.

- *A ten-year-old boy starts to draw weird doodles on scraps of paper.*
Chat informally to the child before deciding whether to take the matter further. Drawings of this kind may be a short-lived phase or can indicate deeper psychological problems. If the child has a talent for drawing it may be possible to divert his efforts more constructively.

- *An 11-year-old girl, through silliness, breaks an expensive piece of science equipment.*
Console the child rather than condemning; after the lesson speak to her and explain your disappointment with her behaviour; discuss with the class teacher before proceeding. Sensible children who behave out of character will normally confide in their parents about an incident of this kind. Don't be surprised if the parent contacts you first. Although a school can insist that a breakage be paid for, it is often not worth the trouble unless there is a serious matter of principle involved. Again, the class teacher is best placed to deal with such matters.

- *A six-year-old, new to the class, swears when the teacher rebukes him for aggressive behaviour.*
Firmly explain that such language is not used in school; reinforce this from time to time during the coming weeks. When younger children use unsuitable language, they have normally acquired it from home in the first place. A child new to school will need time to adjust to the differing expectations. The aggressive behaviour is a more urgent issue and the school's discipline policy will come into play, and may involve the special educational needs co-ordinator (SENCO).

- *A seven-year-old girl is regularly a few minutes late in the morning.*
Ask the child why she is arriving late; consult with teachers of her brothers or sisters. If you are a new teacher to the school or a trainee, seek advice. In some families, especially

where parents leave for work early in the morning, the eldest child has the responsibility for ensuring that the younger ones get to school, with the resulting problem about lateness. If there are concerns about the children's welfare, the head teacher will pursue the case.

- *A reception child frequently falls asleep during the afternoon story.*
  Speak privately to the parent as soon as possible. Some small children simply get tired and need to sleep. Other children stay up too late due, perhaps, to being the youngest in a house full of noisy siblings. Falling asleep may also indicate the presence or imminence of ill-health.

As a guide to appropriate action, the child's immediate safety is always of prime concern. Once this is secured, the child's longer-term security is considered. From this point onwards, any decisions will depend upon the circumstances of the case, bearing in mind agreed school policy, previous experience of similar incidents and the teacher's own judgement. It is usually better to err on the side of caution. The 'funny man' outside the school gate may have been a harmless passer-by with an unusual appearance or a child molester. The boy describing a video nasty might be unsupervised at home or have been told the story by his older brother and was showing off to his friends when he related the story. The reception-aged child falling asleep might be kept awake at night by noisy neighbours or suffering the effects of a hot and stuffy classroom. Suspicions that a parent might be the cause of the distress or responsible for a child's unsettled behaviour means that it would not be appropriate to contact that person directly. Always take advice from the head teacher and monitor the situation informally while advice is sought from the appropriate social service, such as the child protection agency. Trainee teachers do not need to become embroiled in the detail of procedures and processes but have the same responsibility as every other adult to ensure the physical and emotional wellbeing of young lives.

Case study

In many ways Jonny was the ideal pupil and just the sort of nine-year-old child that any teacher would want in the class. He related well to his peers and also to adults. He worked hard and used his natural intelligence to maximum effect. Jonny always strove to achieve a high standard, was sensitive to people's feelings and would apply himself to sporting events with great enthusiasm and competitiveness. Jonny was socially aware in that he fitted in well with the group and was popular with his classmates. Jonny was a capable football enthusiast and a member of the cross-country running team. At the end of the year the teacher, Geoff Ascot, was genuinely saddened when Jonny moved on to the next class.

Twenty years later Geoff was walking through an indoor market when he heard a voice call out to him from behind one of the stalls. It was a beaming Jonny, who to Geoff's eyes did not look all that different from the nine-year-old in shorts that he remembered. After they had exchanged pleasantries, Jonny told Geoff proudly that he was now the owner of three small businesses that he ran from different market stalls. Jonny laughingly described himself as an entrepreneurial market trader. Geoff wondered what Jonny would remember from his days in the class and hoped that he might say something positive. (Even the best teachers need to be reassured sometimes!) Although Geoff recalled the time when Jonny had been in his class as if it were yesterday, for Jonny the same time period composed the majority of his lifetime. It was not long before Jonny's eyes glazed over as the memories flooded back.

'You used to play your guitar in assembly.'

'Yes, that's right, we had some good fun.'

'Mmm. We practised the play for Christmas.'

'Yes, I remember', the teacher replied.

'And you used to run the football team.'

'Yes, I was a bit slimmer then! You were a good player.' Geoff waited, hoping that Jonny might refer to the excellent learning experiences he had in class, but Jonny's priorities were different. Instead, Jonny's mind was saturated with the fun he had experienced, the personal interactions, the joy of being part of a team, the excitement of public performances in front of the rest of the school, parents and friends. Jonny reminisced about the times that the teacher took them out of school on short trips to explore the lanes and bring small treasures back to examine in class, mount them on displays, create large books with pictures and photographs, and include snippets of writing and photographs. Jonny's memories were full of the things that still served to motivate and inspire him.

What will today's children remember of their schooldays? What will be of value to them in five, ten or 30 years from now? School-based education must be an enabling process that creates a desire in children to discover more about the world and to learn skills and attitudes that will ensure a more productive and harmonious society. Education should excite in children a belief that life has purpose and liberate their imaginations and creativity. As Geoff said goodbye to his former pupil, he felt quietly satisfied that at least some of these aims had been fulfilled in Jonny.

Standards

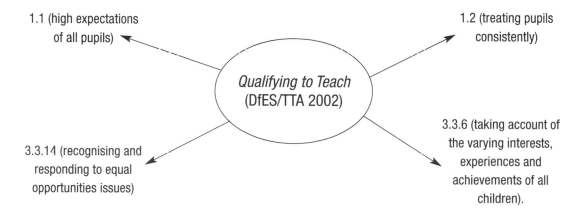

1.1 (high expectations of all pupils)

1.2 (treating pupils consistently)

Qualifying to Teach (DfES/TTA 2002)

3.3.14 (recognising and responding to equal opportunities issues)

3.3.6 (taking account of the varying interests, experiences and achievements of all children).

Further reading

Sharman, C., Cross, W. and Vennis, D. (2000) Observing Children, 2nd edn, London: Cassell.
The authors provide practical advice with a particular focus on the early years of schooling.
Wyse, D. (2002) Becoming a Primary School Teacher, London: RoutledgeFalmer. See chapter 1.
This is an easy-to-read book with useful snippets of advice and a close understanding of primary practice.

2

The Teacher

Introduction

Schools are not just places for children. They rely on committed and conscientious teachers and support staff to make them function effectively. This chapter offers a variety of perspectives on the joys and challenges of being a teacher in school, a role that extends well beyond the act of teaching. The role of other adults in school is dealt with in Chapter 3.

Becoming a teacher

Some people have a sentimental view of the task that teachers face. Visions of children's gentle, eager faces lifting their trusting eyes to gaze expectantly towards a much-loved teacher, waiting on every word, are sometimes far removed from reality. Teachers have to be tough, persevering and determined. The rigours of daily classroom life and the demands of 30 or more children of varying abilities and enthusiasm can be a daunting business for even the most capable and committed.

On the other hand, teaching is an important job offering great reward and satisfaction. There is probably nothing to compare with the thrill of introducing children to new and exciting worlds of learning, to see the glow on their faces when understanding dawns. Not all teachers are loved, but many are and deserve to be. It may sound sentimental but teaching really is a way of life; once a person has entered the world of school, things will never be quite the same again. Equally certain is the exciting truth that most children do not forget their teachers. Fifty years and more from now, many children will still speak some of their teachers' names, refer to their character and the effect they had upon their lives. When much else is forgotten, the memory of a teacher lives on. In a quotation from one of his respondents, Cotton (1998) offers an example of the essential characteristics that teachers must put across to the children if they are to earn a special place in pupils' memories:

> All have human qualities; they made us feel good about ourselves; they made us see things are possible and they justified our existence as unique human beings, not simply faceless pupils (page 42).

Building a relationship with children takes time and perseverance. No one can claim the automatic right to be a respected teacher; it has to be earned. It is the same in every walk of life: if there is no respect, then little account is taken of what someone says or demands unless that person coerces by power. Some inexperienced teachers become despondent when their attempts to establish good relationships with the children are initially rejected. Yet it may be that the class has had some unpleasant experiences with adults and will take some convincing that they can be trusted. Or perhaps they were very happy with their previous teacher and are less certain about the new teacher's ability to take that place. It may be that particular children are shy or fearful and can't respond naturally. In a small number of cases, it may be that certain children are using emotional blackmail – 'I'll give you the satisfaction that comes from seeing me happy and responsive in exchange for staying off my back.' Teachers have to discriminate between children's tentativeness and their wiles. A demonstration of integrity and consistency will convince most children that a good relationship with a teacher is worth the effort, though there may be one or two children who remain aloof or dismissive of the teacher's overtures despite trying to establish a bond with them. If you meet such children it is unwise to dwell unduly on the situation, but rather to persevere gently to establish a working relationship with them. These children are sometimes the ones with whom you ultimately develop the closest bond.

Procedures and rituals

Every school has its codified and unwritten rules and regulations, and trainee teachers and newly appointed teachers to a school have to make sure that they do not unwittingly contravene them. It is worth keeping a record of the procedures and rituals that you observe in the classroom and elsewhere to avoid too many embarrassing moments when you cross the boundaries owing to your ignorance of situations that others take for granted. Most children are ready and willing to offer you information about specific aspects of classroom procedures, and a friendly member of the support staff will usually alert you to school-wide issues if you ask. It is important not to underestimate the significance of ritual and procedures in a school, as these are sometimes unfairly used as an informal measure of a trainee teacher's suitability for teaching.

Knowing about the school policy for discipline and the use of sanctions may avoid problems of inconsistency occurring between you and the class teacher. Similarly, if there is an accepted way for children to move around the school (to assembly, for instance) it is essential that you maintain the required code of behaviour. There are also more subtle issues, dependant on relationships between different adults, that are harder to identify but necessary to discern.

Guiding principles

If anyone suggests to experienced primary teachers that the job is quite straightforward providing they follow standard procedures as laid down in a government document or in a book or theory, they will probably show the speaker the door (once they have stopped laughing). The job of teacher is extremely complex and the act of teaching cannot be reduced to a formula. It requires an array of skills and strategies, intensely careful thought and no small degree of trial and error. Teachers are also learners, and the best teachers show a hunger to find out more about what works best and how they can be even more effective, for once teachers stop thinking and reflecting upon their work, they ossify. Key issues demanding serious attention include:

- Attitude to learning
- Reputation
- Commitment and enthusiasm
- Children's welfare
- Establishing a working relationship
- Attitude to achievement
- Encouragement and praise
- Equal opportunities.

Attitude to learning

Learning does not happen in a vacuum. Teachers need to be clear about the conditions that contribute towards a satisfactory learning environment. Decisions about five key areas are needed:

The best conditions for learning

Learning takes place when pupils are clear about why it is worthwhile and what is expected of them by the teacher. They make most progress when the challenges they face are manageable and allow them to use their knowledge, skills and understanding to achieve the lesson targets. Children learn best when sessions are fun or, at least, not boring. They like working with their friends where possible and respond to an enthusiastic, committed teacher who introduces ideas in an original way. At the risk of being simplistic, it is right to say that learning happens best when pupils want to learn and happens less when they do not!

The degree of co-operation and competition teachers favour

Nearly all children want to do well at school. The only exceptions are a small number who are thoroughly miserable or emotionally unsettled. In some classrooms there is a notable co-operative spirit and children are generally courteous and kind to one another; in others, there seems to be an underlying tension and unhealthy rivalry. The ideal situation is one in which pupils are mutually supportive and celebrate other children's success as well as their own. Teachers who achieve this happy state do so through perseverance, modelling an appropriate attitude to their pupils, and valuing children over and above their ability to attain academically.

Motivation strategies

One of Aesop's fables concerns a dispute between the sun and the wind as to who can make a man walking along the road remove his coat. The wind tries desperately to get the man to oblige by blowing harder and harder; but the man simply wraps the coat more tightly around him. The sun shines brightly and within a short time the man has taken off his coat. Motivation rarely increases as a result of threats or compulsion. The child who is motivated to learn will be more influenced by the warmth of a teacher's personality and encouragement than by icy threats.

The criteria used to evaluate success and failure

One child works hard and achieves little; another makes minimum effort and achieves a lot. A teacher's attitude to each child will reveal a great deal about the criteria that the teacher is using to evaluate success; praise for the latter and dismay for the former will send a signal that attainment is singularly important as a measure. It is all too easy for teachers to make children feel that their worth as a person is directly linked to their success in their schoolwork. Some children like to experiment and do things in a non-conventional way. As a result, they may make more mistakes than their conventional peers but enjoy a richer learning experience. Teachers have to be careful to credit children for showing initiative as well as achieving the correct results.

Acceptable behaviour

It is important for teachers to establish basic classroom rules so that every pupil is clear about what is acceptable and appropriate. This does not mean that there will not be infringements from time to time. Teachers have to decide almost instantly whether a particular behaviour warrants a warning or scolding or whether it is best ignored. Inexperienced teachers find it hard to know what to overlook and what to act upon. Though some behaviour is wholly unacceptable, many forms are merely expressions of children's immaturity. Whatever teachers decide, they should remind themselves that it is children's co-operation that is sought, not their indulgence. Firmness in the early stages may avoid the need for strictness later on.

Further consideration of factors involved in effective learning are considered fully in Chapter 4.

Reputation

Children frequently talk about their teachers. Parents ask their children searching questions about how their day has been and what their teacher is like. Any teacher who wants to play a positive role has to recognise that reputations grow as a result of incidents and responses to situations over a period of time. It is not easy to be a new teacher in school and establish a reputation, but it is worth considering the impact that your presence has on the classroom situation. For instance, the way that you dress and conduct yourself, the tone of voice you use, the way that you react to situations, your attitude to other adults, and so forth, all contribute to the sort of impression that you create. The advantages gained through building a good reputation are considerable:

- Children are proud of you and develop a healthy attitude towards learning
- Children talk positively about you at home, thereby encouraging their parents and building confidence

- Gossip at the school gate about your competence is passed from parent to parent so that they are eager for their child to be taught by you.

For a qualified teacher in school, there are additional benefits:

- Parents and children look forward to being in that teacher's class
- The head teacher is able to speak of the teacher in warm terms to governors, visitors and prospective parents.

A good reputation is not easily established especially if you are only in the school for a short period of teaching experience. Nevertheless, factors such as appropriate relationships with children, adequate preparation for lessons and a vibrant personality are all relevant. The comments of five different groups of people on the subject help to illuminate some of the key issues:

From a four-year-old: 'I like my teacher. She lets us do painting and tells us stories.'

From an eight-year-old: 'My teacher's good. She teaches us to do things and doesn't mind if we talk to her. We do science and stuff and we have a laugh sometimes. She's not exactly strict but she doesn't like us to muck about or she can get really cross. She's alright, though, and I like her because she teaches us.'

From an 11-year-old: 'My teacher's quite cool. He does sports and stuff with us and tells us really terrible jokes! He's good at helping us with maths and gives you a chance to explain if you're stuck. I don't like it when he gets mad, but it's quite funny sometimes!'

From a parent: 'Lisa's teacher, Mr Andrews, is very nice and friendly. He said at parents' evening that he was really pleased with Lisa's progress and that her maths was improving. He said she was near the top in some subjects and one of the best readers. They went on a trip to the zoo and Lisa really enjoyed it. And when Lisa was unhappy about swimming, he phoned me up and asked to have a chat so we could sort things out and Lisa was fine afterwards. He's strict, sometimes, but the children think he's great.'

From a teaching colleague: 'Bella's a super teacher. She's got a marvellous way with the kids, somehow, and she really knows her stuff. She's also very creative and seems to have the ability to get children to think deeply. She did an incredible display for parents' evening, but still had time to help the newly qualified teacher put up her frieze. The thing about Bella is that she's always got time for you. It doesn't seem to matter how busy she is, you always feel that she's interested in what you've got to say. She's the same with everyone – kids, staff, non-teaching staff, cleaners – I don't know how she does it. Even when she's stressed out, she can always raise a laugh! Hope she stays here.'

From one of the ancillary staff: 'Mr Ryan's lovely. He always speaks to you and smiles. He treats you fairly and remembers to say thank you. He's really appreciative if you do something and doesn't mind a joke now and then. Mind you, he's a good teacher and keeps order. I was with Mrs Burton last year and it was terrible. She's very nice and friendly but can't control the class at all. I can work with Mr Ryan; you know where you stand with him.'

From the head teacher: 'I appointed Lela four years ago and she settled down well. She got stuck in straight away and wasn't afraid to ask for advice. Even when she was struggling a bit last year with a difficult class, she was very tenacious and kept going when many of us would have been tempted to give up. Parents like her because she's friendly and efficient and says positive things about the children. She's great at fetes and open evenings because she takes an interest in people. In fact she's very much a 'people person' but doesn't patronise them. As the head teacher, I'm happy because the children learn well with her, she works hard, plans thoroughly, keeps her records up to date and is popular with parents. It's good to have someone so reliable on the staff team who is also willing to learn and take advice.'

Reputation also has implications for the quality of your class discipline, not least because children quickly decide between themselves which teachers are 'soft' and which teachers deserve respect. The most formidable reputations are based on a combination of teaching effectiveness and personal qualities. Gill (1998) captures the essence of the issue: One of the best ways to eliminate discipline problems is to have a reputation as a good teacher who tries to make learning enjoyable but who will do what she says she is going to do (page 42). Sarason (1999) suggests that both teachers and pupils (the audience) should participate in what he calls 'the performance'. Thus:

> Audiences are silent performers. They are silent but not passive; at least they did not come expecting to be inwardly passive. They come expecting to see themselves and a slice of life differently. They do not expect to be bored, unmoved and sorry they came (page 14, my emphasis).

Sarason's description of an audience and performer is easily transposed to the classroom. Pupils have to *believe* in the teacher and be engaged in the proceedings. They are not passively going through the motions of 'being taught' but active learners trying to make sense of concepts, ideas and situations for themselves. In doing so they need to be interested (if not fascinated) by the curriculum, drawn into the lesson through the enthusiasm and 'authenticity' of the teacher and contributing to the proceedings. The use of dialogue in classrooms to explore, test, shape thinking and tease out the unexpected is one such way to ensure that the audience of children is transformed into performers (see Chapter 4). Other methods include free play, experimenting with materials, working co-operatively, collaborating on projects and developing new approaches to familiar pathways. However, in fulfilling these aspirations for effective learning, it is important to be alert to a number of hazards. First, giving children opportunities to explore and be creative does not guarantee satisfactory outcomes. Children can spend hours in aimless pursuits; they can respond to teachers' questions superficially; they can avoid taking risks; they can cloak shallow thinking in a frenzy of activity that yields little in positive learning.

Commitment and enthusiasm

We have noted that it is important for teachers to set a good example to pupils and impress parents by the way they present themselves in school and their general conduct. A small number of teachers spend time complaining about poor working conditions, the government, the head teacher and (sometimes) the children. It is wise to politely avoid being drawn into the conversation, even if you have some sympathy with what is being said. Wise teachers allow themselves the occasional moan but do not let it become a habit. It is surprisingly easy to slide into a negative spiral and depress both yourself and colleagues by constantly complaining, so it is worth persevering to make sure that the majority of your comments are positive ones. It takes effort to develop a healthy outlook on life, but the effect can transform the atmosphere and give hope to you and to others. As a trainee teacher you must strike a careful balance between listening sympathetically to colleagues' comments, yet maintaining a purposeful outlook on life. Do not be fooled into thinking that you will endear yourself to this glum minority by being as miserable as they are sounding! You will simply gain a reputation as a complainer and may be perceived as a burdensome hindrance. By contrast to the despondent practitioner, Fried (1995) promotes the concept of the 'passionate teacher'. Thus:

> To be a passionate teacher is to be someone in love with a field of knowledge, deeply stirred by issues and ideas that challenge our world, drawn to the dilemmas and potentials of the young people who come into class each day – or captivated by all of these. A passionate teacher is a teacher who breaks out of the isolation of a classroom, who refuses to submit to apathy or cynicism. (Prologue).

Research into attitudes of host teachers in primary schools who work with trainee teachers indicates that they value a number of characteristics in trainee teachers who are placed in their schools (Hayes 2002). These include:

Adopting a forthright attitude

Trainee teachers should make sure that they get 'stuck in' from the very start, show a genuine interest in what the children are doing, stay calm, poised and vigilant. They should volunteer for jobs where appropriate, including the messy ones. They should not, however, give the impression to the children that they are assistants or parent helpers. Trainee teachers should let the teacher see that they mean business but avoid becoming frantically active.

Staying focused

Trainee teachers should offer help and expertise to the children whenever possible and make every effort to concentrate their attention on the work in hand. If children start to show off or behave in a silly fashion while they are attempting to help them, trainee teachers should walk away and help another child. They should not allow the children to tease them, treat them like a favourite cousin or distract them from the main purpose of teaching.

Showing concern about the children

Trainee teachers should show that they like the children by establishing eye contact and taking an interest in their activities, but avoid being sucked in to child-orientated conversations. When children approach to speak to them, a trainee teacher should smile invitingly and offer help willingly but also take care that they do not end up doing the work for the children.

Enjoying the work

Trainee teachers should make it clear to the teacher that they are enjoying their time in school and appreciating the opportunities it presents. Those who speak and act to show that they are keen to be in the school will receive a sympathetic response from the staff.

Behaving courteously

As a visitor, trainee teachers are expected to be polite, helpful and well mannered to colleagues and to the children. They should not, of course, be patronising or stuffy, just thoroughly professional in outlook and conduct. Small acts of kindness and courtesy impress staff considerably.

Having a determined attitude to their own learning

Trainee teachers should regularly ask the teacher how they can improve their teaching and should not be fobbed off by general comments to the effect that they are 'doing fine' but ask instead for specific advice. All trainees should be encouraged to monitor their professional progress and acknowledge both weaknesses *and* achievements.

Extending the professional role

Teachers spend as much time working outside the classroom as they do inside it, so trainee teachers should be ready to get involved with other duties. However, in their eagerness to participate, it is important that they take care not to abandon common sense about how much they can cope with.

Expressing appreciation

Learning to thank the teacher regularly for her or his help and support, and showing that they appreciate the effort that has gone into making them welcome and giving them opportunities to gain experience of teaching is seen as a vital aspect of a trainee teacher's responsibility. They must give the firm impression that they value and appreciate what the teacher does but without being patronising or fawning.

There is much for trainee teachers and host teachers to learn about relating effectively to one another for the benefit of the children. Generally, if trainee teachers are willing to learn, respond to advice and make up their minds to be a positive influence in the school, they will receive nothing but support and encouragement. It is obvious that the better that trainee teachers and host teachers work together, understand each other's needs and accept the limitations of their different roles, the more rewarding life in school becomes for all concerned. This ideal state is more likely to happen if teachers and students agree to speak openly and honestly to one another about their feelings and expectations.

Good practice

Each time you respond to a situation, ask yourself if your response is contributing to your reputation as a decisive, forward-looking person.

Some schools have developed strategies to stimulate staff and lift spirits. Mosley and Grogan (2002) suggest that high morale is essential if a school community is to prosper, injecting mystery into the proceedings, having fun together, establishing a 'cheer-up' board and a 'words of inspiration' board, and bringing in outside support. The authors also suggest that just as children's self-esteem and mutual respect can be enhanced through circle-time (see Collins 2001 for numerous practical suggestions), the same principles apply to adults in school. Thus:

- Taking care of oneself as well as taking care of others
- Learning to draw the line and not continually bend over backwards to be helpful
- Recognising that everyone has particular and special needs
- Learning to decline requests without feeling guilty
- Accepting that everyone can only do their best
- Expecting to be treated with consideration and courtesy and as someone with intelligence
- Refusing to be dependent on other people's approval
- Recognising that time for relaxation is not wasted time

The position is well summarised by Suschitzky and Chapman (1998): 'The ways that children view themselves are influenced by the ways others respond to them' (page 8). And one of the most significant 'others' is you!

Good practice

Make a deliberate effort to gradually introduce a larger proportion of positive comments into your conversations. Monitor the impact of your changing attitude on pupils and colleagues.

Children's welfare

All teachers must have a working knowledge and understanding of teachers' professional duties, legal liabilities and responsibilities, so it is essential to be aware of the extent and limits of your duty towards the children. They are protected by the Children Act (1989) which does not allow adults to exert unreasonable psychological pressure upon them, such as shouting in their face and hectoring, or physical chastisement and force (see Chapter 11). There are obvious exceptions to this rule; for instance, screaming out loud may be the only means of preventing a child running in the road, and physical containment may be the only way to prevent one child from injuring another. However, these occurrences are rare and the general principle of treating children with respect and using reason rather than rage is contained within the 1989 Act.

In practice, it may take you a lot of self-discipline to avoid infringing the spirit of the Act, especially with children who persistently and wilfully take advantage of their freedom and seem determined to push adults to the limits of their patience. Nevertheless, you must learn to remain calm and exercise self-control, regardless of the provocation or personal slights you receive. If you are an inexperienced teacher it is unwise to try and deal with difficult situations without support and advice. If you are uncertain about a situation or the appropriate form of response towards children, consult senior colleagues at the earliest opportunity, and keep them informed of subsequent developments.

Children need to feel at ease with one another and also confident about their place in society. The development of PSHE is an important element of effective schooling, as it helps to develop positive attitudes, address issues of significance to children and stimulate an active interest in society and citizenship (see Chapter 1). There are many occasions when a teacher wishes to develop a more intimate atmosphere by gathering the children together in a smaller, well-defined area in which they can all sit comfortably. The children sit in a circle with the teacher to discuss key issues, share ideas and celebrate events (e.g. Curry and Bromfield, 1998). The circle-time approach depends upon everyone agreeing in advance about procedures (such as only one person speaking at a time) and conduct (such as speaking kindly). It is non-threatening (children only contribute when they wish to do so) and is intended to increase co-operation and allow for positive reinforcement, thus raising the self-image of every child. On other occasions, carpet time is used for book sharing, or the teacher or a capable child reading aloud to the class. Although some teachers and their classes make fruitful use of circle-time each week, it should be seen only as a component of the overall teaching method. As with any other approach, its value has to be monitored and evaluated and ensure that the child is left with higher self-esteem and confidence as a result.

Timing can also influence the circumstances. For instance, it may be unwise to gather children into close confinement immediately after a long assembly or inactive playtime. Although the end of the day is frequently used for a story and sharing, other times should also be considered, particularly towards the end of a session when children's minds are buzzing.

Health and safety

Pupils' safety must also be a priority for every adult working in school. Health and safety factors depend on the nature of the activities, the age of the children and adult–child ratio. For very young children, basic cleanliness training may be the priority; for older ones, correct use of tools and equipment may be the priority. There are also some common issues such as ensuring that:

- Children have sufficient space for the task in hand.
- Children are aware of others in the vicinity who may be affected by their actions (such as being sprayed by paint!).
- There is a minimum of hazards on the floor (such as spilled glue) that might be perilous.
- The procedures for movement about the room and the correct place for each piece of equipment have been explained to the children beforehand.

Of course, prevention is always better than cure, so it is essential to think ahead. Sensible health and safety precautions are not for the purpose of limiting what children attempt to do or their enjoyment of practical activities. On the contrary, good working practices liberate the children to work confidently and assuredly. As the responsible adult, you have to make the final decisions about what is permissible.

In science, warn about:

- The hazards of cuts from split plastic and sharp edges. Cuts should be treated by holding the damaged area under free-flowing cold water, direct from the tap, into an empty sink.

- The danger of cord or wire being wrapped tightly around a wrist or tangled around the neck. A pair of wire-cutters should be readily available should instant release be necessary. Unless there is physical damage to the skin, it is usually sufficient to massage the affected area.

- The effect of bright light on eyes and high volume sound on eardrums.

In physical activity guard against:

- Over-exuberant 'warm-up' activities that involve children charging around and the potential for nasty collisions. Instead use more 'on the spot' activities.

- Body movement that may cause strain without suitable 'warm-up' activities. Instead, ensure that you have led all the children through the required muscle-loosening exercises.

- Unstable or damaged equipment. It is essential to check beforehand or, if this has not been possible, to put to one side any item that is in an unsuitable state. If this interferes with the smooth running of your lesson, console yourself with the thought that it is better to have a disrupted lesson than an injured child!

- Hard equipment, especially wooden or solid plastic bats that may hit a child in the face. If bats are necessary, you should not be afraid to enforce strict conditions for their use, especially maintaining a distance between the batter and the rest of the team. One way to achieve this is to insist that the batter stands at a point that is located at the centre of a concentric circle of outer hoops or a chalk/tape ring. No one else is allowed beyond the perimeter of the hoops until it is their turn to bat.

- Equipment that allows children to climb beyond the limits of their capability.

- Long breaks between bouts of physical exertion. If a lengthy break is necessary, a further warm-up should be used before proceeding. Generally, it is better to increase the physical demands gradually and equally gradually reduce them, though in practice this may not always be possible.

- Allowing the noise level to rise too high such that the children cannot hear your commands. The use of clear instructions, explanations about the need for a sensible noise level and a signal on a whistle or tambourine to indicate the need for quiet are all useful control strategies.

- Stopping a lesson abruptly before the children have been led through some 'warm down' activities.

Art, design and technology presents a range of challenges, not least issues relating to resources, grouping and adult supervision of children. Monitoring of activities also makes heavy demands on the teacher. If the whole class is engaged in targeted Arts' activities, you will need to plan well in advance of the event to ensure that there are adequate resources available and children have been taught the necessary skills to make the best use of their time. In addition, additional adult support may require that they are released from other duties or, if parents are being involved, that communication is clear and arrangements are in place. Parent helpers can be a wonderful asset, but they are unimpressed if they have been invited to participate in something that is poorly organised. A basic rule is that the complexity of an activity should never be greater than the educational benefit that the children gain from carrying it out.

Although it is impossible to guarantee that children will never have an accident or suffer some emotional trauma, it is important to take every reasonable precaution without becoming obsessive about it. Casualness about such issues may result in damage to children and stress for you. For instance, you can be sure that the one time you assume that the physical education equipment is in good order or that all the children are safely away from danger will be the one time that something unforeseen happens. Experienced teachers develop a keen sensitivity to where danger and possible hazards lie and take steps to minimise risks. If you are new to teaching, however, you cannot rely on such awareness, so it is important to get into the habit of thinking through in advance where things could go wrong and taking preventative action to ensure that children can get on with their learning without trauma. Simple procedures such as ensuring that walkways are free from bags and keeping items within easy reach, rather than having to stretch for them, make a considerable difference both to the safety of the classroom and its smooth organisation.

Safeguarding children does not mean that they should be wrapped up in cotton wool like fragile ornaments. It does mean that teachers have to undertake a risk assessment about the possible consequences of their work with pupils, especially in less familiar situations such as during out-of-school activities. However, even in regular lessons there may be instances in which special care must be taken. For example, if you are preparing a lesson in which equipment is being used, you must make certain that it is in good working order. Electrical (mains) equipment should not be used unless it has been checked by a qualified electrician and labelled safe for use. If children are involved in any process requiring heat or blades they should be properly trained and organised to use the equipment. Some practical lessons requiring the use of tools necessitate close adult supervision, a point to bear in mind when planning lessons, ensuring that the assistant is fully briefed.

Although accidents are rare in primary classrooms, you should be aware of the correct procedures for dealing with casualties. A course of first aid training, regularly updated, will give you the confidence you need to act promptly in the case of an emergency, though you are not normally permitted to give medicines in school or carry out procedures which require specialist expertise. Should there be an accident in a situation where you are the responsible adult, make sure that it is recorded in the 'accident book' that is often kept in a school's main office or first-aid room. If you are unsure about any aspect of safety law, check with the head teacher and refer to the school's policy and practice document. Chapter 11 clarifies and expands on many of these basic points.

Health and safety is not only concerned with physical wellbeing, as every adult also has a responsibility to be alert to children's emotional condition. This concern should not be confused with the crude notion that taking an interest in children's welfare makes a teacher a social worker. Education involves more than simply teaching facts. It involves helping children to understand their place in the world, the contribution that they can make to society and their responsibilities to one another. Taking time to listen to children, to understand their needs, hopes and desires should not be seen as a burden for teachers, but as a privilege. (See, for example, Corrie 2003.)

Establishing a working relationship

Establishing a working relationship with a class of children requires patient perseverance. In particular, the first few weeks with any new class are always a time of adjustment, trial-and-error and the creation of mutual understanding. Children who are themselves new to school have to make the transition from the relative security of home, playgroup or nursery to the vagaries of school life. Those who may have received exclusive attention at home have to accept that they are only one amongst many other children vying for an adult's time and attention. Those who are transferring to a different class in September will have at least a year of routines and procedures behind them which will differ to some extent from those preferred by the new teacher. And in addition to these changes, a trainee teacher now joins the social mix!

Although this process of establishing a working relationship is rarely without its ups and downs, awareness of the likely course that it will take allows you to be prepared and less likely to be thrown by the circumstances that you experience. It is helpful to think of the route to a working relationship in terms of three stages: preliminaries, courtship and partnership.

Preliminaries

Early encounters with pupils strongly influence the quality of future relationships. Even qualified teachers who change schools take time to assimilate the culture of their new school, so trainee teachers are bound to struggle in the first days or weeks of a new school experience as they grow accustomed to the host teachers' expectations, the class procedures and the 'unwritten laws' (see Chapter 1). Preliminary encounters with children are often very demanding owing to the need to strike a balance between establishing a positive relationship while maintaining control. Although a degree of sparring is inevitable, new teachers can help themselves by resisting the following:

- *Being bombarded with questions by pupils.* If necessary, a curt refusal to answer all but the most basic questions is needed. Otherwise, a pleasant smile and 'that is mine to know and yours to find out' or similar will usually dissuade all but the most persistent questioner.

- *Courting short-term popularity.* You may be the most exciting thing that has come into the children's lives for some time, but the novelty will quickly wear off. It is wise to ease into the new situation and gradually to become absorbed into classroom life, rather than to imagine that the initial enthusiastic welcome will be maintained.

- *Attempting too much too soon.* It is better to build up gradually than attempt too much and struggle to cope. Some trainee teachers want to take major responsibility from an early stage, but it is generally more realistic to work alongside the class teacher for a time and slowly increase the breadth and range of your teaching.

On the other hand there are strategies which help to ease you through these early encounters:

- *Learning names as quickly as possible.* Discipline is so much easier if you can use children's names when addressing them. It is invariably the case that teachers learn the names of the mischievous, minority and assertive children first, but be careful not to use their names too much and reinforce their 'different' status. Quieter children probably hear their names far less often, so may deserve to hear them more!

- *Thorough lesson preparation.* Pupils soon sense any insecurity that exudes from unprepared teachers, so make sure that you know your stuff and, importantly, have thought through the practicalities of the lesson. The more that you are clear about what you are trying to achieve, what the children are trying to learn and how this will all take place, the more likely that they will settle and prosper. At the same time, bear in mind that children sometimes learn things that you did not intend or expect.

- *Ensuring early success for pupils.* Nothing facilitates a smooth passage more than when children receive genuine approval for work well done. However, it is worth remembering that children will not automatically celebrate your positive tones until they have learned to trust and respect you. It is better to slightly understate your praise initially than to be unduly exuberant.

The preliminary stage demands a lot of bridge-building between teachers and pupils, who must learn to relax together as trust is slowly gained through regular interaction, resulting in better understanding. Teachers have to be willing to persevere and hold their nerve through the difficult days. If you refuse to be unsettled, continue to offer interesting lessons, take a genuine interest in individuals, remain alert and maintain a good balance between listening to children's views and insisting on basic conformity to agreed behaviour, you won't go far wrong. However, achieving this state of affairs requires persistence, so don't get discouraged if things take time to fall into place.

Courtship

It is not possible to get to know all the pupils straight away. Some children prefer to weigh teachers up and others almost jump into their laps! Some children remain aloof because they are shy or suspicious of teachers or because they are contented with life on their terms and do not want to be influenced too much by another adult. Children's coolness towards teachers is not an indication that they hold something against them; similarly, effusive children do not necessarily like teachers. Sometimes you will find that the relationships with children that take longer to establish prove to be the most fruitful. Teachers must try to be even-handed with all the children and give them the opportunity to speak when they want to express something and remain silent when they prefer to listen or reflect. Children do not mind a firm teacher, but they despise a gullible or weak-willed one.

As the courtship continues, boundaries between acceptable and unacceptable behaviour can be clarified. Children will test the limits to see how far they stretch. If teachers are too lenient, they may find that the boundary walls are made of elastic! On the other hand, rigidity may lead to resentment. It is important for teachers to explain to their pupils why things are permitted and refused, but done so as matters of fact, not as issues for negotiation. Pupils may not always approve of a teacher's methods but providing they are seen as fair, relationships will gradually settle and consolidate. As a guest in the classroom with a limited time in which to make an impression and learn from your experiences, it is sensible to adopt the class teacher's approach as closely as possible until you feel more confident. Subsequently, you can discuss variations in approach with the teacher and offer your own perspective. In the meantime you may have to persevere with implementing the existing policy.

Partnership

The ideal situation is one in which teachers and pupils are at ease with one another and respond easily and naturally to each other, so that learning is purposeful and children are motivated. Exactly how this state is achieved is not altogether clear but can be recognised instantly because of the shared trust that exists between teachers and pupils as they work harmoniously, celebrate success and handle setbacks positively. Children will have confidence to ask questions and express an opinion. Rules will be adhered to sensibly, though there will be opportunity to discuss their application. The work will be meaningful and, though there may be spells when the children find the work tedious, they will persevere in the sure knowledge that more exciting lessons are never far away. The most striking characteristics of the partnership environment will be the sense of mutual respect, good eye contact and natural use of the voice. Both the teacher and the children will find fulfilment in their work.

Some teachers never get beyond the first two stages (preliminaries and courtship). In exceptional cases the sparring will continue for so long that the classroom climate deteriorates and the teacher resorts to harsh tactics to maintain control and coerce rather than persuade the children to conform. Such circumstances are, of course, very disappointing for those involved. Instead of being relaxed and encouraging, the teacher's relationship with the class is tense and unsatisfactory, with the result that learning is ponderous rather than joyful.

There are always ebbs and flows in the struggle to achieve a partnership but the effort is well worthwhile. Perseverance, a willingness to evaluate your work as a teacher and a thirst to gain advice from experienced colleagues will help you in your quest for an enduring, positive relationship with the children and the enhancement in learning that accompanies it.

Activate your thinking!

Consider your responses in the following situations:

- A ten year old girl keeps asking you if you are married.
- A five-year-old boy wants you to help him all the time and jealously pushes away other children who seek your assistance.

- An eight year-old girl sulkily tells you that you are not her 'real' teacher.

- An eleven-year-old boy angrily accuses you of being unfair.

- A ten-year-old girl spends ages producing work that is inferior in quality to that from much younger children in the class.

- A five-year-old boy produces a colourful painting in half the time allotted and begins to take his apron off.

- An anxious eight-year-old girl constantly seeks your approval and commendation for her work.

- An eleven-year-old boy brings a page of very neat work to you that he has copied from a page on the internet.

Attitude to achievement

Picture the scene. Ben and Angie, identical twins, come out of school clutching their recently acquired swimming certificates. Ben thrusts the creased card under his mother's nose and explodes in mock glee about the 10m award he has recently achieved. Angie saunters up a few moments later, quietly confident about her coveted 50m success. How will the mother respond? Ben knows that his sister is a better swimmer but had secretly hoped that he might match her accomplishments. He had never in his seven years of life shown more determination than in his frantic efforts as he struggled through the final moments of that seemingly eternal swim. The teacher had congratulated him but Ben had shrugged it off, all too aware of his sister's sparkling success a short time before. In his mind he pictured the scene when they met their mother – Angie receiving fulsome praise for her achievements. For himself, the sincere but consoling 'You've done well, too, Ben'.

Achievement is an important aspect of life and some people obviously achieve more than others do. Children need goals as much as anyone else. It is sometimes difficult for grown-ups to remember the thrill and excitement of scoring a goal in a games lesson, winning a prize for a special painting, enjoying a glass of orange after helping the teacher with a job or having a star placed on the chart for finishing another reading book. These are the moments when children's achievements are openly and publicly acknowledged and savoured. A more difficult challenge for adults is knowing how to respond to children whose achievements are limited; where success has only ever been partial and exhilaration has depended upon a surrogate basking in the reflected glow from others.

Central to this matter is the importance of the teacher's concern not solely for children's performance but for children themselves. Achievements are notoriously fickle. Children who depend upon tangible evidence of their own worth can become equally unhappy when achievements remain elusive. The hero of the hour is quickly forgotten. Certificates fade and crinkle. Sparkling reports become an archive. It is the children themselves who are the only consistent factor, and their wellbeing and contentment must outlive the pleasure of achievement. To base the worth of individuals on these certificated or measurable successes while ignoring the other qualities which characterise their lives is to burden children with the need to gain ever further achievements as a means of recognition and approval. That route can be a recipe for heartache and ultimate low self-esteem as the success and the approval that accompanies it diminishes.

There is a need to get this issue in perspective. Achievement is important. It is good to do well. Some children work extremely hard and persevere to attain their goals. They rightly receive recognition and our congratulations. No, it is not the achievement that's at fault but rather our attitude to it as adults if we give children the impression that their personal worth depends upon coming out at the top of the pack. Success should not be measured solely through identifiable and visible outcomes but also in how the outcomes affect the child's character, ability to cope with life, confidence and attitude to others. The child that trails in last at the end of the race, red-faced and sweating but determined to finish, deserves every bit as much recognition as the county long-distance champion who happens to be in the same school. Both children, in their different ways, deserve praise: the winner because of her victory, the loser because of her willingness to try. Both deserve encouragement: the winner to compete for coveted prizes, the loser to take pride in her sporting attitude and gallant endeavours. And we must not forget those between the extremes. It is easy to overlook the also-ran, the average child and the steady-but-unspectacular pupil. Teachers must ensure that the genuine efforts of every child are recognised and acclaimed.

Activate your thinking!

Consider these comments from children, the adult responses and the extent to which they conform to the criteria of being positive, honest and encouraging:

Child 1:   I'm rubbish at this.

Teacher: Well, that's the best I've ever seen you run; I don't suppose you'll ever catch up with mile-a-minute Mandy, but even I can't run that fast!

Child 2:   Sir, John only beat me 'cause he cheated.

Teacher: Well, I'm sorry if that's true, but the important thing is that you didn't give up. You kept going and didn't cheat, so well done.

Child 3:   Miss, I was almost last. That's the worst I've ever run.

Teacher: Yes, I expect you feel quite disappointed. But I know that you can do better and you know that you can, so you'll just have to keep trying. What's more, you haven't made any excuses for doing badly which proves to me that you're a good sport and makes you a winner as far as I'm concerned!

> ## Good practice
>
> Looking the child in the eye, regularly use affirming expressions such as:
>
> Well done, Ben. I'm proud of you.
>
> Top of the class, Vernon.
>
> You should feel very pleased with yourself, Junior. I certainly am!
>
> Champion effort Jenny! Well done!

Snippets of conversation reveal a great deal about a teacher's attitude and the adult–child relationship based on whether:

- The adult took a personal interest in each child.

- The adult's comments were positive and truthful.

- The child was willing to confide in the adult in the first place (a strong clue about previous adult–child encounters).

Contrast the positive teacher attitude in the Activate Your Thinking! box with the following negative one:

Child 1:   I'm rubbish at this!

Teacher: Stop moaning and get changed.

Child 2:   Sir, John only beat me 'cause he cheated.

Teacher: I don't want to hear about it!

Child 3:   Miss, I was almost last, that's the worst I've ever run!

Teacher: You'll just have try a bit harder next time, won't you?

The teacher in this second set of conversations was unable to discern the deeper motives that underpinned the children's comments. Child 1 wanted to be reassured that her poor performance mattered less than genuine effort. Child 2 was upset over the unexpected reverse of fortune and needed a calm adult response to give him space to come to terms with the disappointment. Child 3 was finding failure difficult to handle and looked for confirmation that a single setback was not setting a precedent. The first adult looked beyond the immediate comment to the motive and responded in a sympathetic yet positive manner which assisted the child to come to terms with the reality of the situation without humiliation or condemnation.

A teacher's attitude to achievement influences the creation of a healthy classroom climate and helps children develop a positive attitude towards learning. Teachers who are intolerant of low-achieving children bring about a lowering of self-concept and, consequently, even lower achievement, so as teachers we have serious responsibilities and need to ensure that we:

- Take every opportunity to give praise where it is due

- Encourage children who have tried hard, even if the end product is poor relative to others in the group

■ Ensure that our relationship with the children is one of respect and tolerance.

A proper attitude to achievement for all children is an important element of school life and all teachers must think carefully about where they stand on the issue. Being positive and encouraging should not, however, be confused with giving children a false sense of their achievements. Pupils who do not or will not try and make minimal effort should be left in no doubt about your feelings on the matter!

Encouragement and praise

A small number of people seem unable or unwilling to encourage, but prefer to criticise and look for opportunities to find fault. Others want to be encouraging but somehow can't find the right words. But what is encouragement and what is its place in teaching and learning?

First, encouragement isn't the same thing as praise. *Encouragement* can be given to children at any time to help them improve on their present efforts, complete a difficult piece of work or concentrate harder in order to achieve a higher standard. Teachers can use a variety of expressions to cajole, chivvy, motivate and offer support, accompanied by sparkling eye contact, clapping, smiles, open faces and close body positions. *Praise*, on the other hand, is offered for achievement: good quality work, real effort, instances of sensitivity and responsibility. Praise is usually given with great enthusiasm, openly announced.

Encouragement recognises that the present situation is acceptable but the prospect of better things awaits earnest endeavour. *Praise* recognises that the very best has been achieved in the circumstances. Children won't accept encouragement or praise from someone they don't respect but will see it rather as a subtle form of coercion. It is better to bide your time and be gently approving rather than let loose a flood of commendation in your earliest encounters with the class. You may discover that the efforts and product that you enthused about is below the child's ability level, so it pays to be cautious in making definite judgements before you have a clear view of a child's potential and previous attainment. Further advice about assessing achievement can be found in Chapter 7.

Despite these caveats, it is certainly the case that both encouragement and praise can help children in at least three ways:

1   By revealing that the teacher is interested in what they are doing
2   By helping them to understand the teacher's expectations clearly
3   By opening a dialogue that will help them to consider their attainment and monitor their own progress.

This third point is important. Children must learn to evaluate the quality of their own work and gain a sense of self-satisfaction rather than to rely wholly on adult approval.

With these issues in mind, teachers need to think carefully about the forms of encouragement they use. For instance, to tell a child in a dignified monotone that they can 'do better than that' is unlikely to inspire greater effort or determination. The unspoken message from the teacher's utterance is one of dissatisfaction and the threat of further criticism if there is no improvement. Of course, a lazy or indifferent child needs to be carefully watched, and clear, short-term work targets set, but nine times out of ten children (who are often their own worst critics) will admit if challenged that the work is not their best. This sort of admission opens up the way for the teacher to make specific and non-threatening suggestions about improvement while maintaining an effective level of communication with the child. When children accept that you are trying to understand them rather than looking for things to criticise, they are more likely to confide their reasons for the quality of the work. Perhaps they are bored or uncertain about what's expected or finding it too difficult. Perhaps they are unhappy about their partner. A sympathetic but firm approach unlocks doors that remain tightly shut to a stiffer approach that carries a strong hint of disapproval and reproach.

Similarly, most children will spot insincere praise. The unthinking 'That's good' or dismissive 'Yes, fine' (without paying any real attention to what the child has done or said) is likely to lead to lower standards as children see how little they can get away with and still receive praise. Praise has to be merited and should not be offered lightly.

Encouragement is most effective when it is used constructively, without rancour and in the context of clearly defined tasks and expectations. Praise, publicly and sincerely given, should be reserved for genuine instances of quality work and effort. For children who trust their teacher, there is no greater source of satisfaction for them.

Equal opportunities

In free countries, where the safety of the government depends very much upon the favourable judgement which the people may form of its conduct, an instructed and intelligent people must surely be of the highest importance.

Adam Smith 1776

When planning, teachers should set high expectations and provide opportunities for all pupils to achieve, including boys and girls, pupils with special educational needs, pupils with disabilities, pupils from all social and cultural backgrounds, pupils of different ethnic groups including travellers, refugees and asylum seekers, and those from diverse linguistic backgrounds.

The National Curriculum 2000, page 31.

It is important to understand that discrimination is not allowed in schools on any basis whatsoever. In their publication *Excellence and Enjoyment* (DfES 2003a), the Government confirms the principle that 'Our education system must support all pupils well and unintentionally discriminate against any particular group of pupils' (page 42). Thus, deliberate or unintentional bias towards pupils which can be construed as discriminatory leaves teachers open to charges of unprofessional conduct, so it is important to be as impartial as possible at all times when dealing with children. Not only must pupils be granted the same opportunities, support and encouragement, but it is not appropriate to label children due to circumstances beyond their control such as home background or physical appearance. A teasing pleasantry about a child's looks or domestic circumstances may be more hurtful and do greater damage than a teacher imagines. A useful antidote to discriminatory attitudes is to develop a positive attitude towards achievement and to adopt a 'you can do it' working atmosphere in which all children can fulfil their potential. Remember, too, that it is part of your responsibility to foster an environment in which children treat each other respectfully.

Children like teachers who exercise consistent control and are fair in their dealings with everyone in the class. Teachers who exhibit favouritism or indifference towards certain groups or individuals are resented and pupils who feel slighted are unlikely to make optimum progress in school. Teachers must therefore regularly interrogate the ways in which their own attitudes towards children might affect learning.

At one time, boys were steered towards the skills and subjects that would provide them with a foundation for working life; girls were expected to become homemakers and were taught accordingly. Today, teachers have to be aware that both girls and boys have an important role in the workplace and in the home and it is important to treat each child as an individual, rather than make blanket assumptions about temperament, ability and life chances. Teachers also have a considerable responsibility to use teaching approaches that appeal to lively children, as well as to the compliant ones.

Sometimes gender and not ability or potential appears to be the controlling factor (Brown, 1998; Yelland, 1998). However, results from national tests indicate that the position is more complex, and girls are forging ahead of boys in most areas of work, especially in language and topic work. The experience of many reception class teachers is that although most girls persevere with reading, take their books home faithfully each night and seem to pick up the necessary skills and strategies with little difficulty, the picture with boys is more varied. Some boys are slower, fail to organise themselves as well as the girls and are attracted more by computer games, construction kits, practical activities and competition than by desk-bound exercises. It is ironic that despite girls' tendency to socialise more naturally than boys, it is the independent task of reading which many girls find fulfilling. Paradoxically, the more independent image frequently attached to boys is counteracted by the unease shown by many of them with the solitary task of reading and their preference for collaborative practical work. It is the common experience of teachers that boys who display antisocial behaviour in school often struggle with the basic academic skills.

The spiral of failure now becomes clear. The boy who has experienced constant failure in reading and other aspects of English is marginalised from many of the everyday classroom activities that bring commendation and praise from teachers and peers. Because of his difficulties, he is offered increasing amounts of support in elementary skills by an adult, usually a teaching assistant, sometimes at the expense of involvement in the more attractive practical and creative tasks. This double deprivation (loss of approval for academic success, fewer exciting activities) leads in turn to frustration and resentment and a negative attitude towards school. Teachers, despairing of what to do with these recalcitrant youngsters, resort to strong control strategies or conclude that they are beyond the school's available expertise and are in need of external specialist expertise. Conversations in the staffroom frequently centre upon the impossibility of dealing with such children but there are numerous strategies available for ameliorating the position, including parental involvement, consistency of approach and use of external rewards.

A report by the Office for Standards in Education (OFSTED) found that although girls outperformed boys in almost every area of academic work, some schools and teachers were able to help boys achieve their potential, especially in the problem area of writing (OFSTED 2003a). The issue of schooling boys (Skelton 2001) has become an important issue for teachers in recent years, though 'quick-fix' solutions are unhelpful (Epstein *et al.* 1998). The OFSTED study suggests that in schools where boys progress well there is a culture where intellectual, cultural and aesthetic accomplishment is valued by boys as well as by girls. Progress is most pronounced where positive incentives, respect and encouragement for boys to pursue their own interests combat the 'laddish' anti-intellectual culture. In schools where boys perform well, they are encouraged to read widely and offered choice about the content of their writing, even when the form or genre is prescribed. An effort is made by the teacher for children to write to 'real' audiences where possible. Effective planning and teaching are accompanied by frequent and formative assessment of boys' writing, and a culture that enables them to take pride in the product. Teaching is enhanced when there are opportunities for the boys and girls to write at length ('extended writing') and tackle non-literary texts, poetry and narrative, both as readers and writers. There appears to be a clear link between the development of independent reading habits and enthusiasm for writing on the part of the teacher and the pupils. The OFSTED study also stressed the importance role played by assessment. Thus:

> Boys in these schools know that their writing and their progress as writers are valued by teachers, since this is signalled in the way teachers respond to their work. High quality, close and responsive marking of written work (at different stages of drafting) offers clear advice on how to improve, even to high attainers, and always offers feedback on content as well as skills (OFSTED 2003a, section 24).

This guidance is useful when dealing with boys who already possess some writing skills but the challenge for teachers of children who are disdainful about writing is more severe. Some boys, capable of communicating through speech and visual means find themselves out of favour with teachers due to their reluctance to commit ideas to paper. Wise teachers try to harness their enthusiasm, while firmly insisting that they apply themselves to recording ideas and results on paper, though in practical subjects the children's reluctance can become a significant issue. Although expectations and role-orientation are woven into the fabric of society and are hard to disentangle, relatively small instances may reveal deeper assumptions about gender roles. For example, grouping all the girls' names beneath the boys' names on a register may simply be a method of organising, or it may reflect a belief that boys are more significant. Similarly, in the choice of team leaders, allocation of the order in which children take a turn and selection for prestige positions (in a presentation to parents, say) it is necessary to make decisions based on competence, fairness and academic priorities, not gender or assertiveness. Similarly, a sweet smile from a charming girl should not result in a lesser sanction being imposed on her for a misdemeanour compared with that for an untidy boy with a permanent scowl.

Although impartial decisions are needed as far as possible when dealing with children, male and female, this fact should not be confused with a need to take account of individual differences in children. Children respond differently to situations and circumstances and adults must obviously be prepared to adjust their responses and actions accordingly. However, this axiom results in a dilemma. On the one hand it is necessary for teachers to be consistent in their treatment of children. On the other hand one child will respond to a lighter 'touch' than another child. Teachers are not judges in a court of law handing down sentences regardless of whoever stands before them. They must exercise wisdom in the way that they approach all interpersonal encounters. Nevertheless, the need for discernment is far removed from a blanket stereotyping of children on the basis of gender or any other defining characteristic (such as background, sportiness or even physical height). The key is to treat every case on merit and use a large dose of common sense in making decisions.

Although the majority of concerns about equal opportunities have focused on gender issues, there are studies that suggest that stereotyping is associated with pupil personality. Teachers tend to have expectations about achievement (and behaviour) which are related to their perceptions of children's apparent willingness to learn rather than their true capability. Thus, the child with a bright personality who volunteers to do tasks and errands, and who is comfortable chatting with the teacher, may or may not be a capable learner. On the other hand, the shy, passive children are likely to be perceived as less capable than they really are. This description is, of course, also in danger of becoming stereotypical. Some articulate children with a bright personality are also clever. Some under-confident, diffident types are strugglers (which is part of the explanation for their timidity).

Our awareness of these interwoven factors suggests that it is foolish for teachers to jump to conclusions about their pupils' ability and potential. The outgoing child may, despite an apparently carefree approach to life, be concealing a deep unease which leads to under-achievement. The shy child may be lacking self-confidence or may be an uncomplicated and contented person who does not feel the need to be assertive.

To further complicate matters, the outgoing non-academic children are sometimes skilled in 'losing' themselves in a group of more capable children and benefiting from the reflected glory of their expertise and talent. Against this, the less confident children may lose out in two ways. First, they are unable to articulate their needs, and second, they lack the social and communication skills to find suitable collaborators. Such children often end up being paired with unsuitable individuals who are the remnant after more popular children have been absorbed into the more stable groups or chosen first for teams and collaborative groups. If teachers are to avoid the pre-disposition that may exist that denies children their rights as learners, they must step back from making spontaneous decisions and look objectively at the evidence from outcomes, such as completed work, comments made during question-and-answer sessions, and engagement with tasks.

In every class, therefore, there are children with varied personalities, talents, ideals and potential. Teachers have a responsibility towards all of them and need to employ different teaching strategies to:

■ Ensure that passive children are given as many (though not necessarily any more) interesting tasks as their assertive peers

- Allow children who do not find it easy to learn in traditional ways to have some opportunity to experience different forms of learning

- Make allowance for ebullient behaviour born out of enthusiasm for the task in hand rather than mischievousness

- View basic skills, such as reading, as a socially welding activity through group work and collaborative strategies.

It is essential to avoid situations in which a compliant group of passive children (often girls) are given repetitive tasks (such as colouring) while a few very assertive children (often boys) are kept occupied with the exciting practical activities with which they are most content as a means of keeping them content and better behaved! Teachers have to learn to strike a balance between accommodating children's natural preferences and pandering to their stubbornness or unwillingness to toe the line by allowing them excessive opportunities to enjoy favoured options.

Teachers should also be aware of how many left-handed children are in the class. The DfES provide guidance for teachers on how best to help left-handed children, including the provision of softer-leaded pencils, left-handed scissors, a left-handed ruler, an ergonomic left-handed mouse or a mouse set up for left-handers and a sloping board beneath paper to assist correct writing and drawing. There is no proof that left-handed people differ from right-handers in terms of educational attainment or IQ and various organisations exist to assist children and teachers, including a club for children (www.anythingleft-handed.co.uk). Teachers should watch out, too, for children who sit 'side on' as this may indicate that one eye is weaker than the other, or that the child has a particular spatial preference. Left-handed children write 'into' their bodies and may develop an awkward writing posture.

A teacher's assumptions about children's ability to learn and make progress may have a direct influence upon their attitude to school in general, their willingness to co-operate and persevere, and ultimately their achievements (Lampard, 1994). Attention to equal opportunities yields unexpected rewards.

Activate your thinking!

- Do you pay undue attention to the more articulate and outgoing children?
- Do you make unwarranted assumptions about certain groups of children without evidence?
- Do you have a prevailing view of boys as naughty, girls as biddable?

Special educational needs

There have always been children who struggle with school work or suffer from some condition which prevents them from fulfilling their potential (see, for instance, Heeks and Kinwell 1997). It is important to distinguish between children with special needs and those with special *educational* needs (SEN). Children may have a variety of disabilities which do not, with appropriate support, handicap their educational opportunities, while some children have congenital problems which are exacerbated by the impact they have upon their capacity to learn. This section is concerned with children who are falling behind in their academic work for a variety of different reasons, and who may or may not suffer from a medically diagnosed disability.

Pupils who are labelled as 'less able' tend to fall into one of four categories, though more than one of the factors below may apply:

- Children who do not possess the intellectual capacity to keep pace with the majority of children.

- Children who are of such a high intellect that they find it difficult to fit in to the familiar learning structures.

- Children who are capable of average to high achievement but under-achieve due to their erratic or uncontrolled behaviour. Such children are often referred to as emotionally disturbed or having behavioural difficulties. More recently, the term 'attention deficit disorder' is employed when referring to children who struggle to concentrate.

- Children who, though intellectually capable, possess physical disabilities which have the potential to hinder their ability to attain their full potential.

The DfES publication *Excellence and Enjoyment* (DfES 2003a) emphasises that effective learning and teaching should:

- Ensure every child succeeds by providing an inclusive education within a culture of expectations

- Build on what learners already know by structuring and pacing teaching so that pupils know what is to be learnt, how and why

- Make learning vivid and real by developing understanding through enquiry, creativity, e-learning and group problem solving

- Make learning an enjoyable and challenging experience by stimulating learning through matching teaching techniques and strategies to a range of learning styles

- Enrich the learning experience by building learning skills across the curriculum

- Promote assessment for learning by making children partners in their learning.

The Code of Practice (DfES 2002a) is a document with which every teacher should be familiar. It contains detailed information about the identification of children with SEN and suggestions for appropriate action. It is designed as a positive way of responding to the individual needs of children by means of a systematic process which draws upon expertise from inside and outside the school, and places great emphasis upon parental involvement (Figure 2.1).

Every maintained school must have a member of staff who acts as a SENCO and a responsible person (usually the head teacher or a governor) who acts as a point of reference for the process. The governing body will have a sub-committee to take a particular interest in such

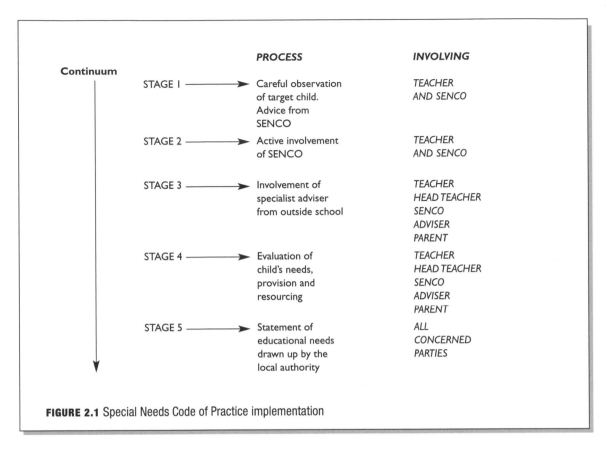

FIGURE 2.1 Special Needs Code of Practice implementation

educational provision and is obliged to report to parents at the annual meeting about policies for children with SEN and their implementation.

The stages of the Code of Practice are not necessarily sequential. A child can enter the process at different points, depending upon his or her circumstances. While all this is going on, class teachers have to do their best to cope with the children in question. The interim period of time can be stressful as events often move more slowly than expected. Long delays prove exasperating for over-stretched teachers as they struggle to help children who may, in certain cases, also suffer from hyperactivity or attention disorders with the accompanying discipline challenges they bring. All this takes place against a backdrop of government demands for higher standards of achievement in core subjects for every child, *including* those with SEN.

Future provision for children with SEN emphasises preventative rather than remedial action and promotes effective school-based support and monitoring. Key principles for provision include the following:

- High but realistic expectations for all pupils.

- Greater support for parents.

- Further inclusion of pupils in mainstream schools.

- Close liaison between schools and the support agencies.

All teachers will need to work hard to ensure that all children are given the opportunity to learn and make best use of their educational opportunities. The increase in teaching assistants to support children with SEN will involve teachers in more sophisticated patterns of classroom management and organisation as they take account of the additional adult help and a wider ability range of pupils (Fox, 1998). The greatest challenges for teachers are likely to come from pupils whose educational problems are rooted in their emotional instability and antisocial behaviour. See Chapter 9 for fuller details about issues relating to inclusion and special educational needs.

Minority ethnic attainment

In the DfES publication *Aiming High: Raising the achievements of minority ethnic pupils* (DfES 2003b) the following characteristics were identified as significant for helping to improve the educational attainment of minority ethnic pupils:

- An agreed strategy that applies across the whole school.
- Effective learning and teaching, including in particular, support for bilingual pupils.
- An ethos of respect, with a clear approach to racism and behaviour.

The study revealed a complex picture of minority ethnic attainment and participation, suggesting that the involvement of parents and the community in the life and development of the school was highly significant. There appeared to be an increased polarisation of how well or badly they fare with increasing age of pupil. Generally, it appears that Black, Bangladeshi and Pakistani pupils performed less well than other ethnic groups during the time of compulsory schooling. By contrast, Indian and Chinese pupils performed better than any of the other ethnic groups that were included in the survey. Proportionately more Black, Pakistani and Bangladeshi pupils were recorded as having special educational needs, though national variations were apparent.

Explanations about the reasons for underachievement of some minority groups are partly explained by the social and material deprivation that characterises those groups, as indicated by the incidence of free school meals. For instance, over 30 per cent of Pakistani and Black pupils, and over half of all Bangladeshi, Gypsy/Roma pupils were eligible for free school meals, compared with 14 per cent for White pupils. However, there was not found to be a simple relationship between these figures and academic achievement, as the biggest gap in attainment was between White pupils with and White pupils without free school meals. Clearly, then, there are other factors that need to be taken into account when addressing issues of under-performance.

(http://www.standards.dfes.gov.uk.ethnicminorities/raising_achievement)

It is one thing to be aware of the trends exposed by the 2003 DfES report, it is quite another to have strategies for improving the situation. The most successful schools have high expectations of staff and pupils, and ensure that they keep close links with parents. Every teacher and trainee should be asking a number of important questions about their teaching approach and attitude towards all pupils, including:

■ Are all children achieving their potential and gaining individual benefit from their education? As a visitor to the classroom, trainees are in a good position to see the situation with fresh eyes and, perhaps, offer insights that will help the regular teacher.

■ If some children appear to be underachieving, what factors seem to be contributing to this state of affairs? You may be able to modify classroom practices that are contributing to this state of affairs.

■ What steps can/should be taken to address the unsatisfactory situation? Regular monitoring and assessment of children's progress will assist in identifying specific problems being experienced by children and begin to remedy them.

■ Are some children underachieving because of lack of access to curriculum opportunities? This is one of the most straightforward areas of difficulty to address, as simply raising the issue often alerts a teacher to discriminatory practices.

■ Would some identifiable groups of children benefit from exclusive attention from an adult or a modified curriculum? This question is one for senior staff to answer but it may be that you are asked to offer such exclusive attention to a child.

The application of an agreed school policy to combat racism and unreasonable behaviour can only be effective if adults in school examine their own attitudes. Every teacher must be honest in confronting covert beliefs about the breadth of issues embraced by inclusive education and address areas of prejudice. This process is a testing one and sometimes uncomfortable, but unless you are willing to face up to any stereotyping or underlying false assumptions about children, it is difficult for you to make a positive difference to the situation. Sooner or later prejudices will be exposed, whether those of pupils, colleagues or your own.

As a trainee teacher you need to be aware of any circumstance in which you may unwittingly show prejudicial attitudes. For example, children may be highly competent in their own language but struggle when expected to use English. It is possible to lower your expectations of the children and assume that they are far less capable than in fact they really are. While it may be tempting to allocate a child with limited English easy tasks to allow for his or her language deficit, it is important to limit the length of time that this happens, for two reasons. First, the child may become the butt of teasing from classmates owing to the simple nature of the tasks. Second, the child quickly becomes under-stimulated and disillusioned with the undemanding work. The strategies employed to ensure that the child is given appropriate tasks depend upon the extent of the adult language support available and the age of the child. Young children benefit from plenty of play activity, where they can immerse themselves in their imaginations, interact naturally with children their own age and become absorbed into the fabric of class life. Older children may struggle to orientate because they are more acutely aware of their language limitations and may not pick up a second language as easily as their younger brothers and sisters. A variety of approaches are commonly used to promote practice that is rooted in positive and high-expectation practice. Thus:

■ Taking account of children's special needs in literacy sessions by implementing IEPs and utilising opportunities to develop language across the curriculum.

- Promoting respect and understanding of diverse cultures, languages, ethnic groups, faith groups, travellers, asylum seekers and refugees in regular interaction with the class and the interest taken in (for example) cultural diversity and special occasions.

- Working with parents from different community groups.

- Ensuring that display work reflects the diversity in ethnicity.

- Discussing issues relating to prejudice with pupils.

One of the keys to successfully integrating all new children into the classroom is to assess their academic competence as accurately and swiftly as possible. In her work as a teacher of younger children, Heyda (2002) describes the strategies she employs when dealing with the arrival of new children in the class who speak little or no English:

- Welcome the child with a big smile and a warm friendly voice.

- Assign a 'buddy', preferably someone who speaks the language, to accompany the child throughout the day.

- Take care not to use 'baby talk' that might embarrass the child or speak too loudly as if the child has a hearing impairment.

- Utilise support staff at an early stage.

- Be encouraging and positive.

- Use the child's mistakes as starting points for progress.

- Use lots of visual aids to get across concepts, such as drawing pictures next to vocabulary and using photographs and diagrams to explain things.

- Give the child plenty of hands-on experiences.

- Label the room with key words.

Heyda's sound advice applies in many respects to work with younger children generally. If there are numerous other children who speak the same first language, the challenges of incorporating the newcomer into the class are usually less severe than if the child is the only pupil who speaks the language. The school is likely to have additional adult support for EAL, though the proliferation of different languages in the school and the involvement of various language assistants present formidable organisation and management issues.

Children for whom English is a second language should, ideally, be assessed by an adult who speaks the same tongue and can give a better-informed picture of their abilities. If such a person is not available, the process will obviously take longer but, where possible, involvement of a bilingual child is the next best option. In the absence of adult or child to act as interpreter, parental or family help may be called upon, as it is likely that at least one person has a sufficient grasp of English to explain the new child's needs, strengths and limitations.

The Commission for Racial Equality web site (www.cre.gov.uk/pubs) contains a useful, though extremely detailed set of guidelines for schools in the form of two audits to monitor whether the curriculum, teaching and assessment and pupils' personal development, attainment and progress are sensitive to ethnic diversity and cultural factors. The curriculum audit contains fourteen statements for the staff and governors of schools to consider whether they are fully, mostly, partially met, or not met at all. As a teacher in training you will not be responsible for decisions concerning the audits, but they provide a useful reminder of the principles of fairness and justice that should underpin the work of every teacher in all schools. The curriculum audit contains a range of useful key words and phrases to help teachers understand better their planning, teaching and assessment of pupils' progress. Thus, paraphrasing some key expressions:

■ 'Needs of all pupils'

■ 'Appropriate curriculum'

■ 'Fair and equitable'

■ 'Assessment methods are checked'

■ 'Assessment outcomes identify needs and inform'

■ 'Teaching takes account of needs'

■ 'Teaching encourages positive attitudes'

■ 'The curriculum draws on areas of interest'

■ 'Diversity is promoted'

■ 'Resources are inclusive'

Similarly, from the personal development audit, the emphasis on caring for and valuing individuals so that they can make the best use of their educational experiences provides a model for all teaching situations (Commission for Racial Equality 2002). With the constraints of the NC programmes of study and the frequent use of the NLS and NNS in schools, it is far from easy for teachers to respond to all of the expectations made of them by special interest groups. However, the essence of helping all children to achieve their potential and the promotion of a secure and relevant learning environment is something to which every teacher can and should aspire.

Activate your thinking!

The following extract is a modified version of a more extensive one offered by Watkinson (2003a) page 33. Examine the list and respond to the questions: (1) On the basis of what you *have* seen in school (2) On the basis of what you would *like* to see in school . . .

■ What books are available in the school to show different cultures and ways of life?

■ Are there books that show people with disabilities as heroes?

■ What resources in terms of musical instruments, fabrics, pictures or artefacts does the school possess?

■ What recorded music is played? Is only Western art displayed on the walls?

■ What relationships does the school have with the local community, organisations, churches or other places of worship?

> **Good practice**
>
> Go to the CRE web site and follow the trail: Publications/ Good practice/Sectors/ Education/Learning for all/audit form (look for hyperlink)/ 'curriculum teaching and assessment' and also 'pupils'. Take special note of (a) item 7 under C, T & A (b) item 5 under Pupils.

A child in your class

What will it be like to be a child in your classroom? A delight, a misery, an endurance test, a laugh, a puzzle? Much depends upon whether you see the pupils as the enemy to be subdued or a group of inexperienced children with whom you will need to develop a working relationship. To help you decide what it is like for pupils in your class, consider the following questions:

Which children do you get to know first?
Is this because you are working closely with them or because they are the noisiest or the tallest or the prettiest?

Do you tend to ignore some children?
Perhaps because they are shy or you feel uncomfortable with them?

What kind of behaviour upsets you most?
Is this because you don't know how to handle it or because it affronts your dignity?

How interested are you in children's opinions?
Do you really care or do you go through the motions of appearing interested?

How much do you want children to like you?
Will you be too soft, try too hard to be nice or perhaps be too fierce and unreasonable? Cullingford (1997a) suggests that successful teachers 'will be fair and consistent, will praise more than blame, will be clear and patient, will ask questions and listen, rather than shout and present repetitive exercises' (page 113). Wyse (2001) recommends the acronym REG, where the R stands for Respect, E for Empathy and G for Genuineness. Thus; 'Respect can come from your positive attitude to children...Empathy is about really trying to understand how the child is feeling and appreciating their point of view...Genuineness is about being honest with the child...' (page 9).

In the light of these points, it is worth thinking about the children you know in your class or groups and how you relate to them:

- The children that show the greatest self-confidence?
- The children that are ill at ease and in what contexts?

- The children that co-operate?
- The children that gain most of your approval?
- The children that seem to have a bright future in school?

And most significantly, what your answers reveal about you as teacher. Remember that children like teachers who are firm but fair, willing to explain things patiently and have a positive attitude to work and people. They are ill-at-ease with adults who hector, complain, agitate and fulminate.

Making progress as a trainee teacher

Fitting in

Every successful teacher has established routines, procedures and patterns of interaction with pupils that contribute to what may be described as a 'classroom rhythm' and do not take kindly if their hard-earned efficiency is disrupted by a well-meaning trainee (or anyone else). Classroom rhythms are not dependent upon the way that the day is structured in a timetable. They are developed through successfully creating a positive learning environment, convincing the children that it is in their best interests to co-operate in maintaining it and providing a momentum for learning that gains a life of its own.

Teachers are charged with the responsibility of clarifying 'the way we do things around here' (Nias, 1989). Class teachers need to establish their priorities or pupils will attempt to do it for them, leading to disharmony and unnecessary tension. Although school policies are sometimes useful in establishing the way things happen in a particular classroom, final decisions about day-to-day interactions and routines still belong to the individual teacher.

Trainee teachers are obliged to adopt the supervising teacher's general approach to routine and procedural matters, regardless of whether they agree with the philosophy underlying them. They can console themselves with the thought that when they have a class of their own they will be in a position to implement some of the things that were denied to them while in training. Nevertheless, it is helpful if teachers are able to explain to trainees the rationale for decisions rather than merely expecting unthinking compliance. Any changes that a trainee teacher wishes to make should be discussed with the teacher first and introduced gradually. Children quickly become alert to any inconsistencies they detect between their regular teacher and the newcomer and may react adversely, usually to the trainee teacher's cost! Sometimes your (apparently) obvious improvement or solution to a problem has already been tried by the teacher and found to be unsuitable.

An essential quality for the development of a successful teaching and learning environment is the ability to organise and manage classroom affairs (see Chapter 6). All teachers want to maintain an orderly environment to facilitate progress but order should not be confused with rigidity or passivity for, as Desforges (1995) points out, 'Parade grounds are often associated with firm discipline, clear control and immaculate performances' (page 183) but graveyards are also orderly places! Neither venue, however, is noteworthy for the quality of the learning that takes place there! It is possible to be efficient without being effective.

At certain times of the year, carefully organised lesson structures are disrupted by events such as a block of the timetable allocated to swimming, play rehearsals, music practices, fire drills and educational visits. Although it is not possible to anticipate every eventuality, an awareness of wider school happenings is essential.

Professional learning

All teachers need to think carefully about their practice, seek advice from more experienced practitioners and try to keep abreast of research findings that provide insights into effective teaching and learning. This process is commonly referred to as 'professional learning' and trainee teachers are normally required by their colleges to maintain a written record of their progress across the weeks of school placement as evidence of their professional development. This type of review should not be confused with providing evidence to show that formal teaching standards have been met. The reviews are intended to be reflective commentaries on school experience to demonstrate an ability to analyse situations constructively as a means of adjusting practice. One trainee, Helena, wrote at length about the first two weeks of her placement, including the following extracts:

Week One

I found week one fairly challenging because of discipline problems. The class has a number of lower ability children and one child with special educational needs who is on medication to help control his behaviour. My previous experiences in school had not prepared me to deal with anyone like him. However, by observing the strategies used by the class teacher and spending time in a one-to-one situation with the child, I began to feel more confident. I have already begun to change my previous ideas on discipline, as I realise that shouting and constant telling-off is not the best option. Discussion with the class teacher helped me to begin to work out the most effective strategies to use with the class. I am also struggling with managing my time. I have spent every night over the past week preparing literacy and numeracy lessons, leaving me quite jaded. After talking to the teacher and tutor, they convinced me that the pressure would grow easier as I get into the swing of things. I can hardly wait! I have identified three target areas next week: (a) improving my time management for lesson planning, (b) developing my discipline strategies, (c) observing how the teacher copes with troublesome children. I also want to teach part of a PE lesson and have a go at organising practical science.

Week Two

This week was much busier than the last one. I spent more than a third of the time teaching literacy and numeracy and learned a lot from the experience. Each lesson flew past and what felt like ten minutes was in fact half-an-hour and work that I thought would be completed was not. The class teacher assured me that this was a common problem. During Friday's literacy hour I did not check the finishing time and had to rush to assembly. In future I must not make assumptions about times. Each morning I take registration. Although this seems a simple task I found it quite difficult. I had to take the lunch time register and add up all of the totals in front of the children at the same time as keeping good order. It made me feel quite insecure with all the eyes looking up at me from the carpet, with the whispering getting louder! During sessions that I taught, the children were less attentive than with the class teacher and I was shocked when some of them back-chatted when I told them what to do. However, I used some of the class teacher's strategies and found that the situation improved slowly. For instance, I separated children if they were noisy together, wrote the names of persistent offenders on the board and made children stay in at break time if they did not respond and concentrate on their work. When I first dismissed the class there was a rush for the door and general pandemonium, so I became much stricter, stood by the door and dismissed them row by row, which improved the situation enormously. I have also come to appreciate the importance of getting resources absolutely ready. I forgot to put spellings examples in order for Thursday's lesson and so produced the difficult words first, which meant that the less able children struggled and became frustrated. Next time I made sure I started with the easiest ones! I have found that annotating my present lesson plans, thinking positively about failures instead of getting miserable, and modifying my plans so that they took more account of children's needs is starting to have an effect on the quality of my teaching. It is all taking time and, unlike the impressive lists we are given in the documentation from college, nothing is straightforward!

Helena did not continue to write at such length. She began to summarise points and be more specific in identifying areas for development. However, she started as she meant to go on by taking time to evaluate her progress, gain advice from the class teacher and tutor, and amend her approach on the basis of what she observed and learned.

The community of practice

It used to be said that if teachers weren't exhausted by four o'clock and on their way home by a quarter past, they hadn't been doing their job properly. Today, with the many different demands upon a teacher's time, most teachers consider themselves fortunate to leave before five, having worked throughout the day with little or no break. After-school and lunchtime clubs and activities are commonplace and every teacher has a curriculum or related responsibility. Paperwork has increased considerably, despite efforts to keep it under control. Accountability to parents and the local community has become a key concern as funding increasingly depends upon numbers of children in school and the traditional safety-net of the local education authority has been replaced in many schools by independent management structures.

We may agree that children need to feel secure in school but forget that adults, too, need to be relaxed if they are to achieve peak effectiveness in their work. Teaching has always been a demanding and sometimes exhausting job but in the recent whirl of national legislation its demands have increased. Many teachers complain that they have been scrutinised more closely than any other profession and expected to cope with an unreasonable rate of imposed change (Cockburn, 1996; Woods, 1997).

All jobs involve some stresses and strains, especially those that require close contact with people, but teaching seems to stand alone in its potential for exhaustion and, paradoxically, for rich reward. One of the reasons for this tension between benefits and losses is the extent to which teachers consider themselves to be responsible for children's learning and personal growth. In addition, the external imposition of targets has done little to relieve the belief that teachers are losing their autonomy. The whirlwind of initiatives from Government has left some teachers feeling breathless and guilty that they are unable to keep abreast of all the changes.

The danger for teachers is that they can grow cynical, struggling to accommodate the new requirements into their busy schedules of planning, teaching, assessing, marking, recording and filling reports. The intensity of teaching can easily lead to over-commitment and increased vulnerability (Cox and Heames, 1999). In the midst of this, a school's prime resource – reflective and enthusiastic teachers – must be safeguarded and *self-management* is crucially important (Thody and Bowden 2004). The situation for trainee teachers is particularly acute. They have little control over where they are placed and enter a school that is largely unknown in respect of the ethos, personalities and patterns of behaviour that characterise it. They have to cope with making an effort to adjust to the prevailing expectations, establish and maintain relationships with staff, learn procedures and adapt to the school's priorities, some of which may be abstruse and difficult to interpret. Furthermore, as Maynard (2001) describes, trainee teachers have to adopt to the class teacher's practices and priorities as part of the process of 'fitting in' to a situation and that it takes time before they become fully aware of the reasons underpinning the teacher's actions. Thus:

> It was through acting like a teacher, initially through becoming someone else, that students began to develop an identity as a teacher. In addition, trainee teachers appropriated their teachers' discourse, even though they did not appear to be aware of doing so, nor initially share the same conceptual understandings as their teachers. The use of this discourse enabled trainee teachers to gain acceptance into the community of practice, the approval of their class teacher, the means by which they could negotiate richer and more appropriate understandings (page 49).

If you want to enter fully into this community of practice you have to make rapid adjustments and learn the unwritten rules that are taken for granted by the staff in the school. This process presents challenges above and beyond the more familiar aspects of school experience such as lesson preparation and class teaching.

Emotional adjustment

The significance of emotions in the work and motivation of teachers has long been recognised. The concept of *Emotional Intelligence*, drawn from the work on multiple intelligences by Gardner (1983), has been made popular by Goleman (1995) who has been instrumental in alerting educationists to the central role played by the emotions in decisions and actions. First, three general principles to underpin practice as you focus on recognising that:

1 *Your role is important.* Without secure and confident teachers and other adult workers, children are unlikely to receive a fully effective education. You and your colleagues are undertaking a vital task in helping to educate the nations' children and provide for the future stability of the country and, ultimately, the world. This notion is not a fanciful one. You do not know whether a child sitting in front of you is a prospective genius, leader or entrepreneur. Let that thought motivate you.

2 *It is essential to use every means to encourage and support colleagues.* Teachers who spend time praising and helping children to feel positive about themselves and their classmates may need to offer the same level of support to their co-workers. There is a saying that you should not judge a book merely by looking at the cover. In any staffroom there are folk who need reassurance, a word of comfort, a kind smile and a pat on the back. Schools rely on active collaboration across the whole team, and even if you are a trainee teacher with little direct control over events, a word of appreciation, a short note of thanks or willingness to listen can help to transform someone's day and give that person hope. Such actions not only demonstrate compassion for fellow-humans but also provide a foundation for a successful school placement.

3 *It is better to focus on your achievements and successes than dwell on failures.* Teachers possess and exhibit daily a range of skills and knowledge that are taken for granted: organising, planning, summarising, public exposition, dealing with children and adults, curriculum expertise and so on. A bad day often simply means that the call upon these skills has been excessive. It is frequently the case that what you consider to have been 'a bad lesson' was, in fact, simply less good than it might have been. In evaluating your progress as a teacher and the distance yet to be covered, don't lose sight of how far you have already travelled.

There are a number of warning signs that all teachers need to be alert to in their own experience and in those of others that signal negative emotions and the likelihood that stress is affecting health:

- *Persistent anxiety:* This emotion is deeper than worry and eats into every aspect of life in and outside school. Some people say that they are unable to 'switch off'. They fall asleep straight away at night but find themselves wide-awake in the early hours. Sometimes a persistently anxious person takes on more and more responsibilities, well beyond the ability to cope, as a means of blocking out feelings of distress. If you experience such deep emotions, it is sensible to seek help urgently. Do not imagine that you can somehow 'pull yourself together' or that you will be thought the worse of by asking for assistance.

- *A lack of enthusiasm for the job:* Every teacher entertains feelings of doubt. Every trainee teacher has times when fervour diminishes and may even entertain vocational uncertainty. These emotions are commonplace and are often due to fatigue and poor health. During such periods the quality of lessons may suffer, which in itself creates further anxiety. At such times it is essential to remind yourself of two things. First, no teacher is perfect and everyone has off-days. Second, children will learn despite your feebleness. A good night's sleep and a talk with a sympathetic friend will usually remedy loss of appetite for the job.

- *Reluctance about going to school:* Even experienced teachers admit that their confidence can sink to a low point prior to going in to school, but that once they are there they feel completely different. Although as a trainee teacher you are probably not earning a salary (or, at best, just a small remuneration) teachers are paid to teach! Sometimes the pleasure that teaching engenders can cause us to forget that it is a form of employment and, like any other job, requires effort and perseverance and a reasonably consistent standard of performance.

■ *Resentment towards pupils:* It is undeniable that some pupils are more troublesome than others. Occasionally, a child gets 'under your skin' and you find that it is hard to resist becoming irritated or feeling that your professional identity is being undermined. A small minority of teachers become disillusioned with the job and express their concerns publicly. Others fall into the trap of compensating for their own shortcomings and difficulties by criticising others. Such behaviour quickly becomes endemic and wise head teachers and senior staff act quickly to stop the spread of disillusionment. It is often the case that a teacher who makes negative comments is merely letting off steam and does not normally feel that way at all.

■ *Unnatural ill-temper or intolerance:* The most even-tempered adults sometimes become unsettled by children's behaviour and overreact. For the most part the reaction consists solely of a strong word or impatient remark and is soon forgotten. However, if you find that you are regularly employing authoritarian tactics to enforce discipline, it is time to seek help from more experienced colleagues.

Although these stress signs can be associated with a time of ill-health or other unsettling experience, their recurrence can signal the need for rapid action (Woods and Carlyle 2002). A teacher who works in a school where such feelings and attitudes can be openly expressed and discussed is fortunate. However, many teachers find that the opportunities for such openness are few, either because the school ethos does not espouse it or because life is too busy and colleagues too preoccupied with their own worries to listen. Good team spirit, however, comes from support and encouragement.

The skills of listening carefully, sympathising and affirming should not be reserved for work with children; every adult needs to hear that they are needed, valued and trusted, too. Publicly expressed statements of gratitude for advice, guidance or example can enliven an ailing colleague. Teachers who are at ease with school life should support those who presently are not. Comradeship and empathy can strengthen and heal. Just as children's experiences and attitudes affect their performance in school, it is similar for adults, though they are usually more skilled and often see it as part of their professional responsibilities to conceal their feelings. If consolation and encouragement are not available within school, it is essential to spend time in building an informal network of confidantes outside school as an alternative. Lawrence (1997) offers some sensible advice on keeping things in perspective when he suggests that while teachers should be careful to take their work seriously they should never take themselves so seriously that they lose their sense of humour. Life in school relies on every member functioning efficiently, so effort expended in supporting others benefits all.

Care of the voice

Your voice is probably the single most valuable teaching resource that you possess, so it pays to take good care of it. Teachernet, the on-line counselling service for teachers (www.teachernet.gov.uk) recommends that teachers should avoid placing undue pressure on their voices by sudden switches from a normal speaking tone to a fierce or forced one. In addition to avoiding smoke and polluted atmospheres, teachers are encouraged to breath carefully through the nose (and out through the mouth) refrain from eating unsuitable foods (such as very spicy ones) and use alcohol and dairy products sparingly. General health can be improved through humming quietly before speaking, standing upright (not slouching) and taking regular pauses for breath. Teachers should also keep to a minimum the amount that they clear the throat (which causes the vocal cords to collide), talk too quickly (which leads to inadequate breathing and chest tension) and use an unnatural pitch or forced whisper. Teachers can help themselves by sipping water during the lesson, breathing deeply and making a determined effort not to 'push' the voice when it is tired or hoarse. It goes without saying that the ability to relax the whole body during teaching assists the health of the voice, too, with the accompanying improvement in speech clarity that results.

Activate your thinking!

On your way home every night make a mental list of your many achievements during the day. Do not allow negative thoughts to enter your head.

Whatever the stage of your career, you will be aware that being a teacher is a demanding, exhilarating and emotional experience. There will be good days and not-so-good days. Learn to take it in your stride, reflect upon your practice, keep buoyant and don't allow the job to become such an obsession that it smothers your life outside school.

Good practice

Write down the six things that frustrate you most about being a teacher. List them under three headings: those I can change by myself; those I can change with the help of others; those I cannot change. Begin to work on the items in the first two categories; destroy the third!

Case study

It is difficult to compare and contrast two teachers at work for the simple reason that no two classrooms are identical. Nevertheless, there are characteristics which can be weighed and evaluated. Let's take two fictitious characters from the same school, Martha and Diane. Both teachers have taught children at Key Stage 1 for about the same length of time; both have had similar opportunities to attend in-service training; both hold curriculum responsibilities; both run a midweek extra-curricular activity.

Martha

Martha's classroom seems to flow with paper. Her desk is littered with exercise books, worksheets and half-finished drawings. The walls drip with numerous charts, pictures, unmounted writing and the remains of an earlier display. Tables are pushed together in groups of three and some chairs are touching the wall. There are corners: a play area, large construction, a dressing-up box and a row of CD players strewn about the shelf. The atmosphere is exuberant, with children moving freely about the room, chattering, laughing and busy. After a few minutes observation, it becomes clear that much of this activity is rather purposeless. The noise level rises as Martha, immersed in a queue of children, calls out instructions and general warnings that many children appear to ignore or respond to for a short time before resuming their unsatisfactory behaviour.

This teacher likes the children to get down to their work quickly. She regularly uses photocopied sheets full of tasks which the children have to work through and hand in when completed. The tasks are varied, some requiring the application of library skills and investigation, the majority desk-bound and requiring a single correct answer.

To cope with the constant flow of queries and questions, Martha spends much of her time dealing with children on a one-to-one basis, repeating answers to the same query from different children. Occasionally, she stops the class to remind them of the need to behave or of what they are supposed to be doing.

Although the tasks are not differentiated, the worksheets gradually become more demanding so that although all the children can attempt the first one, less able children find later ones too difficult. As the session continues, some children become restless as they tire of the work and begin to copy from more confident neighbours; others work very slowly, choosing the easiest elements and avoiding anything conceptually difficult; a few hurry through to be ahead of friends. The standard of work is variable. Martha often warns individual children to 'get on with your work'.

At the end of the lesson, she tells the class to clear up and put the completed sheets in a box on her desk and the uncompleted ones in their trays. There is a scramble to do so and some sheets are crumpled. Martha raises her voice and tells the class to 'be more sensible'; one child is strongly rebuked and told to sit down on his own in the corner. Children find their snacks, chatter about 'swops' and playground activities as they noisily leave the room; no one remains behind to talk to the teacher about the work. She sends out the last child after saying that she is 'tired of your behaviour'. She walks down to the staffroom and is the first to make a drink before flopping down in an armchair. When the head teacher mentions that it is her turn to have a trainee teacher next term, Martha pulls a face and says that she hopes that this one is 'a bit better than the one I had last year; she was useless; couldn't keep control'. The head teacher smiles to herself but says nothing.

A few weeks later, Martha comes across the uncompleted worksheets and throws them away. During the tidying-up prior to a parents' evening, several children ask her what they should do with their completed work from earlier this term found in their trays. The teacher collects them all in and, when the children have gone home, hurriedly ticks the best of them and mounts them on an empty display board together with some colourful, bold labels and an impressive title.

During parents' evening, Martha speaks loudly to parents, extolling the merits of their children and offering comments about their achievements, edged with inferences about their potential 'if they concentrated better on the work'. Parents are quite pleased to hear positive things but feel unaccountably troubled as the teacher's report does not square with their children's diminishing enthusiasm for school.

Diane

Diane's classroom, with its interactive displays, selected examples of children's work, due regard to safety and easy access to equipment is the envy of her colleagues. Children's work is mounted with bold labels that enhance the room's appearance. Most displays consist of children's contributions, though here and there the teacher's artistic touches are evident. Photographs of the children in a variety of formal and informal poses, together with dates of birth and a list of their favourite foods and animals, are arranged on a small board. Well-thumbed documents in carefully labelled folders are in place on a shelf behind Diane's desk. The room is orderly but not clinical; the atmosphere is purposeful yet relaxed.

The class always seems business-like without being rigid; children work singly and in groups and relate together comfortably. There is little acrimony and many moments of genuine laughter and smiles. On other occasions, there is a serious intent about the children as they concentrate on the task.

Diane has a brisk but friendly manner. She begins a session by reviewing previous work and asking thought-provoking questions, trying to involve as many different children as possible. The children sit up straight in anticipation of what the teacher might say and don't seem afraid to venture an answer even if they are unsure. In turn, Diane treats every response seriously and tries to make a positive comment about its merits; children are encouraged to speculate and offer their own thoughts. She insists that other children respect what is said. The overall impression of these whole-class times is one of mutual respect and a healthy learning environment.

Diane introduces the lesson by telling the children what she hopes they will learn and do, explains the activities and gives some specific instruction to each group. It is clear that the children are used to showing initiative as they sort themselves out, gather resources, settle to work and discuss the activities. Different children are engaged in similar tasks but there are subtle differences between the groups: some are using an open-ended worksheet as a starting point for discovering new facts by way of a library search; others are using books pre-selected by the teacher to check some facts; a further group is using a computer data-bank to extract information. While offering close guidance to one group of children, Diane nevertheless spends some time with each group in turn and tries to give each child some personal attention. Some individuals wander out of their place to see her but generally the children collaborate and appear to have a shared sense of purpose. When a child occasionally becomes over-excited or silly, Diane stands and looks hard at the culprit without saying anything; other children alert the transgressor to the teacher's concerns and normality resumes. Once the situation is calmer, she walks across to the group and quietly enquires if she can assist with anything but does not mention the incident.

From time to time, Diane stops the class to point out an instance of good work or to commend someone who is trying hard; the children listen attentively. Towards the end of the session, she tells the class that in a few minutes there will be opportunity to share with others; one or two children explain anxiously that they have yet to finish and she reassures them that they do not need to rush. About five minutes before the end, the teacher stops the class and invites the children to turn to someone nearby and explain what they have done or discovered; a hum soon fills the room as children share together. After a minute or two, Diane stops the class and asks a few children to tell the rest of the class about their findings. Several children do so with confidence and enthusiasm; others listen carefully, occasionally thrusting their hands in the air to indicate their own willingness to add something. After each contribution, the teacher thanks the person warmly and briefly summarises what has been said. When she tells the children that they have to finish, there is a quiet groan of disappointment and several children ask her whether they are going to continue after the break; several more ask if they can stay in to finish during playtime.

After clearing up thoroughly, the children slowly slide out of the class, some still talking about the work, others engaging the teacher in animated conversation. Diane stops one noisy girl at the door and gently places her finger on her lips. The offending child smiles an apology and saves her exuberance for the playground. Diane is often one of the last into the staffroom and one of the first out; she always asks if anyone else wants her to make them a drink and has time to offer a brief word of encouragement to a trainee teacher who is struggling with his class.

At the open evening, she does as much listening as talking. When she speaks, she impresses parents with her sincerity and knowledge of each child. Diane speaks considerately and positively about the children but does not try to conceal their shortcomings or weaknesses. She has detailed notes about the children, each on a separate page to which she occasionally refers for fuller information. When parents make a significant comment, she notes it on her pad and promises to follow it up; parents feel confident that she will.

The head teacher overhears two parents talking as they cross the playground later that evening: 'I wish our Becky had Diane Jones again this year', sighs one parent wistfully. The other parent nods in agreement.

Standards

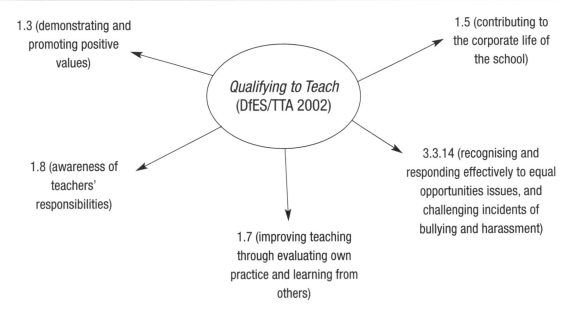

1.3 (demonstrating and promoting positive values)

1.5 (contributing to the corporate life of the school)

Qualifying to Teach (DfES/TTA 2002)

1.8 (awareness of teachers' responsibilities)

3.3.14 (recognising and responding effectively to equal opportunities issues, and challenging incidents of bullying and harassment)

1.7 (improving teaching through evaluating own practice and learning from others)

Further reading

Acker, S. (1999) *The Realities of Teachers' Work*, London: Cassell.
Based on research, highly informative and to the point.
Holmes, E. (2004) *Teacher Well-Being*, London: RoutledgeFalmer.
The author presents strategies for teachers who want to be proactive in dealing with their own welfare.
Zucker, J. and Parker, D. (1999) *A Class Act*, London: Sapphire Publishers.
A book that is fun to read and opens up the mystery of a teacher's world.

Working with Parents and Other Adults

PARENTS

Introduction

Parents are the first educators of their children. Once formal schooling begins, teachers assume some of the responsibility, but the closer the partnership in learning, the more likely that children will benefit. The first part of the chapter explores the relationship between teachers and parents, including professional boundaries, informal and formal liaison, parent meetings, dealing with difficult parents and the role of parents in the classroom. The second part of the chapter considers the importance of the many other adults that contribute towards enriching children's education.

Home and school

A report for the DfES by Desforges and Abouchaar (DfES 2003) about the impact of parental involvement on pupils' education found that what parents do with their children at home is the single most significant factor. They quote from Kreider (2000) that the greatest success occurs when parental development is integrated fully into a school's development plan. Although a few parents will not always be able to help with homework tasks, they all have the potential to contribute to their children's learning in other ways. Some schools provide training evenings for parents who are interested in knowing more about how they can help directly.

Adults in school spend a great deal of time working with children, so much time, in fact, that it is possible for teachers to believe that they are the sole educators. In truth, parents may not teach their children much of the formal curriculum that they encounter when at school, but they impart other forms of life knowledge. They teach them about living in a community, learning to cope with people, discriminating good from harmful and spending time wisely. Parents teach their children particular sets of values. They set boundaries for behaviour and the consequences of not obeying the rules. Most parents take children out into the open air to experience the elements, observe the changing seasons and marvel at creation. They take them into the city to savour the sights and sounds of urban life. They show them books, introduce them to games and, most importantly, offer them opportunities to play alone or with friends, and talk to them. A parent can give close attention to one child, whereas in school 30 or more pupils have to share one or two adults. Children are educated at home, either implicitly (absorbing what happens without being consciously aware of it) and explicitly (having their consciousness raised and their attention drawn specifically to items).

All parents want the best for their children, though some do not have a clear understanding of what 'best' means in terms of school-based learning. School reports offer them a limited amount of information about specific aspects of their children's learning, but parents also want to know about their children's behaviour, attitude, friendships and potential. If their children are unhappy in school, parents will be concerned, regardless of academic results. If children are seriously underachieving, then this obviously requires urgent attention, normally through the school's Special Educational Needs Co-ordinator (SENCO), who will ensure that parents are aware of the problem and involved in its solution.

It goes without saying that some parents do a better job of educating their children than others do. When children arrive in school they vary in the extent and quality of their experiences and so-called 'baseline' assessment of their capability is a standard procedure for teachers of reception age children at the end of the Foundation Stage (see below). This initial assessment is not only an evaluation of children's academic ability but of their social skills, and it is often in this area that teachers soon become aware of the differing ways in which children have been prepared for life in school. McEwan (1998) claims that 'skilled teachers can often identify several children with problems before the first week of school is over' (page 42). The growth of pre-school education has helped to compensate for the minority of children who have not received adequate parenting, but no strategy can wholly redress the limitations placed upon children whose parents are uninvolved in their education. Nevertheless, children do have a life outside school and it is important for teachers to recognise that theirs is only one of many influences upon an individual child's learning.

By the time 'rising five' Sharmilla joins the reception class, she will already have had four years of experience of adults, most of it helpful, some of it confusing or frightening. A few of these adults will have carried out a teacher role – playgroup leaders, nursery assistants – but most have simply been 'the grown-ups' who have, in one way or another, influenced Sharmilla's life. The likelihood is that she has spent most time interacting with a few close family members – mum, dad, brothers, sisters. Her own behaviour will reflect their attitudes, preferences and personality, and affect her willingness to learn and her satisfaction with school life. Parents, in particular, will remain the most important influence in Sharmilla's world, a world that she carries into school with her every morning (Tizard and Hughes, 1984; Hughes *et al.*, 1994; Hallgarten 2000).

The vast majority of parents co-operate fully with teachers to ensure that children receive the best education in the most pleasant environment. However, two of the major changes in parental attitudes in recent years have been an increasing awareness of their rights and a willingness to express their views about school individually or through group pressure. Wise teachers are not intimidated by these changes but take account of them in their dealings with parents (see later in this chapter).

Activate your thinking!

Consider what it means for your relationships and professional attitude to see parents as *clients* or *customers* or *partners*. Reflect upon how parents may perceive the relationship.

Home–school contacts

Over recent years, legislation has established the rights of parents to be well informed about the curriculum offered by each school and to know about their child's progress through reports and informal access to teachers (see, for example, Stierer *et al.* 1993; Hughes *et al.* 1994, Chapter 8; Vincent 2000; Beveridge 2004). With each school's budget depending in large measure upon the number of pupils on roll, there is extra incentive for head teachers and governors to ensure that parents are welcomed and made to feel part of the school community. Inevitably, this new relationship has caused schools to re-evaluate home–school links and establish procedures for coping with parental concerns. Parent areas are a common feature of primary schools and almost every school has regular meetings with groups of parents in a parent–teacher forum. This often provides the impetus for fund-raising, school events, and (sometimes) policy decisions.

The greatest level of interaction between parents and school staff is commonly found at nursery, reception and Key Stage 1 (Stacey 1991; Lindon 1997, part 4; Fitzgerald 2004) owing to the fact that parents tend to bring their young children into the classroom and meet them after school. Although every school has its own particular ideas about establishing and maintaining good quality relationships with parents, contact in the foundation years (for children aged three to five years) and at the start of Key Stage 1 often includes:

- Home visits by the reception class teacher close to the start of a child's formal schooling
- Visits to and from nursery schemes and playgroups by teachers from the mainstream school
- Informal meetings between teacher and parents at the start and end of the day when they are leaving or picking up their children
- Involvement of parents in the classroom, both to assist, and in some cases to help ease the transition of their child from home to school (Henry 1996).

Many head teachers actively promote home–school liaison through invitations to participate in aspects of school life from practical and mundane tasks such as mending library books, making tea for special events or tidying classroom cupboards, through to an active contribution to teaching and school effectiveness (Jowett and Baginsky 1991; Wolfendale and Bastiani 2000).

As children progress through the school, contact with parents tends to become less regular. Older children may travel to school on their own or with friends. Parents, freed from the demands of caring for young children, may find a job or decide that they have 'done their stint' as parent-helper and look elsewhere for fulfilment. Junior-aged children sometimes find their parent's presence in the school an embarrassment and ask them to stay away. So although it may appear that parents lose interest in their child's education over time, in reality parental interest merely changes perspective (Tizard *et al.* 1988). Early on, parents are chiefly interested in basic considerations such as:

- Is my child happy in school?
- Is my child being properly cared for?
- Does my child have friends?
- Is my child getting on well with basic skills such as reading?
- Is my child behaving satisfactorily?

Later on, when parents are satisfied that these basic needs are being met, they are more likely to concentrate on specific aspects of teaching and learning:

- How is my child progressing in subject work relative to others in the class?
- Is my child being offered a full range of educational opportunities?
- Are extra-curricular activities available?
- Does my child have the ability to achieve success in future education?

Parents of all children are also concerned that their children are not disadvantaged at school, that teachers treat them fairly and that they are offered opportunities to succeed. It is worth remembering that when adults in school interact with a child, they are not only affecting the child but indirectly influencing the parents and families, too.

Children from certain cultures will be used to the continual presence of family members at home and may have had little experience of separation from them until they enter school. Some cultures emphasise the importance of maintaining close family ties and several generations may live in the same household or close to each other. In addition, close chaperoning of children (girls in particular) mean that the concept of complete privacy, so cherished by many in the Western World, is largely unknown to some children from different backgrounds.

Professional boundaries

There will be a variety of parents represented in a single class of children, from (possibly) teenagers to (even) grandparents who are the guardians of their own grandchildren. Some parents will have enjoyed their time at school, others will have unhappy memories, and this experience has a strong influence on their attitude. Some parents are constantly in and out of school, others are never seen. A few parents will be keen to give their time helping the school in whatever way possible. The majority will be too busy earning a living to afford such luxury.

Parents who are struggling with life will sometimes come into school to seek comfort or reassurance from a sympathetic teacher but it pays to be cautious about being drawn into delicate social situations. If a distressed parent approaches you, the general rule is to listen a lot and say little. If there are sensitive issues involved (especially about a teacher in the school or another parent) take particular care not to say anything which might be relayed to the person in question or misconstrued as being critical. It requires a disciplined approach to avoid being swept into an ongoing dialogue with anxious or unhappy parents who begin to see you as their ally. On the other hand, a few moments spent listening and showing some interest in their plight is an important humanitarian role. If possible, try to steer the conversation away from personal issues and towards the progress currently being made by the child of the parent in question. Think of something positive and optimistic to say. If you find that a parent is keeping you from your duties, it is perfectly in order to say something to the effect that you are sorry to have to interrupt them but you will be in trouble if you don't get back to work. A cheery goodbye as you walk away may provide the spark of encouragement that the parent requires. If the parent repeatedly comes to see you, ask for advice from a more experienced colleague. It is important that you never release information about another child or discuss his or her progress to anyone other than the parent or legal guardian. If you feel uncomfortable about the episode, mention it to the head teacher and make a brief record of your conversations with the parent in your private diary.

Communicating with parents

Sometimes, parents may receive conflicting or confusing messages about school life, so good communication is essential. If face-to-face contact is not possible, communication is usually carried out in one of three ways:

- Printed correspondence, such as a school circular or letter, if the issues affect the whole group or class.
- Verbal messages given to an individual child.
- Handwritten notes.

A number of practical points are worth noting.

Printed correspondence

Printed correspondence in the form of general circulars normally come from the head teacher and unexpectedly arrive on the teacher's desk or are brought in by an assistant or administrator. It is a sensible policy always to check the instructions about sending them out and to follow the head teacher's wishes precisely. A delay (or sometimes premature release) in sending a letter home can cause problems if some parents receive notification and others do not. In the busy end-of-day activity, it is easy to overlook a letter intended for home.

If there is time, and particularly in the case of younger children, each child's name should be written neatly at the top of the sheet. Many circular letters never reach parents, and, although they usually emerge some weeks later from a deep coat pocket, it is useful to be able to tell the parents that the circular really was sent home with the child's name on it.

It is sensible to maintain a file for copies of all circulars; this ensures that they are available for parents who arrive to complain that their children never received the letter. A quick photocopy, pleasant smile and gentle apology can diffuse the situation. Many schools have a special noticeboard for copies of important circulars, such as those from the school governors. If you are especially busy and liable to forget to send the letter home, ask the children to remind you. One of them is bound to remember!

Written messages often have to be produced in a variety of languages. Although the child may speak good English, parents do not necessarily do so.

Verbal messages

Adults tend to speak quickly and although a child may nod when asked if the message is understood, there remains a good chance that it will not have been heard properly or will not be remembered, especially in the case of younger children.

It is important to be careful when relaying verbal messages. If teachers hear themselves saying, 'Tell mummy that...' or 'Ask at home to see if...' then they should not be surprised if the next day a bewildered parent contacts them asking what the school can possibly want with a pair of grandpa's old socks or why David has to bring sausages for the school rabbit! Children will rarely alter a message deliberately; more likely they will forget what was said or will become confused. It is like the game of Chinese Whispers in which the message becomes distorted out of all recognition by the time it reaches the person for whom it was intended. More significantly, a special effort should be made to communicate effectively with parents for whom English is not their first language.

If circumstances oblige you to send a verbal message home, then the child should be asked to repeat what has been said before leaving. Generally, though, it is far better either to write it down or to contact the parent in person. It can be worrying and irritating for a parent to receive a jumbled verbal message in the evening and have no idea whether it is urgent or important.

Handwritten notes

Teachers do not often have the time or inclination to write notes to parents, but if you do it is important to remember that parents expect teachers to maintain high standards, so scruffy handwriting will be viewed badly by parents and they will focus immediately on spelling errors. Under such circumstances, a teacher's carefully polished image can quickly evaporate. The same is true of everything teachers write that is placed on public view, such as labels for displays.

If you feel it necessary to send a note home, great care should be taken to be accurate and thoughtful. Many inexperienced teachers have caused themselves considerable anguish through writing to a parent about a child without giving the matter necessary consideration. It is one thing to drop a note to Meena's mum to ask if she would mind coming in to help on Friday instead of Wednesday; it is quite another to send Sam's parents a formal letter to say that he is banned from recorder club because he hasn't bothered to practise. If in doubt about taking action that has implications for a child's learning or for relationships with parents, it is always worth consulting a senior member of staff first. Whereas an ill-advised off-the-cuff remark can usually be smoothed over, a letter in the teacher's own handwriting is harder to dismiss.

If a note goes home to parents, the opportunity can be used to compliment the child who has tried hard or made a special effort. Parents are pleased to receive those personal comments. Children are equally delighted.

In any communication home, it is essential to be careful about addressing letters. If in doubt, the safest way is to ask the child discreetly what you should write or simply put: 'To the parent (or guardian) of Jody Adamson, class 7, from Miss Eddis' and seal the envelope. If you are a trainee teacher it is unlikely that you will need to send a note home, but following the common-sense guidance outlines above may save you a lot of trouble if you do.

Communication with parents takes many forms and can help or hinder a teacher's attempts to build a good working relationship. One of the greatest communication challenges comes when a new teacher meets parents, often for the first time, in the formal circumstances of parent interviews.

Face-to-face with parents

Face-to-face formal encounters with parents take many forms. Some schools operate a rota system, in which a set of appointment times is drawn up for parents to come in to the school during the late afternoon or evening. Other head teachers like to foster a less formal approach in which parents are encouraged to wander in and out of classrooms during the teaching day and chat to the teacher. Some schools have experimented by encouraging parents to have their child present during the discussion with the teacher as a means of giving the child some ownership of the process. Each of these (and other) systems has various advantages and shortcomings, but whatever the form of parent interview adopted, all teachers find their first formal meetings with parents rather nerve-racking and stressful. With time, it becomes easier, but never easy. Teachers have variously described it as frightening, exhausting and exhilarating, but ultimately very worthwhile. If you are still training, then you probably won't have to undertake anything more than a practice event with (say) a teaching assistant playing the part of a parent. You should take every opportunity to sit alongside the teacher during a formal event, both to learn and to experience the strong emotions attached to the occasion.

There are ways of reducing the sense of burden and making the experience positive and beneficial for all concerned. First, the groundwork for a parents' evening is done in advance of the first parent entering the room. The teacher's personality, attitude to children in the classroom, pleasantness during informal contacts, willingness to take time finding out something of a child's interests and approach to learning will already have made a mark. Teachers are talked about regularly at home and at the school gate; their reputation goes before them and influences parents' reactions and inclination when they visit the school.

Second, some parents are nervous about school and (occasionally) have a negative attitude towards teachers in general, which is often a reflection of the parents' unsatisfactory schooling or fear of teachers when they were pupils. Little wonder that the parent concerned can find it difficult to relax and act naturally, and is either rigid and hesitant or unnecessarily abrupt. It can help the teacher concerned to understand that merely entering the school premises requires a considerable mental effort for the small number of disillusioned parents. On the other hand, most parents come into school because they are deeply interested in their child's education and want to find out more about their progress, both academically and socially. Teachers have access to this information and therefore something of value to share with them. Very few parents want to trip teachers up or intimidate them. It is worth viewing parent-interviews as a wonderful opportunity to share information, ideas and concerns, in addition to giving facts and figures about a child's academic attainment.

Activate your thinking!

Questions parents might be asking themselves:

- Will the teacher take a personal interest in my child?
- Can the teacher maintain good order and control?
- Does the teacher have an interesting and lively personality?

Fostering positive relationships with parents:

- Make your classroom a welcoming place.
- Use informal opportunities for developing positive relationships with parents.
- Give advice to parents about helping with their children's education at home.
- Utilise parental help as partners in education.

Preparing for parents' meetings

Every meeting with parents has the potential to enrich an existing situation. There are a number of practical and organisational points that can facilitate a more successful meeting and increase the likelihood that parents will go away feeling satisfied and that you will also be pleased with the outcome.

Check that the classroom is in good order

Parents are only partly aware of what happens in a classroom from day-to-day, so it is the teacher's responsibility to offer evidence of the vitality and effectiveness of the learning that takes place. Trays must be tidied, marking completed, wall displays arranged, examples of children's work named clearly and boldly. View the meeting as an opportunity to show off your expertise and express your personality. Neatly labelled cards with useful information about the nature of projects focus parents' attention on important elements of learning.

> ## Good practice
>
> Invite a friend into the classroom before the parents' meeting for an objective opinion about its appearance.

Prepare thoroughly

In the hurly-burly of school life, even important events like parents' meetings can arrive with alarming speed and find teachers ill-prepared. It is said that great wartime leader Sir Winston Churchill was the best prepared impromptu speaker the House of Commons has ever known. This paradox (well prepared yet apparently spontaneous) has an easy explanation, as the great man prepared so thoroughly that he could speak with authority without constant reference to his notes. This gave the impression of mastery and spontaneity. Teachers should emulate his example.

Thus, when a parent comes to talk about her son, Tom, the teacher ought to be clear about Tom's general strengths and weaknesses without the need to fuss about searching for notes and files. It is important to begin the meeting with a clear, positive statement about Tom that will help to create a bond with the parent. The amount of detailed information needed will depend upon the purpose of the meeting and access to notes may be necessary but it is essential that your detailed knowledge about Tom as a person as well as a scholar comes across clearly (Johnson *et al.*, 1992).

At the start of the school year, a parent will probably be satisfied to hear about how Alice has settled down, whether she has made some friends and if she is making good progress overall. Later on, the same parent will look keenly into Alice's exercise book, scan the wall for examples of her work and make rapid comparisons with other children's work. If the teacher needs to disclose or discuss test scores, it is essential to give clear explanations about the circumstances under which the test was carried out, the status of the result and the implications for Alice's future progress. It is important to be honest with parents but not brutally so. If there are serious concerns about a child's work, do not leave it until the formal meeting before revealing them or parents will rightly ask why you waited so long to inform them.

Know the child

It may seem unlikely, but in the intensity of the moment it is surprisingly easy to confuse the progress of two different children. It is helpful to have a photograph of each child on a separate page in a folder and write down brief notes for every child prior to the meeting. Having a separate page that you can turn over after each interview also prevents parents reading information about other children. Generally, parents are always impressed by a teacher who takes a close and personal interest in their child.

Keep things orderly

Assuming that the background preparation is satisfactorily completed, two guiding principles are important during the meeting: (a) keeping to time by adopting a systematic approach and (b) keeping the conversation focused on the key issues.

Keeping to time is essential if an appointments system is used. Parents rightly become cross if they have to wait for an unreasonable length of time because a teacher is running late. Sometimes it can take a few minutes before the conversation 'warms up' and the allotted time is used up before the serious business begins. Thinking through in advance about the way the meeting will be handled is invaluable and can both help avoid over-running and keep the conversation focused on the relevant issues. The following procedure often proves successful:

- Stand up as the parents approach.

- Make immediate eye contact, smile, extend your hand, greet them by name (or, if in doubt, say: 'You're Andrea's parents, aren't you?') and invite them to sit down.

- Tell them that it is good to see them and thank them sincerely for coming.

- When you need to refer to the child's performance, make sure that you have already turned to the page on which their child's photograph and details are noted. Don't leave another child's details open in front of a different set of parents.

- Begin positively and truthfully: 'I'm really pleased with John's progress this term; he's made a terrific effort' or 'Richard is so persevering. I won't pretend that he has found the work easy, but I have tremendous admiration for the way he refuses to give up' or 'Where did Louise learn to play the piano? She was wonderful in the class assembly the other day'.

- After this item of conversation has run its course, change direction and state the purpose of the meeting. For instance: 'In the next few minutes I've got to tell you about Stephen's progress in the core subjects' or 'We've got just five minutes to chat about Astra's report and another couple of minutes for you to ask me any questions about the class visit next week'. It is, of course, important to be clear yourself about the purpose of the meeting or you and the parents will either stare at one another blankly or indulge in small talk.

- When the time is nearly used up, begin to bring an end to the conversation by saying something like: 'I'm sorry we haven't more time to discuss this. I'm happy to talk again on another occasion if you need to do so. Perhaps you can let me know when you've had chance to think about it but we'll have to draw to a close now'. Stand up and extend your hand.

- As you conclude, close with a positive summary comment that gives the parents something to take away with them:

  Peter's a lively young man and certainly keeps me on my toes. We're doing all we can to help him and there are already signs that things are improving.

  We want Amy to grow more confident in her own abilities because there's no doubt that she can do well.

  Lisa is doing her best and I'm convinced that with a little extra help in maths she'll start to make real progress. We love her sense of humour.

David's a bit anxious about the trip but we'll keep our eye on him, so don't worry. If you've got any concerns, don't hesitate to contact us.

■ As the parents walk away, thank them again for coming. Note the name of the next parent and turn your file to the appropriate page.

Notice how often these examples include the plural forms 'we' and 'us'. This strategy reinforces the teacher's own comments by emphasising the team effort in what is said and gives parents confidence that the issues are being addressed. Parents expect teachers to act and behave like professionals but also to show compassion and understanding. As the meeting proceeds, make a brief note of any parental concerns, action needed or points of interest. Parents can see that you are taking their child's needs and their comments seriously and will go away feeling happy and satisfied.

Activate your thinking!

Restawhile Primary, has been refurbished and given a cash injection after coming through several years of disruption owing to staff changes. Your class, Year 3, is drawn mainly from a white, working class population, with a small but growing minority ethnic community and a few middle class families who want their children to attend the school because it is representative of 'the real world'. The aim of the Parents' Evening at the end of September is for the teacher to let parents know how their children have started the year and begin to cement a working relationship. Detailed information about children's progress is not on the agenda for this ten minute meeting. Consider how you would deal with the following parents:

Parent 1: Miss Small, a shy, retiring person, did not have a successful time at school when she was young. Her daughter, Charlaine, is also timid and underachieving but has shown a growing ability in gymnastics. Miss Small has several younger children and regular contact with Social Services for support. Charlaine has a small cohort of quiet, compliant friends.

Parent 2: Rupert's parents are among the wealthiest in the school. They are professional people and well aware of their rights, but have agreeable personalities and understand that teaching is a challenging job. They also have high expectations for their son, who is a bright cheery lad but not a high-flier. Rupert is passionate about football, sensitive to his parents' aspirations for him and has a growing awareness of his academic limitations. Rupert has a highly intelligent older sister.

Parent 3: Mr and Mrs Singh are very proud of their eldest son, Gulwar, and desperate that he should do well in school. They have considered moving him to another, more academically successful school, but are afraid he will lose his friends if they do. Gulwar excels in mathematics but is ambivalent about literacy and restless during formal teaching sessions. He is an enthusiastic, popular boy and prefers to work unaided.

Parent 4: Mr and Mrs Tuffnutt have twins in the class, Marty and Ocean. Marty is a sharp-tongued, irritating child who often succeeds in getting under a teacher's skin. He is adept at being subtly rude (especially to the support staff) yet charming at the same time. He is always on the fringe of trouble. Ocean is a sad-looking child with few friends, who would, given the chance, spend her time drawing and colouring. She rarely initiates conversations with adults. Mr Tuffnutt is a loud character and can be dismissive of other people's opinions. Mrs Tuffnutt seems to be a little in awe of her husband.

Parent 5: Ms Monroe has five children, allegedly by three different fathers. She has a gushing, breezy manner and teachers consider her to be a genuinely nice person, very willing to help out with school events. Her son, Brixton, is far more intelligent than anyone else in the family but chooses to mask his abilities for fear of being thought of as 'a swot' by his mates. He is very helpful in class and completes his work without fuss.

Guarding your words

It is obvious that a person who wishes to be treated like a teacher must behave like one. This particularly applies when parents are present. Parents do not expect teachers to be casual or indifferent, but rather to be pleasantly professional. Many teachers enjoy chatting with parents and sharing a joke with them, but it is important not to get carried away with the friendliness. Even informal comments from teachers are remembered and taken very seriously by a lot of parents, so careless remarks should be avoided. Teachers in staffrooms may sometimes say outrageous things about serious matters but it is unwise to do this publicly. A pleasant smile and responsive laugh at the right moment is helpful when dealing with parents, but clever remarks and subtleties should be saved for when you are mixing with friends outside school.

In a small number of cases, a parent will befriend you in the hope of gaining inside information about the school and staff. Some parents may wish to know about the current state of thinking in the school about issues where a firm decision has yet to be made. It pays to be cautious and say as little as possible, without giving the impression that there is something to hide. Even if you feel strongly about a particular matter, resist the temptation to vent your feelings in front of parents, as rumours about staff disharmony spread rapidly. Gossip can be fuelled by a throwaway remark from a teacher in an unguarded moment, so be careful that you do not allow yourself to be ensnared in this way. Special care and wisdom is required in discussing matters in front of parents who regularly help in school (as mealtime staff or teaching assistants).

The intensity of parents' meetings and the heavy demands they make on a teacher can easily lead to elementary blunders. These can be avoided with a little forethought and discipline. The following are five common mistakes in teacher–parent dialogue to be aware of:

Saying too much

Teachers must learn to listen as well as speak and not become carried away by the sound of their own voice. Nerves can sometimes make a teacher too talkative but there is still a need to pause for breath occasionally.

Patronising the parents

Parents may or may not know much about formal education but they know a lot about their own child. Even if a teacher feels that they are not doing a very good job in bringing up their child, it would be unwise to betray such thoughts in conversation. The key is to listen sympathetically to parents wishing to share their private thoughts but avoid passing judgement. If parents ask your advice, offer a gentle response without sounding too assertive, leaving the final decision with them.

Promising to do something that cannot be done

Parents will sometimes come to a meeting with their own agenda relating to what they want for their children from academic work, extra-curricular activities, sports events or relationships. The frequency with which parents mention these matters reinforces the important truth that they see their own child's needs extending beyond the academic. Most teachers try to be as accommodating as possible in responding to parental requests, but there is a danger of promising too much. Some parents hope that a teacher will provide opportunities for their child which, by rights, are their own responsibility. For example, it is unrealistic to offer to establish an individualised teaching programme for a child that cannot be maintained. Teachers put under pressure in this respect should first check with the head teacher or suggest that the parents do so. Promises are easy to make in the intensity of interaction with parents but more difficult to keep.

Imagining that parents are full of ill-intent

The vast majority of parents are not teacher-consuming monsters. Some are critical and others are not easily satisfied, but most are supportive and as keen for their child to do well as anybody. It would be a mistake to be defensive when meeting parents. Assuming the best, trying to be positive and enthusiastic, and looking upon the parents as allies and partners in teaching and learning provide the basis for happy encounters.

Parents need reason to be hopeful and have confidence in you and it is unusual for them to be negative or abrasive. It is important to give parents hope and the clear message that you can be trusted with their child's education. If you are an inexperienced teacher or do not have children of your own, you may not realise what a transformation a good report can make to the atmosphere in the home.

Difficult parents and parents with difficulty

From time to time, teachers come into contact with challenging or unco-operative parents; this likelihood is increased with parents of children who are struggling educationally (Greenwood 2004). However, there is a difference between 'difficult parents' and 'parents who have a difficulty with an aspect of school life'. Difficult parents may feel intimidated in the teacher's presence or have bad memories of school or be experienced parents who are hoping unrealistically that their younger child can emulate an older child's success. Sometimes the parents may have had a bad experience with another teacher in the school. Of course, they may just be nasty people. On the other hand, 'parents who have a difficulty' may be signalling something important about the school or the teacher's own teaching, skills of communication or attitude towards the children.

It is uncomfortable to be confronted by a parent who seems intent on finding fault and very difficult to remain detached from the issues. However, it helps to remember that only teachers have the power to influence the classroom situation directly, whereas parents do not have. Always listen. Never be tempted to belittle parents or allow them to intimidate you. Keep the channels of communication open. Maintain a professional attitude at all times but don't tolerate abuse or threats. A more positive way of viewing parents who express dissatisfaction is that they are taking the time and trouble to become involved in their child's education, however clumsily it may be expressed. Nevertheless, when faced with sour or indignant parents, it is important to think through the practicalities:

- If the confrontation is public, the parents should be asked to accompany the teacher to a more private spot, but not out of sight. If they refuse, ask whether they would like to arrange another meeting in the near future. Quite often, the parents have already 'had their say', will refuse the offer and march off. In this case, it is essential for the head teacher or a senior colleague to be informed as soon as possible. The head teacher will probably want to contact the parents directly and clarify the nature of the grievance. Don't allow matters to remain unresolved in the hope that they will somehow fade away. Always seek advice from senior colleagues.

- If the parents agree to sit and talk about their concerns, the teacher should maintain eye contact and show interest in what is said, resisting the temptation to refute any allegations or become defensive. The teacher may want to summarise the parents' concerns in order to clarify the nature of the grievance. In most cases, a simple explanation will suffice and the parents will go away satisfied. The teacher should thank the parents for taking the trouble to come and encourage them to return should there be any further concerns.

- In the unlikely event of parents becoming very agitated or threatening, the teacher should state that the conversation is terminated, stand up and inform the parents that the matter should be shared with the head teacher (or the most senior person available). It is important (though far from easy) to maintain a calm demeanour. Walk quickly away and find a colleague to talk to.

Aggressive behaviour from parents is extremely rare and is normally avoidable by following the advice given in the earlier part of this chapter. It is quite possible that you may never experience such unpleasantness. Remember that an increasing number of children live with only one parent or with a substitute parent and this can sometimes create additional pressures for all concerned. Bear this fact in mind when tempted to be judgemental. Most parents, whether in a stable relationship or not, are keen to offer their support and will do all in their power to ensure that they maintain a good relationship with their child's teacher. An aggressive parent can leave a teacher feeling vulnerable and shaken, but console yourself with the fact that you have 29 other satisfied clients!

Parents in the classroom

Over the past 20 years, the number of parents working alongside teachers in the classroom and around the school has increased significantly. There are many reasons for this:

- The publication of numerous reports stressing the importance of closer home–school links
- A recognition of the useful skills possessed by parents
- The need to have more adult support in the classroom.

Most schools will have a policy for parental involvement and teachers need to work within these guidelines. Parent helpers are volunteers and could, under other circumstances, be receiving payment for their work. Parents in the classroom can be a bonus or a problem depending on the care with which they are selected and the skill with which they are deployed. When a parent approaches a teacher with an offer of help, it is essential to check first with the head teacher, as some parents are unsuitable for reasons which may not be known to the teacher. Once a teacher is committed to accepting an offer of help, it is difficult to tell parents that they are no longer wanted. Good parent helpers are worth their weight in gold; poor ones can cause problems for a teacher.

It is important to appreciate that a parent who is in and out of the classroom and staffroom picks up a lot of information about individual children and staff, so care about disclosing information which may or may not remain private beyond the school gate is essential. Further discussion about the deployment of teaching assistants is found later in the chapter.

Remember that a large percentage of a school's budget depends upon the number of children attending the school. The loss of just a few children, especially in a small school, can make a substantial difference to the overall financial position and put pressure on governors and staff to cut resources. Establishing harmonious relations with parents is not simply a matter of good educational practice; it is necessary to ensure that they are sufficiently satisfied to keep their children at the school and recommend it to others.

OTHER ADULTS IN SCHOOL

As noted earlier, parents provide the emotional and practical bedrock for pupil progress, by stimulating interest in learning, encouraging the children to persevere, assisting with homework and, in some cases, working as a volunteer helper. The next section deals with the different roles of the many other adults apart from parents that form part of the school community and contribute to the teaching and learning programme, and to the nurture and care of children (Hughes 1997).

Working together

Children have their own views on who matters in school and who does not. For instance, mealtime assistants are rarely accorded the same respect as teachers, whereas the school administrator is seen as being very significant. Nevertheless, in different ways, every adult makes a contribution to school life and their co-operation, support and encouragement are vitally important in shaping the school ethos and the children's progress (Mills and Mills 1995). The more successful schools are usually those in which there is a high level of collaboration and a good team spirit (Nias *et al.* 1989), both between members of the same group (such as ancillary staff) and across groups (such as the relationship between teachers and assistants). Teachers, in particular, as the most influential people in the children's education, have a responsibility to consider ways in which they can develop positive links with other employees and volunteers for the benefit of children's learning.

Trainee teachers are included in the variety of adults who contribute to this complex amalgam of influences. It is not easy for them to go into a strange school and begin to establish a good working relationship with children and colleagues that they have never met. This is, however, exactly what has to happen in most school placement situations. The skill of trainees in relating to their class teacher and mentor can make the difference between an effective and a disappointing school experience. This does not mean that they have to like the teacher or approve of his/her methods. It does mean that they have to make every effort to show that they appreciate what is being done on their behalf and support the teacher fully. The large majority of host teachers value trainees in the classroom and want to see them succeed, not least because of the benefit to the pupils.

Because of the commitment of the host teachers to trainees, under no circumstances should you ever admit to having doubts about your vocation. Teachers are understandably dismayed if they think that they are wasting their time helping trainees to progress when they have little intention of teaching after qualifying. Teachers will give their full backing if they perceive that students are determined to be a positive influence in the classroom. They expect them to be willing to listen, learn, respond, acknowledge mistakes and do all that they can to improve their classroom practice. Teachers will judge your commitment by the thoroughness of your preparation, awareness of opportunities to enhance children's learning and positive contribution to classroom decisions where appropriate. Although it is important to demonstrate a willingness to be an active member of the team, it does not mean that you have to passively accept all that is said to you without ever questioning or offering your own opinions. Trainee teachers have to be prepared to question, reflect, ponder and establish an intelligent dialogue with those who are responsible for their mentoring and training.

Developing a supportive attitude

When you are qualified and have responsibility for a group of children, you will understand more fully the concerns that teachers have about allowing a stranger to take charge. Every teacher has some idiosyncratic practices and ideas which others find difficult to accept. At the heart of the collaborative endeavour must be a strong inclination on the part of trainee teachers to co-operate with the host teachers for the benefit of the children, even when they don't fully approve of some of the things that are done. For instance, you may not feel that they want to use the same system of rewards and sanctions as the teacher. You may want to do more listening and less speaking than the teacher does. You may wish to give children more or less freedom to make choices, and so on. However, it is important for every trainee teacher to take an unprejudiced view of these sorts of issues, as the more that teachers at all stages of their career can develop an open dialogue with colleagues and mentors about the managing and organising of learning, the more confident they will become in adjusting their approach from a well-informed and considered perspective. However, in pursuing a dialogue, it is particularly important to be courteous and non-judgemental, as well-intended comments may be construed by a colleague as subtle criticism. A school ethos founded upon positive attitudes and affirmative comments towards pupils should also apply to adult–adult relationships, and facilitate open discussions about serious issues. You must still try your best to be positive and supportive, whether or not you are sympathetic towards the host teacher's priorities.

Activate your thinking!

In what practical ways can you make a positive contribution to the school ethos?

Fostering understanding among school staff

As a means of gaining a better understanding of other adults in school, it is important to consider some of their roles and examine the ways their work impinges on others. The rest of this chapter provides a synopsis of the work, needs and priorities of some key personnel.

The head teacher

Every report about schools stresses the importance of the head teacher. Together with governors, the head teacher is responsible for the whole running of the school. For instance, the head teacher has immediate responsibility for achieving agreed aims, safeguarding curriculum entitlement for pupils, maintaining links with the community, involving parents closely in school life and establishing appropriate forms of pupil assessment, in addition to staff welfare, training, development and appraisal.

Many head teachers work long hours and this exacts a high cost (Clegg and Billington, 1997). Local management of schools (LMS) brought with it new demands for control of the school budget and associated financial decisions. A large proportion of the head teacher's day is spent dealing with administrative tasks, meeting people and attending meetings. Unless the school is very small, it is unlikely that the head teacher will have a substantial teaching commitment. While it is true that head teachers are often less informed about the detail of the curriculum than their class teachers, they are certainly interested in what goes on in the classroom. A good head teacher will spend a lot of time encouraging staff to work as members of a team, to attend courses to enhance their work and promoting high standards of pupil attainment and discipline.

Whatever head teachers' strengths and weaknesses, they are entitled to expect every teacher's support and enthusiasm. Some new teachers are in awe of the head teacher, but need to remind themselves that the head was once a classroom teacher and only asks that staff work hard, respect their colleagues and help to promote the school's reputation and achievements.

Teachers are most likely to have contact with the head teacher during assembly, at staff meetings, when decisions are being made or when their advice is sought. Head teachers also write references for teachers who apply for other jobs, so it is in every teacher's interest to maintain an open, courteous and professional relationship with them.

The head teacher expects staff to:

- Be trustworthy and hard-working
- Prepare thoroughly and to teach efficiently
- Show enthusiasm and determination
- Relate well to parents
- Show respect towards colleagues and visitors
- Have a bright and tidy classroom with evidence of good quality children's work on display.

Governors

The role of governors has changed considerably in recent years (see, for instance, Doust and Doust 2001; Adams 2002). At one time, they were merely figureheads and rarely involved in school life other than for special functions and emergencies. Until the 1980s, governing bodies had few powers and relatively little influence in schools. The head teacher determined most school policies, and teachers decided what they taught their children. The Education Acts of the 1980s and 1990s drastically altered the responsibilities and status of governing bodies, all of which must now include representatives from the teaching staff, parents and local community.

People become governors for a variety of reasons. The majority have a desire to help the school community. A small number get elected so as to wield influence on behalf of a particular social or religious cause. They are normally people of considerable ability and experience, and although they may not have a background in education, they normally have other skills and attributes that allow them to offer a different perspective on issues. Many governors are delighted to offer their help and support wherever possible, and although they may not have the time or inclination to give regular classroom support, the best sort of governor will always listen and provide sound advice. If you are a trainee teacher, take every opportunity to meet governors, as they have responsibility for every aspect of school life, including the work of trainees.

Each year, a formal meeting of governors and parents is held at which governors give an account of the school's work and progress; teaching staff are normally present. Although in practice only a small number of parents attend, this annual meeting highlights the governors' accountability and significance in the life of the school. Governors also have the right to enter the school at any time and examine aspects of its life and work, though convention dictates that this should only be done with the permission of the head teacher and, if teaching is to be observed, with the consent of the teachers concerned. Many head teachers arrange informal gatherings of teachers and governors each term to help cement relationships and celebrate successes. These meetings form an important element of professional life. It is also reassuring to know that at least one colleague will be representing the views of staff by being elected as the 'teacher governor'.

Governor elections

Parent and teacher governors are elected. Elections are held for parent representatives to serve for three years. Ballot forms are distributed to parents of the children in the school and the candidate with the most votes is elected. If a number of parents wish to stand for the vacancy, they have a right to circulate their views and win over support; this is sometimes carried out by the simple expediency of allowing each candidate a given number of words in which to set out their position. Their manifestos are then copied to all parents. Ballot papers have to be carefully monitored and returns counted carefully. Governors (often the chairperson) have to be involved in the process to ensure that procedures are correctly followed. Procedures for appointing the teacher representative are less complex, though equally rigorous. In very small schools with only a handful of staff, there is sometimes a problem in finding a teacher willing to stand.

The head teacher can opt whether or not to be a governor, though nearly all do so. When school inspectors visit, their report is sent to the governors (not just to the head teacher), who are charged with the task of ensuring that the recommendations are followed and perceived shortcomings dealt with. Head teachers often refer to 'my governors' indicating the close relationship which ideally exists between them. A school in which the governors and head teacher have a harmonious relationship is likely to prosper. Head teachers who enjoy this harmony know that when there are difficulties and problems, they will be assured of support and encouragement from the governing body.

Governors' responsibilities

Whatever their motivation, the role of governor is a demanding one and requires people with stamina, determination and the ability to grasp fairly complex issues and make sense of a large number of government missives and local authority circulars. Governing bodies are responsible for the upkeep of the buildings, curriculum development, staff, finance, special needs provision and maintaining satisfactory community relations (see, for example, Advisory Centre for Education 2001).

Governors also have the responsibility for ensuring that school policies and decisions accord with the large number of government edicts which have been issued in recent years, including managing the curriculum, publishing an informative school brochure for parents containing test results and other information about the school, staffing, health and safety, special needs provision, employment contracts, disciplinary procedures, buildings and numerous other aspects of school life. Governors also receive, comment upon, and act upon inspection reports and other consultation exercises. They are expected to be involved in establishing and monitoring 'target setting', relating in particular to the percentage of pupils who reach level 4 in their Standard Assessment Tests (SATs) in core subjects (notably English), which is supposed to improve year upon year. In theory, the head teacher is responsible for the day-to-day running of the school and the governors act as an executive. In practice, the roles can overlap and there may be uncertainty about where the head teacher's role ends and the governors' role begins. The balance between governing bodies offering adequate support to a teaching staff and becoming intrusive is a fine one, but the trend is towards more, rather than less, governor involvement (Dean 2001).

Most governing bodies are sub-divided into groups responsible for different areas of school life. The groups report back to the main body at each governing body meeting. Some decisions can be made by sub-groups, but there are guidelines on which decisions require the full governing body and which do not. In some schools, governors take a particular interest in one curriculum area or age-phase. For instance, a governor may be attached to mathematics, another to science; similarly, a governor may develop links with the nursery class or with classes at the end of Key Stages. Governors do not have the right to interfere with curriculum planning and implementation but the more they know about the detailed situation, the more able they are to argue the case for additional resources for it. Schools should have a governor with a brief for monitoring the implementation of policies for special educational needs (SEN).

In the past, governors have not paid much attention to trainee teachers. However, as their contribution has come to be seen as part of the teaching and learning, and forms an element of the inspection process, governors now need to show more interest in what they do. If appointed as NQTs, of course, they become the subject of intense interest because:

■ Governors appointed them and will want to feel that their decision was a correct one.

■ In any inspection the performance of every teacher (recently qualified or otherwise) is significant.

■ Governors regularly talk about the school staff, their needs, concerns and aspirations.

■ One of the parent-governors may have a child in their class or will know several people who do.

Teachers are most likely to have contact with governors:

■ During specially organised meetings for the purpose.

■ When a governor has been delegated to collect information about a given curriculum area

■ With teacher-governor colleagues.

■ Informally with parent-governors who collect children and attend parent teacher association meetings.

Things that governors expect from teachers:

■ To do their job to the very best of their ability and be willing to learn how to do it better.

■ To support and be enthusiastic about all aspects of school life.

■ To be willing to develop and extend their expertise and influence within the school and community.

Over and above the regular issues, governors' chief concerns are about the head teacher's welfare, financial constraints, individual teacher's competence and school inspection. Governors are also charged with making important decisions about internal promotion, the head teacher's salary and restructuring the workforce to ensure that teachers are able to enjoy a reasonable balance between work and home commitments (DfES 2003c).

Teaching assistants

The use of teaching assistants is very common in primary schools. They may be voluntary or paid. If voluntary, it is up to the class teacher to negotiate when the adult comes into the classroom and for what purpose. If (as in most cases) the assistant is paid, then she or he is called a Teaching Assistant (TA) and will have a job description to which she or he needs to conform. TAs have been employed in larger primary schools over many years for general duties but they are gradually assuming more responsibility for pupils' learning and there has been a large increase in their numbers to support the work of class teachers. Some teaching assistants are responsible for the needs of one child, for whom the term Learning Support Assistant (LSA) was often used in the past. However, assistants are now graded as a TA or as a Higher Learning Teaching Assistant (HLTA). HLTAs in particular are likely to work more closely with the teacher with respect to teaching and learning, though all adult assistants can be used in one or more of a variety of ways (see Waters 1996 for a summary of ideas). Although some assistants have their own clear view of what they are and are not prepared to do, it is up to you to be specific about your expectations, especially with early years' classes where additional adult support is often interwoven into the fabric of the teaching day. It is important to recognise, however, that the role of the TA is being restructured (DfES 2002b) though the distinction between teacher role and TA role is not always as clear-cut as official publications suggest.

Nearly every class teacher who has the services of an assistant is grateful for the help and support. Salaried teaching assistants have tended to be more common in younger age classes than in the upper primary range. Increasingly all paid assistants possess a qualification and attend further in-service courses to develop their expertise (see Watkinson 2003a, 2003b). Some assistants are former teachers who no longer wish to teach. The majority are local people who enjoy working in school, have their own children there and have been appointed to support the work of teachers, particularly those with larger classes. Due to funding limitations, assistants may be employed on temporary contracts.

In many primary schools TAs have been principally used to work alongside children in core subjects rather than in the more creative and aesthetic areas, with the result that some of their traditional responsibilities (such as assisting with basic practical tasks and putting up displays) have assumed secondary importance. However, the situation is altering rapidly and a new breed of better-trained and remunerated assistants is emerging. The Government is keen to recruit tens of thousands of support staff and exploit their expertise in the classroom. The principle to increase their number of assistants is supposed to mirror the situation in hospitals where a senior professional (such as a consultant) is involved only with key decision-making and advanced practice, leaving the subordinates (junior doctors, nurses) to carry out the orders and perform most of the regular work. Training for teaching assistants is now a required and necessary element of the strategy and for those wishing to pursue further study there are career routes into teaching. There are a number of elements to this strategy of employing more TAs:

- More flexible models of teaching and learning, so that teachers can use professional judgement in leading support colleagues

- Teachers becoming principally responsible for learning outcomes than every aspect of the teaching and learning process

- Teachers being freed from more routine tasks so that they can concentrate on the more specialised elements of their role, such as planning, preparation and assessment of pupils' learning

- Ensuring that support staff are given suitable training to ensure that they possess the appropriate skills and knowledge to complement the work of teachers

  (See www.teachernet.gov.uk/remodelling)

It is evident that additional support staff must be flexible and able to respond rapidly to a teacher's requests. Although a lot of lesson planning is done in advance, a great deal of a teacher's day consists of making spontaneous decisions and sometimes adjusting plans at the last moment to fit the events of the moment. On the one hand a TA is not a lackey, waiting obediently for the teacher's command; on the other hand a TA must accept that effective teachers modify and adjust priorities and that not everything can be predicted. Thus, it is essential that the relationship between teacher and assistant is comfortable for both parties. Any action that might upset the delicate balance of mutual trust and endeavour that is the mainstay of effective schools must be resisted. In addition, primary schooling involves an array of rich learning opportunities, such as the visit of a theatre company, outdoor pursuits, educational trips and whole school productions. The value of experienced adults to help administer and organise such events is invaluable. Note the important legal implications for schools and teachers outlined in Chapter 11.

The strategy for involvement of large numbers of TAs is posited on the assumption that having additional support staff is advantageous in releasing the teacher from onerous tasks and supporting children's learning. However, there are new management skills that teachers need to develop, both in knowing how to relate to TAs and use them profitably. There are 25 routine tasks that teachers have often carried out and are now deemed more suitable for classroom support staff. Not all of the items in the list are equally important or relevant to primary schools. The full range of tasks is shown in Figure 3.1: Possible tasks for Teaching Assistants.

It is clearly a waste of time and money to employ a capable assistant and fill their time with menial tasks when they have other talents to offer. The tasks more relevant to primary education might include some of the following:

- Collecting money
- Collating pupil reports
- Stocktaking
- Bulk photocopying
- Record keeping and filing
- Classroom display
- ICT trouble-shooting and minor repairs (acting within health and safety guidelines)
- Ordering supplies and equipment

1   Collecting money
2   Chasing absences
3   Bulk photocopying
4   Copy typing
5   Producing standard letters
6   Producing class lists
7   Record-keeping and filing
8   Classroom display
9   Analysing attendance figures
10 Processing exam results
11 Collating pupil reports
12 Administering work experience
13 Administering examinations
14 Invigilating examinations
15 Administering teacher cover
15 ICT trouble-shooting and minor repairs
17 Commissioning new ICT equipment
18 Ordering supplies and equipment
19 Stocktaking
20 Cataloguing, preparing, issuing and maintaining equipment and materials
21 Minuting meetings
22 Co-ordinating and submitting bids
23 Seeking and giving personnel advice
24 Managing pupil data
25 Inputting pupil data

FIGURE 3.1 Possible tasks for teaching assistants (based on DfES 2002b)

- Issuing and maintaining equipment and materials
- Seeking and giving personnel advice
- Managing pupil data and inputting pupil data

Although assistants can carry out these tasks, they still have to be co-ordinated and monitored by a teacher. In addition, whereas a simple job such as bulk photocopying does not require specialist expertise, it is not acceptable (for example) for an assistant to carry out minor repairs to technical equipment without full training. Similarly, it is useful if a TA can relieve you of important but time-consuming jobs in the area of health and safety (such as checking the state of games' equipment) providing that legal responsibilities are met. Again, it saves a teacher a lot of time if an assistant carries out the administration of ordering (say) consumable resources, but the teacher still has to spend time in being familiar with what is needed and liaising with the assistant before the order is sent. In other words, the mere availability of an assistant does not of itself free you to concentrate on the tasks that require more sophisticated professional skills such as planning and preparing, teaching, assessing children's progress, marking and reporting. It is also the case that an assistant will not always be available when you need assistance, so there are bound to be times when you have to do the task yourself. Consequently, although you may want to delegate jobs, it is important that you do not lose touch with them entirely or allow yourself to become deskilled.

Good practice

Working with reception-age children, one teaching assistant's responsibilities included the following:

- Hearing children read orally and maintaining records
- Assisting with a maths extension group
- Assisting during the lesson time, working one-to-one with particular children
- Mounting and displaying children's work around the room and corridor
- Producing some resources for teaching as requested by the class teacher
- Taking children to the library to select books and other general library duties
- Assisting the teacher when children were moving around the school and being taken outside the premises
- Keeping accident report records and overseeing health and safety requirements
- Designing and producing scenery for school plays
- The collection and distribution of refreshments, including drinking water
- Voluntarily running an after-school craft club

The level of involvement of support staff will be affected by the size of the school. In particular, small schools with fewer than one hundred pupils do not have the infrastructure, physical space or finance to operate like a secondary school of (say) a thousand pupils, with dedicated spaces and specialist support staff. Small schools are more likely to utilise voluntary adult help or employ part-time assistants, often shared across several classes. Consequently, the deployment of support staff involves considerable flexibility and close teamwork to ensure consistency and equity.

The need for developing expertise will become even more essential if proposals to allow assistants to act as substitute teachers in certain circumstances are enacted. There are legal implications involved in leaving a TA in charge of a class if incidents or injuries occur. If you are a trainee teacher you do not have to worry about this particular issues as the class teacher has overall responsibility, but as a new teacher with your own class it is something to clarify with the head teacher.

One way and another, the involvement of assistants in a variety of activities previously considered the sole province of qualified teachers is likely to become increasingly significant in schools but is not of itself a panacea for reducing teachers' workload. The most important factor is that the benefits that accrue from having an assistant outweigh the additional demands that managing another adult involve for the teacher.

Activate your thinking!

Imagine that you have responsibility for managing two teaching assistants, one of whom works with a blind child, the other on general duties, shared half-time with the adjacent class. What factors will you need to consider in managing the situation?

Special needs assistants, though now subsumed under the TA title, undertake a specialist role in working alongside children whose learning needs have been formally identified through a 'statementing' procedure involving the parents, school, educational psychologist and local education authority. Due to the policy of integrating children into mainstream schooling, the status of learning support assistants has been enhanced over recent years. Ideally, if there is a child who has been formally identified as having special needs, an assistant will be available for part or all of the day, depending on the nature and severity of the need. However, the concept of one adult clinging like a leech to a single needy child throughout the day is becoming outmoded (see Chapter 9).

Teaching assistants are nearly always hard-working and dedicated. They may not have the teacher's level of professional expertise but will often have a store of experience about what happens in and around the school. Every assistant has an agreed job description but most enjoy some variety in their routine and are happy to undertake other tasks when it is appropriate to do so.

Although all assistants have specified priorities, they rely on the class teacher to direct them and provide support. If this does not happen, they understandably become frustrated or insecure and begin to create their own patterns of working which may not suit the teacher. It is therefore essential for teachers to maintain good and open relationships with TAs. If the assistant has been at the school for a long time and has become attached to a particular way of working, it may be more difficult to bring about changes in the working brief. Under such circumstances, teachers need diplomacy and patience to effect change and make adjustments. If the assistant is a parent, the teacher's reputation can hinge on the informal conversations about the teacher that the assistant has with other parents outside school, so be warned!

Good practice

To ensure that your teaching assistant contributes effectively to classroom life and gains satisfaction from doing so, it helps to incorporate the following good practice into your weekly schedule:

■ Take time to clarify her duties and your own expectations.

- Offer her the chance to develop her skills and be involved in aspects of classroom work that she finds enjoyable and fulfilling.
- Set aside a time each week to discuss matters of mutual concern.
- Take every opportunity to thank the TA for her efforts, raise her self-esteem and acknowledge her contribution to the life of the class.

Teaching assistants are not assistant teachers and this must be taken into account when deciding the tasks they are asked to undertake. For instance, if you ask an assistant to hear children reading aloud, it is essential that she has enough knowledge about the process of learning to read to make a positive impact. The quickest way to damage a TA's dedication is to make unjustified assumptions about her capability and level of responsibility or to take advantage of her goodwill (Balshaw 1999; Fox 1998). Teachers have to take care to assign to them appropriate duties and responsibilities rather than the mundane tasks that no one else wants to do! Teaching assistants expect from teachers appropriate respect and understanding, clarity about the nature of their work and being kept informed. TAs' chief concerns include opportunities to engage with tasks that use their expertise instead of lower level activities, and the positive responses of the children they supervise. In common with every other adult in school, assistants merit and enjoy sincere praise and encouragement.

Caretakers and cleaners

Over the past few years, the demands upon caretakers and cleaning staff have grown. A school which at one time had three or four staff to safeguard and clean the premises may now make do with one or two on reduced working hours. Some schools employ contracted staff who may or may not have a commitment to the particular school and will probably be poorly paid. Caretakers work prescribed hours and are possibly also on call. For instance, if a child is sick over the classroom floor, it is normal policy that only the caretaker clears it up, using specific procedures and designated chemicals. Unfortunately, the caretaker may be unavailable or live at a great distance from the school, in which case there will be a school policy about the appropriate procedure. Caretakers are not allowed to perform certain tasks such as climbing ladders above a certain height, lifting heavy weights and carrying out property maintenance. Although many caretakers will loosely interpret these rules, it is important for teachers to remember that an innocent request for assistance may meet with a shake of the head if the request means breaking the contractual terms. The first rule for teachers who hope to develop a good relationship with the caretaker is to discover what duties are specified.

One of the caretaker's most demanding tasks in a larger school is to supervise cleaners. Cleaners sometimes work in the early morning before school begins or, more often, for two or three hours after school. In that time they have a lot to do and the caretaker is responsible for ensuring that the work is carried out satisfactorily. In a very small school, one person may be both cleaner and caretaker and will have to do everything from locking and unlocking the school to mopping floors, collecting and depositing rubbish, and controlling stock. Even in a medium-sized primary school, there may be as few as two persons involved.

All teachers should be sensitive to the pressures on cleaning staff and bear in mind that the most frequent complaints about the state of classrooms made by cleaning staff include the mess made by clay and plasticine trodden into carpets, inappropriate use of paper towels, chairs not stacked according to the school's agreed procedure, messy sinks and graffiti on table tops. It is also fair to consider that cleaners need to come into the room after school, so a little consideration to allow them to do so is both courteous and practical. A little effort to train the children to clear up and follow sensible rules will avoid irritating cleaners as well as improve your organisational skills.

Activate your thinking!

What does the cleaner say to colleagues about the condition of your room? How does your attitude to the caretaker help in generating a positive working relationship?

Good practice

If your caretaker has an interesting background, extend an invitation to talk to your class about it. Remember that this volunteer may not be used to addressing children and will need your support and guidance. It is usually better to have two short sessions on different days than a lengthy monologue. The caretaker (or any other adult you invite to speak to the children) may be loquacious with adults but feel constrained when addressing children.

Caretakers expect respect and courtesy from teachers, an acknowledgement of the demands of their job and advance notice about forthcoming events. Caretakers' chief concerns are a visit from their supervisor, cleaner absenteeism and a lack of basic resources to do the job effectively.

Mealtime assistants

Many people feel that mealtime assistants (MTAs) have the least enviable job in schools (Fell 1994). Playground supervision, in particular, places great demands upon them as they attempt to control large numbers of excitable children, sort out squabbles, mend damaged knees and broken relationships, and direct children to the right place at the right time. Inside the school, there are lunch boxes to open, tables to wipe, slow eaters to encourage and poor manners to correct. Although the majority of MTAs are dedicated and conscientious, their lack of authority can cause them to struggle with unco-operative children, and the sound of strained voices is a familiar one in some schools.

An increasing number of head teachers and governors have come to recognise that as MTAs play an important role in the life of the school, it is worth investing time in the provision of training and guidance. As a result, issues such as behaviour management, assertiveness, interpersonal relationships and first-aid are addressed through regular sessions. MTAs need to have a good sense of humour, plenty of stamina and a strong personality. Due to the low wages, most of them will be local parents and a number of them may have a second job. When MTAs are seen leaving school the moment the dinner break is over, it is tempting to think that this reflects a low level of commitment. In fact, they are likely to have other responsibilities or are (understandably) refusing to do unpaid overtime. Until relatively recently teachers were all expected to take a dinner duty and although in some schools there is still a voluntary rota of teachers who wish to help, very few do so. Some schools now employ a more highly qualified person to supervise lunchtime arrangements, generate interest in traditional games and activities, and manage the other mealtime staff.

With the youngest children, it is quite likely that an MTA will come to the classroom a few minutes before the official end of the morning to take responsibility for the children who stay for lunch. If so, it is important that teachers consider the organisational implications of completing work and tidying up before she arrives. This last point is especially significant if the room is used for children to eat their packed lunches. If it is a wet day, the MTAs will be trying to look after the children all together in the school hall or flitting from classroom to classroom attempting to entertain and subdue the restless children. MTAs are only responsible for children who remain at school to eat their lunch, not for children who go home. Younger children who are going home for lunch have to be supervised by the teacher until an adult collects them. If children return to school too early from lunch, they are not, strictly speaking, the responsibility of MTAs.

When children are together in the playground, it is inevitable that there are disagreements and conflicts from time to time that require adult intervention. Occasionally, MTAs cannot cope on their own and may bring a naughty child to the teacher for admonishment. There are a number of principles to consider in evaluating your interaction with MTAs:

- As a teacher, MTAs believe that you are never fully off-duty.
- MTAs expect teachers, however inexperienced, to be able to deal with instances of pupil misdemeanour.
- It is important to remain detached from the emotions of the moment until explanations are sought and the situation can be properly resolved.
- There is a need to balance the MTA's expectation that she will receive your support with the possibility that the child concerned may also have a genuine grievance.

Conflict situations are never easy to deal with but teachers must expect to meet them from time to time. Frustration can lead to overreaction and a rapid deterioration of the situation. A useful guide to the success achieved in deploying and training MTAs in a school is the length of the queue of children outside the head teacher's or deputy's room at the end of the lunch break: the longer the line, the more urgent the problem. Effective MTAs lead to happier children and a more settled start to the afternoon, so it pays to support them in their attempts to do the job well.

Guidelines for lunchtime situations

- Do not jump to conclusions. Make sure of your facts first.
- If in doubt about the appropriate course of action, delay in making a decision until you have chance to consult a senior colleague.

- In the case of serious incidents, always inform the head teacher or deputy as soon as possible. Make a brief note about the details of the incident as soon as practically possible.

- Never use platitudes with an angry adult. Try to find out the facts and remain calm until the position is clearer.

- Be constructive with your comments and search for a resolution or strategies to improve the situation.

- Always support the MTA where possible but remember that children have rights, too.

What MTAs expect from teachers:

- To be courteous and pleasant

- To acknowledge the demands of their job

- To offer constructive support when necessary but not to undermine their position.

MTAs' chief concerns are individual mischievous children, uncomfortable relationships with fellow MTAs and worries that they have done or said too much to a particular child.

Good practice

Allocate some time in your schedule to get to know one other adult better each week. Decide how you can demonstrate your gratitude for their contribution to school life without appearing patronising.

The role of adults on educational visits

Children love to go out of school on visits and many claim that it is the most exciting part of the school year for them. In addition to numerous practical arrangements, the role of many different adults is vitally important in making the visit a safe and successful one. There are now strict rules governing charges made to parents for school visits and no child may be excluded from an educational visit on the grounds of cost. In other words, visits are for all children, regardless of status or a parent's ability to pay. Teachers have to consult with the head teacher about the procedures for outings and any constraints before committing them-selves or the school to any financial agreement.

School trips, educational visits and other field activities can be great fun and a wonderful opportunity to seal your relationship with the pupils. They can also be times of hazard and potential danger, so a lot of planning is required to ensure that a visit is safe and educationally worthwhile (Smart 1995). In addition to checking that the venue is suitable for the age group and is properly managed, trip organisers have to send letters home detailing the itinerary, receive permission slips from parents, order transport, confirm insurance, liaise with colleagues whose lessons may be affected. They also have to ensure that every part of the day has been considered in detail. The DfEE (now the DfES) has produced a 'good practice guide' known as *Health and Safety of Pupils on Educational Visits* (DfEE 1998b) designed to help head teachers, teachers, governors and others to ensure that pupils stay safe and healthy on school visits. It includes chapters on Responsibilities for Visits; Planning Visits; Supervision; Preparing Pupils; Communicating with Parents; Planning Transport; Insurance; Types of Visit; Visits Abroad and Emergency Procedures. It also includes a number of model forms that can be copied or adapted. The guide is not intended to replace local or other professional guidance or regulations and local education authorities should be the first source of advice to clarify finer points in the guide.

Even when all the planning and organising is complete, there is still a lot of work to be done in ensuring that the day runs smoothly. In particular, it is essential to anticipate problems or hazards and the action needed to respond to a situation should something go wrong. It is not only important to have access to a mobile telephone for making immediate contact with emergency services should this prove necessary, but to carry a list of key contacts.

In practice, most schools have a well-ordered programme of visits and NQTs will normally discover that there are well-trodden paths to museums, landmarks, ancient monuments and adventure courses. Nevertheless, thorough preparation is essential if the trip is to be a success. In doing so, check the following:

Costs

Some visits are not viable due to the cost of travel (coach hire is expensive) or entrance fees.

Timings

Coach travel is slower than travelling by car and an apparently short car journey through country lanes can become a long jaunt as the coach driver is obliged to follow a much longer prescribed main road route. Always leave a few minutes leeway for the journey time.

Safety

Coaches must conform to minimum safety standards. It is better to pay a little more and ensure a high standard of service from a reputable company. Regulations have become much stricter in recent years, but a few rogue companies still exist. Although it was at one time possible to put three smaller children per double seat, the requirement for coaches to fit safety belts means that this option is no longer available. This ruling also has cost implications. If private cars are to be used, a list of experienced drivers with current licences should be compiled and checked with the head teacher. If the venue involves any activity that carries some risk (such as adventure courses) then basic health and safety regulations must be observed and the activity centre's own safety procedures verified. Safety first means thinking ahead and following guidelines closely.

Communication with parents

Parents should be notified at least six weeks before the proposed visit. For standard visits, a brief note should be prepared about the purpose of the visit and the intentions for the day with information about clothing, lunch arrangements and possible physical demands, together with an invitation for parents to contact the teacher in charge with any queries. A detachable permission slip is normally included. This should include space for the child's name, address, contact number and for the parent to mention any special circumstances (such as the child's need to carry an inhaler, fear of heights or water, etc.). It is better to send two letters: one a preliminary note with the basic details requesting parental permission; the second, nearer the time, including more detailed information.

Itinerary

Each stage of the visit should be allotted a time: setting out, stops and starts, breaks and arrival. Parents and children should be given a copy in advance of the visit. A little more time than anticipated should be allowed for longer journeys. If the visit is likely to continue beyond normal school hours, it is important to stress this fact to parents beforehand.

Resources

Clipboards, paper, pencils, activity sheets, maps, measuring tapes, cameras and other necessary equipment need to be prepared in advance. Educational visits have a habit of creeping up unawares on busy teachers and it is very stressful to be scurrying about on the morning of the visit in search of an essential item when it should have been ready the previous day. Teaching assistants have an important role to play in the preparation and monitoring of equipment.

Adult–child ratios

Local authorities have guidelines for the amount of adult help required for an educational visit. Younger children obviously require more supervision than older ones and under-fives need a large adult presence. The experience and competence of the adults involved should be taken into account and they should all be fully briefed before the visit.

School arrangements

It is essential to check whether the canteen staff has been informed that children will be away during that day as well as the teachers who normally hold clubs. A playground duty may have to be swapped. Children bringing dinner money may need to bring money for one day less than usual unless the canteen is providing a packed lunch. Children whose parents do not have to pay for meals are entitled to a packed lunch. All these details need to be sorted in advance.

Educational potential

The effort required to plan a successful educational visit demands that in the days and weeks following the visit there is opportunity for children to draw upon their experiences and utilise their new-found skills, understanding and knowledge in a variety of contexts. Many teachers use a visit as a starting point for innovative teaching and learning and the production of stimulating displays and events.

No teacher who has planned an educational visit will underestimate the effort that is required. Trainees and new teachers are advised to collaborate with a more experienced colleague and plan the enterprise jointly.

Case study (Parents)

Grace was nervous about meeting parents. She knew it was irrational to be so fearful but had never found it easy to relate to adults, though she had a natural way with children and her tender manner endeared her to her colleagues. It was a shock, therefore, to be placed with Foundation Stage children, where home visits and close liaison with parents formed an important dimension of the job. Grace was relieved to hear that she would be accompanied by an experienced TA for the visits, but was still daunted by the prospect. In addition, the head teacher had arranged a series of informal meetings for the parents of new school entrants at which they could ask questions, express concerns and provide information about their children. Grace understood the benefits of such gatherings but still wished that she could just be left alone to get on with the job of teaching the children. However, over the following weeks, Grace's attitude changed completely as, to her surprise, she enjoyed the meetings and found that she was able to relate well to the parents. Furthermore, the knowledge that she gained about the children helped her to understand their concerns more clearly and respond to their social and academic needs more appropriately. In addition, Grace discovered that her self-confidence increased sharply and such was the excellent rapport that she established with parents that she found herself actively looking for opportunities to further their relationships.

Case study (Other adults)

Miss Burns is pinning up some children's work on the display board, when the MTA, Mrs Adams, marches in, tugging a reluctant nine-year-old by the sleeve.

'Miss Burns, I'm bringing Terry to you because he won't do as he's told. I said to him "Don't throw your trainers up in the air" but he insisted on doing it and now Vicki's got hit on the head and ended up crying. Then him and Shaun set to, and Shaun ends up in tears. And I can't find Mrs Carlevale [the head teacher] or Mr Halpern [the deputy] so I found you instead.' [Sullen looks from Terry.]

'Well, Terry, what have you got to say for yourself?' the teacher ventures. [Shrug of shoulders.]

'He's always the same, Miss Burns; I tell him and tell him but he takes no notice.' [Terry looks at Mrs Adams fiercely but says nothing.] 'Anyway, I'm sick of him.'

'I'm sick of you picking on me,' retorts Terry, provocatively and angrily. The mood is blackening. Mrs Adams and Terry begin to argue in what is clearly a continuation of a long-standing feud. Miss Burns has a few seconds to decide what should be done: shout louder than either of them; walk off to find a senior colleague; deal with it herself. She wisely decides to take firm action.

'Thank you Mrs Adams; you did the right thing; I'll deal with Terry now. Thank you very much.' Mrs Adams, much relieved to unload the problem, returns to her duties. Miss Burns sensibly stands still for a moment to allow Terry time to regain his composure, then quietly but firmly asks him what happened. Terry is on the verge of tears and clearly frustrated. As Miss Burns listens to his story unfold it becomes clear that the eposide with the trainers was a minor issue and that the real problem has its roots in an argument that took place between Terry and Shaun about team selection. As a result of Shaun's taunts and cutting comments born of superior intellect, the less competent Terry hit back in the only way he knew how. Mrs Adams observed the moment when Terry punched his adversary and, owing to Terry's reputation for fighting, took immediate action. Miss Burns did not blame the MTA, who was only doing her job, but had some sympathy with the boy as he stood in front of her, miserable, resentful and defiant. She told him that she would have to think about what should be done and told him that he must see her straight after the lunch break. She would also ask Mrs Adams whether he had tried hard to behave. After extracting a muttered promise that he would 'do his best to behave' Miss Burns let him go. She immediately started to worry about whether she had done the right thing. After all, the rule was that anyone seen fighting should stand outside the head's door. She did not want to appear to be soft or failing to support the MTA, but she was also aware that the circumstances were not as straightforward as they seemed and wanted to give Terry, who was a child from a very unsettled background, another chance.

Activate your thinking!

Imagine that you are Miss Burns: What next for Terry? Whom else will you involve? What will happen tomorrow lunchtime? Terry goes home and tells his mother that Mrs Adams is picking on him at lunchtime. His mother comes in to find out from you what is going on. What will you say?

Standards

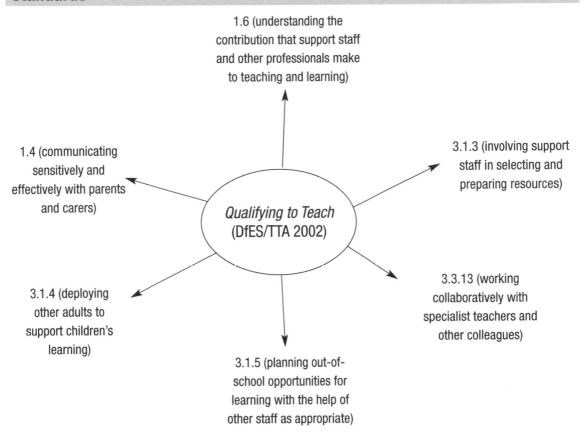

1.6 (understanding the contribution that support staff and other professionals make to teaching and learning)

1.4 (communicating sensitively and effectively with parents and carers)

3.1.3 (involving support staff in selecting and preparing resources)

Qualifying to Teach (DfES/TTA 2002)

3.3.13 (working collaboratively with specialist teachers and other colleagues)

3.1.4 (deploying other adults to support children's learning)

3.1.5 (planning out-of-school opportunities for learning with the help of other staff as appropriate)

Further reading

Kay, J. (2003) *Teaching Assistants' Handbook*, London: Continuum.
Contains primary school examples, including the role of assistants in helping to teach English, mathematics and science.

Stern, J. (2003) *Involving Parents*, London: Continuum.
A concise exploration of the potential benefits associated with parental involvement with children's education.

Learning and Teaching

The Process of Learning

Introduction

This chapter is about how children learn and the way in which a teacher's decisions and priorities affect the quality of the learning. Throughout the chapter there is a recognition that learning relies on motivation, working relationships and curriculum relevance. By considering these issues carefully, both trainee teachers and newly qualified teachers will be better equipped to help children achieve their potential. The value of dialogue in learning and the needs of gifted and talented children are also examined.

Learning

The process of learning is complex and unpredictable and no one fully understands how it takes place. There are occasions when even the slowest children amaze everyone (including themselves) by grasping a difficult concept, mastering a skill or retaining some knowledge when their more illustrious classmates struggle to do so. Although teachers' enthusiasm and commitment play an important part in bringing about the best conditions for learning, it is essential that they consider things from a child's perspective if effective progress is to be made. Children are not merely recipients of learning but active partners and initiators of it. Three essential elements of learning are knowledge, understanding and the development of skills.

Knowledge

Knowledge has a safe ring to it but can be slippery and deceptive. There are many different forms of knowledge, including knowledge of facts, of controversies, of situations, of procedures and of people.

Knowledge of *facts* involves more than memorising. It needs to take account of new understanding; for instance, we now know that the earth is round, not flat. Knowledge of *controversies* requires an awareness of the disputed information; for instance, whether Columbus discovered America. Knowledge of *situations* demands a wide view of the relevant factors and an ability to make judgements about their relevance and importance. Knowledge of *procedures* is necessary when a task has to be completed or decisions made about effectiveness. Knowledge of *people* is needed to prosper in social situations.

Although at one stage of a child's development it may be sufficient to 'know' something is 'true' it may subsequently be appropriate to point out that things may not be as straightforward as they appear. For example, seven-year-old children can be told that all objects fall towards the ground at the same rate, but 11-year-olds also need to be aware that the principle only holds for objects over a certain density and under normal atmospheric conditions. A 15-year-old may be interested in the variations according to air pressure, the effect of a vacuum, and so forth. Knowledge evolves and deepens with age, experience and a greater facility with language use.

Knowledge may also be thought of in terms of being *transitory*, such as remembering a telephone number for as long as it takes to dial it but no longer. It can be *accessible*, such as recalling a spelling rule for use when writing but not holding the knowledge at the forefront of thinking for regular use. It can be *immediate*, such as knowing a friend's name or the route to school without needing to think deeply about it. Sometimes, children seem to remain locked in the transitory knowledge zone. They appear to have learned something during the morning lesson but cannot remember it during the afternoon. Sometimes the knowledge is locked into a child's recall system but cannot be accessed, either because it is too deeply stored, the child is tired or circumstances (such as stress) create a barrier to remembering.

Finally, children gradually need to gain wisdom about the use of knowledge, its appropriateness, its relevance and its application. Teachers therefore have the difficult task of helping children to locate what they learn in social contexts.

Many of our teaching techniques rely on children's immediate access to knowledge. A teacher may use a question-and-answer session to draw out what pupils know and understand. One child has her hand flapping in the air every time a question is asked; another remains as still as a statue, eyes lowered, hoping that the teacher does not choose her. We may reasonably conclude that the enthusiastic child has a higher level of knowledge than her timid classmate, but this is not necessarily the case. The second child may have stored the knowledge and, in the intensity of the moment, been unable to draw it out of her memory bank. She may be weighing up other options rather than the obvious response or simply hate answering questions publicly for fear of being wrong. Teachers should be careful to ask both closed questions that test immediate recall, and open questions in which a variety of answers are acceptable. The child who may have prompt immediate recall may or may not be able to offer a more considered and thoughtful response. Able children are often the most successful in responding to open and closed questions but all children benefit from time to think. The best teachers have fun shooting out closed questions to a class, but also ask speculative types of questions that test a child's ability to ponder carefully and suggest unlikely possibilities. When working with children, it is helpful to think of knowledge from their perspective:

Received knowledge: I know because I can repeat what you have told me.

Descriptive knowledge: I know because I can observe it happening.

Explanatory knowledge: I know because I can explain why it happened.

Applied knowledge: I know because I can understand the implications for its use.

Walker and Soltis (1992) use the term 'knowledge in use' and identify three forms: associative, applicative and replicative. *Associative* knowledge allows links to be made with previous learning. *Replicative* knowledge is being able to remember and reproduce facts when required. *Applicative* knowledge is for use in solving questions. Walker and Soltis argue that applicative knowledge is the most significant of the three as it 'requires seeing the connection between what one knows and what one wants to achieve' (page 41). Thinking about how knowledge is used allows pupils to move from basic comprehension to being able to analyse and evaluate situations. The most powerful forms of knowledge involve higher levels of understanding that permit its use in a variety of contexts. Knowledge without understanding is merely information. Knowledge that cannot be applied may be superfluous.

Understanding (conceptual development)

One of the most common questions that teachers ask their pupils is whether they understand something. In the majority of cases, the children chorus 'yes' and the teacher, pleased at her skill in explaining, proceeds to the next stage of the lesson. But do the children really understand? And what does 'being able to understand' mean? These are complex questions involving complicated answers. Having asked if the children understood, the teacher might usefully say: 'Well done; now tell the person next to you what I have said'; and after a suitable time has elapsed: 'Now put up your hand if you think that your partner really understands!' The chances are that a number would be less clear than they imagined they were before having to explain it to a friend.

Understanding is usually gained gradually. Like knowledge, it operates at a variety of levels and requires considerable reinforcement before a thorough grasp of the issues has been accomplished. Understanding comes initially through *raising awareness* as many children simply do not realise that there is anything to be understood! After raising awareness comes *raising interest*. Children are naturally inquisitive, a characteristic which needs to be exploited (by the teacher posing relevant questions or wondering out loud about a situation). Inquisitiveness results in children raising their own questions, and this is the point at which the teacher's skill in explaining is important as queries are dealt with and uncertainties are clarified. Subsequently, children should have opportunity to explore, discover and test propositions, experiment with ideas and raise fresh issues. This cycle of raising awareness and interest, followed by further questions can be continued until pupils reach the limits of their understanding.

Knowledge and understanding are inextricably entwined. For instance, a young child may understand through observation that seeds grow into plants with roots and a stem. The teacher will probably have to supply the terminology and, as the process takes place, enthuse with the child at the visual growth, raise significant questions about how it happens, and speculate about what might happen next. Older children not only understand the significance of the root system and the influence of different types of soil but can also offer explanations as to *why* it happens. The five-year-old who gazed in wonder at the bean plant's speed of growth becomes the 11-year-old who can not only describe what is happening but also use evidence to prove underlying principles. The steady progression from the five-year-old who wonders at the way things happen, to the 11-year-old who can provide insights about the unseen processes at work, is testimony to the levels of understanding that children can attain. Examples of this progression can be found in every area of the curriculum. For example:

- In moral and social development, children's understanding of ethical issues, social justice and fairness emerge over time as they gain a more complete picture of the prevailing circumstances and conflicting claims of varied viewpoints.

- In maths, a child may initially understand concepts such as 'smaller and bigger than' but will later apply more varied terms which involve expressions such as 'multiples and factors of'.

- In science, the use of a coloured dye in the water used to sustain the plant (such as a piece of celery) results in a gradual discoloration. Young children talk about the colour change; older ones will, if provided with the necessary vocabulary, discuss issues relating to capillary action and metabolism.

- In art, the four-year-olds, random dabs of paint are gradually replaced by rainbows of colour, which lead to paint mixes and experimentation with other substances.

The development of understanding (concepts) therefore involves a combination of intellect, maturity (especially the ability to think abstractly), the opportunity to explore ideas and 'play' with alternatives, combined with the teaching skills of teachers who give children appropriate information, strategies and encouragement to speculate, make discoveries, articulate their claims and uncertainties, and eventually reach firm conclusions.

Continuity of learning experiences through concept development is a foundation stone of the National Curriculum and the Literacy and Numeracy Strategies. It is facilitated by lessons that build on previous knowledge and experience, encourage children to explore and question, and allow time for understanding to grow and consolidate by using it in a variety of learning situations. Higher levels of understanding come through experimentation and opportunities to explore ideas, discuss findings and investigate possibilities.

Activate your thinking!

Consider how the following statements from a child might apply to some of your lessons:

- I hear what you say and understand a little.
- I reflect upon the ideas and get them straight in my mind.
- I explore the ideas for myself and understand more fully.
- I ask questions to clarify the issues and my mind becomes clear.
- I explain to others using my own words and gain confidence.
- I speculate about possibilities and grasp the concept.
- I use my understanding to some purpose and grow eager to find out more.

Skills

The term 'skills' is used to describe a wide range of abilities that children need in their lives. Skills cover two broad areas: (a) abilities that children need so that they can find out things for themselves and enhance their existing knowledge and understanding; (b) abilities and attributes that children will need to acquire if they are to take learning forward. Skills can also be thought of in terms of those that are principally *cerebral* (mainly to do with active thinking) such as the skill required to present an opinion, and those that are *manual* (mainly to do with physical co-ordination) such as throwing a ball accurately or kneading a ball of clay. This distinction is not to suggest that manual skills do not require thought and judgement, but that the predominant form of learning is represented by a visual outcome in such cases.

Mastery of skills is necessary to support learning. For instance, there is little to be gained from a child being able to open a book and find the index, but then being unable to use it effectively. Similarly, it is interesting to study the trajectory and flight of a ball in the air, but this does not ensure that the child will hit the target. Every skill involves judgement, decision-making and evaluation as to the effectiveness of the procedure and the quality of the end result.

The National Curriculum originally used the word 'skills' to denote transferable abilities in areas as diverse as communication, numeracy, problem-solving, personal and social relations, and information technology. These skills are intended to be used across the curriculum and apply to every subject area. For example, children should be able to express themselves in speech across the whole curriculum and use computer software to produce visual representations of findings. The NC2000 (DfES/QCA 1999) now specifies six 'key skills' that are intended to help learners to improve their learning and performance in education, work and life as follows (based on pages 20–1):

- *Communication*, using speaking, listening, reading and writing. Skills required include the ability to take account of different audiences, to understand what others are saying and to participate in group discussions. Pupils should be able to read both fictional and non-fictional texts fluently and with understanding. Although most direct development of communication skills takes place during literacy lessons, consideration should be given to the development of language across the curriculum.

- *Application of number*, including the development of a range of mental calculation skills and their application. The use of mathematical language to process data, solve problems and explain the reasoning behind solutions also forms part of this skill.

- *Information technology*, developing the ability to use a range of information sources and ICT tools, and to make critical and informed judgements about when it is appropriate to use ICT to access information, solve problems and for creative expression.

- *Working with others*, including the ability to contribute to small-group and whole-class discussion, and to work collaboratively. The interaction requires the development of social skills and an awareness of other people's needs and perspectives.

- *Improving own learning and performance*, involving pupils in reflection and critical evaluation of different aspects of their work, assessing their own performance and establishing targets for learning.

- *Problem solving*, including identifying and understanding problems, planning ways to solve them, monitoring progress and reviewing solutions.

Five 'thinking skills' are also identified in NC2000 as important in assisting children to know how, as well as knowing what (page 22): information-processing, reasoning, enquiry, creative thinking and evaluation skills. The NC provides definitions for each of the skills. Thus, information-processing skills 'enable pupils to locate and collect relevant information, to sort, classify, sequence, compare and contrast, and to analyse part/whole relationships'. These skills require that pupils are not satisfied with gaining a single piece of information but draw from a variety of sources. Reasoning skills 'enable pupils to give reasons for opinions and actions, to draw inferences and make deductions, to use precise language to explain what they think, and to make judgements and decisions informed by reasons or evidence'. These skills move beyond mere information-gathering and encourage children to express their beliefs and opinions. Enquiry skills 'enable pupils to ask relevant questions, to pose and define problems, to plan what to do and how to research, to predict outcomes and anticipate consequences, and to test conclusions and improve ideas'. These skills require that children think beyond the immediate circumstances and project into new possibilities and opportunities. Creative thinking skills 'enable pupils to generate and extend ideas, to suggest hypotheses, to apply imagination, and to look for alternative, innovative outcomes'. The key word in this definition is *imagination*, where the children are actively encouraged and liberated into fresh modes of thought and activity (see, for example, Carter 2002 for ideas for creative writing). Evaluation skills 'enable pupils to evaluate information, to judge the value of what they read, hear and do, to develop criteria for judging the value of their own and others' work or ideas, and to have confidence in their judgements'. These critical skills (Quinn 1997) are considered to be amongst the most difficult for children to grasp, as they require considerable experience and maturity if they are to be anything more than superficial responses.

Skills do not exist in isolation from knowledge and understanding. Children need knowledge and understanding in order to consolidate what they have already grasped and open up fresh areas for enquiry. For instance, the skill of being able to solve problems systematically can provide insights that may not be gained by other means such as direct instruction or information served up in neat chunks from a database.

Skills, therefore, involve both thinking and dexterity. To possess thinking skills is important, but without having the necessary skills to complete the task, children quickly become frustrated. The application of practical skills that involve only a small amount of thinking leads to inertia and passivity, limiting children's capacity to think more widely and imaginatively. Thus, knowledge, understanding and skills are mutually dependent. Wenham (1995) helpfully expresses the relationship between the three elements: 'Without understanding, experience is blind; but without experience, knowledge and understanding are empty; and without skill, all of them are dumb' (page 133).

Learning to learn

Learning is a word that rolls easily off the tongue but it is difficult to define and even harder to explain the processes that combine to produce a learning outcome. Although learning comes relatively easy to some children, others find that they have to work hard over a long period of time before things fall into place. Some children seem unable to master quite elementary principles and are adjudged to have special educational needs. They require a considerable amount of adult help in remedying the situation. By the time children leave the infant sector (Key Stage 1) and join the big boys and girls in the juniors (Key Stage 2) teachers are normally in a position to predict with some certainty which pupils will succeed academically and which will not. It is not unusual for the strugglers to exhibit symptoms such as lack of motivation and general dissatisfaction with life. Some of these children may also have few friends and, occasionally, exhibit poor behaviour. In addition to academic achievement, therefore, the learning process has implications for children's emotional and social wellbeing.

When asked by the teacher how she understood what was happening, Cordie, a five-year-old girl thought for a moment before replying: *When I want to understand something I draw a picture of it in my mind*. This small insight into a child's thinking suggests that definitions of learning must be rooted in the effect that it has upon the learner, rather than the actions of a teacher. With this principle in mind, a number of suggestions have been made to describe learning; for instance:

- The process of making sense of information and creating something new from it.
- A process that transforms our current understanding into fresh and more elucidated understanding.
- The process of utilising the knowledge and insights that we have gained from our previous experiences to respond to new ones.
- The process of taking risks and moving away from the security of certain knowledge and exploring less well considered areas.

None of these definitions offer a complete picture, but they share a common thread in emphasising the transformation that takes place in the learner. The teacher's role in the process is to provide the resources, guidance and wisdom that facilitate the learning. Such teaching recognises that learning does not consist merely of the linear transfer of an adult's superior intellect to a less knowledgeable pupil but rather an accommodation of fresh understanding into the child's existing conceptual framework. As such, the teacher must be aware of the child's present understanding, not in order to 'tailor make' the teaching programme to fit the needs of all the children (as this would require 30 different approaches) but to graze contentedly across the pastures of knowledge. The grazing metaphor promotes the idea of 'sampling' from the variety of food available as opposed to being force-fed.

Although it is popular to emphasise the importance of making sure that children have 'learned' something, the term has a variety of different meanings, depending upon the context in which it is used. For instance:

- Learned for now but likely to be forgotten soon
- Learned, never to be forgotten
- Learned within specified limits
- Learned but requiring updating and reinforcement
- Learned and understood so thoroughly that the learning can be used successfully in different situations.

Thus it is possible for children to learn how to use a piece of computer software early in the school year but without regular practice they are likely to forget the procedure by the next term. In this case, the learning has been functional and the fourth of the statements given above is relevant. A child may 'learn' how to multiply two numbers by using a certain technique but flounder when given the same problem in a different form. In this case, the third of the statements is relevant. The ideal is for children to have such a grasp of knowledge, skills and understanding that they can use their existing abilities to forge ahead confidently into new areas of learning. If learning is only *functional*, it relates solely to the work in hand and has little value outside the immediate context in which it is being used; if it is *pervasive*, it moves outside the boundaries artificially imposed by the task or activity, and has wider applicability.

Learning, then, may be of the restricted type or the transferable type. Take, for instance, the earlier example in which children learn to use a software program. Some children will doubtless become adept at using the program and may even be used by the teacher to inform other children about its functioning. However, only a proportion of the same group of well-informed children will make connections with the implications for using other, similar programs. The first group, knowing only how to operate the program, will possess a restricted form of knowledge. The second, who can use their knowledge, skills and understanding more widely, are of the transferable type. Again, children who learn a set of spellings for a test may get them all correct, yet misspell some of the words in free writing. The aim is, of course, to ensure that children not only master the word list but can also utilise their learning in a variety of active, writing situations where spelling is only one of the required skills.

Some learning is short-term; other forms need to become embedded and for all practical purposes permanently etched in the memory (long-term memory). The child who learns lines for a drama sketch in front of the school will memorise them carefully, prompted no doubt by an anxious parent who is keen for the child to do well. This learning may require repetition, frequent reminders, and a move from artificial to more natural speech as the words become familiar. A few months after the performance, the words may be largely forgotten, though odd phrases may spring to mind for a while. Contrast this temporary memorising with the ability to interpret words on a page for the purpose of reading, in which the regular use of the words in a variety of contexts (books, work sheets, text on a whiteboard, screen) will ensure that they are never forgotten.

Every teacher is keen for their pupils to learn in such a way that they can use their abilities widely and thereby achieve intellectual freedom (or conceptual autonomy). Conceptual autonomy allows children to free themselves from reliance on the teacher as they develop the skills, confidence and determination to be self-motivated, ask suitable questions and evaluate answers.

Activate your thinking!

You can teach a child, but the child being taught is not always learning what you teach!

Enhancing learning

Most learning is gained or enhanced by 'experiencing' for which no amount of direct teaching will substitute. For example, pupils' understanding of industrial change is brought to life through a visit to a working museum. Similarly, listening to poets and authors read from their own work, enjoying practical drama, playing with construction materials, touching unusual objects and buying vegetables from a market stall, all help children to understand the world better. Children's learning is also improved through 'investigations' in which the outcome is uncertain. For instance, science experiments, paint mixing, library searches and computer simulations all involve investigations which assist conceptual understanding, skills acquisition and factual knowledge.

Enhanced learning also depends upon the opportunity for children to ask questions and raise issues in the expectation that teachers will respond positively (Wragg and Brown 1993; Lawrence 1997). Most children are extremely curious and will, if their interest is aroused, ply adults with queries and questions about how and why. Teachers sometimes need to understand the reason for a child asking a question. An apparently innocent question from a five-year-old about 'Where did I come from?' may be the first sign of a wish to understand the wonders of human reproduction but is far more likely to relate to the fact that her friend said that she came from Birmingham! Interpreting children's questions is time-consuming but essential if teachers are to help them in finding answers to things that are of real interest to them. Whatever the age of pupils, teachers need to capture their curiosity, encourage a questioning attitude, engage with issues that concern young minds and provide enough stimulus to arouse further interest.

It is important to be mindful of ways to help pupils to be creative in their work. That is, to encourage diverse thinking, risk-taking and innovative practice (see, for instance, Jeffrey and

Woods 2003). A report by OFSTED (2003b) about developing creativity in schools concluded that it was most likely to be found in schools where teachers did not feel bound by orthodoxies, use was made of cross-curricular themes and the physical environment was enlivening. Creativity did not emerge by simply giving children time and space to 'create something', but by providing stimuli and appropriate adult support within a culture of self-expression where new ideas were actively sought and encouraged. Grainger (2003) argues that teachers should spend more time on discussing literature, oral storytelling, poetry performances and improvised drama if children are to be offered the chance to 'interpret, communicate and *create* meaning for themselves' (page 44, author's emphasis) in their learning. She stresses that a willingness to take risks with creative and artistic activity enhances teachers' confidence and pupils' imaginative engagement. Teachers who are excited and personally involved with the literacy curriculum are much more likely to communicate its joy and wonder than a plain transmission of the necessary facts.

Children need to be given some ownership of their learning. After all, it is they who have to use it in their present and future lives. Learning is not, therefore, principally about accumulating enough information, knowledge and understanding to gain high scores in national tests and examinations; rather, it is about empowering pupils to live their lives more positively and successfully. Examination success may assist this process of self-fulfilment, but there is a danger that anxious teachers may see scores gained during a test as the sole yardstick of achievement. Nevertheless, Williams and Ryan (2000) argue that teachers should view the tests as an opportunity to gain information that will help to improve their teaching and raise standards.

Ransom (1993) contends that curriculum entitlement and rational planning are inadequate unless pupils are adequately motivated within a community context. He argued that teachers need to develop an 'empowerment curriculum', characterised by the following elements:

- Citizenship in learning
- Active learning through practical reasoning
- Democratic and public organisation
- Partnership.

Consequently, pupils' learning can be enhanced by the following:

Valuing pupils' capability

By celebrating the untapped reservoirs of capability in individuals in order to create active rather than passive learners, endowed with skills to make responsible choices and co-operate with others.

Offering a comprehensive curriculum

By providing a broad and balanced curriculum, relevant to learners, enabling them to draw upon their experience of living within the community.

Promoting active learning

By involving pupils, thereby engaging their interest, sustaining their motivation to succeed, and encouraging them to take responsibility for their learning experience and that of others.

Creating partnership with parents and the community

By promoting education within the community, notably by involving parents and local people.

A lot of children seem to have a 'product' attitude to learning, often abetted by adult expectations. They are set tasks for completion or activities to perform, and they strive to finish the work to the teacher's satisfaction. The children soon become aware that they will be rewarded with praise and approving comments from adults if they accomplish precisely what is expected of them. If children deviate from the set task, they are guided back onto the right path or scolded if they insist on pursuing their own inclination. If children become obsessed with an objectives-driven agenda, they tend to display one or more of the following characteristics (based on Fisher 1995):

- Success is viewed as absolute, being either achieved totally, or missed completely. There is no halfway house for such children and they become depressed if they do not fulfil or exceed expectations.

- Excuses are given to explain away shortcomings in their work. Children view anything less than perfect or below the achievements of their rivals as a personal affront.

- Ability to learn particular things is seen as fixed rather than something to be improved. Children will say that they are 'no good' at some things and brilliant at others. In response to a teacher's prompting they will resist being coached or trained to get better at something.

- Difficulties dominate their thinking rather than possibilities and solutions. Two men looked through prison bars; one saw mud, the other saw the stars. Such children see the mud!

- Initial failure or problems result in depression. Children with a product orientation evaluate success only in terms of achieving the objective. They do not regard the process as significant, only the end result.

Focusing exclusively on an objectives-driven agenda might lead children to become anxious about making errors, which in turn paralyses their minds and creates mental stagnation. Fisher also comments that pupils 'often resist the invitation to think for themselves. It is easier for them to be told than to think' (page 116) but also that 'extended contact with a child gives a teacher opportunities to become a significant and influential model in that child's life' (page 117). One means by which this can be achieved is through the teacher modelling the behaviour that they want the children to imitate, such as listening to one another, taking time to think, allowing other points of view, thinking things through properly, being curious, questioning and keeping setbacks in perspective.

Lessons have to be properly organised, of course, and in the pressure of school life there is a limited amount of time that can be spent exploring and interrogating a given area of work. Teachers also have to be reasonably clear about the things they hope that children will learn (learning objectives) and provide a facilitating structure to make it more likely that they will do so. However, learning encompasses more than children satisfying the designated objective. Just as children can convince themselves that they must have learned something if they get the right answer by an approved method, so teachers can slip into the same way of thinking and believe that task-completion is the primary goal. In fact, finishing a task may or may not involve deep learning. Too many so-called experiential lessons, for instance, consist of little more than mechanically 'predicting' and 'testing' and 'recording' without properly engaging with the principles underpinning the work or employing problem-solving skills. Completing pages of sums may or may not demonstrate that the underlying principles have been mastered. In this regard, MacGilchrist (2003) makes five important points about the nature of learning that have implications for classroom practice:

- Learning is an active process of meaning-making. Learners construct and integrate new knowledge in a way that makes sense to them.

- Learning about learning (metalearning) and making sense of experience is a hallmark of effective learners. Learners become increasingly aware of the thinking and learning processes that are taking place and thereby assume greater control over them.

- The relationship between learning and performance is complex and is influenced by motivation and self-image. Some children are capable of completing tasks ('performance-orientation') without thinking hard about the implications of the work and gaining personal satisfaction other than through a tick at the bottom of the page.

- Learning involves the understanding and mastery of emotions, both personal and viewing things from other people's perspectives. Learning can be enhanced through developing a variety of social skills and a willingness to persevere and stay on task.

- Learning is situational. The social contexts of the school and classroom are significant in promoting or inhibiting learning.

The implications for classroom practice can be summarised as follows:

- Pupils need the opportunity to discuss what they are doing and understand where it fits into their overall understanding. The teacher needs to spend time explaining the context, where the present lesson content fits within the larger picture and the links with previous learning. The use of familiar examples and experiences will help children to grasp the concepts more easily.

Good practice

When discussing the lesson with the children, use phrases such as 'You remember that last time . . .' (links with previous learning) and 'It is the same as when you . . .' (linking with familiar experiences).

- Pupils will often complete tasks and engage in activities solely because they are set before them by a teacher. Metalearning encourages children to talk about what they are doing and express how they feel about learning, both verbally and through different media (such as drawings).

Good practice

Spend small amounts of time regularly talking to the children about ways in which they can approach the work, suggesting alternatives and encouraging them to speculate about the challenges and opportunities. These conversations should be underpinned by a positive 'can do' attitude and an acknowledgement that trying different approaches and searching for creative solutions sometimes results in failure/set-backs.

- Pupils should be encouraged to satisfy their own aspirations rather than those of the teacher and be self-motivating rather than compliant.

Good practice

Make a habit of asking children what particularly pleases them about the work that they are undertaking. Encourage them to think about their achievements and share their excitement with others.

- Some pupils fear failure and worry about getting things wrong and being in trouble as a result. Other pupils are unwilling to persevere when faced with challenges, because either they are unable to cope with the situation or they try to avoid making more than a nominal effort to achieve a satisfactory outcome. As these negative responses are the result of emotional insecurity, teachers' reactions need to focus on finding solutions to the root cause rather than merely treating the symptoms. In other words, it is important to make a priority of strengthening children's emotional security.

Good practice

Make it clear that children can use an adult or another child as a source of advice, confirmation or guidance, but that, as far as possible, they should persevere with work and not be afraid of making genuine errors. At the same time, use mistakes positively by expressing an interest in how the child has gone about the work, explaining the alternatives and using the opportunity formatively to assist understanding. A mistake can be a springboard for progress or a barrier, so ensure that the first of these prevails.

- Teachers should put themselves in the child's place. Is the classroom environment stimulating or depressing? How does the attitude of adults (teacher, assistants) serve to motivate or discourage? How do patterns of social interaction, such as friendship patterns, grouping of children and peer support, impinge upon children's appetite to engage with tasks?

> ## Good practice:
>
> Observe a child unobtrusively throughout a full day and try to evaluate his or her experience with regard to classroom environment, adult attitudes and social interaction. What does it 'feel' like to be that child? How does s/he perceive the learning experience?

It is preferable for children to have an 'adventurous' attitude to learning, where they are eager to try things out, experiment and find solutions to problems. Challenges are seen as opportunities to use their ingenuity and determination to break through the uncertainty rather than obstacles. Children with an adventurous spirit towards learning are not fazed by setbacks. They are persistent and willing to approach the problem from a variety of positions. They are reluctant to take 'no' for an answer and will seek ways to improve their abilities.

The term *praxis* is sometimes used to describe action that is informed by reflection with the aim to free those involved into more productive forms of learning. Some educators (notably Jurgen Habermas) argue that the teacher's role involves emancipating pupils through the curriculum and developing a liberated and fair world. With regard to classroom teaching, Morrison (2001) refers to the eight principles of pedagogy (the principles and practice of teaching) that Habermas and others propose:

1   The need for co-operation and collaborative work

2   The need for discussion-based work

3   The need for autonomous, experiential and flexible learning

4   The need for negotiated learning

5   The need for community-related learning to explore a range of environments

6   The need for problem-solving activities

7   The need to increase [pupils'] rights to employ talk

8   The need for teachers to act as 'transformative intellectuals'

This critical form of pedagogy is built upon a belief that 'educators must work with, and on, the lived experiences that [pupils] bring to the pedagogical encounter rather than imposing a curriculum that reproduces social inequality' (page 219). Setting aside the social equality issues that these educators argue can be addressed in part through the curriculum, the eight principles outlined above provide a useful basis on which to develop a positive teaching and learning environment. Thus, pupil collaboration facilitates a 'fusion' of minds as children grapple with problems and combine their intellects. Discussions allow issues and contradictions to surface and demonstrates that nearly every situation has a multiplicity of perspectives. Experiential learning allows children to touch, sample, feel, manipulate and handle substances, equipment and circumstances directly. Negotiated learning encourages children to advance their own ideas, priorities and suggestions about what is important. Community-related learning promotes the value of involvement in the local environment and draws on the expertise of those who live there. Problem-solving helps children to see that the skills and knowledge they acquire in school has a practical outworking. Children's right to venture their own opinions and ideas, when coupled with an appropriate sense of responsibility, encourages self-confidence and willingness to be innovative. Teachers who view themselves as 'change agents' approach their work with a greater sense of purpose than those who merely see themselves as curriculum technicians.

The learning context

Learning does not take place in a vacuum, of course; it is influenced by three factors: situation, motivation and emotion. If it were not so, we could dispense with schools and teachers and send 'electronic teaching machines' to do the job! Every learning experience is 'situational' and affected by the physical and social context. Within the physical environment, the many interactions that take place daily between child and adult, and between different children, impact upon the quality of learning. The nature of these interactions depend on the power relationships that exist in a classroom. If children feel relaxed and confident when seeking adult help, they can channel their energies into the work rather than worrying about doing or saying the acceptable thing. Similarly, if there is an ease of relationship between children, they can concentrate on the task and not on worry about friendship patterns. It is the teacher's responsibility to establish a facilitative and co-operative climate such that learning can proceed unhindered by social conflict or emotional insecurity. There is also the broader social context to consider, not least the fact that technological and social changes have influenced the skills needed for daily living, people's priorities and their expectations. As Turner-Bisset (2003) argues, classrooms must move with the times and consider the teaching and learning needs of primary education in this century rather than those that existed in the last. To ignore such factors can cause learning to seem less relevant and to become less interesting.

Teachers' attitudes to the work also affect learning. The depth of a teacher's motivation and expectations about pupil achievement make a profound difference to the way in which children approach the work. A teacher who is enthusiastic about the tasks that the children are engaged with, clarifies what is expected from them and gives clear guidance about what can be achieved will not be disappointed with the outcome. Children respond well to an adult who displays a positive attitude and belief about what can be achieved and celebrates small successes rather than highlighting minor errors. All teachers need to ask themselves what sort of social context they are producing in the classroom.

Pupils' attitudes towards themselves influence the quality of learning and the impact of emotion on learning is increasingly viewed as being of crucial importance. Some children are very positive despite their apparent limitations, while others are negative despite their obvious ability. Too much anxiety can hinder learning. By contrast, enthusiasm pumps oxygen to the brain and stimulates its operation. There are three sets of conditions that assist pupil confidence in learning: to feel secure, to know the rules, to be clear about the lesson. Thus:

Children need to feel secure

This is particularly important when teachers are asking questions or inviting responses from the class. Timid children are unlikely to risk answering if by doing so they incur the teacher's wrath or ridicule. Teachers who treat all answers seriously (including incorrect ones) and encourage the children who give them by praising their efforts will soon have the class clamouring to participate. Similarly, if a new skill or concept has to be mastered, the teacher's patience and understanding can transform children's tentativeness into boldness. The maxim to 'have a go and find out what happens', if promoted and practised, will act as a springboard for progress.

Children need to know the rules

Teachers who spend time explaining and clarifying the details of an activity or the procedures for involvement at the start will have to spend less time during the lesson in reminding children of the expected standards, repeatedly answering queries and rebuking transgressors. Boundaries for behaviour and action allow children to be positive and confident. Learning has more chance to be effective when everyone understands the rules of the game!

Children need to be clear about the terms and conditions of the lesson

Some lessons are specifically for the purpose of gaining knowledge. Others are more concerned with understanding processes, and yet others demand skill mastery. Many lessons involve all three dimensions. Children should be told about the lesson purpose as well as what they have to do or complete. Some classrooms have a small whiteboard affixed to the wall on which the teacher writes the lesson purpose prior to commencement, though it is a mistake to imagine that teaching and learning can be neatly packaged. Nevertheless, the more that teachers are prepared to involve children in their learning and make explicit, both its purpose and usefulness, the more the learning climate will improve.

Reinforcing learning

It is important for teachers to take every opportunity to reinforce learning. The final few minutes of a lesson or session is often a useful time to extract key points from the work and emphasise them or offer examples of them and extend thinking by providing a challenging question about 'where next?' or 'what if?' Similarly, during question and answer sessions it is useful to repeat a good or thoughtful answer for the benefit of all the children, some of whom may not have heard the original response. In appropriate cases, an answer can spark ideas and open possibilities that may not have occurred to you. You can promote learning by employing targeted praise and disseminating the information; for example:

- Yes, Toby, well done. Did you hear what Toby said, everyone? He said that...

- What a lovely idea, Georgia, I hadn't thought of counting them in that way. I think we could all have a go at...

- Now that's a brilliant suggestion, Raj. I love the way you used the things we've been doing and added your own ideas. I hope that everyone heard when Raj explained how we could...

- Alice, what a clever technique! Come and stand by me and show everyone else in the class what you did, please...

Teaching style and retention in learning

Suffice it to say at this point that the methods employed strongly influence the effectiveness with which children are able to learn. For instance, Koshy (2000) refers to the fact that different teaching approaches in mathematics have markedly different outcomes in terms of retention rate. Thus, whereas only about 5 per cent of the information presented in a formal lecture is retained, the figure increases with other strategies:

- 10 per cent when the same words are read
- 20 per cent when audio-visual aids are used
- 30 per cent for a demonstration
- 50 per cent for a discussion group
- 75 per cent for practising by doing
- 90 per cent when teaching others the immediate use of the learning

Although retaining facts is only one dimension of learning and the above figures are only approximations, they suggest that direct transmission of information to children is unlikely to be effective if it is the sole means to present the curriculum. The opportunity to read relevant text, listen to sounds or see images, watch an adult showing how something is done, discuss the lesson content with others, engage in practical activities and make use of peer tuition, can all enhance the quality of learning. In addition, children learn best in different ways. Some children find it easy to understand written information, others prefer to hear it explained verbally, others like pictorial representations and yet others benefit from diagrams. Most children benefit from a combination of approaches, so it pays to bear this fact in mind when planning lessons. For instance, you may want to read an extract of text (with or without involving the children), explain the concepts/issues/key points, provide visual aids and use the board to demonstrate stages of progression. It is also helpful to allow children some degree of choice when it comes to representing their answers. While you will not often want to give latitude to a child who dislikes writing to use pictures instead, a little flexibility on your part to encourage a little of both types of recording is sometimes worth considering. While some boys (in particular) are averse to writing things down and need to be cajoled into doing so, the value of employing alternative representations should not be underestimated.

Using homework to extend and reinforce learning

In their guidelines for homework, the DfEE (1998c) underlined the importance of regular tasks, particularly those that require reading. Teachers must provide relevant forms of homework and other out-of-class tasks that help to consolidate and extend the work that has been carried out during the school day, thereby promoting independence in learning and, where possible, the active involvement of parents. In setting homework tasks, bear in mind that it has to be just as appropriate to the age and ability of the pupil as the work in school is intended to be. Homework also has to be realistic and manageable (Kidwell 2004), as there is little point in having grandiose schemes that are impossible for the children to complete, even with adult support, or that require sophisticated equipment or expensive resources. For instance, tasks should not assume that ICT equipment is available in the house. Suitable homework might include giving the children an observation activity (such as noticing pattern formation on wallpaper and carpets), consulting with an adult about living history (such as life in the 1950s) or paper and pencil activities (such as learning key vocabulary or completing as many sums as possible in a given time). The most straightforward homework is when the same task is given to all children such that they are all able to engage with it at their own level, and the end product can be marked easily or shared with others. For younger children, additional reading, supported by an adult if possible, is frequently used, with an adult signing in a 'reading record book' to confirm that it has been done. It is wise to remember that homework has to be monitored and assessed if it is to be fully effective, so the more elaborate you make it, the more time and effort has to be expended in dealing with the results.

Homework tasks need to be organised in such a way that children can cope unaided if necessary and, ideally, be directly linked to the learning objectives that you have established in class work. The tasks, therefore, provide consolidation and extension opportunities that would have been available in school had time permitted it. Formative feedback on homework tasks is not always possible, owing to time constraints and the many other demands upon a teacher. However, pupils can be inducted into sharing their work with a classmate, though this apparently simple procedure is more difficult than it sounds, as evaluation is demanding enough for adults, let alone for children! One way or another, comments must be made about the overall quality of homework tasks with indicators about improvements or implications.

Homework is only useful if it builds on previous school-based work or begins to open up new avenues of learning. Some homework consists of 'finishing off' incomplete work from the day; however, this penalises slower workers and does little to extend the more able. Other than familiar paper-and-pencil types, the best type of homework is of the project kind, where children are given a number of activities that have to be completed over a period of time (a half term, say). Homework can provide a starting point for discussion and sharing experiences, the very heart blood of learning, and a useful spur in promoting dialogue in learning (see later in this chapter).

Invigorating learning

Katz and Chard (2000) remind us that from a child's point of view, school is real life, not contrived or pretend, so children need to make learning an adventure that is sometimes challenging, sometimes perplexing but always motivating. Although some parts of the curriculum are less appealing than others, teachers should strive to create a learning environment that offers diverse experiences, excites children's interest and, wherever possible, builds on their enthusiasm. The following four principles apply to every age group and situation:

Help children to feel that learning is worthwhile

Learning becomes worthwhile when four factors apply: (a) The content is interesting and relevant (b) The lesson is presented imaginatively, see second bullet point below (c) The tasks associated with the lesson present a reasonable challenge (d) The learning climate is lively and encouraging. Teachers obviously have a vital role to play in each of these four factors. Thus:

- Even when the lesson content is mundane, you can explain its usefulness
- By the tone of your voice, the passion of your delivery and the incorporation of visual material, story, verbal exchanges and collaborative activity, you can stir the children's imaginations and engage their minds
- Differentiating tasks so that each child can succeed and feel pleased with her/his efforts helps to enhance self-image and motivation
- Your friendly but purposeful approach to teaching, emphasis on positive aspects of learning and patient explanations can transform the climate from one of stale conformity to energetic vibrancy in a short time

In promoting effective learning, it is important not to dismiss underachievement by using tired excuses such as 'boys will be boys or 'that sort of child never makes an effort' or 'well you cannot expect anything more' (see also Chapter 1).

Feed and exercise children's imaginations

As noted in the second point above, stirring children's imaginations is important in learning. The root of the word is 'imagine', which can be thought of as a 'mental picture' or 'seeing in the mind's eye'. Although the methods by which this can be achieved vary with age of child, there are a number of common stimuli that can be employed:

- Posing questions that cause the children to think deeply
- Offering real-life or fictitious scenarios to highlight key points or offer examples
- Using familiar objects in unfamiliar ways to offer differing perspectives on a subject
- Using unfamiliar objects as a source of awe and wonder
- Using powerful music, expressive poems or stimulating pictures to evoke an emotional response
- Giving children opportunity to share their own life experiences with others in the class

Stirring children's imaginations may be an end in itself (for sheer joy) but is more often used as either a starting point or an accelerator in the learning process.

Answer a child's unasked question: 'Why are we doing this?'

It is not possible to ascertain how many children ask this question but unease about the lesson's relevance is sometimes expressed by younger children through their superficial commitment to the task, yawning or restless behaviour. Older children will also exhibit these tendencies but will often be more assertive and even ask directly about why an activity is necessary or its purpose. These responses can be minimised in two possible ways: (a) most importantly, by explaining the purpose to the children beforehand; (b) by being honest with children when they express misgivings.

The process of explaining the purpose beforehand is rooted in the learning intentions for the lesson but more pragmatic explanations are sometimes equally valuable. For example, you may tell the children that they need to spend time practising their sums because you want to move on to a different topic. You might tell them that you want them to finish writing the story because it is parents' evening soon and you want to show mum what they have achieved. Being honest with children is not the same as being apologetic, though there are occasions when you will need to admit that although the content is not particularly interesting, it is a necessary prerequisite for subsequent, more exciting work. Your responses will vary according to circumstances but should be an explanation and not indicate that the child has a choice (unless, of course, this is the case). You may be faced with an option when dealing with a recalcitrant child about whether to insist or compromise, but dealing with stubborn children is an issue for Chapter 8 and will not be pursued here.

Convince children that they can be successful

Children need to develop self-motivation, but this is often enhanced by an adult's attitude towards success. Merely encouraging a child to do well will not, of itself, produce a sudden transformation from uncertainty to optimism. However, a positive approach, coupled with appropriate support and direction will allow a child to persevere in the certain knowledge that there is an adult 'safety net' underneath. Over time the buoyant and cheerful mood you exude will spread throughout the class and, coupled with appropriate external rewards (such as stickers and merit cards) will influence the children's expectations and sense of determination. Your positive attitude may not affect pupils in the same way. There will always be occasions when, with your very best efforts, a child simply refuses to take an upbeat view of his or her potential and prefers to remain sullenly defeatist. Occasionally, someone who is inwardly quite confident will pretend to be downcast because it invites the teacher's close attention. Nevertheless, if the classroom exudes a 'we can' approach to learning, the increase in self-esteem, work of high quality and co-operation soon becomes tangible.

Activate your thinking!

To what extent do you sympathise with the following statements?

1 Each child learns in a different way from every other child.
2 Boys' and girls' learning needs differ from each other.
3 Adults can unintentionally constrain children's learning.
4 Children need time to observe, think, try and experience first hand.
5 Enthusiasm is contagious.
6 Teachers should learn to be skilled observers of children.
7 Self-belief is a necessary pre-requisite for effective learning.
8 There are times when it is difficult for children to learn and times of great significance.
9 Children's imaginations need to be activated for effective learning.
10 Pupils should be empowered in their learning.
11 If teachers convince themselves that they like children, they grow to like them.
12 Criticism is invariably damaging.

13 Children need to have something to hope for and look forward to.

14 The best teachers have deep personal humility.

15 Children are more likely to succeed if they feel welcome and valued.

16 Children have many things to teach one another.

17 Children benefit from having an accurate view of themselves as learners.

18 A fear of consequences constrains children's learning.

19 Children learn better if they understand the process of learning.

20 The heart is at the heart of education.

What are the implications for classroom practice?

Good practice

Read how one trainee teacher was able to enthuse all the children in the class. This sparkling description shows how an ordinary lesson can be transformed when children are liberated within a secure framework.

'This week's session gave me a real sense of shared pleasure, with the children and I enjoying the music, each other's company, and creating real joy. We had worked hard listening to Vivaldi's *The Four Seasons*, thinking about what he was trying to say with his music and then, as the piece called 'Summer' built to a crescendo, the children were finding it hard to keep still. Toes were tapping, bottoms wriggling and heads moving. I encouraged them to take on the role of the conductor, using their hands and arms, but also moving with the music. We turned the music up really loud and got completely caught up in it. It was a wonderful sight to see them all enjoying the music so much. Hannah, a little girl with Down's Syndrome, had a huge grin on her face and was dancing around to the rhythm.'

Dialogue for learning

Many experts have argued that pupils learn more effectively when they are given the opportunity to talk about their work, express their feelings and offer comment on issues. Teachers who taught in primary schools during the 1970s and 80s will be familiar with the term 'Oracy', which was a shorthand for the speaking and listening that took place during collaborative sessions. A lot of emphasis was placed upon the potential for learning when children were given properly constructed opportunities to explore issues, make decisions, experiment with ideas and draw conclusions through working together rather than singly. Oracy as a learning tool was predicated on a belief that by allowing children the space and time to talk together about a common interest their combined contributions, knowledge, understanding and wisdom would lead to a more satisfactory outcome than one person working alone. Teachers commonly interact with pupils by inviting contributions and the children responding appropriately. The teacher approves the response and comments further (or perhaps asks a question). The children respond again and the teacher confirms or casts doubt on the responses. The pattern is set: teacher speaks, children respond, teacher praises. Superficially there is an active dialogue, especially if the teacher invites the children to suggest alternatives, give another example or offer suggestions. Yet even this apparently rich learning environment may be less effective than it seems. For instance, it is the teacher who raises all the issues and asks all the questions. It is the teacher who determines the efficacy of the children's responses. It is the teacher who decides when to move on to the next point or lesson phase. In the practicalities of teaching lessons within a given time frame these practices are difficult to avoid. After all, the lesson content has to be 'covered' and there is not an endless amount of time available for child-initiated talk. On the other hand, such a strongly teacher-led approach assumes that all ideas must be from adults and that children cannot learn without close guidance. Such assumptions merit close scrutiny.

Using pupils' talk for learning can be accomplished by identifying the nature of the talk and the conditions for its use. Three opportunities for talk are commonly used in classrooms:

- Discussion
- Debate
- Decision-making

Discussion

Discussion involves verbal contributions that approach a topic from a variety of directions and requires that pupils know enough about the subject to offer an opinion, suggest alternatives or summarise a position. To ensure effective discussion, participants must gain a variety of skills:

- Talk meaningfully to one another
- Listen carefully to one another
- Respond constructively to what others say
- Express their own views carefully
- Acknowledge that a variety of views exist
- Be determined to develop their knowledge, understanding or judgement.

As with all spoken language, discussion necessitates careful listening as well as marshalling and articulation of ideas. Such qualities are not easily acquired but can be shaped and steered sensitively by a teacher who is willing to give children the time and opportunity to express their thoughts. One of the challenges for teachers is to help children to understand that discussion is not merely an opportunity to put a point of view but to acknowledge and receive another person's perspective. Even adults find it hard to be disciplined in discussions, so little wonder that children find it hard, too! Dillon (1994) provides a helpful definition:

> Discussion is a form of group interaction, people talking back-and-forth with one another. What they talk about is an issue, some topic that is in question for them. Their talk consists of advancing and examining different proposals over the issue (page 7).

It is evident that pupils can only discuss something if there is something that merits being discussed. For instance, the merits of a cause, the correctness of a decision, the ethics of a controversial issue all provide fertile ground for talking to one another. Thus, younger children may discuss how best to take care of their 'snacks', ways to share toys or whether it is right to speak to strangers in the street. Older pupils may discuss issues of 'fairness', equality and classroom sanctions. Children of all ages can contribute to a discussion about local issues (such as a proposed road scheme) national issues (such as how to care for the elderly) and world issues (such as conservation). Opportunities also exist through personal, social and health education and citizenship. Teachers who wish to promote discussion should take account of four factors:

The physical environment

The environment should be stress-free and settled but also purposeful, as additional noise and distractions detract from the concentrated attention that discussions deserve.

The size of group

With older children it is sometimes better to split into smaller units of (say) four or five children to discuss the issues, with a subsequent report-back and plenary in which further comment can be made by a child from each group. Younger children are usually better off working within a whole-class situation (such as a 'circle time' situation) where the teacher can exercise a more immediate influence upon the proceedings and ensure that timid children are included.

The sophistication of ideas

It is important that issues do not lie beyond children's experience or imagination. The best discussions deal with things that are of direct concern to the children involved but allow them to think beyond the immediacy of present circumstances.

The teacher's role

A lot depends upon the nature of the discussion as to how intimately the teacher is involved. If the teacher intervenes too much, discussion will be stifled; if too little, discussion may stray too far from the intended topic or dissolve into a series of trivial comments.

Debate

Debate follows more closely prescribed rules than discussion and is more carefully structured. It therefore requires more formal organisation and is more common in Key Stage 2 classes. Prior to the debate, pupils need time to find out about the given topic, talk informally to one another and, perhaps, record some of their findings in a form that can be later shared. The search for information can also be extended into homework tasks. During the debate, children who have volunteered to speak are given a period of time (say two minutes) in which to do so without interruption. The rest of the class have to sit patiently until the contribution has been concluded before being given about one minute to think about a helpful question or speculative comment. When the opportunity comes for questions and comments, no one is allowed to preface their comment with the words 'Yes, but...' or similar. No responses are allowed at this point. Once the questions and comments are exhausted, another speaker is allowed the same amount of time to present information and ideas. Ideally, speakers should offer contrasting views so that when the process of contributing, questioning and commenting is complete, a more interactive plenary is able to take place. During the debate, the teacher needs to ensure that time is carefully monitored, issues are noted and contributions of all types are considered fairly by pupils. At the end of the lesson, teachers also have an important function in drawing together the different threads, thanking the main participants and (most importantly) reminding the class about the significance of the debate in terms of the overall learning objectives. Although debate is of itself a valuable means of stimulating interest and thought, it is doubly valuable if it can be seen as directly contributing towards longer-term curriculum goals.

Decision-making

Decision-making is a strategy used in collaborative problem-solving and investigations. It is most effective for groups of about four children working towards a shared aim. Teachers sometimes give individuals specific roles (such as chair, secretary, scribe, time-keeper) though it is normally more successful to allow children to sort themselves out or take turns in different roles. Decision-making processes require a lot of teacher preparation in setting the scene, explaining the parameters of the task and organising groups. As with discussion and debate, teachers have a responsibility to encourage all children to participate, to discourage some pupils from dominating the talk and generate sufficient enthusiasm for children to feel that their efforts are worthwhile. Time must be allowed for feedback from selected children and, where appropriate, questions and comments. If necessary, some 'overspill' time must be allowed to save rushing the concluding phase.

It takes time to train children in making the most effective use of their opportunities for talk, and many teachers find that it is several weeks before the strategy is working smoothly. The teacher's role is crucial in planning and organising, managing the lesson and maintaining a sense of purpose and direction without crushing pupils' enthusiasm or causing them to feel that they can only express opinions of which the teacher approves.

Activate your thinking!

Consider the following questions:

(a) Do people always think first, speak later?
(b) What is meant by 'getting your brain in gear' before you speak?
(c) Is thinking the same as talking to yourself?
(d) Can you think without words?
(e) When do people talk to themselves?

Allowing children opportunities to talk to others enables them to move outside their familiar world and explore different avenues of thinking, recognise life's complexities through the eyes and mind of another person, and occasionally fantasise. The opportunity to hear their own voices and opinions taken seriously allows insecure children to gain confidence and can enhance their self-belief. Not only does dialogue help children to learn through sharing ideas with others but, with guidance from a sensitive adult, to learn to evaluate different opinions and, where appropriate, to offer peer support in search of solutions.

There are many forms of talk that help children to learn cerebral and social skills. They can recount an interesting experience, tell a joke, comment on what is said by others, wonder out loud and express concerns. Children can be taught how to debate, offer advice and disagree. They can provide knowledge, explain how something is done and suggest alternatives. In other words, children's insights are a rich resource waiting to be unearthed. However, it cannot be assumed that children will be able to handle all these elements of talk, so you need to offer them guidance about doing so.

Promoting dialogue

Learning through dialogue does not and will not happen automatically because children are split into groups and given something to talk about. It needs to be developed in the same way as any other learning technique such as scientific enquiry, manipulating figures or shaping a clay pot. Dialogue is, perhaps, an inadequate word to explain the complexity of multiple interactions between a selected group of children and the learning that ensues. A more satisfactory expression might be 'critical dialogue' to indicate the interrogative nature of the happening or 'focused dialogue' to indicate its purposeful nature. Some children are naturally talkative and dominate conversations to the detriment of more passive types. Other children find it difficult to express themselves and may, therefore, prefer to remain silent rather than expose their inadequacy. Teachers need to take these factors into account when planning their strategies for teaching and learning.

If learning through dialogue is to be effective, a number of things need to be in place. First, a suitably positive classroom learning climate must have been developed such that teacher and children are mutually supportive and encouraging. If, as a trainee teacher, you find that such conditions are not ideal, it does not preclude collaborative work of the kind described above but means that you will have to work even harder to establish and maintain the right atmosphere. Second, children must be inculcated into thinking about their learning rather than passively receiving it. This process takes a lot of perseverance and, despite the ubiquitous use of 'creative' in recent literature, a lot of teaching in the core subjects is dominated by a philosophy of 'teacher provides, pupil receives'. By posing interesting and speculative questions, encouraging children to think aloud and providing alternative explanations for events and phenomena, you can gradually foster a more inquisitive attitude and thirst for knowledge in them. Third, children must be given strategies for taking turns and offering an opinion. Even adults struggle to conform to the conversational 'rules of engagement', especially when the topic is controversial, so little wonder that some children find it difficult to contain themselves and blurt out what they are thinking at the first opportunity. Last, and importantly, children must be taught how to listen to one another. This apparently 'natural' ability is anything but natural for a lot of children! The skill can be improved and refined in a number of ways, including:

- The teacher models the importance of careful listening by repeating or summarising for the benefit of the whole class what a child has said.

- Children are given opportunity to summarise what another child has said after being selected by the teacher to do so.

- Play a 'repeat after me' game based on the US Marines' strategy of the group echoing the leader's statements (this is also great fun for the children).

Despite the growth in interactive teaching involving teacher–pupil exchanges, the incidence of extended dialogue has become less evident in primary teaching because teachers have been encouraged to inject 'pace' into the lessons and plan sessions under specific time constraints, most notably in the 'literacy hour'. As a result, some teachers do not feel comfortable in allowing children room to pursue an argument, explore an issue or express an opinion unless it can be done succinctly. In addition, some younger children speak slowly and others need to deliberate, pause and retrace their steps, so that even more time is used to complete what they want to say. If time is taken up by a child's extended verbal contribution, the squeeze on the remaining lesson phases (e.g. group activity, recording, plenary) becomes a serious factor in covering the curriculum.

On the other hand, the partitioning of lessons into units of equivalent length (usually about an hour each) is for convenience rather than being based on children's learning needs. Trainee teachers are sometimes fearful that they may invite trouble if they do not adhere to the conventional lesson structure. However, if you are in a position where you want to develop children's verbal skills but are sensitive to time constraints, there are a number of ways in which the problem can be addressed:

- Discuss the issue with the host teacher and find out whether there is any flexibility allowable.

- Introduce the strategy of 'tell a friend what you think before you tell the teacher' during interactive and 'carpet' sessions.

- Make stronger use of collaborative work, where a number of children work together to discuss and solve problems.

- Allocate specific slots in the timetable for the purpose of discussing issues. It is sensible to start with a familiar issue and introduce more challenging ones when the children become familiar with the process.

A scan of the above factors shows the difficulty and complexity of trying to promote learning through dialogue. As teacher, you have to model the attributes and carefully guide children's attitudes so that they gradually learn to speak and listen effectively. It is far from easy to involve all the children in a whole-class discussion, so if the children are inexperienced in verbalising their thoughts and ideas, it is best to begin with discussion in small groups. Once the children become more confident, you can consider having a reporting-back time and wider debate.

The concept of learning through dialogue has been resurrected to an extent through the emphasis on teacher/class verbal interaction that forms such a crucial part of formal literacy and numeracy sessions. More recently, attention has been focused on the significance of pupil/pupil interaction through the establishment of collaborative learning that can take a number of forms:

- The teacher establishes a practical problem-solving situation related to the existing curriculum work for the children to resolve by discussing approaches and then acting upon the agreed procedure. For example children may be offered three possible ways to improve the tidiness of the playground, such as (a) to erect a larger number of bins, (b) for each class to take a turn in being playground monitors, (c) for the establishment of regular playground 'guardians'.

- The teacher establishes a theoretical problem-solving situation based on present curriculum work in which the members of the group have to discuss the options and arrive at an agreed solution or position on the matter. The teacher outlines the issues, invites preliminary comments from the children and presents them with the problem to be discussed in groups of (say) four or five children. For example, in the area of citizenship the issue may relate to an issue of *fair distribution*. Younger pupils might be asked to talk about ways to ensure that every child has an equal chance to use the classroom-based computers. Older pupils may be asked to discuss ways in which money raised for good causes overseas will not be squandered through bureaucracy or the actions of corrupt leaders.

- The children raise an issue about which they feel strongly with the teacher during the teacher/class interactive session. The teacher then helps the children to shape their ideas into a proposition, which each group discusses. For example, children have firm opinions about friendship patterns, school rules, homework, children's television programmes, playground behaviour, and associated topics, all of which may provide fertile ground for exploring important principles.

In each of the three circumstances, the groups combine after a suitable time to contribute their ideas and, after further discussion, arrive at a consensus or the teacher summarises the conflicting positions. Children need to be shown that having different views about issues is perfectly acceptable, providing there is evidence to support their assertions.

Activate your thinking!

During the collaborative activity, which children were the thinkers and which children were the followers? How do you know?

Good practice

Think of a 'discussion topic for the week' and introduce it each Monday morning. Allow brief opportunities throughout the week for discussion and on Friday afternoon gather thoughts and ideas in a forum.

The teacher role in dialogue

In promoting the concept of learning through dialogue, it is important to keep your eye on the central purposes, namely, to learn from one another by pooling ideas and expertise, and enhance social cohesion through shared experiences. However, the teacher has an important role to play in the proceedings, expressed in one of three ways:

Acting as an *expert*

That is, you provide knowledge, information and advice as you consider necessary. Being an expert may militate against free discussion and expressions of opinions if the children perceive that there is a 'right' answer and that you are the final arbiter of what is acceptable.

Acting as a *facilitator*

That is, you ensure that the conditions are right for children to learn through talking. You keep a low profile in respect of what is being said but monitor the way in which contributions are made and pupil involvement.

Acting as a *participant*

That is, you take part as a 'temporary' member of a group or the class. In this role, you take your turn in the same way as everyone else. In such a case, there is no hierarchy and no imposed authority.

Although it is tempting to set children to work in groups and stand back, not interacting with them until work is finished or a child asks a question, your role in stimulating children's verbal contributions is significant. While you will not want to swamp the children so that they are unable to express their own ideas, it is overly optimistic to imagine that you have no part to play in the proceedings once the children are talking. However, it has been known for trainee teachers to become so engrossed in one group that they forget what the remainder of the class is up to!

A variety of practical considerations has to be taken into account in making the most effective use of time spent on dialogue:

- On the whole it is better to put children into homogeneous groups (capable pupils together, less capable pupils together) rather than mixed ones. In mixed groups the dominant children tend to do all the talking and although you can monitor the situation to some extent, less confident children often merely sit and listen rather than participating. In homogeneous groups, a group consisting of assertive children is invariably loud and bold as the personalities compete for dominance. A group consisting of quieter children usually struggles to make headway but the under-confident children are more likely to have opportunity to say something.

- It is worth giving pupils something to talk about by providing them with a subject for debate. Sometimes the issue arises naturally from the curriculum work that you are covering with the children. Sometimes a national or international event will trigger considerable interest and you decide to 'catch the moment' (a necessary part of teaching at all times). However, you may decide that as a means of promoting dialogue and stimulating discussion you are going to set up a contrived situation and maintain close control over what happens, at least initially. The close control approach allows you to teach or reinforce the necessary skills for effective speaking and listening before exploiting other learning opportunities.

- Children should be encouraged to think and organise their thoughts before speaking. There is a fine balance to be achieved between verbal spontaneity and talking nonsense! Saying the first thing that comes into their heads can lead to children being ridiculed. On the other hand, too much time spent deliberating can result in missed opportunities. It takes some children a lot of courage to make a verbal contribution, so it may on occasions be necessary to employ a strategy to facilitate it without causing embarrassment. For example, children can be taught to jot down a few ideas on paper prior to the main discussion.

- It is helpful to encourage children to speak aloud what they want to say in their heads before opening their mouths. This is a useful strategy for trainee teachers, too! Telling children to 'hear it in your head first' is particularly useful for diffident pupils and an alternative to writing ideas down first (see above).

Classroom management considerations include the need to structure opportunities for one-to-one listening and group-to-group listening, to teach children to rephrase what others have said and ask them sensible questions and to enthuse about other children's verbal contributions as a means of encouraging them. In working with young children, skills can be enhanced through games and fun activities that foster listening. For example, well-known games such as 'Simon Says' and Chinese Whispers require children to concentrate on what is being said. There are many opportunities through so-called circle time to facilitate taking-turns and concentrating on what other children say.

Activate your thinking!

Write down some responses that a six/seven-year-old or a ten/11-year-old might give to each of the following questions . . .

1 What do you like to talk about?
2 When do you talk to your teacher?
3 When does the teacher talk to you?
4 What do you mainly talk about in class?
5 Who does most talking in class?

Good practice

Other organisational considerations for learning through dialogue include:

- Deciding how much (if anything) should be written down.
- Having paper, pencils, computers or other recording instruments available and accessible.
- Seating arrangements for the groups.
- Roles for different group members.
- Specific targets for achievement in the time available.
- The way that ideas will be shared between groups.
- The activity that follows the dialogue.

Play in learning

We noted in Chapter 1 that all children love to play and that a lack of desire to do so is viewed with anxiety by parents and teachers. Bruce (2001) maintains that play helps children to learn in a number of powerful ways (based on page 8):

- To become symbol-makers by making one item stand for another (such as a stick becoming a wand)

- To think in abstract ways that take them beyond the here and now

- To develop theory of mind, an understanding of the way others think and feel, and relate to people

- To make changes, transforming their lives and events, using imagination and creating alternative possibilities

- To be flexible thinkers, so that intelligence continues to develop throughout life.

Most teachers of young children use play as a means of enquiry-based learning; teachers at Key Stage 2 tend to encourage play only within the confines of a controlled learning environment. For younger children, who are familiar with school routines and able to cope with more structure, play may be timetabled or used informally as an incentive to complete formal tasks. For older children, play can be a vehicle to explore issues and confront life choices through improvisation, and to be introduced to the demands and responsibilities of team membership. A teacher's planned intentions for a child of any age will always be limited by the child's enthusiasm for learning and ownership of the task. This applies to play as much as any other form of learning.

Johnston (2002) stresses the importance of adult–child and child–child interaction as the basis for effective early learning. She suggests that adults affect children's learning through interacting with them in two principal ways. First, the adult provides a role model for the children and can show them by example (such as showing enthusiasm). Second, adults can focus the children's attention and raise issues by asking questions. Johnston underlines that by interacting with children, adults can learn alongside them, as 'It is important that children do not see adults as having a complete set of knowledge, understandings and skills' (page 29).

O'Hara (2004) suggests that there are four broad types of play: structured, free, exploratory and social. Structured play is planned and initiated by the adult. Free play is spontaneous. Exploratory play is when children experiment with tools, equipment and materials (including sand and water). Social play provides 'opportunities to learn about and practise the rules, rituals and norms of society' (p. 79). Play as an essential part of the educative process and a powerful learning agent (see, for example, Griffiths 1998). Orr (2003) presents a compelling argument for play as a vital agent in the development of children suffering from disabilities. Garrick (2004) argues the importance of outdoor play. This book does not provide an in-depth analysis of the arguments supporting the educational value of play as there are many other texts dedicated to this purpose (for instance, Smith 1994; West 1996; Beardsley and Harnett 1998; Drummond and Pollard 1998; Manning-Morton and Thorp 2003; Kalliala 2004).

Nevertheless, teachers need to be clear about a number of principles before they incorporate play into their repertoire of enquiry-based learning strategies. These relate to ways in which children learn, how they understand the world and their need to express themselves imaginatively. If teachers believe that children learn by engaging with issues and life-situations through play, then there needs to be evidence to support that view. If teachers are disparaging about play and see it as a holding activity to keep children happy while the real work goes on around them, then it is difficult to justify play as an essential element of a teaching and learning strategy.

Teaching able children

A lot of attention is given to the needs of less able children: however, rather less has been paid to the needs of the more able (sometimes referred to as 'gifted'). There are numerous definitions of the terms 'gifted' and 'talented'. However, a commonly held view is that *gifted* is an exceptional ability in the core subjects, history, geography, design and technology, religious education. The word *talented*, on the other hand, tends to be reserved for children who display exceptional ability in other curriculum areas where there is more of a public performance element: art and design, music, PE, dance, drama. Gifted and talented pupils will typically comprise between five and ten per cent of the class. In other words, in a class of thirty children there are likely to be two or three children in the gifted and talented category.

The prominence of gifted or talented ability should not be considered as being either innate or absent; that is, either a child has 'got it' or has not 'got it'. Although it is normally quite easy to distinguish the very able children (i.e. those possessing exceptional innate abilities) from the majority (i.e. those who do not have innate abilities) the learning environment can also have an impact on the *emergence* of the gift or talent (see Hymer and Michel 2002 for practical ideas and suggestions). It is possible for one teaching approach to draw out such ability and another teaching approach to suppress it.

Part of the problem for teachers lies in the fact that some gifted and talented children may be unconventional and their behaviour interpreted as being anti-social because they push the boundaries, ask probing questions and insist on being innovative rather than compliant. Some talented children may not shine at mathematics and literacy; as a result they are obliged to spend additional time on these subjects, which reduces the opportunity for them to display their creative abilities elsewhere. Yet other children have latent talent that requires a stimulus before it is released. For example, children from less affluent homes may not have a chance to attend (say) out-of-school ballet, dance, craft or sporting sessions, at which they might have excelled. These are difficult issues and the heavy demands made by planning, teaching, assessing, meetings, marking, reporting, extra-curricular activities, and so forth sometimes mean that a teacher is already stretched to the limit and has little time to identify individual talents. Nevertheless, you owe it to the child to make every effort to help them exploit their potential (see, for example, Eyre and McClure 2001).

Helping *gifted* children is easier for teachers in that there is a considerable amount of time spent on literacy and numeracy, so it is easier to spot exceptional ability and differentiate the work accordingly. Advice on assisting gifted children suggests that they need time and opportunity to develop their knowledge within a secure classroom environment. In fact, this advice applies to all children at every level. However, the learning culture should ideally take account of:

- The learner's own interest
- The learners' preferred style of learning
- Opportunities for learners to be independent and autonomous
- The need for openly sharing ideas and initiatives with others
- The need to find connections across areas of learning
- Opportunities for wider application of knowledge
- The use of a variety of resources, ideas, methods and tasks
- The importance of encouraging a reflective attitude about the process of learning.

Teachers are encouraged to develop a learning climate in which mistakes are used constructively, children are encouraged to discuss their learning with adults and other pupils and opportunities are afforded for them to explore challenging forms of learning. Teachers should, therefore, ask the children questions that force them to think. (Based on information from http://www.nc.uk.net/gt/general/05_environment.htm, modified and amended.) While it is unlikely that anyone would disagree with such sound advice, there are practical reasons why such an approach may prove easier to say than to do!

Findings from a study of more able pupils in Year 6 indicated that many teachers tended to leave them alone to get on by themselves or simply gave them additional work to keep them busy (National Primary Centre 1993). The study concluded that good provision at this level required careful planning and appropriate task implementation. The highest levels of performance were achieved when teachers interacted with pupils in a way that encouraged them to grapple with more demanding concepts and levels of understanding than other children. The imposition of artificial ceilings in tasks led to pupil frustration. Similarly, Dickinson (1996) found that able pupils wanted to be challenged and find fulfilment through active dialogue with the teacher. They wanted to be 'challenged within the curriculum rather than by special provision outside it' (page 8); that is, able pupils did not want to be isolated from the regular tasks and activities, but rather to be given the opportunity to extend their thinking and be innovative. More able pupils were motivated by teachers' comments more than grades and wanted to receive truthful, realistic and challenging feedback.

Able pupils are not always easily identifiable as teachers sometime struggle to disentangle pupils' *potential* from their visible performance. Able pupils can underachieve in the same way as other children, especially if they lack motivation or if, due to their quizzical attitude, teachers diagnose them as unco-operative instead of intelligent. Denton and Postlethwaite (1985) offer a useful list of characteristics that help teachers to identify very able (gifted) pupils (see Table 4.1).

The majority of able pupils take their work seriously and want to do well. Their attainment can be suppressed, however, by teacher insensitivity, mundane tasks and being treated 'differently' from everyone else and thereby gaining a reputation as a 'swot'. The challenge of

TABLE 4.1 Characteristics of gifted pupils (based on Denton and Postlethwaite, 1985)

superior powers of reasoning	alertness and quick responses to new ideas
intellectual curiosity	quick memorising
ease of learning	interest in the nature of humanity
wide range of interests	unusual imagination
broad attention span	able to follow complex directions
superior vocabulary	rapid readers
independence in working	enjoy a range of hobbies
advanced reading skills	wide ranging reading habits
keen powers of observation	effective users of the library
initiative and originality	superior in maths problem-solving

presenting academic success as desirable is most acute among a small percentage of older primary age boys. Disillusionment with schooling is an attitude that can easily be carried with them into secondary education and lead to underachievement, so you have an important task to persuade them otherwise! Teachers also need to be aware that able pupils do not necessarily possess the full range of fundamental skills that may be assumed. For instance, Dean (1998) notes that boys, in particular, struggle to keep pace with the demands of writing and sometimes underachieve, and offers suggestions about helping able pupils to reach their full potential in reading and writing. Some very able pupils may exhibit odd characteristics that mark them out as being atypical and invite teasing from other children. Others will excel in every curriculum area (including sports) and thereby attract excessive admiration from their peers. Howe (1990) warns that although able children may not react in expected ways, close parental involvement, coupled with high expectations, yields rewards. Teachers need, therefore, to be alert to the possibilities and challenges that such children present. Few children are naturally good at everything but, with perseverance and determination, many are capable of achieving a high level of success.

In recent years there has been an increase in interest in the principle of 'multiple intelligences' developed by Howard Gardner (1985). This awkward phrase reminds teachers of two important principles. First, children can be successful in a variety of ways and not only in the more obviously measurable ones. Gardner suggests that we each have at least eight different intelligences for expressing ourselves and solving problems. Because we experience life in different ways and have different emotional responses to the same stimuli, it is appropriate for us to express those responses in a variety of ways. For example, emotions may be expressed through language or the employment of visual images or in movement. Second, that intelligence is not fixed and can be enhanced, developed and matured through appropriate teaching, high levels of motivation and determination. The stereotypical comment made by children that 'I am rubbish at such-and-such a subject' betrays a belief that they are either good at a subject or not good at it for ever. However, numerous studies have shown that this is not the case. Skilled teachers try hard to develop in the children a different attitude towards themselves and wean them off adopting a negative view of themselves. You may have a larger number of gifted and talented children in the class than you imagined!

Activate your thinking!

Use the list in Table 4.1 to identify the most able children in your class. Consider ways in which you can help them to achieve their potential.

Case study

The children in Year 4 were learning their five times table and every member of the class or group was able to chant the table without a mistake and give correct and immediate answers to individual computation questions asked by the teacher. Initially, the teacher was very pleased but quickly recognised that although superficially every child had 'learned' their tables, their conceptual grasp varied considerably...

- Shena could respond correctly when asked a straight question, such as the answer to four times five, but had little understanding beyond the immediate answer. For instance, she did not realise that 20 is composed of two tens.

- Gareth could work out the answer by adding five and five and five and five very rapidly. He was slightly slower than Emily but understood that multiplication is equivalent to multiple adding.

- Nicu knew the answer, too, but he had grasped that five times four is also 20. He also realised that the total bill for four items costing £5 each came to £20.

- Skye not only knew the answer but could also tell the teacher what 40 times five equals.

Although the teacher was initially satisfied that each child was equally competent the reality was quite different. Once he spent time talking to the children about the work and setting them a variety of tasks to test their grasp of the concepts, he was able to structure future lessons accordingly. Although all the children were able to respond at a functional level and get the correct answer to the computation problem, some had a sound conceptual grasp of the mathematical principles and a small number were able to apply their learning to other situations.

Standards

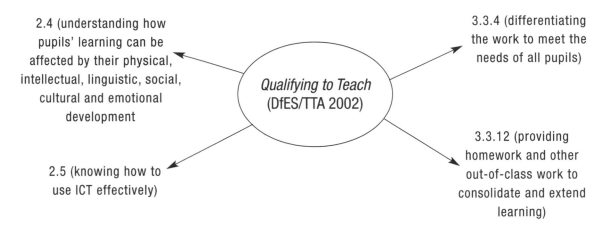

2.4 (understanding how pupils' learning can be affected by their physical, intellectual, linguistic, social, cultural and emotional development

Qualifying to Teach
(DfES/TTA 2002)

3.3.4 (differentiating the work to meet the needs of all pupils)

2.5 (knowing how to use ICT effectively)

3.3.12 (providing homework and other out-of-class work to consolidate and extend learning)

Further reading

Dixon, A., Drummond, M. J., Hart, S. and McIntyre, D. (2003) *Learning Without Limits*, Maidenhead: Open University Press.
The authors explore ways in which effective teaching and learning can take place, based on a belief that children's potential is not predetermined and can be transformed.
Wallace, B., Maker, J. and Cave, D. (2004) *Thinking Skills and Problem Solving: An inclusive approach*, London: David Fulton.

5

Planning and Teaching Skills

Introduction

In this chapter we focus on the range of teaching skills and strategies needed to develop effective classroom practice and enhance children's learning. Of all the many teaching skills that teachers have to master, planning and the production of lesson plans is presented as being of prime importance. Issues relating to differentiation, body language and interactive skills, including questioning are also considered in depth.

Lesson planning

When trainee teachers begin teaching, they go into their first session clutching a lesson plan like a life saver, fearful that it may slip from their grasp and leave them exposed and helpless. As they become more confident, they are able to set the plan aside and concentrate on improving their lesson presentation, interacting with pupils and exercising control. Over time, they begin to think less of surviving and more about what the children are learning. They realise that the best laid plans can prove to be unsatisfactory unless they are clear about what the children already know, the most effective way to organise for learning and how to make an accurate assessment of what has been learned.

Inexperienced teachers gradually become aware that children take differing amounts of time to grasp concepts and remember facts, and that most children do not learn in a smooth, uninterrupted way but are like the tide moving up the beach in a series of waves; sometimes gaining ground, sometimes slipping back, occasionally surging forward. Lesson plans become more comprehensive as they make allowance for faster and slower workers, less able and more able pupils, and the vagaries of classroom life. A short lesson at the end of the day following PE is treated differently from one of normal length during the early part of the day. Lesson plans are developed with respect to previous learning and anticipated future progression. Both immediate and cumulative learning outcomes are taken into account. Spontaneous opportunities are seized and 'milked' for all they are worth.

Lesson *planning* is an active process, requiring some knowledge of the school's existing plans and schemes of work. In drawing up successful lesson plans, it is important for trainee teachers to do so in accordance with the school's medium-term school curriculum plan (often spanning half a term) and to collaborate with other teachers who have responsibility for the same age group or subject (often done weekly or fortnightly).

At the start of a school experience, it is likely that you will teach isolated lessons and there will be little chance of developing continuity from session to session. You may have little grasp of the overall curriculum direction for the class and feel slightly bewildered about priorities and content. If so, do not be overly anxious, as most teachers concentrate the majority of their efforts into the immediate lesson patterns and the week or two that lie ahead. Over time, you will become more knowledgeable about the curriculum and the selection of material from the extensive amount of information now available.

As more teaching responsibility is allocated to you, teaching and learning has to be perceived as a continuous unfolding of related knowledge, skills and understanding across days and weeks, rather than within a single session. When you start teaching a series of lessons rather than individual and isolated ones, each lesson can begin by rehearsing some of the key points from the previous one. Assessment of one lesson enables the next one to be planned more accurately by using evidence about the way that the children responded to the tasks, answered questions and so forth. The planning process supports progression in learning through continuity from one session to the next as the threads of learning are woven together and teaching is targeted using information from previous lessons. *Continuity* refers to the close relationship required between the learning objectives from lesson to lesson. It is achieved when there is a discernible thread of knowledge, skills and understanding running through a set of lessons. *Progression* refers to the need for children to build upon their existing knowledge, skills and understanding in a systematic fashion so that they reach higher levels of attainment. To be effective, every lesson plan should contain a number of key elements, as follows, notably:

Lesson purpose or purposes

These are often referred to in the form of 'learning objectives', though 'learning intentions' is a more appropriate term, as it not always possible to predict what children will learn. Lesson objectives should be clear and specific. Vague ideas about purpose and broadly based aims are inadequate, especially in mathematics and literacy. Sometimes the same learning objectives apply to several consecutive sessions, requiring only minor adjustment over the period of teaching them. Although the objectives apply to every child in general terms, the specific needs of particular children must be taken into account through differentiation.

Lesson content

The lesson content should be set within a National Curriculum Programme of Study (PoS) or relate to the Literacy or Numeracy Strategy. Schools follow a variety of subtly different programmes, using units of work or utilising guidance material from (notably) the Qualifications and Curriculum Authority (QCA). Many schools have incorporated the precise wording of the particular document source into their planning and even provided details of suitable tasks and activities to support learning in that area. The use of ICT enables the process of information transfer to be carried out more efficiently.

Knowledge

It is essential to note what pupils are expected to know as a result of the lesson or (in many cases) series of lessons. This is often closely related to PoS ('knowing what') but may include less obvious forms of knowledge, such as 'knowing how' and 'knowing why'. In considering what knowledge children should acquire, it is important not to confuse it with 'information'. There is a surplus of information available through many sources. Children need careful guidance about ways to access information (through the internet, for instance) and how to be discriminating about the facts that are presented. For example, it is relatively simple to accumulate information about Queen Victoria and inventions of that era (a popular theme in schools) but more challenging to consider Victoria as a person and why inventiveness was such a characteristic of the 19th century.

Concepts

These are composed of the main ideas and principles which are important to the lesson, often referred to as 'understanding'. As with skills, those concepts from previous teaching that require reinforcing or revising and those that are being developed or introduced by means of the present lesson should be identified. Conceptual development is more difficult to pinpoint in a lesson plan than knowledge or skills, as it encapsulates a large number of variables and modes. Understanding something is rarely a one-off event for children. It requires careful and persistent explanation, engagement with practical tasks, talking about the issues, trying things out, making errors, adjustments, revision, rehearsal and repetition. Every teacher has experienced the frustration that comes when children appear to understand one day, only to have forgotten by the next!

Skills

Most learning requires the application of particular skills. These may be of a practical kind (such as knowing how to use equipment) or cerebral kind (such as knowing how to orientate a map or manipulate data). Skills should be listed as (a) those which pupils have already mastered that are needed to complete the tasks and activities; and (b) those which are being introduced or developed through the activities. Occasionally, one of the key skills to develop in children is an ability to work collaboratively or as a member of a team. Note that more information about knowledge, concepts and skills is available in Chapter 4.

Links with previous lessons

Few lessons happen in isolation. Mentioning the links with previous lessons strengthens the sense of continuity and helps strengthen the developmental nature of learning. Children are not thinking about the details of lesson planning like their teachers are doing, so regular reminders are essential if they are to engage fully with the process of learning.

Resources

Resources can consist of practical items or human assistance, so details should include (a) a list of the equipment needed by you and for the children; and (b) the role of adult helper. If equipment requires special training or there are health and safety factors to consider, these must, of course, be taken into account when planning the lesson. Even commonly used resources can pose dangers if procedures are not correctly followed. Resources should always be appropriate for the task. It is unwise to 'make do' if such action increases the risk attached to it. For example, using PE equipment that has loose parts would be reckless.

Vocabulary

Significant words and expressions, especially subject-related ones, should be noted on your plan. In some lessons it is useful to write down examples of sentences containing the key words to use as part of the teaching. If vocabulary is needed for written work and pupils' anxiety about spellings will detract them from the main lesson purpose, it is worth writing a list of the words in bold pen on a large sheet of paper and putting the list in a prominent position for children to use. Children should, ideally, try to spell words for themselves first. Subject-related terms may be a mystery to the children unless explained.

Special needs provision

Less able and more able children must be catered for in the lesson. This may entail them doing separate tasks from the majority of children or modifying the lesson so that the less able are able to find success in the elementary component tasks and the more able can extend their learning through open-ended activities. If less able children are extracted from the lesson for tuition purposes, you need to take account of the way in which they will be incorporated back into the lesson on their return.

Questions

Questions should be listed under two broad headings:

- Those to assess pupils' knowledge ('closed' types)
- Those to make pupils think and reflect ('open' types).

More details about questioning can be found later in this chapter.

Assessment criteria

Assessments should always relate to the original lesson objectives. Although not all assessment is possible during the lesson, careful observation of children's progress and purposeful use of the plenary will provide a lot of information about their understanding and progress. Although it is impossible to observe every child closely during each lesson, you should make it your aim to categorise the children under one of three broad headings in respect of the tasks they do: coped comfortably, struggled to cope, required more challenge. The use of the three categories is a starting point for more sophisticated assessment strategies. Assessment following the lesson (sometimes referred to as 'summative' assessment) usually relies on an evaluation of children's written or pictorial output after work has been handed in.

Lesson review

The process of review is an important part of the learning process, as it allows the teacher to draw together some of the various task and activity threads that have characterised the lesson. The word 'plenary' is sometimes used to denote the fact that the whole class/group are present and involved. Sometimes a review requires the teacher to spend just a minute or two summarising outcomes. Sometimes it involves the teacher selecting children at random to tell the rest of the class what they have found out or done. Occasionally it involves one child speaking on behalf of the collaborating group to explain what they have found out together. Other strategies include children:

- Showing or reading aloud their work to everybody
- Saying what surprised or pleased them about their work
- Voting on which idea or approach they preferred
- Telling someone other than their partner about what they did.

Children normally love the opportunity to talk about their work and show off their models, charts, pictures and drawings. Teachers have a vital role to play in the process of gathering the class together and enthusing about pupils' achievements. Whichever method (or combination of methods) is used to involve pupils, it is important to ensure that every contribution is received enthusiastically by the teacher. Even comments from children that are self-evident or replicating what has already been said should receive praise and commendation. Very young or shy children also need to feel that they have contributed towards this phase of the lesson, even if they have not actually spoken. This can be achieved by asking for a show of hands about different aspects of the lesson and praising everyone. One way or another, a plenary session, however brief, should reinforce learning and provide encouragement and a sense of fulfilment. There are many occasions when the last moments of a lesson can be used to remind the children of what is coming after the break or during the next lesson in that subject. One way or another you should make a conscious effort to conclude the lesson on a positive note.

It is worth noting that the most effective lessons are those in which teachers have high expectations, offer their pupils clear instructions, help them to identify their own learning targets and encourage an active, purposeful dialogue about the lesson content. By contrast, weaker lessons are vague, teacher-dominated, routine or repetitive and badly paced. The best lessons are those in which the teacher uses an appropriate range of teaching strategies, monitors and intervenes progress, and sets appropriate challenges with respect to the ability range of children.

It is useful for teachers to share with pupils the learning intentions and, perhaps, provide a visual reminder (usually through a written notice displayed for children to see). Children need to reach a point where they understand that the activity is not an end in itself but part of a wider lesson intention. Contrast the following exchanges between a visitor and two children engaged in the same activity:

Visitor to classroom: What are you doing?

Child: I'm cutting out words and sticking them in the gaps.

Visitor to classroom: What are you doing?

Child: I'm finding a way to use more interesting adjectives in my poem.

The first child was concerned solely with the activity in which she was engaged. The second child saw that the activity served a larger purpose. It is similar to the story of two men cutting stone for a building. On being asked what they were doing, the first replied that he was cutting bricks, the second that he was helping to build a cathedral.

Activate your thinking!

It is important to make it clear to children that their lack of understanding about what we intend is our fault, not theirs.

Planning for learning involves much more than finding appropriate activities for pupils to do. In particular, it is extremely important to be certain about the lesson purpose (represented through learning objectives/intentions) and the method for carrying out an assessment of the lesson or, in some cases, series of lessons if they all contribute to the same broad goal. Furthermore, the lesson purpose will vary according to the class circumstances, as even tried and tested lessons have to be modified for different groups of children depending upon their previous experiences, the level of their knowledge and their grasp of the concepts to be learned. The lesson that succeeded with one group may prove inadequate with another unless attention is paid to the underlying principles described earlier. As Hart (2000) rightly reminds us 'Classroom dynamics are so complex that it is impossible to predict or fully control what will happen when decisions made at the point of planning are translated into practice' (page 7). Nevertheless, careful and detailed thought about the practicalities of lesson implementation prior to the commencement of the session, as well as during it, increases the likelihood of success.

Activate your thinking!

There's a difference between lesson objectives (your overall purpose), learning intentions (what you hope children will learn) and learning outcomes (what they do learn!)

Lessons that span several sessions

Unless there is a specific and easily measured lesson outcome it is usually not possible or desirable to try and 'achieve' learning objectives through individual and isolated sessions, though in some subjects the limited curriculum time makes it unavoidable. The unsuitability of trying to match closely a single task or activity with a single objective was explored in Chapter 4 and also referred to earlier in this chapter. Deep learning is best achieved in stages by being initiated during one lesson, developed in a subsequent lesson or lessons and concluded at a later stage after a lot of rehearsal, practice, discussion, problem-solving and investigation. Although the process of introducing the lesson, allocating tasks and evaluating outcomes during each teaching session is a useful method of managing lessons, it is also important to take a longer-term view of the teaching-and-learning process. Lessons do not always fit neatly into a one-hour slot (say) and the lesson purpose often requires more time to fulfil than a single timetabled session allows, other than at a superficial level. For instance, the main purpose may be to inculcate in children the skills of discernment about the value of primary sources as historical evidence. To accomplish this purpose, the teacher may wish to spend a whole lesson simply introducing the significance of historical evidence to the class through demonstration and transmission teaching, the visit of an expert to the classroom, the use of video, and so forth. This opening lesson in the sequence would not, therefore, involve much practical pupil activity to consolidate learning. A second session might consist of sub-dividing the class into collaborative groups for the purpose of examining archival items. In this case, pupils would be involved in a lot of practical experience. A third session might involve drawing together the threads of the two previous sessions, sharing findings, raising issues and drawing conclusions. In such a situation, the overall structure of the 'lesson' would involve a number of sessions, as no single session would be sufficiently long to incorporate all the features needed to achieve the stated purpose. Thus, the principal learning objectives would be achieved in stages; for instance:

Session 1: Introduction to historical evidence (teacher-led).
Session 2: Hearing from, and putting questions to, an eyewitness (guest speaker).
Session 3: Collaborative tasks: to begin writing up findings and incorporate further information.
Session 4: Complete writing up findings.
Session 5: Publicly sharing results (initially in class, then more widely).

Three factors have to be taken into account when planning lessons which span several sessions. First, short-term lesson objectives (per single session) have to be subsumed within the overall lesson purpose. Second, the sessions should be reasonably close together to minimise loss of continuity. Third, children who have been absent will need to catch up. The introduction of tightly defined teaching sessions through the literacy hour and numeracy hour, and the strong advice from school inspection reports about the importance of systematic lesson structures may deter teachers from thinking more imaginatively about the ways that learning can be organised. However, lessons which straddle a number of sessions provide the opportunity to explore ideas within a more natural and less rigid framework than attempting to cram every element into a single, artificially designated period of time. Although the principal learning objective will require a longer period of time to be achieved than a single session, the short-term objectives for each session all contribute to the final outcome.

Spiral curriculum

All learning intentions must take careful account of pupils' existing abilities, experience and knowledge. It is important to recognise that there is often a need to rehearse, reinforce and restate ideas before a child's grasp of the ideas and concepts involved is secure. The term 'spiral' or 'cyclic' curriculum is sometimes used to describe the process of returning to an area of learning in order to remind children of previous learning and enhance their understanding. Sometimes the reinforcement will take place within a single session, but more commonly over a greater time span. Some concepts take years to mature. For example, imagine trying to explain to a class of six-year-old children about the change of state from a tadpole to a frog. Now consider doing the same thing with a class of 11-year-olds. Although the learning objective would be similar ('understanding the process of change') the level of detail and complexity would differ greatly.

Although lessons are usually planned within an overall framework in which the learning outcomes are identified with reference to the National Curriculum or NNS/NLS, it is essential to allow opportunities for reinforcement and the development of new ideas through more demanding work and challenges. More able pupils can use these opportunities to forge ahead by using their initiative to explore fresh avenues of thought and build upon their existing knowledge. Less able pupils can gain confidence and raise their self-esteem by dealing with familiar concepts in novel ways. Reinforcement is most effective when children are offered the chance to engage with a variety of stimulating tasks through which they can develop, practise and rehearse their ideas. Tedious repetition is not a substitute!

Reinforcement of previous learning is facilitated if you use the introduction to each lesson as an opportunity to remind children of what has gone before, ask some suitable questions to stimulate thinking, point out the implications and so forth. Similarly, the end of some sessions is not only useful to rehearse the key points of the lesson but to draw together the threads across a series of lessons and consolidate the key themes.

Differentiation

All classes and groups of children are of mixed ability. They contain slower and faster workers, less and more intelligent, keen and apathetic, confident and insecure (Bearne 1996). No matter how carefully pupils are divided on the basis of ability, each group will contain a range of different types of children whose learning and academic needs have to be taken into account. In the light of this diversity, teachers are faced with a choice about the way they plan lessons. The first type is differentiation by *outcome* in which all pupils are dealing with similar curriculum material at a variety of conceptual levels. For example, differentiation by outcome may be appropriate during the 'guided and individual work' of the literacy hour. In this situation, the teacher's expectations for groups would differ according to their academic competence. Second, differentiation by *task* in which pupils of different ability work with distinctive curriculum material. For example, different groups (or 'sets') in mathematics will attend to different tasks. In this situation, the activities and tasks involved would differ substantially from group to group. For older primary children this is frequently organised so that pupils of similar ability across several parallel classes are brought together to be taught ('setting'). This allows the planning to be more specifically targeted towards the academic needs of those children and requires less differentiation, though even within a single ability group there can be considerable variation in ability.

Less able children will normally need more time to reach the same point in their learning than more capable ones. A small number of capable children are slow and methodical in their work, not because they lack the ability but because they are conscientious and anxious to avoid making mistakes. Some less able children complete work quickly because they can only engage with the concepts at a relatively superficial level and need to be encouraged to try more demanding tasks. More able children need opportunities to extend their thinking, rather than merely doing more of the same thing. It is important to ensure that planning allows for every child to gain initial success and move on to interesting tasks that require determination to complete.

Some able children struggle to complete their work on time because they want to divert from the standard approaches and try out their own methods or simply like to spend time pondering issues. Your introduction to the lesson must clarify the amount of flexibility you are prepared to allow, taking account of the fact that children are stimulated by opportunities to consolidate their learning through open-ended activities, problem-solving and investigations.

In addition, all children need to be given the opportunity to transfer what they have learned to new situations; this is often the acid test for whether or not deep learning has been achieved. Even if all the group or class appear to have grasped the principles and ideas contained within a particular learning objective, some children will retain what they have learned; others will require regular reminding and refreshing. However, the more that children see the relevance of their learning, the more likely it is that they will engage enthusiastically with the lesson content and retain what they have learned.

Finally, every teacher has to take account of the resource and time implications of trying to develop too many tasks and activities for children in an attempt to cater for everybody's individual needs. Such a personalised curriculum is impractical other than for classes numbered in single figures! Planning must rely on a satisfactory grouping of children so that each group can cope with the demands of the work, and individuals can further their own understanding, knowledge and skills in the subject.

Body language

To effectively implement lesson planning, every teacher needs to have a repertoire of teaching skills to promote learning, including the effective use of body language. Teachers are performers, not in the same way as a stage artist who aims to receive public acclaim, but rather to improve the quality of their communication with the children. Although it is important for teachers to behave naturally and react spontaneously in the classroom, there are techniques that are effective in gaining and maintaining children's attention, particularly during interactive phases of a lesson. These techniques are based on the premise that variations in a teacher's body language (stance, voice tone, gesticulation, eye contact, etc.) can generate and maintain interest among the children, enhance interaction and thereby improve the learning climate. There are five principal areas in which body language is important:

1 Speech patterns
2 Head position
3 Eye movement
4 Pauses
5 Stance

Speech patterns

Speech is used by listeners as an indicator of a speaker's competence and attitude. Some inexperienced teachers make the mistake of thinking that they will endear themselves to the children by using casual expressions. In fact, the opposite is true. If teachers want to establish and maintain their authority, they should speak plainly at all times and (other than with children who have specialised language needs) never attempt to modify it for the sake of effect. Some teachers gradually slip into using an unnatural tone when addressing children (and parents) which can sound patronising and false. Good speech comes through correct breathing and posture and, as the voice is of prime importance in teaching, it is worth taking care of it (Hayes 1998).

Some teachers have mellifluous, natural voices that sound like a mountain stream: clear, cool, and smooth. Other teachers sound more like an old steam engine whistle: shrill, scratchy and hard on the ears. Pity the poor children who have to listen to them day after day! Most teachers' voices lie somewhere between these extremes, but all practitioners need to improve their voice quality and technique by learning to relax when they speak, breath naturally and stand or sit comfortably. It is not necessary to have a very loud voice to deliver your lines effectively, though those teachers with quiet voices have to work hard on diction to ensure that all the children can hear what is said. If you have a strong dialect, you may need to improve the roundness of your vowels and the crispness of your consonants. In addition, it is worthwhile varying your speech pattern by occasionally slowing, accelerating or changing pitch as a means of emphasising key words, stimulating interest in a phrase or adding character to the voice tone. The impact of changes in speech pattern can be increased by the use of strong eye contact and, where appropriate, adopting a fresh physical stance (see below). Variation in speech pattern is important during the opening phase of a lesson when seeking to maintain the interest of all the children with their varying enthusiasm, propensity to listen and academic prowess. It requires considerable skill to keep every child 'on board' and actively engaged, so it is essential to develop a repertoire of verbal delivery modes when explaining, reading aloud, questioning and responding to children's comments.

Good practice

Practise varying your voice tone by:

- Injecting expression during story-telling
- Speaking slowly, firmly and deliberately to emphasise points
- Showing enthusiasm when introducing a topic
- Explaining things with precise and accurate phrasing.

Head position

When addressing a group of children, it is important to keep the eyes level and speak directly ahead of you as much as possible. However, moving the position of the head slightly can be used to good effect. For example, staring down momentarily (especially with arms folded) carries the message that you are deep in thought, and may serve to increase the children's curiosity. Staring straight ahead with a serious face for a few seconds without looking at anyone in particular can be used to convey the fact that you are waiting for the children's close attention. A gentle nodding of the head, with soft eye contact and affirmative sounds, indicates that you are very interested in what children are saying and happy to be patient until the child has finished speaking. By contrast, staring up at the ceiling denotes a degree of impatience and unwillingness to tolerate the situation any longer. Of course, head position alone is not going to provide an automatic solution to the vagaries of classroom life or convince the children of your mood, but in conjunction with words and eye movement can be positively effective. It is also important to stress that the less often you have to turn your back on the class, the more direct eye contact with them is made possible and the less chance you have of injuring neck muscles as you swivel back and forth. There are three possibilities to reduce the amount of 'back-turning':

- Have resources available; for example, cards or a sheet with key words prominently displayed. If you use a series of individual cards, attach them to the board using plastic adhesive in advance of the lesson.

- Invite children to come forward and write the words, draw the diagram or list the numbers. However, be aware that the involvement of children in this way tends to slow the pace of the lesson and may be practically difficult.

- Use electronic means (such as an overhead projector, interactive whiteboard or PowerPoint). The employment of any electrical equipment involves space management and attention to health and safety factors.

Eye movement

The eyes are probably the most expressive part of the body and often reveal a great deal about what someone is thinking. They betray the truth about us, and disclose whether we are sad, mad, glad or bad! Teachers in a variety of teaching situations use their eyes a great deal to bond with the children, transmit unspoken meaning and influence actions, so it is worth being aware of how you might use them. For instance, wide eyes convey your enthusiasm, amazement or incredulity, whereas narrowed eyes suggests to children that you are concentrating or mentally interrogating the facts. Many teachers develop what is often known as the 'hard stare' with fixed eyes as a method of discouraging children from unwise behaviour without having to say a word to them. On the other hand, teachers also find that a twinkling eye, a flashed smile and a simple nod of approval can transform a child's attitude and enthusiasm for learning. Since approval by touch has become more problematic in school, affirmation through the use of the eyes has assumed even greater significance and must be fully exploited if you want to communicate actively with the class.

Pauses

Although it is generally wise to maintain a steady flow of words, delivered in an interesting way (see speech patterns, earlier) there are numerous occasions when intentional pauses are useful. For instance, in the midst of speaking, you may gaze thoughtfully at the children, make a brief diversionary movement (such as stroking the chin or tapping a pencil on paper) before continuing. This technique has three benefits. First, it allows you to gain some thinking time. Second, it offers a moment of respite from talking so that the children can re-focus on the lesson. Third, the silence causes the children to gain a sense of anticipation about what follows. The impact of interrupted action is enhanced if the first few words after the pause are spoken deliberately and slowly. If the pause is part of a discipline strategy, it is sometimes worth adding a soft but firm 'sit up and look at me please' at the same time. Although it is important not to use this strategy too often or impose an extended silence, using the opportunity to scan the class and make numerous eye contacts often provides a psychological 'cohesion'. Remember, too, that what seems to be a lengthy pause to you feels much shorter to the children.

Stance

Maintaining a set position from which you speak to the children is useful in that it gives them a single focal point and does not cause any distractions that constant movement back and forth tends to invite (the 'tennis match' syndrome, from one side to the other and back again!). At the other extreme, a rigid pose does little to transmit a message to the children that the lesson is going to be exciting or worthy of close attention. By deliberately changing your physical position and occasionally adopting a fresh stance, however, you are encouraging the children to follow your movements closely and, if used in conjunction with some of the other strategies described in this section, will help to keep them on their toes. Thus, to sit for a short time when you have been standing, turn your back momentarily on the class before gently spinning back to face them, putting hands on hips, and even fold and unfold your arms, can recapture children's attention. If the change of position is accompanied by a slight adjustment to another feature of the physical environment (such as straightening a chair), the impact is even more pronounced. It is important to limit the number of occasions that you adopt these fresh stances but with concomitant changes in voice tone it can have a surprisingly powerful impact on children's concentration level.

The strategies described above should be viewed as teaching skills that can be used to enhance effectiveness, and not as clever gimmicks to cover inadequacies in planning and knowledge of the subject. Whatever decisions you make about your use of speech, head, eye, pause and stance, it is important to constantly review and evaluate your classroom presence and the way that you engage with the children, especially when you are leading and they are listening. Exaggerated body language can lead to discipline problems if children perceive the way that you behave as whimsical. Equally, a lifeless lesson presentation results in a lack of stimulation and a dreary learning environment. Having focused upon the significance of body language, we now consider a variety of other teaching skills commonly used in teaching, starting with forms of interaction between teacher and taught.

Interactive teaching skills

Teachers are called upon to make dozens of small decisions every day and cope with a large number of demands, not only with respect to the activity of teaching but also ways to respond to individual children and colleagues. Although some judgements are born of wisdom and classroom experience, the development and refinement of teaching skills provides the foundation for success in learning. The following section explores a variety of those that are commonly needed by primary teachers, some of which require fine judgement, others that deal with pragmatic considerations.

Addressing the whole class

In recent years the ability to address the whole class and hold their attention has assumed increasing importance. Successful whole class teaching requires a combination of seven inter-related qualities. First, a firm grasp of the subject material so that you don't have to keep referring to notes. Second, familiarity with the lesson structure assisted, perhaps, by having a summary written in bold letters on a large sheet opposite your main teaching position. Third, use of a calm and clear voice, aided by careful articulation and a rich tone. Fourth, developing a lively (but not frenzied) manner to engage children's interest using strong eye contact and varied facial expression. Fifth, having access to relevant resources, including basic items such as board pens. Sixth, using questions effectively. Seventh, knowing when to invite, encourage and monitor children's responses. Each of these seven qualities can be improved through practice. Thus:

- Grasp of the material requires dedicated study and, importantly, translating the content so that it can be presented to the children using vocabulary and concepts that are appropriate for them. If you only have a partial grasp of the material, this insufficiency will be reflected in the quality of your explanations, which are likely to be overly complex and convoluted. It is not difficult to make something simple to sound complicated. However, it takes a great deal of careful thought and study to create something straightforward and understandable from complex material.

- Familiarity with the lesson structure is not merely a case of knowing the sequence of events, though this is clearly a fundamental requirement. It involves weaving together the lesson elements so that the total experience makes sense to the children who are on the receiving end. Each part of the lesson is referred to as a 'phase' and the move from one phase to the next is often the time when a lesson can lose momentum, so your ability to link the phases is crucial to successful learning.

- You do not need to possess a loud voice to be effective but you must be able to speak distinctly in such a way that the children enjoy the sound of your voice. Anxiety can cause inexperienced teachers to speak too quickly or slur their words or 'drop' their consonants. It can also lead to a colourless or monotonous tone. You can improve your facial muscles by gently rubbing your cheeks, moving your lips around in a circular motion, sticking out your tongue and opening your eyes widely for a few seconds, repeating the process several times. Momentary slowing your speed of speech and occasional bursts of speed to punctuate the regular delivery can help to add colour to your talking.

- Some teachers can make even the dullest lesson material sound interesting by effective use of the voice (see above), raising rhetorical questions, reminding the children of what they already know, rehearsing ideas and summarising viewpoints. The use of illustrations, stories and occasional humour help to oil the wheels of an exposition, though it is important to restrict the number of these assisting strategies lest the lesson loses its direction or becomes trivialised.

- Resources should not only be available but accessible. You should give plenty of thought to the practicalities of handling them while speaking to the children and interacting with them.

- The use of questions is so important in teaching that it merits a full section to itself later in the chapter. You can begin to hone your questioning skills by clarifying in your own mind the purpose of the question, and whether it is to assess what the children already know, expand their thinking, raise issues or generate interest in a topic. Once you know the purpose for asking the question it is easier to frame it meaningfully. By mentally putting yourself in the children's place you can anticipate the sorts of responses they might provide.

- Perhaps the most difficult aspect of whole class teaching is developing an ability to 'think on your feet' and involve the children in the lesson through verbal contributions, responses to questions, feedback and practical actions (such as writing on a whiteboard). For inexperienced trainees it is better to maintain close control over the proceedings rather than be too ambitious. Thus, to use predetermined questions, give instructions and limit choice. Over time, you can gradually introduce greater spontaneity to the proceedings. As with all teaching skills it is sensible to practise the session in your mind and 'hear' yourself speaking to the children. In the pressure of handling the whole class it is possible to allow the lesson to 'accelerate' and find yourself carried along much faster than you intended, with the result that what was meant to be an interactive phase deteriorates into a monologue! One way to reduce the likelihood of this happening is to write in deliberate pauses into your lesson plan and discipline yourself to count to five in your head from time to time.

Good practice

Begin whole class teaching in a situation in a straightforward way, such as reading or telling a story, giving a single piece of information or instruction, gradually increasing the tempo and complexity.

Working with children seated

The intimacy of group interaction, especially 'on the carpet', raises class management issues that are different from those when the class are seated on chairs. Some younger children in particular are inclined to call out, move around the floor and sit where they cannot see. You have to decide whether or not to be very firm about such behaviour or accept that it is an acceptable price to pay for increased involvement. During interactive sessions (teacher inviting verbal participation) watch out for less able children who do not think for themselves but merely 'cue' from more able or confident children around them. It is difficult to spot that a child is feeding off his or her more illustrious classmates but there are a number of indicators:

- They raise their hands/boards/fans a second or two after the majority.

- The less able children sit towards the back so that they can be concealed from the teacher while having a view of other children.

- They shoot their hands in the air before anyone else and feign enthusiasm for answering the question but if selected to answer offer a lame response, suddenly 'forget' or repeat a whispered answer from a more able child.

Such forms of behaviour have their origins in low self-esteem, an inability to cope with the conceptual demands of the questioning or (in a very few cases) an unwillingness to make the necessary effort to think. To remedy such behaviour, consider whether the teaching is sufficiently targeted and differentiated. If not, it is likely that you will have to introduce some simpler questions or explain concepts using more straightforward vocabulary if you are to involve the less able and under-confident children. Second, decide whether you are placing more emphasis on speed of response than thoughtful replies. Some children need a little longer than their classmates for their brains to process the information and become despondent if they are constantly upstaged by quick thinkers. Third, determine whether some children are cloaking their unwillingness to make a genuine effort by going through the motions of eagerness, not expending any mental energy to solve the problems that have been posed. One positive way of combating such deceit is to ask a question and insist that children work in pairs to produce a response.

When drawing attention to a significant key word, phrase or idea, use it in a sentence and encourage the children to do the same. This process of contextualising reinforces the meaning and aids children's understanding. The strategy is useful for words that are spelt the same but pronounced differently; for example 'wind' and for unfamiliar words and phrases.

Activate your thinking!

How can you involve children who think a lot but rarely volunteer answers?

Children reading in unison

When reading a passage in unison with children (during a literacy lesson, say), it is important to read much more slowly than you imagine to be necessary, or the middle range and weaker readers will soon get left behind. Whereas the whole class read the text at the start, numbers gradually drop off as the pace quickens and by the end of the passage only the teacher and the best readers (usually sitting near the front) are still reading. The other children are merely 'mouthing' the words or will have stopped trying to keep up. There are also a number of strategies that you can use to maintain involvement. For example:

- You stop reading and allow the children to continue on their own for a short time.
- You stress certain words (such as adjectives) and encourage the children to do the same during a second reading of the passage.
- You ask the children to speak specified words in a different way (such as whispering the first word in a sentence or emphasising the last one).
- You and the children read alternate lines or sentences.

Depending upon the length of the passage, there is much to be gained from a second reading or repeating key phrases to reinforce understanding, allow children another opportunity to grapple with difficult words and spellings, and help slower learners catch up. Although bodies of text are valuable as starting points for exploring aspects of language, their vocabulary and syntax should not restrict the breadth of your questions and explanations. By asking the children if they can, for instance, suggest alternative words, provide a variation in the sentence construction, think of rhyming words, and so forth, you extend the range of their thinking beyond the immediacy of the passage and begin to enlarge thinking. Most children, regardless of age, benefit from being invited to evaluate aspects of the text, such as whether it conveys meaning clearly and if the writing excites interest. Depending on the lesson purpose and time available, more able/older children can be asked to speculate about what the author was trying to achieve and to what extent s/he succeeded or even what mood the author was in when the piece was written! Explorations of this sort that move children beyond the immediacy of print and get them to think hard about deeper meanings serve to enhance interest and excite a mood of reflection and questioning.

Reinforcing concepts

One way to reinforce a concept after receiving a correct answer from a child is to repeat the answer, several times if necessary, to ensure that all the children have heard. For instance:

Teacher: If I have five sweets and Jenny gives me five more sweets, put your hand up if you know how many sweets I will have altogether.
Child (selected to answer): Ten.
Teacher: That's right, Sam, well done. I'll have ten...but ten what?
Child: Ten sweets.
Teacher: Yes, ten sweets, because five and five is ten, so five sweets and five sweets mean that I will end up with ten sweets. Let's look at some pictures to prove that Sam is correct when she says that adding five sweets to five sweets gives us ten sweets.

Notice that the teacher in the example is reinforcing the concept both verbally and diagrammatically to accommodate the children's different learning modes. Some children can grasp a concept simply by listening, other children by speaking to another and yet others by seeing it presented visually. Less able children may need some tactile (touching) experience, so if time permits, one such child can come to the front and help the teacher while s/he counts (say) two lots of five cubes into the child's hand.

The time spent in reinforcing concepts in this way is not wasted. On the contrary, coverage of the lesson content without ensuring that all the children grasp the principles leads to a flurry of questions from anxious children and disappointing outcomes when they tackle any associated tasks you put in front of them.

Responding to changing circumstances

The longer that a lesson phase continues, the less likely that the less able children and those with limited concentration will attend to what is said. There is a fine line to be drawn between persevering with a lesson, refusing to be deterred by daydreamers and restless children and insisting on full attention, and curtailing what you are presenting because the children's flagging attention indicates that they are bored or 'saturated' with content. To guide your decision bear in mind four points:

- Boredom comes because the work is irrelevant or too hard/easy to understand or you have talked too long without involving the children in something meaningful for them.

- There is a difference between deliberately disruptive behaviour and restless behaviour. A useful rule of thumb is that restlessness begins to affect normally compliant children as well as the usual characters.

- While it is sensible to try and keep to your intended lesson timings, they should be viewed as flexible rather than inviolable.

- Your awareness of the class's general mood rather than the inappropriate behaviour of a few children should drive changes in lesson direction.

Your lesson plan obviously has to accommodate the various lesson circumstances and if you are inexperienced it is wise to conform to your plan and allocate the time accordingly. However, as you grow more confident you will find opportunity to make on-the-spot modifications. For example, if the children take longer over tasks than anticipated or are immersed in fruitful collaboration, you may opt to extend this phase of the lesson and reduce the end phase. Similarly, the introductory phase usually involves a lot of teacher questions and pupil answers, but the introduction of more speculative questions can generate bursts of ideas and the generation of children's own questions. To make best use of this creative energy and maximise the learning that results, you may decide to let the discussion run for a few more minutes than you planned. This is good educational practice and should not be confused with slackness.

Using whiteboards and fans

If children are using individual whiteboards and markers, suggest from time to time that they show what they have written to a friend before showing it to you. This strategy has three advantages. First, it breaks the monotony of 'write it down and show me'. Second, it helps less able children to gain confidence from working co-operatively. Third, it gives you space to look around more carefully than is normally possible to see if any children are uncertain or mistaken. If you note that a child or some children have made an error, it may be appropriate to say something to the effect: 'Well done everyone for being so sensible. I noticed that one or two people got a bit muddled about . . .' rather than drawing attention to specific individuals.

Response boards (whiteboards) and number 'fans' are often used during interactive sessions to elicit a whole class response to a question, rather than merely selecting a single child whose hand is up in the air. There are practical points to consider when using white-boards (see also later in this chapter):

- It is essential to have a supply and reserve supply of pens.
- Forbid children to elaborate what they write by drawing fancy patterns on the board.
- The boards need to be properly and regularly cleaned.
- Watch for less confident children that conceal their answers from you by keeping the board out of view.
- Be aware that less confident children will sit so that they can see what a more able child writes, then hurriedly copy before raising the board.

There are also a number of practical points to bear in mind with use of fans:

- Small fingers may struggle to manipulate the fan.
- It is difficult to scan all of the children to see how many answers are correct and if there are errors.
- Younger children may reverse numbers.
- The fans need to be put to one side when finished with or they may be used as . . . fans!

The advantage of whiteboards and fans is that they have the potential to stimulate a higher degree of participation from a larger number of children. However, as they can generally be used only for 'closed answers' (where there is only one correct response) they encourage teachers to use fewer speculative or 'let us imagine' or propositional questions. Consequently, the session becomes dominated by questions asked by the teacher and correct/incorrect answers given by the children. This scenario can lead to an extreme situation in which the teacher is using question-and-answer to extract responses, when it would be much easier to tell the children directly! Another factor that can intrude into the dynamics of questioning is that whereas it is important to praise good responses, offering equally effusive praise to unexceptional replies demeans the commendation given for outstanding ones.

Organisational skills

Organising and managing for learning is dealt with more fully in Chapter 6. Suffice it to say at this point that clarification of task, clarification of expectations, appropriate intervention, support for writing tasks and knowing how to end a session successfully are basic skills that every teacher must grapple with.

Clarifying tasks

When children say that they 'don't get it' or sit staring miserably at the page, you have to determine whether they are bored, confused or out of their depth. More often than not the child does not have the confidence or the knowledge/understanding to tackle the work, in which case you have to decide which of the two reasons (low confidence or weak knowledge) is relevant, a job made much easier when you get to know the class. Some children are academically capable but very tentative when faced with a task to complete. This category of children are doubly disadvantaged because they feel (probably correctly) that they ought to be able to do the work and hesitate to ask an adult for fear of being told so! By contrast a less able child may feel more comfortable asking for adult support. It is best to engage the timid academic child in a cheerful manner, using a question and answer approach to reveal the nature of the blockage. In doing so, you should avoid giving the impression that you are surprised or disappointed with the child.

Clarifying your expectations

It is important to distinguish between instructional and invitational comments. The instructional comment anticipates compliance. The invitational comment is a recommendation rather than a command. Inexperienced teachers sometimes confuse the two and find that they have to revert to an instruction after initially using an invitation. It is possible for what is intended as a command to end up sounding like a choice or an aspiration. For example, consider the difference between:

- Can you keep your fingers away from the equipment, please? (Choice)
- I'd like it if you did not touch the equipment. (Aspiration)
- Do not touch the equipment. Keep your hands under the table. (Command)

It is important to be clear in your mind which of these three types of comments (question, aspiration, command) you are employing and make it equally clear to the children.

Intervening

Decisions about how much to intervene when children are working are rarely straightforward (see also Chapter 7, assessment issues). Sometimes, children do not understand the concepts involved. Sometimes they have not grasped the nature of the task. Over-eagerness on your part to assist a child can mean that the child does not flex his or her intellectual muscle and engage with the challenge. On the other hand, reluctance to offer help may mean that the child is left floundering and becomes demoralised or demotivated as a result. As a rule, if you have explained the task carefully, clarified procedural issues and provided resources, there is every reason to assume that all the children will be able to make a reasonable effort to address the work. Their failure or inability to do so should not be taken as a signal that they cannot or that they will not. It is sometimes the case that children lack the confidence to proceed, in which case your intervention (explaining, directing, posing questions, prescribing etc.) offers the necessary reassurance for them to move ahead. Once children engage with the work, your role changes from manager to assessor. That is, you cease offering advice and support about how to tackle the work and begin to make a judgement about the understanding that a child demonstrates during the activity phase.

Offering support for writing tasks

After enjoying a stimulating interactive session, children are often asked to record their ideas on paper. More able and confident children can usually make a 'running start' at such a task but other children may spend some time in applying themselves, either because they are unsure what to write or aware of their shortcomings as writers and hesitant to commit themselves in print. Teachers differ in the extent to which they believe it appropriate to 'pump prime' the children so that they can make a more positive beginning. Some teachers feel that it is important to give the children time to mentally grapple with their ideas. Other teachers foster peer support, whereby children work in pairs to share ideas before committing to print. Yet other teachers believe that leaving less confident children to struggle invites restless behaviour and little being achieved during the lesson, so provide structured guidance. All three approaches are appropriate on different occasions and rely on professional judgement as to when to employ which approach. The most effective teachers discern when it is best to leave children alone to grapple with their ideas, when to promote peer support and when to intervene directly and give specific guidance. You may decide that it is sensible to offer the children some 'starters' in the way of (say) opening phrases or an outline consisting of subheadings as a means of avoiding the 'blank page' syndrome that sometimes has a paralysing effect on children. For younger children, the same principles obtain, though there may be several adults to provide immediate support. A lot depends on what you are trying to achieve in the lesson or sessions. If you want a tailored piece of writing then it is probably appropriate to offer closely structured support and guidance, such as supplying key vocabulary, suggesting phrases and insisting on correct presentation. If the work is being used for formal assessment purposes, then you will need to spend much longer in explaining the task so that subsequent adult intervention is kept to the absolute minimum and the children are left to cope in the best way they can (see Figure 5.1 Support for tasks). Thus:

TYPE OF TASK	PREPARATION	ADULT INVOLVEMENT	OUTCOME
Formally assessed	Exact instructions	Overseeing completion	Grading
Specified	Task allocation	Intervention & support	Criteria-evaluated
Creative	Discussing options	Advisory role	Collaborative

FIGURE 5.1 Support for tasks

Lesson ending

If you incorporate a plenary into the lesson plan, you should be clear about its purpose. For example, the following are common possibilities (with nominal times attached to each):

- A brief time to celebrate achievement and give a few morale-boosting comments (two or three minutes).

- A time to share a few examples of good practice; for example, reading aloud samples of written work, holding up pictures/diagrams and pinpointing their qualities (five–ten minutes).

- A longer time to 'report back' findings randomly from (say) an investigation (10–12 minutes).

- An extended time for representatives from groups to report back and demonstrate outcomes to the other groups (12–15 minutes).

Before clearing away, invoke a 20 second 'freeze' while you explain that nobody leaves before the room is spick-and-span. You will need to ensure, however, that in their haste, the children don't cut corners and cram items into trays and containers. It is also right to insist that the children not only put items in the proper place but also correctly orientated. For example, that books have the main title showing, book spines are upright, uncompleted work is face up with the child's name clearly visible, and so on. These procedural niceties are not being fussy but contribute to an orderly well-run classroom that benefits you and the children.

As a general principle, it is worth inculcating basic, clean working habits into your lessons from the outset. Attention to small but important details make a large difference to classroom efficiency, such as insisting that aprons are folded before being carefully placed into a box or hooked properly onto pegs and not allowed to slide on to the cloakroom floor.

> ### Good practice
>
> Use a 'pat yourself on the knee' rather than 'pat yourself on the back' when the class has done well. If you ask the children to clap for any reason, teach them how to do it using their middle three fingers on a flat palm. This technique gives a clearer, sharper tone to the clap and minimises the chances of a cacophony!

Instruction

The importance of establishing learning objectives and the need to clarify learning intentions for the children in guiding lesson planning was emphasised earlier in this chapter, together with a caution that it was possible for children to spend time engaged in activities without actually learning very much. One of the direct teaching strategies that aims to combat this unsatisfactory state of affairs is through *instruction*. Despite the rather dated sound to the word, instruction is an essential part of effective teaching and a necessary skill for every teacher. Instruction takes a variety of forms but is associated with one or more of three inter-related approaches: explanation, exposition, demonstration.

Explanation

Explanation is a method by which a teacher offers information, explores situations and justifies decisions or positions in a rational, structured manner. It is a technique often used in response to the question 'why?' and frequently employs examples to illustrate key points. Explanations must pay careful attention to the age of the children by using suitable language and terminology. As explanations are purely verbal, the information must be presented in such a way that children are given time to absorb what is said, think about the implications and ask questions of clarification. Like all good teaching, explanations should build on the children's existing knowledge and understanding.

Exposition

Exposition is a step up from explanation, involving graphic illustrations, critique or commentary on an activity or occurrence. Exposition is literally an 'exposing' or 'opening up' of a situation as viewed from a variety of perspectives. During exposition, teachers use persuasion, project their personalities into the verbal element and exhibit a little flamboyance or indulge their enthusiasms. For instance, an exposition may focus upon the harmful exploitation of indigenous populations by foreign explorers. In this case, illustrations may include statistical details of economies before and after foreign intervention, a critique of the benefits and losses which result and encouragement for the children to raise their own questions after carefully considering the issues. With younger children, an exposition may deal with issues of road safety, healthy eating or moral issues such as kindness.

Demonstration

Demonstration includes elements of exposition but makes use of more varied resources and equipment, together with presentations of the techniques, skills or procedures associated with the activity. For instance, a teacher may demonstrate the correct handling and techniques associated with a variety of percussion instruments or the way to access an index or thinking strategically in a games session. Demonstration depends on the teacher having a firm grasp of the processes and able to show them to an audience at the same time as talking them through the stages. A summary of the three types of instruction are shown in Figure 5.2 (Forms of instruction).

Trainee teachers may be tempted to reduce the introductory phase and get children working on the set tasks quickly in the hope that lesson management will be more straightforward. However, curtailing the instructional element is often counter-productive as the lesson lacks a strong foundation and time is wasted in answering children's queries and rectifying later misunderstandings. Like any other approach used obsessively, direct instructional teaching may lose its freshness and become another tiresome teaching method so, as with other teaching skills, the guiding principle should be 'appropriateness for purpose'. Instruction can be enhanced in a number of different ways:

TYPE	VERBAL ELEMENT	PRACTICAL ELEMENT	VISUAL ELEMENT
Explanation	Major	Minor	Minor
Exposition	Major	Minor	Major
Demonstration	Minor	Major	Major

FIGURE 5.2 Forms of instruction

1 Keep the monologue succinct. Avoid droning on and on until the children lose interest. Children sometimes appear to be listening, when they have 'switched off'. Making a provisional decision in your lesson planning about the amount of time you intend to spend on the instruction will act as a constraint on your excessive use of monologue.

2 Concentrate on gaining good eye contact with as wide a range of children as possible. It is tempting to select the dependable children to answer questions, respond to your points and offer positive non-verbal reinforcement (such as nods, smiles and sitting erect) and avoid the same level of interaction with the others. In an interactive lesson phase you should make it your aim to catch the eye of every child as often as possible. You can increase the quality of the interaction by widening your own eyes and brightening your face when you look at a child and momentarily holding their eyes with your own.

3 Pause from time to time to recap, allow questions, encourage discussion with partners. In doing so, it is important to guide children into what precisely they should be discussing and how to go about it.

4 Distinguish between children exchanging comments during an exposition (due to boredom or uncertainty) and the excited buzz of chatter that may occur due to their enthusiasm about the ideas being presented. Inexperienced teachers become unsettled if children start to exchange comments during the presentation, assuming it to be the start of misbehaviour. It is not worth getting cross with the children concerned unless it is obviously a wilful action. Instead, try to catch their eyes while continuing with the exposition and give a little shake of the head to indicate displeasure. If normally sensible children start talking it is often the case that they are excited about an aspect of the lesson rather than bored. A simple 'hold on girls, please, you will get your chance to say something in a moment' (or similar) is normally sufficient to restore order.

5 Deal as calmly as possible with any inappropriate comments from pupils without losing the flow of ideas. Children sometimes call out because they cannot contain themselves, sometimes because they forget that they should remain silent and occasionally because they are being mischievous. You have to make a rapid decision about the reason and respond appropriately. For instance, holding your arm outstretched, palm facing the transgressor, is often enough to put an end to comments. Meanwhile, you can continue with the instruction.

6   Ensure that resources are close at hand before the session begins. Their availability is an important factor in successful exposition and, especially, in demonstration. It pays to think through resource issues carefully beforehand. Efficient use of resources not only facilitates a smooth passage for your teaching but promotes a strong sense of security among the children as they see that you are coping confidently.

7   Use children's excitement positively. For instance you can say something like: 'I'm glad that my idea appeals to you. From your reaction, I shall expect you to come up with plenty of useful suggestions'. Although a small number of children get carried away with enthusiasm, especially when they observe a stimulating practical demonstration, console yourself with the thought that it is better for them to be excited than to be bored!

8   Avoid following a stimulating period of instruction with a mundane activity. For instance, children quickly lose enthusiasm when a stimulating visual demonstration is followed by a dull writing task.

Morgan and Saxton (1991) stress that all effective teaching depends upon recognising that effective learning takes place when pupils are active participants in what is going on. In this respect, lively exchanges and use of interesting questions from teachers and pupils has the power 'to generate ideas, spur the imagination and incite both teacher and (pupils) into a shared creative learning experience' (page 7).

Consolidation

Instruction may be followed by consolidation of children's learning using strategies such as *imitation*, whereby the children copy the teacher's technique. For instance, five-year-olds may copy particular letter shapes; ten-year-olds may use a specific catching technique in PE. Imitation is followed by *practice*, in which children perfect the technique. For instance, five-year-olds use the letters in a variety of interesting contexts; ten-year-olds spend time catching the ball when it is thrown to them from a variety of positions. Other reinforcement activities include *experimentation*, where children are given the opportunity to plan and execute their own ideas. For instance, five-year-olds make patterns with the letter shapes; ten-year-olds make up their own game incorporating the catching technique. It may also be appropriate to encourage children to become innovative, where children use the ideas for a variety of purposes and outcomes. For instance, five-year-olds might produce paintings based on the letter shapes; ten-year-olds may develop variants on a basic technique that has been introduced to them by the teacher.

Activate your thinking!

Do you agree that the more talking you do, the less opportunity children have to think?

Questioning

Teachers ask hundreds of questions each day in their teaching, broadly categorised into two types. *Closed* questions have a single correct answer. *Open* questions require children to speculate and evaluate alternatives. Both open and closed forms of questioning are widely used in teaching, though there is a tendency for teachers to use far more closed than open ones. Teachers normally ask closed questions when they want to stir children's memories about previous work or to assess their knowledge and understanding of a specified content. Teachers use open questions as a means of stimulating interest and discussion, and extending children's thinking by making them consider possibilities that lie beyond those that are immediately obvious. Both types of question are necessary, though the overuse of closed questioning can make children anxious if they know that the teacher is looking for a specific response. The best teachers do not become irritated by wrong answers but try to probe the reasons for the incorrect responses. Sometimes, however, in the pressure of an intensive interactive session or in their desire to ensure that the lesson maintains pace, the opportunity to follow up children's errors is missed. Open questions invite children to be more adventurous in their responses, though open/speculative questions require more time for answers, so fewer of them can be posed. Sotto (1994) reminds us that it is useful to follow a factual question with a more probing one:

> Teachers might first ask a question which requires the recall of information, but good teachers follow that with a question which requires a reasoned reply. No job in the world can be done by (only) remembering facts (page 175).

To take a simple example of this, the closed question might be 'Which city in America is known as The Big Apple?' After receiving the correct answer, follow-up questions might include: 'Where did the name come from?' or 'Who decided the name?' or 'Why isn't New York the capital city of America?' or 'If New York changed its name, what would you call it, and why?'

Questions tend to be productive or unproductive. Productive questions include those in which children answer as they consider appropriate, those that scrutinise issues closely, those where further information or clarification is sought and those in which the children have to consider and evaluate propositions. There is also a value in posing more hypothetical questions for older children, in which they are encouraged to consider situations and convey opinions, values and perceptions. Unproductive questions, on the other hand, are poorly focused, require a right or wrong answer (unless teachers are using this as an assessment tool or as a source of gaining responses) and oblige the children to guess what the adult is thinking. In this last case, the teacher spends too long selecting from raised hands until a correct answer is forthcoming. The productive/ unproductive polarisation is not absolute, as your ability to put across the question, make it relevant to the children and interact with the class also contributes to the value of the question and its value in learning.

As in so many teaching situations, careful listening and affirming comments are prerequisites for successful interaction and creating a positive climate of 'yes, have a go', as opposed to 'dare not even try'. Curriculum work at the University of Southampton (2002) concluded that questioning techniques fall into five broad headings (pages 1–2). First, it provides increasing attainment through developing wider skills associated with literacy and communication, discussion and enabling pupils to examine/question their own learning. Second, that it enhances retention, such as reinforcement that can happen during the plenary. Third, it encourages participation. Fourth, it aids classroom management, such as keeping pupils actively involved in lessons. Fifth, it supports personal and social education, such as encouraging self-assessment, team-building, developing enquiring attitudes and expressing personal opinions. Inexperienced teachers do not necessarily take full advantage of the opportunities that questioning offer. These include failing to acknowledge correct responses by pupils, not waiting for their attention before asking the questions and not providing the learning climate for pupils to ask their own questions. Less experienced teachers also tend to be impatient in waiting for answers from pupils, ask questions in a monotone, allow the pace of the lesson to falter and forget to praise genuine efforts.

Questioning skills do not come naturally: they have to be practised and developed in the same way as any other teaching ability (Kissock and Iyortsuun 1982). Younger children have to be inculcated into the process of question and answer, as many of them will be used only to answering straightforward questions the moment that it is asked. They will find rhetorical questions more difficult to handle and may, in their excitement, call out answers randomly. As children get older, their attitude towards teachers' questions not only depends upon their knowledge of the area under scrutiny but also whether they feel confident to answer the particular questions. This reluctance is particularly evident if the children are anxious about the adult response that an incorrect answer might induce. Children will understandably prefer to say nothing if they feel that their responses will be trivialised or if they fear humiliation in front of their classmates. It is part of your role as teacher to encourage every child to participate in question and answer sessions and to acknowledge every opinion that is offered. Kerry (1998) insists that the children must be convinced that the aim of questioning is to share knowledge and ideas within a supportive framework where each serious comment is valued. The creation of a learning environment in which children are encouraged to respond to open questions and teachers display a genuine interest in their answers is therefore essential. Harlen (2000) claims that this supportive style of teaching motivates children to answer questions without fear attached to being wrong. In this way, misunderstandings can be used constructively as a basis for formative assessment and future learning.

Activate your thinking!

How many questions do you ask in each lesson? How many are necessary? How many are productive?

Using open-ended provocative questions are less easy for trainee teachers to employ because they are difficult to think of and children's responses are harder to manage. The teacher not only has to select a child to give his or her response but also has to *evaluate* the quality and appropriateness of the reply. This process requires alertness, careful listening to what children say and sensitivity when trying to encourage responses from children.

Another important issue concerns the length of time that teachers are prepared to wait for answers to the questions. Some children think slowly and deeply, while others are more spontaneous and willing to risk making mistakes for the pleasure of being chosen by the teacher to give the answer. Owing to the emphasis on maintaining pace in lessons, a lot of teachers are nervous about silence and giving children time to consider their replies. However, allowing children to cogitate for longer improves the quality of their answers, whereas peppering questions at them in the expectation of immediate responses tends to lead to superficiality. Waiting for a little longer is likely to result in answers of a higher cognitive value and produce deep, rather than shallow forms of learning. It is, therefore, essential to be clear in your mind about the purpose that the questions are serving and adjust them accordingly. Teachers should avoid asking questions that necessitate children reading their minds.

Good practice

To avoid marginalising the less able and less confident children, employ the following strategies occasionally:

- Offer an either/or pair of answers and ask children to wink at you with one eye if they agree with the first and both eyes if they agree with the second.
- Ask a question but only allow responses from a defined group of children (such as those with birthdays in months ending with –ber).
- Ask a question, give the children 30 seconds to whisper what they think in their neighbour's ear, reveal the answer, then ask them to raise their hands if their neighbours were correct.

Use of the board

Despite the availability of overhead projectors and other sophisticated equipment, many teachers still rely on some form of wall-mounted board, normally a 'whiteboard', though so-called interactive (computer linked) boards are increasingly common (see Chapter 6). There are many different ways of using (and misusing) the whiteboard, and this section provides some suggestions for more effective use. A number of basic principles should be adhered to carefully:

Ensuring that the surface of the board is in good condition

There is little point in trying to write on a greasy or scratched surface; it sets a poor example, ruins the marker and makes accurate writing or drawing a problem. A few minutes spent preparing the board each week pays dividends.

Having the proper markers available

Some boards require special markers and will be damaged by others. It is essential to replace tops firmly to prolong the life of the pen. (This also applies to children when they use miniature whiteboards.)

Checking that the board is at an appropriate height

It is easy for children to strain their eyes or adopt an uncomfortable position in order to see clearly, so be aware of this fact when organising the seating.

Keeping the surface smooth

Although a fixed board is a tempting target for special displays, the damage inflicted by staples, pins and adhesive can be irreparable.

Remembering your pupils' learning needs

In doing so, note the following:

- Many children find it difficult to copy off the board due to the need to look up and down while transferring information to paper.
- If asked to write quickly, less able pupils are likely to make spelling, punctuation and letter formation errors.
- Teachers' handwriting varies in quality. If children need to read something off the board, teachers must ensure that their writing is large and clear. In particular, children seated at the sides of the classroom may find it difficult to read certain words if the light creates a glare. Unless the lesson is specifically for the purpose of handwriting, it usually pays to print on a board rather than join letters or to use other means, such as printed material.

Good practice

To check that all children can see adequately it is worth positioning yourself before the lesson begins at different points around the room (preferably at chair height) to see whether you can see without squinting.

In direct teaching to a group or the whole class, the teacher can use the board as a memory aid by writing a list and referring to each point in turn. Sometimes the board is useful to demonstrate the correct way to set out a piece of work (in maths, say) or the heading for a letter. Similarly, it is useful to write up spellings or note words supplied by children in advance of free writing sessions. Some teachers encourage the children to use the board during a lesson for noting ideas or recording findings.

These uses are valid and can facilitate learning, but there are times when board work can lead to bored work. For instance, it is not sensible to expect a class of 30 children to strain their necks or have to keep coming up to the board to read something because it cannot be seen from the back of the room.

Using worksheets

'Worksheets' (also known as activity sheets) is a general term used to describe written material which has been produced by a teacher or taken from one of the many activity books that allow multiple copying. (*Note*: Replication of copyright material without permission is an offence.) Worksheets fall into one or more of four broad categories:

Information sheets which children can use as a starting point for thematic or topic work. Typically, the sheets will give some background information and children will be encouraged to research further to uncover fresh insights or enlarge their knowledge base.

Practice sheets which give examples for children to work through to reinforce previous learning. Computation and English grammar are commonly practised in this way. Practice sheets often require a series of single correct answers.

Investigation sheets which set out problems for children to solve using their own ideas and ingenuity. Investigative sheets are normally used by groups of children engaged on a collaborative project.

Task sheets that contain the requirements for completion of a project, areas to investigate, problems to solve or that serve a variety of different functions. Task sheets are used in situations in which pupils are expected to demonstrate a high level of autonomy in organising their work. For instance, a task sheet might set out what the teacher expects each child to complete over the course of a day.

Worksheets can provide a useful additional tool in the teaching and learning programme. They ensure that teachers plan ahead, think through the work and, if produced by the teacher, relate closely to the work in hand. Unfortunately, there is a tendency to use worksheets obsessively and neglect other important teaching strategies. In particular, practice sheets can be over-used (with little preparation or introduction) as a means of keeping children occupied or as a substitute for proper teaching strategies such as instruction, exploration and collaborative approaches. Although the first few minutes of practice sheet work can be orderly, the lesson often degenerates into a situation in which bored and frustrated children call upon the teacher for assistance.

Worksheets, if sparingly and imaginatively used, can provide children with ready information, opportunities to practise examples, a starting point for more innovative work or a reminder about key aspects of the work. However, a number of safeguards are needed:

- They should not be seen as a substitute for other teaching methods
- Limited information should be placed onto a single sheet
- The purpose of the sheet should be clearly explained to the children
- Practice sheets must allow for variations in ability, beginning with easier examples and

gradually increasing the level of difficulty or using separate sheets, each one slightly more demanding than the previous one

- The teacher should try to review the key points following their completion rather than simply collect them in for marking
- Opportunities for collaboration should be exploited.

Worksheets can be very useful for a busy teacher but there are hidden time costs: preparation, reproduction and assessment. There are large numbers of worksheets available from different sources but they must always be contextualised. That is, they must serve the particular learning needs of the class. Too often, worksheets end up half completed, languishing in children's trays until the next clear-out, when they are discarded without exploiting their value. Although worksheets provide a tempting option as a holding task for one group while dealing with other children who require direct teaching or supervision, these occasions should be kept to a minimum.

Case study

As he had previously only worked in KS2, Bart was anxious when he heard that his school placement was with Year 1 children and, though he was reluctant to admit it, the thought of working with infants rather alarmed him. Bart's friends at the rugby club had teased him when they heard the news and his friend Ian told him to practise tying shoelaces and wiping noses! However, the female student teachers specialising in early years' education with whom he shared a house warned him that he would be in for a shock if he thought that teaching young children was easy. These conflicting comments and his own insecurity weighed heavily upon him, but he decided that he would grit his teeth and make the most of it. After all, he needed to 'pass' the school experience if he wanted to continue training to be a teacher, so it was best to be positive.

When he commenced the placement, Bart found that the class teacher made handling five- and six-year-olds look simple. Perhaps teaching young children wouldn't be so bad after all. From the moment Bart was first introduced to the children, he was amazed at how small they were. In turn, they stared up at his six-foot frame with wide eyed astonishment. One little girl asked him if he was the new head teacher. A diminutive little boy called Devon (who was to be the bane of Bart's life in school) pointed at him and screeched out that he was a giant! The class teacher, Mrs Williams, introduced him to the class as a 'new teacher who has come to help us', which made Bart feel much better. He hated being referred to as a student. The first few days came and went, and as he settled into the situation Bart realised that there was a lot more to teaching young children than he had imagined. For a start, they were much more dependent on adults than he had been used to with older primary children. Their concentration span was shorter and they lacked some of the most basic skills that he had taken for granted with ten-year-olds. Procedural matters had to be explained carefully and some children still got into a muddle. On the other hand,

Bart found himself enjoying the attention he received as the only male teacher in the school and quite liked the spontaneity that characterised certain parts of the day. He also noticed, and was a bit surprised by, the formality of some teaching. Bart had in his mind that little children just played! Mrs Williams explained that although she would not choose to teach so formally, it was important that the children did well in tests or the school could be marked out as a 'failing school'. Bart shuddered at the prospect.

After a few days getting to know the children by working with small groups, Bart began to teach his first whole-class lessons. He used a modified version of the plans that had been successful with older children and decided to demonstrate his interactive abilities as early as possible to impress the class teacher and establish his authority. The topic was 'Colour' and Bart had a large poster of a rainbow to use as a visual aid. He sat the children on the carpet and they waited with anticipation. Mrs Williams sat behind them, smiling encouragingly. Bart began briskly, asking the children to tell him about their favourite colours. He had not anticipated the flurry of answers that came flying at him. Some children shouted out their preferences, one little girl began telling him that her bedroom had been painted yellow, and Devon, the diminutive boy, started laughing and shaking his head from side to side. Bart was stunned and held up his hand for them to stop, urging them to sit still and be sensible. The noise subsided, but Amy stood up and tapped him on the shoulder to tell him that her bedroom was also painted yellow. Bart did not want to know! Mrs Williams uttered a few 'shush' sounds and spoke directly to Devon, who immediately sat bolt upright before shrinking and burying his face in his lap.

Bart continued and got out the picture of the rainbow from behind the table, pinning it to the board. Several children called out what it was and several claimed loudly to have seen a rainbow yesterday. One boy said that his uncle had flown through a rainbow, another pointed out that the corner of the picture was creased. Bart smiled and pretended to be pleased that the children were responding so enthusiastically. Inwardly he felt vulnerable and wanted to be stern but feared that it might be inappropriate with young children, so he commended them instead: 'Well done; well done everybody'. He then read the class a short poem about a rainbow in a slightly breathless and exaggerated way to keep their attention, a strategy that was only partially successful.

Bart decided to take a direct approach to impose some order and began talking rapidly, telling the children about features of the rainbow and how it was created. He did not venture further questions and talked 'over' the children when they tried to interrupt him. After about ten more minutes, Bart told them to sit up and listen, which to his relief they did almost immediately. He explained that they were going to draw a picture of the rainbow and complete a work sheet (a scaled-down version of one that he had originally prepared himself for older children) in which they had to match words and provide the correct 'describing' words for blanks in sentences. The children moved to their tables and got down to work very quickly. Bart was pleased at first but soon became alarmed to see that a number of children were using the wrong colours for the rainbow; others were pressing the pastel crayons too heavily and a few were colouring the words that they were supposed to use for sentences. The TA asked him gently whether he wanted the children to work alone or together (he said he didn't mind). He heard Mrs Williams tell her group that they should try on spare paper before attempting the proper drawing. Two children told Bart that they didn't know how to draw a rainbow. A steady drift of children wandered from their seats to look more closely at the picture on the board before skipping back, adding some detail, then returning to the board again. Bart had simply not expected that such an apparently simple task would become so involved.

To Bart's credit, and with the patient assistance of the class teacher and assistant, he managed to hold the lesson together and was even able to bring the children together at the end for a useful sharing time. After the lesson he was extremely relieved to see the children leave for playtime and felt quite exhausted. Mrs Williams gave him a reassuring smile and steered him towards the staffroom for a cup of tea.

After school that night, Bart and Mrs Williams sat down and talked about the lesson. 'I know it was a disaster' Bart began, but the teacher shook her head. 'Not a disaster at all. It's not at all easy working with young children and very tiring.' Bart had begun to realise the truth of what she said and when he went home that evening and was asked how the day had gone, he admitted ruefully that it had been a challenge. 'I told you it wasn't easy with younger ones,' sympathised one of the female students. Bart agreed ruefully and realised that he would need to think hard about his teaching approach if he were to do better next time.

Evaluation of Bart's lesson

- Planning for younger children needed to take account of their experience and existing knowledge; modifying an old plan from KS2 was unsatisfactory.

- It was a good idea to use a question to invite interest, but also important to clarify the ground rules for children's responses.

- The use of an interesting story involving a rainbow was a useful alternative strategy for gaining interest and raising questions.

- The direct transmission of information (keeping talking so that the children do not!) was useful as a temporary control strategy but hopeless in terms of children's learning.

- Young children need more time to absorb, reflect and explore concepts, so it was important for him to speak quite slowly and deliberately, to pause between statements and use appropriate vocabulary.

- Clarification of task demands and expectations needed to be reinforced to prevent a tide of queries from children.

- It was important to be aware of children with special learning and emotional needs, such as those who lacked confidence and need a lot of reassurance.

Footnote
After qualifying, Bart was appointed as a teacher for a Year 1 class!

Standards

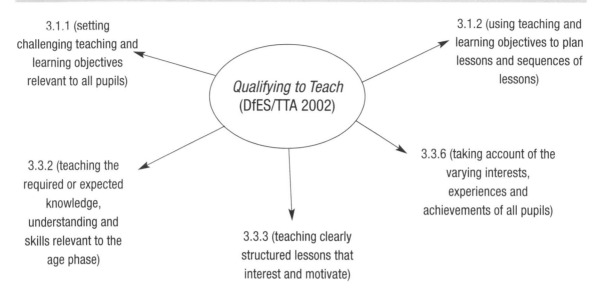

3.1.1 (setting challenging teaching and learning objectives relevant to all pupils)

3.1.2 (using teaching and learning objectives to plan lessons and sequences of lessons)

Qualifying to Teach (DfES/TTA 2002)

3.3.6 (taking account of the varying interests, experiences and achievements of all pupils)

3.3.2 (teaching the required or expected knowledge, understanding and skills relevant to the age phase)

3.3.3 (teaching clearly structured lessons that interest and motivate)

Further reading

Butt, G. (2003) *Lesson Planning*, London: Continuum.
Contains a lot of advice, schedules and suggestions for effective planning.

Otterton, M. (2004) *Teaching Techniques*, London: Continuum.
This practical book looks at the ways in which teachers can change and improve their teaching techniques by looking at a variety of innovative approaches.

Overall, L. and Sangster, M. (2003) *Primary Teacher's Handbook*, London: Continuum.
This book is an A to Z of guidance that includes suggestions about teaching skills that primary teachers use regularly.

6

Organising and Managing for Learning

Introduction

We noted in the previous chapter that learning is not a random process, so teachers need to be clear about the conditions that contribute towards a satisfactory learning environment. If organisation is the structure that facilitates effective teaching and learning, management is the means by which it is achieved. This present chapter underlines the fact that effective organising and managing are both necessary to maximise teaching opportunities and promote sound learning and discipline.

Effective teaching

We saw in the previous chapter that successful lessons do not happen by chance, but result from a combination of careful planning, sensible organisation, skilful lesson management and enthusiastic teaching that also allows for spontaneous opportunities, creativity, and the needs of pupils of all abilities. All effective teaching is enhanced by paying attention to three factors:

1   The ability to think ahead.
2   Purposeful reflection about ways to improve teaching and learning.
3   The significance of interpersonal relationships.

Thinking ahead

The ability to think ahead is crucial to success. Effective teaching is not only about coping with the immediate situation but relies on advance thought about resource provision and activities appropriate to the age and ability of the class. Inexperienced teachers tend to stare fixedly at the path beneath their feet; they must learn to look up and see the road stretching ahead.

Purposeful reflection

Purposeful reflection to improve practice lies at the heart of improvement. Teachers are professionals for many reasons: their length of training, the significance of their job to society, the extent of their responsibilities, level of expertise and, above all, in their capacity to critically evaluate their teaching (e.g. Alexander, 1997; Cotton, 1998; Silcock and Brundrett 2002). The need to go on learning applies as much to seasoned professionals as to novices. Over recent years, there has been an increased emphasis upon establishing continuity between initial and in-service training, reflecting the need for all teachers to enhance and update their professional skills, and understanding the significance of new initiatives, surveys and research findings. It is important that all teachers learn to evaluate their own teaching through discussion with colleagues, engagement with scholarly activities such as reading professional journals and gaining further professional qualifications. All of this endeavour must be grounded in regular reflection on their teaching approaches and strategies.

Interpersonal relationships

It is not merely in a deliberation about the mechanics of teaching that professional progress is made, but also in understanding the significance of human interaction, emotions and behaviour. Constant interrogation of the role of relationships in learning is not only important for the general classroom ethos and children's wellbeing, it also has implications for effective organisation. For instance, it is not sufficient merely to inform the children about standards of behaviour or expected procedures, but to explain why they are necessary, thereby involving pupils in decisions which influence their lives. Children are more likely to develop an affinity with a teacher who takes the time and trouble to include them in the decision-making process, if only to inform them about why something has been decided, than with one who treats them like passive recipients of adult decisions. The teacher is, of course, ultimately responsible for what happens in the classroom, but in the meantime the children will increase in self-confidence and awareness of the issues if they develop a sense of ownership over events that directly impinge upon their lives. For very young children the decisions might involve something as simple as determining a sensible way to deal with wet paintings. For older infants involvement might be at the level of discussing ways to organise the fiction books. For older children the issue might relate to classroom seating arrangements. Whatever the issue, the process of teaching-and-learning is enhanced when children's opinions are taken into account and valued. Furthermore, children are attracted to teachers who take their views seriously.

ORGANISING LEARNING

Classroom environment

Most primary teachers spend the majority of their teaching time in the same room. Despite the increase in subject specialists, advanced skills teachers, teaching assistants and curriculum co-ordinators, the familiar pattern of one teacher taking responsibility for the learning, welfare and motivation of around 30 youngsters remains commonplace in schools. We saw in earlier chapters that teachers' job satisfaction depends principally on the success they make in shaping the lives of 'their' children. The conditions they create for learning is one factor which contributes to the extent to which this aim is achieved. One sign of a teacher's commitment to children is the appearance of the classroom, including its cleanliness, order, decorative appearance and purposefulness (sometimes referred to as the classroom 'climate'). Despite the increasing demands made on teachers to achieve ever higher standards in English and mathematics, primary teachers and their assistants show a determination to give sufficient time to their environment. Adults and children spend many hours there each day and need to feel comfortable in their surroundings (see Hastings and Wood 2002 for advice about classroom layout).

Classrooms vary in size and shape; few are ideal for every purpose. Some will suit a particular teaching approach; others will be a source of frustration to the teacher due to the room's odd shape, lack of access to resources or location (such as being separated from the main school building). Whatever the conditions, however, visitors will use its appearance as one of the measures to assess the teacher's professionalism and, perhaps, the quality of the school. Head teachers frequently show prospective parents around and make a habit of delaying in some classrooms and passing hastily through others! The reason for this behaviour is obvious.

First, it is important to examine a classroom from the pupils' perspective. What do the children see when they first enter the room? Does it look inviting, tidy, thoughtfully arranged? Is there an air of disarray and confusion, or of dowdiness? Are tables and chairs of suitable size? Are trays, books and resources clearly marked and accessible? A useful exercise is to kneel down in various parts of the room to take a 'pupil eye' view, including the doorway, and scan it for a few moments to see how things might be improved with a small amount of effort. The room can also be examined from an adult's perspective. Is there an air of efficiency due to the arrangement of furniture, tidiness and the obvious care that has been given to the overall layout? Does the classroom look cared for and the sort of place where everyone can work safely and efficiently? Is there a feeling of purpose, enriched by interactive displays, examples of good quality children's work on the walls, and well marshalled resources? A classroom like this can bring prestige and attention from the people who matter: children, parents, governors and other members of staff.

Seating arrangements

In making decisions about seating, it is important to be clear about the basis on which decisions are made. A few teachers give the children complete freedom about where they sit; others allow children to sit where they prefer for a week or two until the children's academic ability, self-discipline and inclination to work become apparent, when changes are made accordingly. In most cases, children are allocated a place for the majority of lessons and remain there unless they are moved for a specific purpose (e.g. a collaborative task or art and craft activity).

Most teachers take account of friendship patterns in making decisions. In doing so, there are a number of factors to consider. First, if children sit with their friends it can result in them chattering and disrupting proceedings; on the other hand, they are more likely to co-operate with someone they know and get on with. Second, if friends are separated they may be tempted to wander across the room to make contact, send hand signal messages or (worse) call out to each other. Third, although a seating arrangement made on the grounds of friendship may be popular with children, it may create problems when pupils of similar academic ability need to work together. Finally, less capable children may be tempted to copy from their more able partners, though this tendency should not be confused with genuine co-operation, when children are encouraged to provide peer support for one another.

Teachers who dictate the seating pattern will reduce some of these potential problems but generate others. For instance, many children feel more secure when sitting next to a friend and may be unhappy if separated. Teachers may inadvertently place children together who dislike each other, with the inevitable disruptive consequences. Most teachers try to strike a balance between keeping friends together in situations where grouping does not rely principally on academic ability, and separating them where this is necessary because of the differentiated requirements of tasks and activities.

In making decisions about seating arrangements, teachers need to be aware that the term 'academic ability' can be defined in different ways. The majority of teachers group according to the children's ability in English (especially reading and writing) except during timetabled maths sessions. During work outside the core subjects, pupils' expertise in areas as diverse as ball skills (in PE), computer skills (in ICT), communication skills (in discussions and collaborative problem solving) and organisational skills (in team work activities) need to be taken into account. In addition, two other factors have to be considered:

The age of the children

Younger children are likely to need guidance about where to sit but are unlikely to be antagonistic towards the children next to them. Nursery age children may be given considerable freedom of movement, depending upon the availability of adults to supervise their activities. Older children are much clearer about their friendship preferences and more assertive as a result. On the other hand, older primary children tend to be academically grouped.

Teaching style

If the class is taught as a whole rather than in groups, single tables with two pupils per table may be best. If collaborative tasks predominate, groups of about four are often appropriate. The structured patterns of the literacy hour and numeracy strategy do not leave much room for manoeuvre, as pupils are together at the start and conclusion of the lesson and separated into ability groups for the other parts of the lesson. If teachers use a board to illustrate what they are teaching, children must be seated in such a way that they can see clearly without getting a stiff neck or having to use a telescope!

Most teachers have a basic pattern of organisation but vary the set-up according to the circumstances. For instance, tables may be placed together for the purpose of sharing resources for a large-scale project. Children may need to move around the room if there is a 'circus' of various tasks to be completed in a given time, each task in a different area of the room. There are also practical factors to be taken into account if children have special learning needs and, for example, require more space for wheelchair access or specially adapted working surfaces for children with limited upper-body mobility.

Health and safety

Whether a classroom is brand new or an ageing Victorian relic, the children need to be able to move around easily and use equipment safely. Every lesson should be planned with 'risk factors' in mind. If the risk factor is high, more adult supervision, discipline measures and training about the correct use of equipment is needed (see also Chapter 2).

The teaching approach also has an impact upon the level of safety required, especially in respect of children's movements around the room. Generally, less pupil mobility reduces the likelihood of accidents; greater mobility necessitates more stringent safety measures. Pupils have less need to move when all the resources required for the task are within arm's reach and where the teacher moves about the room to see pupils, rather than the pupils leaving their places to see the teacher.

Classroom climate also plays a part in health and safety. Some classrooms have a settled feel to them as pupils move about purposefully and get on with their tasks without undue fuss. Other classrooms seem like a disaster waiting to happen, as pupils mill about aimlessly, lacking motivation and arguing about resources. Most classrooms vary between a settled feel during teacher-led phases, and noise and bustle when pupils are engaged in tasks which require independent thinking and initiative. It is difficult, for instance, to imagine a time when design and technology experiments with eight-year-olds can be carried out in sterile, near-silent conditions! There is, however, a big difference between enthusiastic application to the job by keen young minds and irresponsible behaviour from pupils who are determined to take advantage of the freer conditions. Teachers have to strike a balance between allowing children the liberty to exercise initiative and being insistent on proper codes of conduct. Nevertheless, there are at least ten health and safety rules that teachers need to be alert to at all times:

1   Pathways should be clear so that pupils can walk unhindered. Tables and chairs should be set out so that children do not have to squeeze past or risk tripping over obstacles such as bags.

2   Pupils carrying out activities which require large areas should be given the appropriate spaces in which to work.

3   Equipment and resources should be stored so that they can be reached without stretching or pulling items down from the shelf, especially heavy items.

4   Wet activities should be kept to a designated area away from main walkways, and sink areas should be kept free from furniture.

5   Pupils must be taught how and when to wash their hands thoroughly, especially before meals.

6   Pupils' view of the board and other visual aids should be unhindered.

7   Pupils should not have to sit next to a draughty window, hot radiator or a tall piece of furniture with objects resting on top.

8   Pupils should only use specialist equipment with adult supervision and after proper training.

9   Pupils must not be allowed to put small objects in their mouths.

10 Pupils should walk and not run in the classroom.

Health and safety issues are particularly relevant for vulnerable pupils; for example, the very young, those with disabilities and children with allergies. However, all children should know how to use equipment correctly and should never be 'let loose' without training. In a situation where a number of different activities are taking place in the room simultaneously, teachers must ensure that sufficient adult help and supervision is available. In 'large space' activities involving heavy or hazardous equipment, all possible safety checks should be made beforehand and limits imposed upon access. It is better to use a limited range of equipment safely than to attempt too much at one time, lose control of events, and create unsafe working conditions. Even young children will, with encouragement, offer their own suggestions about improvements in safety procedures. If your instincts alert you to possible danger or hazards, take additional precautions and seek expert advice.

Resources

The level of resourcing can make a considerable difference to the quality of teaching and learning, and contribute towards higher standards. Teachers are wonderfully inventive and make a little go a long way, but there is a limit to what can be accomplished. A good supply of resources, accessible and clearly labelled, makes life easier for everyone and smartens the appearance of the classroom. Pupils need to be taught how to use equipment, care for materials and, most important, return items to their correct place after use.

The type of resources will, of course, vary according to the nature of the task. A messy, creative activity (such as clay work) necessitates the availability of raw materials, tools, protective clothing and suitable working conditions such as a cleanable, flat surface located some distance from other activities. By contrast, a deskwork activity involving a single, self-contained worksheet requiring only writing implements is relatively easy to set up. Teachers need to be sensitive to the way that a shortage of resources (such as a lack of aprons) and insufficient time spent on training children to use things (such as a measuring scale) can result in arguments, unsatisfactory quality of work and avoidable accidents.

There are also financial and practical implications if resources are abused. For instance, lined paper is expensive and if used inappropriately can result in it ending up in the dustbin with just a few mis-spelt scrawled words at the top of the page. Meanwhile the child has another fresh piece and is busy making the same mistakes. Similarly, incorrect use of tools can lead to expensive breakages. The rule is simple: use the correct tools for the job and monitor use of consumables to minimise waste.

In addition to the familiar resources, all schools now have a range of computers and other equipment to support ICT. Sometimes they are held in a central area, sometimes they are allocated to different classrooms, frequently both options are utilised. Each situation creates different organisational challenges. If there is a computer suite away from the classroom, supervision of children and careful timetabling is essential. If computers are located in classrooms, managing access is a priority.

Preparing resources for a lesson can be time-consuming. Most of it needs to be completed during the previous evening and, where possible, left in place for easy and immediate access, especially in the first session of the day. However, it is sometimes better to wait until the morning before distributing your precious wares. For instance, if the equipment is delicate or expensive, it is preferable to wait until the last moment before setting it out. If an equipment cupboard key is required, allowance must be made for the time it will take to collect and return it. Some resources for the afternoon session have to be organised during the lunch break. Again, logistical considerations are important, such as whether the room is being used for (say) a lunchtime activity; or whether a sudden downpour of rain will bring the class back inside to descend on the lovingly prepared items that you carefully placed on tables when the room was empty!

Large space activities and 'design and make' tasks inevitably carry resource implications: sticky tape and adhesive pots have to be distributed in advance; clay has to be accessible; tables have to be reorganised, and so on. Similarly, equipment has to be checked in advance of PE lessons; drama 'props' have to be put in position; the floor space has to be cleared before a dance session; computers have to be switched on, programs set up and paper trays filled for printing. If arrangements are not in hand, the lesson gets off to a bad start as organising resources absorbs the time and effort that ought to have gone into active teaching, the exception being when the involvement of the children in the organisation forms an important part of the lesson.

Activate your thinking!

Well organised lessons lead to settled children and improved learning. A summary of questions helps to point up ways of increasing the likelihood that lessons will run smoothly.

- Is there sufficient time during one lesson to achieve all that you planned or are you being too ambitious?
- Have you sorted out in advance the activities that different children will be involved in doing?
- Does the teaching assistant know what is required of her?
- Are there likely interruptions to take into account during the lesson?
- Are lessons immediately before or after any events (such as assembly, singing practice or play rehearsals) which might affect the time available or pupils' concentration?

Attention to the details of organisation and daily priorities pays dividends. A few minutes spent reflecting systematically upon the working day is amply rewarded by the improved efficiency. It is worth developing the habit of sketching out each day's predicted pattern and needs during the previous evening, as having a well-considered framework allows unanticipated events and disruptions to the programme to be more easily accommodated.

> ## Good practice
>
> Before the start of each day and each session, take a moment to rehearse your programme in your mind to foresee possible hindrances and opportunities.

Displays

Many primary school classrooms are enlivened by displays of children's work, paintings, models and exhibits. Some corridors are festooned with colourful motifs and stimulating pictures, all of which take a lot of time and energy to produce (see Jackson, 1993; Cooper 1996). In recent years, the increased emphasis upon the core subjects has been matched by a similar reduction in time spent on the creative subjects; as a result, many teachers find that preparation, planning, marking and target setting consumes some of the time they might formerly have spent on displaying work. Although teaching assistants can take responsibility, they are often used to support the teaching of literacy and numeracy and consequently have less opportunity to be involved in other tasks (see Chapter 3). Some assistants do not possess display skills or may not produce in the display what the teacher had in mind, so active liaison is essential.

Despite the objectives-driven nature of modern primary school life, many teachers emphasise the need for colourful and well displayed classrooms and invest a lot of energy into ensuring that pupils' work is visible. In addition, teachers of younger children often establish different areas to stimulate the children's imagination: a *story corner* surrounded by lavishly painted pictures of characters from fairy tales; a *writing corner* separated from the rest of the room by curtains from which hang samples of completed stories and pictures; a *mystery corner* with unusual items of interest; a *home corner* full of household items. The same classroom may have a number of tables with specimens from walks, maths equipment and small scale construction materials to handle, play with, and enjoy. Cards with carefully framed questions or challenges will be placed alongside the displays, prompting children to extend their thinking by handling the objects and talking about them to their friends. The pupils in these classrooms encourage their parents to come and admire their contributions. The class teacher is known throughout the school as having a 'fantastic classroom'. Even so, head teachers worry that time spent on display can mean time lost in promoting standards in the core subjects. Displaying classrooms should certainly not be a competition between teachers. Nevertheless, if displays are going to serve a useful purpose, consideration must be given to the following four factors:

Selecting work for display

Criteria are needed for selection. For instance, a teacher may want to display a single piece of work from every child, in which case some poor work will be on general view; or alternatively select the best examples, in which cases the less able children will never see their work on display. Gathering large amounts of completed work into a simply produced homemade book is sometimes preferable to pinning up the work.

What displaying the work achieves

While displaying work has the benefits mentioned earlier, the quest to cover walls with work can become wasteful unless the purpose for doing so is clear. Displayed work should act as an incentive for pupils to complete work of similar quality, assist learning by offering interesting ideas, and stimulate children's imagination. Teachers can use work on display to point out high standards of attainment, commend the children who have produced it, and praise the unity of a whole-class endeavour.

Changing the displays

The fresh colours of a newly finished painting, the visual impact of a recently completed model and the charming eloquence of a poem about autumn leaves can quickly fade into an untidy collection of curled edges, cracked paint and out-of-season writing. Teachers are sometimes embarrassed to discover that the display of tessellations is more than a term old or the winter frieze is gathering dust in a revealing stream of summer sunshine. Time passes rapidly in the bustle of classroom life and displays soon become dated. A simple plan of action for changing wall displays will help to avoid the discomfiture of snowmen in June!

The destiny of old displays

Wall-mounted displays are often in a poor condition by the time they have completed their useful life and it is sometimes best to quietly dispose of them. On other occasions, the children want to take their work home, in which case it is essential that teachers have checked first that they are happy for parents to examine the work close up. Sometimes a piece of work is required for a pupil's Record of Achievement folder (see Chapter 7); if so, details of the child's name, the date of completion and a brief note about the circumstances under which it was produced are needed.

Good practice

Discuss your plan of action for changing displays with the teaching assistant and draw up a schedule. Make sure that the assistant has the necessary skills to make a good job of it.

MANAGING LEARNING

Forms of management

It is imprudent to think that because the classroom organisation has been carried out efficiently in advance of the lesson, everything will proceed without a hitch. The best teachers not only organise but ensure that they manage classroom affairs (monitoring, intervening, guiding, assessing) so as to ensure the most favourable conditions for learning. The concept of effective management is now strongly rooted in classroom practice and poor management is likely to result in weaker teaching and underachievement.

Management is derived from the root 'manage', a word we use in a variety of expressions that emphasise a successful outcome. Examples of how the word is used include:

- 'I managed to get there on time.' That is, I succeeded in meeting the deadline.
- 'She managed the final question.' That is, that she had sufficient knowledge to ensure success.
- 'He managed to control the class.' That is, he had the ability to cope successfully.

The use of such expressions points to three different aspects of management that teachers need to take into account: (a) time management; (b) information management; (c) human management. For example, in the expressions noted above, there are underlying assumptions about each of the three forms of management:

- That the person has taken responsibility to meet the deadline (time management)
- That the person needed to be sufficiently well informed to meet a requirement (information management)
- That the person coped with the challenges presented by a class of children (human management).

The significance of these three elements for teachers, who need to meet deadlines (such as finishing lessons on time), be well informed (in particular, to have good subject knowledge) and cope with pupils (establishing and maintaining order) is considerable. A summary of the practical implications helps to underline these points.

- *Time management*. Good time management establishes a framework for working, both within individual lessons and across a whole day. It allows for the quirks of classroom life, accommodates the unexpected and ensures that time is used appropriately. This does not mean that every moment is accounted for in the planning process or that pupils have to keep their 'noses to the grindstone' but rather that time is utilised purposefully and effectively. More information about time management can be found below.

- *Information management*. Good information management ensures that the teacher has a high level of subject knowledge and knows how to access additional sources as required. Teachers who are good at managing information will have the confidence to share ideas with pupils, show interest in their discoveries, monitor their understanding and encourage them to find out more.

- *Human management*. This involves finding ways of relating effectively to pupils and assistants, and engaging them in the teaching and learning process. Human management is facilitated by clarifying boundaries of behaviour for pupils, using stimulating teaching approaches and presenting ideas in a comprehensible form. Good human managers respect pupils' genuine concerns and make allowances for their failings. The learning environment is characterised by a sense of wellbeing, mutual respect, high expectation and undisguised celebration of progress.

Organisation and management are mutually dependent for successful teaching and learning. A good organiser and poor manager promises much and delivers little. A poor organiser and good manager make the most of the situation despite the low level preparation. A good organiser and a good manager not only promise much in advance but make the fullest use of teaching opportunities for the benefit of every pupil.

Managing time effectively

We have seen that one characteristic of successful teachers is their ability to organise and manage their time. The best teachers are normally skilful in making the best use of the available opportunities, and seem to achieve more than their colleagues and produce work of a higher standard. Brown and Ralph (1994) argue that although time itself cannot be managed, our *use* of it can. In other words, we manage the way that we manage our time! They suggest that a well ordered routine not only leads to higher standards of achievement but reduces stress levels. Brown and Ralph summarise the position as follows:

> Time is irreplaceable and has no substitute. You can't borrow or steal time or change it in any way; all you can do is to make the optimum use of the time you've got (page 58).

Every teacher finds that, unless priorities are established, the hours slip past and essential things remain untouched while trivial issues or those that emerge unexpectedly take precedence. For example, imagine putting up a display during the break when the resources for the literacy session that followed were still not in place. Imagine chatting casually to a parent at the start of the day while the nursery nurses were waiting for you to discuss a particular child's needs. Imagine arriving late for the lesson because you had been doing some photocopying. Imagine spending the first ten minutes of a lesson in sorting children into groups because you had not bothered to do it beforehand. Imagine arriving in the hall for a Movement session, only to discover that because you had been late that morning, you had left the music CD at home by mistake.

The above examples demonstrate the principle that poor time management is detrimental to your work as a teacher, so it is essential to learn to 'think ahead' by deciding in advance what is *essential*, what is *necessary* and what is *non-essential*. You then decide what is *pressing* and what can wait. To avoid being overwhelmed it is useful to make a determined effort to categorise tasks under one of the following four headings:

1   NOT PRESSING and TRIVIAL

2   PRESSING but TRIVIAL

3   PRESSING and SIGNIFICANT

4   NOT PRESSING but SIGNIFICANT

It is not worth wasting time on things that are neither pressing nor significant, even if they interest you, and pressing tasks that are relatively unimportant should be dealt with as quickly as possible without trying to be a perfectionist. On the other hand, if something is pressing and significant it obviously has to be done as soon as possible. The fact that you have a hundred other things to do cannot be used as an excuse. You simply have to spend less time on other tasks and respond to the new priority. As a trainee teacher, lesson preparation will nearly always take prime position. Seek advice from your mentor if you are suddenly faced with an urgent task and feel overwhelmed. As much of a teacher's work is ongoing, use of a *planner* with interim targets is essential if you are to avoid last-minute panic.

In doing so, recognise that completing forms, filling-in lists and other mundane tasks often have a greater significance than you realise when you are training. Experienced colleagues will advise you about priorities and the categorisation listed above will help you to negotiate them. Papworth (2003) in his 'secrets of time' suggests that effective time management relies on four factors:

- Have an excellent reason
- Have an excellent plan
- Do the right thing
- Do the thing right

Despite Papworth's useful guidance, there are always unexpected demands being made of teachers, and you need to ensure that you don't get submerged through a lack of forward planning or allowing minor tasks to metamorphose into major ones because of time pressures. Obviously a task that is pressing and significant has to be tackled first; everything else can wait. However, if too many tasks fall into this category, it should act as a warning to you that you are failing to plan far enough in advance of the deadline. The majority of essential tasks should be non-urgent because you have left sufficient time for them to be dealt with. In the hurry and scurry of school life there are occasions when unexpected events conspire to upset your carefully laid plans, but make it a rule not to be caught out too often. Effective management of time is a necessary skill for the smooth flow of lessons, administration and decision-making, but it also has more profound implications. Carlyle and Woods (2002) in their longitudinal study of stress among teachers in school found that poor time management was one of a number of factors that contributed to exhaustion and demoralisation. The intensification of work practices and increasing societal expectations of educators placed further time pressures on practitioners and exacerbated feelings of helplessness and being unable to cope.

As one strategy to protect against unnecessary time stresses, it is helpful to compile each evening a list of things that need to be done before school begins, during the lunch break and after school. For example, a telephone call about arrangements for an educational visit can only be made out of lesson times. It is important to balance the time it will take to make the call with what may need to be organised for the lesson that follows. There may not be time to do both. Again, information may be needed from pupils at the start of the day about numbers who wish to participate in a particular event or you may have to transmit information about (say) changes in the timetable pattern. If a parent has requested a brief informal discussion after school, it needs to be made a priority over putting up a wall display or marking books. The balance of each day is likely to be different and unexpected events can disrupt the best laid plans; nevertheless, the importance of looking and planning ahead is crucial to success. Failure to do so means that events control you when you should be controlling the events.

Managing individuals, groups and the whole class

The successful management of lessons relies heavily on selecting the most suitable teaching strategy to accomplish the intended outcome. In the following section, we focus upon using teaching strategies with children in three different settings and evaluate the differing demands each makes upon the teacher's skill and expertise: one-to-one, in groups and with a whole class.

One-to-one

One-to-one opportunities exist in both the regular monitoring of progress during a lesson and in giving specific attention to a child's particular learning needs (Ayers, 1996; Goldthorpe, 1998). Due to large class sizes, the chances to give one child exclusive attention for any length of time are few but extremely worthwhile, as a breakthrough in learning often takes place when a child has an adult's exclusive attention. There are at least four reasons for this acceleration in learning:

- The child can receive individual help.
- The child can ask the teacher questions without publicly exposing his or her ignorance.
- Work can be closely and accurately monitored.
- A close relationship often develops between teacher and child.

However, there are possible disadvantages if the individual attention is prolonged:

- The child may become over-dependent on adult help.
- The child has less opportunity for collaboration with other children.
- The child has little opportunity to reflect and develop solutions.

One-to-one interaction is intensive and demanding, and can make surprisingly heavy demands upon the teacher or assistant. In addition, during regular teaching sessions, too much attention given to one child can lead to a suspicion of favouritism. Although it is often necessary to offer a struggling child extra support, the danger of teachers neglecting their responsibility to the rest of the class is always present. Younger and more timid children especially need to be helped to bridge the gap which exists between what they can do alone and what they can do with support. Work by Crozier (2003) with pupils across the full primary age range indicates that shy children participate less in class, hesitate to respond and tend to use shorter and less elaborate answers to adult's questions. The shy child's hesitation appears to have more to do with anxiety about being evaluated than about lack of ability. If teachers have a teaching assistant, they may be able to manage priorities in such a way that one or other of them has the opportunity to spend additional time with the needy child. A large number of schools offer additional support for children who might benefit from extra tuition, though these tend to be related to those who have the potential to achieve a higher level in the national tests. Otherwise, space has to be found during assembly time, break-time, quiet reading sessions, shared class times and the like to give extra support. None of these options is ideal as they place an additional burden upon the teacher; nevertheless, certain one-to-one tasks are unavoidable and have to be accommodated somehow in the teaching programme, including:

- Hearing children read
- Conferencing (discussing the child's work in depth on a one-to-one basis)
- Discussing homework tasks.

Even experienced practitioners find that hearing readers is particularly challenging; they use various means to cope with the problem of fitting them in during each week. Teachers of younger primary children utilise parents, teaching assistants and odd occasions when the majority of the class are engaged in self-sustained play activities in order to hear readers. Teachers at Key Stage 2 find that although good readers enjoy reading to them, it becomes less and less useful as the children can read silently much more quickly than aloud, with the consequence that reading aloud may reduce their fluency. A balance has to be struck between hearing readers to monitor their grasp of concepts, pronunciation and intonation, and wasting valuable time working one-to-one with a child who is an independent reader and does not need to practise aloud. Many teachers, accepting that one-to-one engagement is unrealistic, utilise whole-class reading (such as in the literacy hour), group reading (where a number of children have the same book in front of them) or paired reading (where a more capable child assists a less capable one) as a means of coping with or enhancing the quality of reading. None of these methods are free from problems and despite the cost in time and effort, individual attention is sometimes the only option. Children who have severe problems with reading will normally receive targeted attention, though care must be taken that time spent on providing additional support does not deprive them of other learning opportunities or make them feel an oddity.

Conferencing normally takes place at least once each term and is a means of reviewing work and setting longer-term learning targets with (rather than for) the child. The teacher spends a few minutes exclusively with one child, discussing his or her work, considering the progress that has been made and, perhaps, selecting pieces of work for the Record of Achievement folder that will accompany the child through the school. These occasions need to be planned carefully and consideration has to be given to issues of privacy, confidentiality and the means of sustaining uninterrupted contact. Some schools have a policy of using a substitute teacher during the 'conferencing season' to supervise the rest of the class. Other situations are less straightforward and require the sort of imaginative strategies demanded for hearing readers. It is likely that experienced and trained teaching assistants will also be available to undertake such a task. Some schools utilise a 'target review sheet' (TRS) to help children and teachers reflect upon the work that has taken place and what lies ahead. Typically, a TRS will contain such information as the following (child perspectives are shown in brackets):

- Name of child and the date of completion
- Past achievements *(In child-speak: what I have achieved so far)*

- Analysis of previous success *(the reasons I have done well)*
- Future plans *(things I still need to persevere with to achieve)*
- Analysis of struggles *(reasons I have found things hard)*
- Aspirations *(new goals I set for myself)*
- Strategies to achieve future success *(how I can do better at my work)*
- Celebrating success *(things I can feel proud about)*

The format can, of course, vary according to the age group of children and specific purpose for which the TRS is used. With young pupils it is helpful if each child shares with an adult, who writes down what is said and agreed. In many ways, the exact nature of the written evidence is less important than the conversation itself and the opportunity to reflect on individual progress. In practice, there are so many different things that could be written down that some selection is inevitable. If the child is 'driving' the agenda, then the adult has to accept that the priorities may differ from what might be expected! The ongoing assessment of individual children is addressed further in Chapter 7.

Activate your thinking!

Consider the truth of this principle: Groups can be taught but only individuals can learn.

Groups

We have already seen that the dividing of the class into groups is an important part of organising for learning. Division into groups is most often based upon the academic ability of the children for core areas (maths, science, English), friendship groups for creative activities (notably PE and art) and a mixture of friendship and ability for collaborative work in other non-core subjects. For instance, there might be three ability sets for maths, friendship groups for drama, and a mixture of children for project, thematic or topic work in the humanities (see **Table 6.1** Group type by subject area).

TABLE 6.1 Group type by subject area

Subject area	Group type
CORE SUBJECTS	Based on academic ability
CREATIVE TASKS	Based on friendship patterns
PROJECT WORK	Mixed composition

In determining the pattern of group work, the demands made of teachers grow in proportion to the number and complexity of groups operating, so handling several groups engaged in similar tasks is easier to cope with than groups working in different subject areas. Dividing the class into groups at the beginning of a session is followed by the challenging process of monitoring, recording of children's progress and bringing the session to a satisfactory conclusion.

All teachers have had to recognise that the National Curriculum and national strategies for literacy and numeracy has resulted in less opportunity and time for spontaneity and has forced them to become highly specific in their direction of group work. This has sometimes resulted in less time for exploratory, enquiry-based learning.

Note that teacher input is normally required before children can purposefully explore their own ideas. Thus, explanation about the computer program precedes exploration of options; similarly, the creativity in drama emerges from a close study of the original example. This means that in addition to direct teaching, teachers have a responsibility to provide the necessary structure and circumstances within which the children can subsequently explore ideas and investigate processes, a function sometimes referred to as 'scaffolding'. This procedure does not imply that children do not possess original ideas of their own; on the contrary, a well-structured approach to experiential teaching and learning will facilitate children's contributions by providing a knowledge base or equipping them with the necessary concepts or skills. The assumption is that children will find out many things for themselves and learn more thoroughly providing they are given appropriate knowledge, guidance and resources as a foundation on which to build their ideas and innovate.

As children work together they experience a range of emotions and challenges which have as much to do with learning to get along with one another as with solving problems or exploring concepts. Biott and Easen (1994) comment on the significance of friendship groups in particular:

> Friendship groups offer opportunities for children to learn social competences in situations where they feel they can act upon shared understandings of how to be both cooperative and assertive (page 65).

While there is always a danger of friends spending too much time talking about out-of-school affairs when they should be concentrating on the work in hand, the risks should be weighed against the advantages to be gained through close social interaction and mutual support in the pursuit of common aims. See Figure 6.1, Social factors in collaboration and the section on learning through dialogue in Chapter 4.

Teachers also have to decide whether group work is intended to enhance collaboration or used as an organisational tool. That is, whether children sit together in groups to achieve a common learning objective (collaboration) or whether they sit together and are generally co-operative while working. Experience has shown teachers that although children sit together they do not necessarily collaborate for three reasons: (a) they do not want the interaction to be interpreted as 'cheating', (b) they lack the necessary skills, (c) they prefer to work separately. If you want children to collaborate, you need to explain the process, teach the skills and clarify the boundaries. It is important to stress that assisting a classmate is not cheating and to insist that everyone has a responsibility to contribute, not merely the

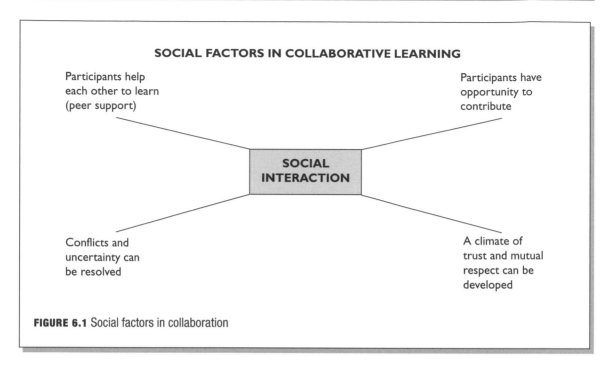

FIGURE 6.1 Social factors in collaboration

assertive pupils. Collaboration is typically associated with investigative, enquiry-based tasks whereas co-operation is associated with children working independently or in pairs but being mutually supportive while they do so. Thus:

investigative task > collaborative grouping > joint outcome
independent tasks > co-operative grouping > separate outcomes

Collaborative tasks require the active involvement of every child to achieve the objective. Between them, pupils in a group need to offer a range of skills, principally the ability to speculate, predict, justify, evaluate and generalise (see Figure 6.2, Cognition skills needed for collaboration). However, even collaborative grouping can result in the exclusion of individual children from the process due to their insecurity, lack of experience as a group member or dominance by the strongest characters. Collaborative group work needs crew-members; there is no room for passengers. The joint activities do not detract from the principle that each child has a personal responsibility for learning, as no one can learn for somebody else, but only help others to understand while reinforcing concepts for themselves while doing so.

Activate your thinking!

Evaluate the way in which pupil groupings facilitate (a) co-operative learning; and (b) collaborative learning. Reorganise the tables or seating arrangements to minimise unhelpful conversations and maximise learning.

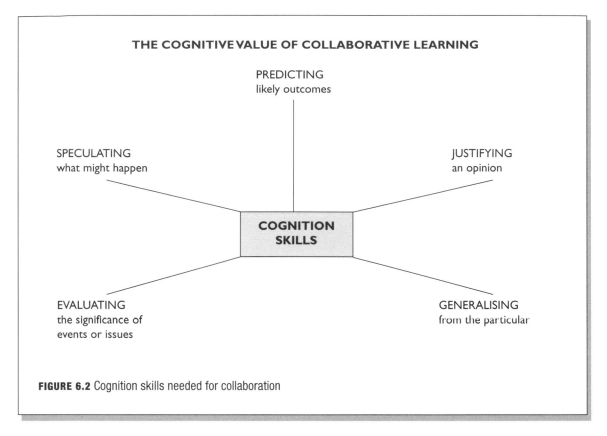

THE COGNITIVE VALUE OF COLLABORATIVE LEARNING

PREDICTING
likely outcomes

SPECULATING
what might happen

JUSTIFYING
an opinion

**COGNITION
SKILLS**

EVALUATING
the significance of
events or issues

GENERALISING
from the particular

FIGURE 6.2 Cognition skills needed for collaboration

Close attention to a single group of children is very difficult when the whole class has to be managed. Inexperienced teachers may find themselves involved with one table of children, attempting to give them their full attention, while the remainder of the class drift along restlessly or form long queues in an endless wait for attention. Even with the support of a TA to offer guidance, control issues can soon emerge if the children are unclear about the work. Consequently, in designing tasks for groups, a number of important considerations have to be taken into account:

- Ensure that the children understand what is required of them, are offered some ownership of ideas and given opportunity to interpret the task.
- Provide the resources and clarify the extent to which children can be autonomous.
- Make decisions in collaborative enterprises about who handles the resources, who takes responsibility for recording results, who reports back and how each child is to be involved.
- Match task to ability and ensure that the activity lasts sufficiently long to allow children to become fully involved but not so long that they suffer from discouragement or task fatigue.
- Keep noise levels suitably restrained.

- Regulate the children's movement around the room.

- Explore cross-curricular links.

- Repeat activities as necessary to allow children to gain a fuller understanding of the principles and concepts.

Group work often makes heavy demands upon teachers who need to find the opportunity to review their classroom management, intervene where necessary and maintain a whole-class perspective. The involvement of a teaching assistant is important as a means of spreading the responsibility for advising, monitoring progress and maintaining order. Opportunity for groups to share findings helps to strengthen and extend learning.

Whole class

Dealing with the class as an undifferentiated whole requires additional and different skills from one-to-one and group work, and even from setting. Kutnick (1994) describes whole-class teaching as 'an efficient means of transmitting information to a large number of children simultaneously' but alerts teachers to the extent of their 'didactic control of knowledge and socialisation in the classroom' (page 25) as they do so. Whole-class teaching therefore demands a high level of skill and application to keep pupils attending and interested for the given period of time. There is some evidence that more frequent and regular use of whole-class teaching helps to raise standards in literacy and numeracy (OFSTED, 1998) though there are limitations attached to this approach, too.

Many teachers find that their public performance in front of the whole class is central to successful teaching, and for inexperienced teachers it is essential that adequate practice of performance skills is undertaken prior to the teaching session. There are few experienced teachers who can stand up and offer accurate information, demonstrate ideas and control a question-and-answer session without thorough preparation. Some teachers write out a memory aid on a sheet of paper which they carry around or on a large card which they pin to the back wall and glance at occasionally as a reminder of key points. As a trainee teacher, there is no shame in referring to your lesson plan, though the more that you can operate without having to stop and look down at your notes, the more in control of events you will look, feel and sound.

Good practice

If you lack confidence in front of the whole class, practise on a tape recorder before-hand and write down the questions that you are going to use with them. Listen to the clarity with which you are expressing yourself. Give some thought to the types of responses your words and questions might elicit from the children and how you will use their answers to enhance learning.

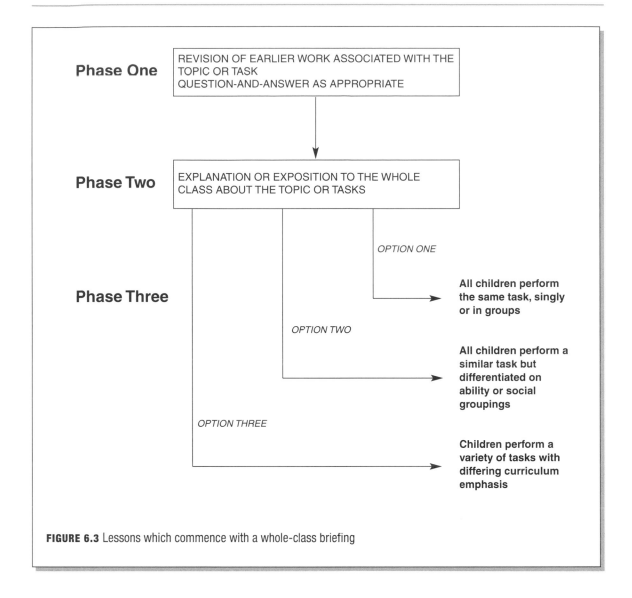

FIGURE 6.3 Lessons which commence with a whole-class briefing

Whole-class lesson procedure

Instructing is an essential element of whole-class management and if it is linked with the variety of organisation discussed earlier in this chapter, it is possible to represent this diagrammatically (Figure 6.3, Lessons which commence with a whole-class briefing).

In broad terms, Phase One links the lesson with previous work, reminding children of what went before and explaining the relevance of previous learning. In your haste to get the present lesson moving, it is essential not to overlook the importance of this phase. One way in which pupils' memories can be stirred and the new lesson opened up is by the use of question and answer. The opening phase is followed by a second phase consisting of instruction, followed by a whole-class briefing phase. In the third phase, the class is divided up for activities using one of the options selected by the teacher. Most often, therefore, the introduction is followed

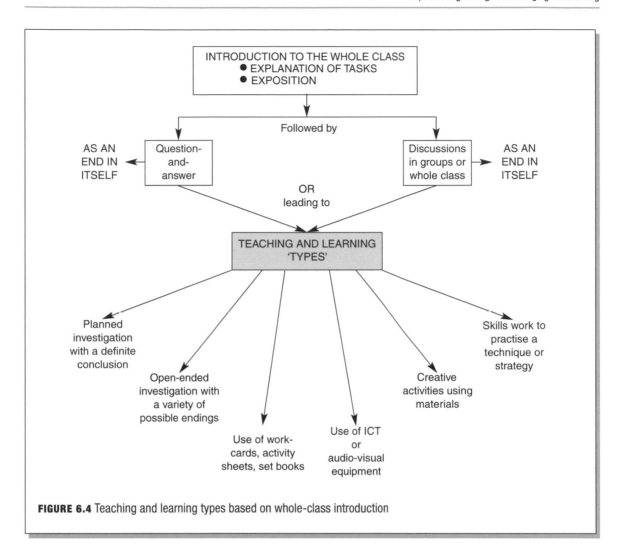

FIGURE 6.4 Teaching and learning types based on whole-class introduction

by a question-and-answer phase for the purpose of task clarification or raising ideas which in turn leads to one of the teaching and learning types indicated in Figure 6.4, Teaching and learning types based on whole-class introduction.

Time spent on the introductory part of the lesson should be seen as an investment, ensuring that you do not have to repeat the same information and explanations to different children who are still confused about what to do. Although some children will require an adult's close direction during the lesson, the greater the independence they ultimately achieve, the greater the freedom for the teacher to monitor progress and to engage in one-to-one or group interactions.

Teaching the class as a whole for part or all of a session is an opportunity for teachers to perfect their ability to articulate clearly, assert their authority and pace their delivery in a stimulating way that engages the children's interest. The teacher's personality is a critical factor in the prevailing mood: dictatorial or responsive, warm or aloof, humorous or sullen, encouraging or demoralising, harsh or sympathetic. There are issues of class control and discipline to consider but these should not detract from the value and sense of achievement that come about as a result of dealing with the class as a whole.

Whatever the lesson structure adopted when working with the whole class, a number of issues are central to success:

- Children need to sense the teacher's *enthusiasm* for the subject matter in the way that the task is introduced, expectations are explained and questions are invited.

- Children learn more if they are given some *ownership* of the task and are allowed and encouraged to be flexible in their method of approach during the experiential phase.

- Children must be allowed some flexibility to *interpret* the work according to their understanding, ability and experience.

Varieties of whole-class management

Whole-class lessons are often associated with the formal structure of literacy or numeracy lessons; however there are a number of other variations in organising lessons, of which six approaches are seen in primary schools. For ease of reference, these forms of task management will be referred to as **linear**, **circular**, **staged**, **spoked**, **single** and **stepped**. Each approach has advantages and limitations.

Linear task management

This approach consists of a single whole-class introduction followed by tasks that gradually increase in difficulty. All children attempt task one, some will proceed to task two, fewer still to task three and so on. The teacher monitors progress by checking that a particular task has been completed successfully before permitting children to proceed to further tasks (Figure 6.5, The linear approach). Only the more able or those who work harder or faster are likely to reach the later tasks. Consequently, linear management lends itself to a straightforward form of differentiation in which a single task, progressively more difficult, is used as the lesson spine. There are a number of implications:

- The later tasks must be more challenging than the earlier ones.

- There is a danger that the more able and less motivated children will linger unduly on the less demanding tasks.

- If children work in mixed ability groups on a task organised within the linear approach, the more able may be slowed down or the less able may be carried along without gaining proper understanding.

A further challenge for teachers is how best to pick up the threads of learning next time the class meets for that particular subject or topic as different groups and individuals will have reached a variety of end-points during the previous session. A good introduction becomes essential for the purpose of reviewing earlier work, clarifying understanding and setting fresh

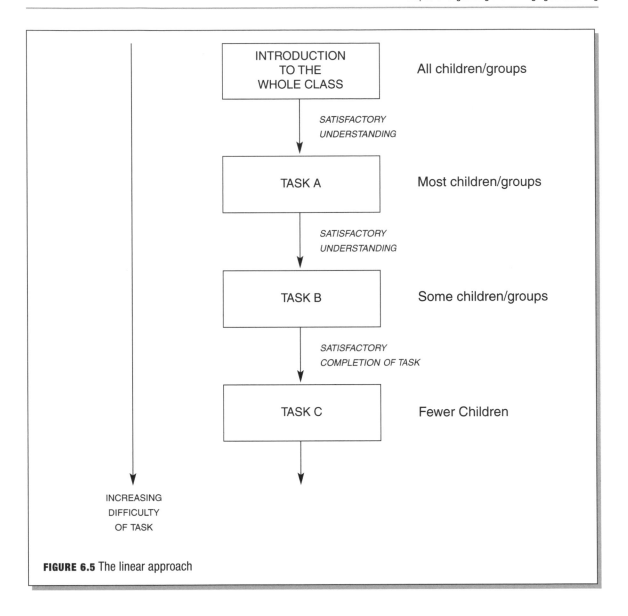

FIGURE 6.5 The linear approach

targets based on progress to date. The same issue applies to the children who were, for whatever reason, absent in earlier sessions.

Linear task management is sometimes used with worksheets in subjects like mathematics in which sequential learning is more easily planned or in topic areas where there are a number of different experiences and skills to be covered sequentially over a period of time. However, there are a number of challenges for teachers adopting this approach:

- Some children view the process as a competition to see who can be furthest along the line and consequently tend to rush ahead.

- Teachers can become overwhelmed by monitoring during the lesson, as they keep track of children completing different tasks at various times throughout a session.

- Children may be demoralised as they compare themselves unfavourably with their more capable classmates.

- Resourcing may become a problem if several groups reach the same task at the same time.

- Subsequent lessons can deteriorate into 'Carry on with the work you left off last time' and lack any direct teacher input.

- The gap between the less and more able becomes pronounced.

Teacher manuals usually stress the importance of maintaining a balance between teaching, task completion and review of work; nonetheless, it is possible for teachers to ignore the manual advice and lapse into a sedentary practice using the text as a surrogate teacher or make excessive use of activity sheets.

Activate your thinking!

All five groups in the class have completed task A, three have completed task B, one is part-way through task C and one group is ready to begin the final task. How will you begin the next session?

Good practice

Make sure that you, and not the textbook, do the teaching.

Circular task management

A second type of task management, following a whole-class introduction, is to organise learning using a circular approach. It differs from the linear in two important respects:

- Whereas with a linear approach children can work individually, in pairs or in groups, the circular approach relies on group work.

- Whereas children can proceed through the range of linear tasks at varying rates, the circular approach requires synchronised completion.

The circular approach can be used where groups are involved in working on different tasks from the same curriculum area (say, history) or tasks from different subject areas within a common theme (e.g. Festivals). Following the introduction, each group is allocated a specific task and given a time limit within which to complete it. To ensure that groups finish at about the same time requires meticulous planning. Teachers need to form groups so that they are of comparable size and ability, and provide sufficient resources so that each group engages with the full range of tasks. Managing resources is particularly important to the smooth flow of sessions. For instance, a lot of disruption can be caused if a group finds that some of the batteries are dead and the bulbs fade when it is their turn to try the circuit experiments. Circular tasks must be of equivalent length if the system is to have any chance of operating successfully. However, despite organising the activities in such a way that they require the same length of time to complete, some tasks inevitably take longer than others. This fact sometimes leads to an excessive reliance on 'holding tasks' for some groups (if they finish early) and undue pressure on others (if they take too long to complete).

Holding activities should not be confused with pointless ones! They are simply a device for ensuring that children who complete work earlier than expected are usefully and independently occupied before the time arrives for moving on to the next task. Groups that take longer than expected to finish will, of course, often receive additional help from the teacher or be encouraged to modify the original idea. However, it is inevitable that some slower workers will fail to complete the task fully in the given time.

Time is therefore an important factor in the circular approach, so as to maximise resource usage and maintain control, all groups must change task simultaneously (Figure 6.6, The circular approach). Once the allocated task has been completed by every group, tasks are reassigned. The children involved in the open-ended task may be given a creative task; the group practising skills may be given a planned investigation, and so on. The circular approach aims to give every child the opportunity to be involved in many different types of work over a given period.

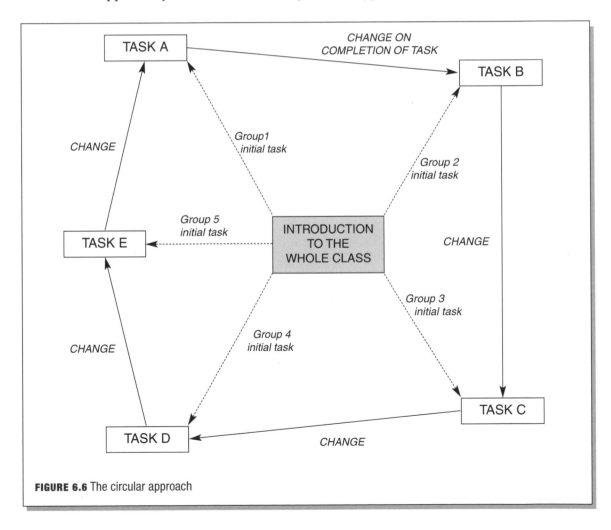

FIGURE 6.6 The circular approach

Many teachers discover that although the circular approach is challenging and difficult to organise, it is also motivating and stimulating when it works well. It is not advisable to attempt the circular approach unless you are convinced of its benefits over-and-above other approaches or in specialised situations with well established resources and prescribed activities (such as the whole class working on a series of designated science experiments).

Activate your thinking!

Half way through a set of activities based on a circular form of organisation, Angie returns from a music lesson, having missed a considerable amount of her group's previous two tasks. How can Angie be helped to catch up?

Staged task management

An alternative means of managing learning for the whole class is for children to be engaged in different subject activities at the same time within the same general topic. This form of organisation is rarely used owing to the introduction of structured teaching in literacy and numeracy, but offers an exciting alternative for ambitious teachers. Groups are normally based on academic ability. One group may be working on an aspect of maths, another group employing written English, a third group on artwork. If the groups consist of children with varying academic ability, then within each of these broad groupings, differentiation takes place *within* a single group rather than across groups. For instance, group 1, consisting of 12 children, may be sub-divided into two ability sub-groups for their maths work; group 2 may be in two sub-groups working in pairs on different aspects of reported speech for English; group 3 may be working together but be found at different stages in developing a composite picture in art. Thus, the following organisation exists in the same classroom:

Maths group: Two ability sub-groups
English group: Pairs work
Art group: Collaborative activities.

Sometimes the broad curriculum groupings are within the same topic or subject area. Thus, for the History unit about Explorers, group 1 may be finding out about the lives of individual explorers, group 2 plotting their courses on outline maps and group 3 writing about the realities and hardships of travel:

Group 1:   Researching the lives of explorers (cross-curricular skill)
Group 2:   Plotting journeys on a map (geography)
Group 3:   Writing about the hazards of travel (English).

In the subject area of music, a class of Year 1 children may be developing ideas about performing and composing:

Group 1:   Creating simple musical patterns using resonators

Group 2:   Experimenting with low notes using different shapes

Group 3:   Making plucking instruments.

A high level of organisation and planning is necessary where a number of groups of this type are involved, not only to ensure that they are clear about the tasks but also to manage their progress.

Sometimes a modified version of the staged approach is used if a whole-class enterprise is intended whereby the briefings all take place before any of the groups begin work on their specific activity. For instance, in a large space session where groups of children are working in the hall on a theme (different dance forms, say), the teacher may speak to the assembled class about each activity first so that when the groups are later drawn together, all the children are aware of what the others have been doing. If groups change activity at some point, the whole class briefing enables the transition to take place without further lengthy explanations. This approach demands that the children listen attentively throughout the teacher's explanations and understand the purpose of the final combined enterprise. In this modified version:

Stage 1:   All the children listen while each group is briefed.

Stage 2:   Separate groups are involved with their activities.

Stage 3:   Groups are brought together to discuss and share ideas.

Stage 4:   Activities are reassigned and the process continues.

The staged approach makes a number of demands:

- Instructions must be explicit
- Resources must be in place before the children are briefed
- The last group to be briefed should not be kept waiting too long
- The opening and closing minutes of a session are likely to be quite intensive.

In common with the linear and circular methods, the staged approach requires careful planning, attention to learning objectives and close monitoring of children's progress. Many teachers of younger children use a form of staged approach but only when there is a teaching assistant or another reliable adult available, as this makes this approach more manageable and less demanding on the teacher. In common with the circular approach, if groups swap activities at some mid-point in the session, the staged approach requires that tasks are of similar duration, that there is account taken of more and less able children, and that early finishers are not left without a purposeful activity.

Spoked task management

Probably the most common form of managing learning is to organise children into ability groups and provide a separate but related task for each of the groups. The introductory phase of the lesson brings all the children together for the purpose of explaining and exploring the topic, raising issues, asking questions and so forth, before sending the children to their activities. The number of groups will vary according to the pupils' ability and experience. Group size is typically around eight to ten children. Thus, in a class of 30, three or four different and suitable tasks have to be provided for the session, usually in the same subject area. At the end of the task phase, children complete their work and, where relevant, reconvene as a whole class to evaluate the learning, share findings and clarify points.

The spoked approach places a heavy burden of preparation on teachers, as it requires them to design a variety of activities, monitor progress across the range of tasks and evaluate separate outcomes. It has the advantage of targeting learning and facilitating differentiation.

Single task management

We have already been alerted to the importance of matching the demands of tasks with the ability and experience of the children. Poor matching leads to under-achievement (if the task is too easy) or frustration and low esteem (if the task is too hard). Alternative ways of differentiating are discussed more fully in the next two chapters.

The single task approach is used when every group is engaged on a similar task in a particular curriculum subject or area but the *teacher has different expectations* for each group, depending upon their ability and previous experience of the work. Following the introduction and explanation of the task, each group is allocated the same resources and given a similar length of time to complete the investigation, experiment or research. As part of this process, children write up the work in different ways. For instance, a low ability group may use more diagrammatic representations than the extended written forms used by a more able group. Towards the end of the time, the groups report and compare findings. The teacher is able to draw the various strands together, acknowledge the diversity of outcomes and weave them into a comprehensible set of conclusions (Figure 6.7, Single task approach). The single task approach offers a number of advantages:

- A single set of learning objectives can be established which apply to all pupils
- The process is relatively easily managed
- All the children are involved throughout the lesson
- Groups of children do not have to wait around to receive instructions before commencing their task
- The teacher is able to make reference to the progress of other groups working on the same or similar task.

There are also disadvantages, as follows:

- The single task has to be carefully planned and appropriate to every child
- There have to be sufficient resources for everyone to do the same activity at the same time
- Group composition has to be appropriate to avoid children becoming marginalised
- The teacher requires a high level of skill to draw out all the learning points in a way which can be understood by all the children.

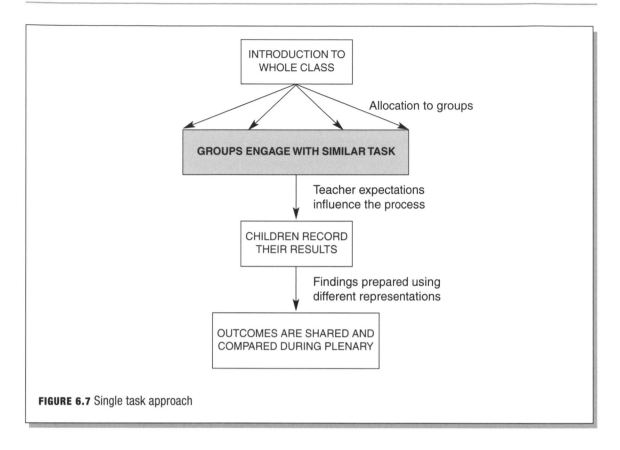

FIGURE 6.7 Single task approach

The single task approach, like any other, is better under certain circumstances than others. In particular, it has value in investigative, open-ended tasks in which collaboration and whole-class sharing are significant. However, the principle is also embodied in the NLS and NNS in which lesson objectives are common for the whole class and the children tend to be allocated similar group tasks to support learning. Owing to the fact that the single task approach is relatively easy to manage compared with others referred to above, it dominates much of formal primary education.

Stepped task management

The stepped approach is most commonly used in organising and managing large space lessons (PE, gymnastics, games and drama) and requires specific and detailed explanations/demonstrations by the teacher, followed by more independent activities by pupils. In the stepped approach, all the children are introduced to an elementary task, which they then explore or practise for a given length of time, followed by increasingly complex tasks, each of which is engaged with. Thus:

TASK ONE (elementary) leads on to TASK TWO (more involved) leads on to TASK THREE (most complex)

It is often the case that the teacher encourages children to try a form of the activity on their own initially, then (say) in pairs, then as a small group. Depending on the theme and subject, it may even be appropriate to bring the whole class together to demonstrate progress, group by group. The overall whole-class management for each task may look like this, beginning with the elementary task:

- The teacher introduces the activity and explains/demonstrates what the children have to do.
- The children practise the skills individually or in pairs.
- Individuals or pairs combine to create small groups, who work together.
- Each group takes a turn to show what it has done to the rest of the class.

Once the teacher is happy that the first task is successfully completed, the class is brought together and the second task is explained or demonstrated. Depending on the nature of the task, children repeat the sequence noted above or work in small groups immediately. The pattern is repeated for the third task, and so on.

One advantage of the stepped approach is that it enables you to explore each step fully until you are satisfied with the product. If the children are not progressing as you hoped they would, you can spend longer on enhancing the skills or techniques required, rehearse the ideas and repeat the activities. If they make more rapid progress, it is relatively simple to move on to the next task with minimum delay or offer the children the opportunity to explore the theme to promote initiative and creativity. An example will help to illustrate the approach. Example: *The impact of heat on life forms (movement and drama)*

- Year 4 children have been working with their teacher on the cross-curricular topic of 'heat', noting the variations in climate in different countries and the effects of extreme temperatures on human habitation, fauna and flora. The teacher wants to employ some of the concepts in drama and, as it is November, decides to use the familiar phenomenon of melting ice (as the weather is getting colder) and burning branches (after Bonfire Night celebrations).

- In the hall, the children warm up 'on the spot' individually by stretching and moving different parts of their bodies, to raise awareness of the movement possibilities and limitations, guided through each step by the teacher. Children with limited mobility are encouraged to contribute at their own level of physical comfort.

- The teacher concentrates the children's attention on fine motor skills and less obvious body movements, such as use of fingers, facial muscles, shoulders, hips and toes. Children are asked to 'melt down like a snowman in the heat' as a task that will enable them to practise the movements. Initially, the children just collapse in a heap, but the teacher uses a tambourine to sound out first ten, then 15, then 20 beats as the time frame for the task.

- After a minute or two of individual effort, the teacher then asks the children to work in pairs and rehearse the 'melt down' while facing each other, again using a 20 beat time frame, trying to co-ordinate their actions so that they finish simultaneously (as puddles on the floor).

- The teacher asks for volunteer pairs to demonstrate their actions to the rest of the class and selects three of them, commending and pointing out features of their actions.

- While the children sit and listen, the teacher plays some music from the film *The Snowman* to remind them about the dance of the snowmen scene and the melting that happens to the main snowman character at the end of the film. (The TA is responsible for controlling the CD player so that the teacher can concentrate on class management.)

- The children individually explore larger movements associated with the dancing, each child in a separate area of the hall to avoid accidentally hitting one another. The teacher moves about commenting on the actions, suggesting alternatives and offering advice.

- The teacher asks the children to explore in pairs, then in double pairs to create a foursome.

- The teacher asks for volunteers as before to demonstrate their ideas to the rest of the class.

- Finally, the teacher asks the children to combine their dance and the 'melting down to a puddle' movements, first individually, then in pairs, then in groups, using the music as before.

- Realising that there is insufficient time to explore the burning tree activity, the teacher decides to postpone it until the following lesson rather than force it into the small amount of remaining time. Consequently, the children stay in their prostrate positions while the teacher moves quietly around the room, sprinkling some 'magic dust' on them as a signal that they are to 'come alive' and sit up straight.

- Before returning to the classroom, the teacher spends the last two minutes raising some of the issues from the movement and drama, praising their hard work, inviting comment about the impact of heat and cold on life forms, and linking the comments to work being undertaken for the topic.

- The children return to the classroom.

During the next movement lesson, the teacher spends a short time reminding the children about the previous work, practising some of the movements associated with melting, and introducing the 'burning trees' theme. She stresses the importance of fire safety issues and the devastation that can occur when people are careless, but also explains that burning can destroy pests and reinvigorate growth. The lesson follows a similar pattern to the one described above but concentrates on the effects of wood as it turns to charcoal/ash 'from the tips of fingers (twigs) to the end of toes (roots)'. In the later stages of the lesson, the teacher puts the children into groups to explore fire spreading across a forest, tree by tree, until all the children have become piles of charred and smoking charcoal/ash. The process is then reversed as the 'new growth' eventually creates young saplings that bend and sway in the breeze as they reach for the sky. Finally, the process is brought together in an extended performance, with appropriate supporting music, from the first burning to the final resurrection!

There are many teaching skills employed in this example but for the purpose of this section on managing the whole class, it may be seen that although the basic format was straightforward, it required a lot of thought and preparation to ensure the best outcome. In practice, the lesson did not progress in the smooth way that the above description might portray (it seldom does!) but the stepped principle of exploring thoroughly a relatively easily-controlled task before moving on to a slightly more complex one is clear to see.

Managing the learning of young children

There are numerous teaching strategies required for the effective management of young children, such as clarity of explanation, use of repetition, setting a number of short-term goals, active use of TAs and development of reading skills. Drake (2003) offers a variety of practical ideas and activities for all early years' practitioners. However, the most important reference document for the Foundation Stage is *Curriculum Guidance for the Foundation Stage* (QCA/DfES 2000). The information is intended to help practitioners plan to meet the diverse needs of all children to take them beyond the Early Learning Goals by the end of the Foundation Stage. The document offers guidance on teaching and learning, planning and assessment for children before they commence on the formal National Curriculum programme. Use of the term 'foundation' in government documentation is a controversial one (Fisher 2002), implying as it does that early learning provides the necessary bedrock for further learning and is not valuable in its own right. The early learning goals include six areas of learning and 'stepping stones' of progress towards the goals. The guidance provided in the document clarifies strategies by which teachers and other adults working in educational settings can help children to make optimum progress. The six areas of learning are organised as follows:

- Personal, social and emotional development
- Communication, language and literacy
- Mathematical development
- Knowledge and understanding of the world
- Physical development
- Creative development.

Curriculum Guidance for the Foundation Stage contains examples to help teachers and support staff identify the progress that children are making and suggests how the practitioner can use this information to support and consolidate learning and help children to make progress. The Foundation Stage guidance is intended to help teachers and other adult practitioners ensure that each child is given the opportunity to make good progress towards the early learning goals and in a few cases to go beyond them. The sections entitled 'communication, language and literacy' and 'mathematical development' cover the Foundation Stage for children aged three to the end of the reception year. The early learning goals synchronise with the objectives in the frameworks for teaching literacy and mathematics throughout the reception year, facilitating ease of planning. Reception teachers have a choice about whether to cover the elements of the literacy hour and daily mathematics lesson across the day or in a single unit of time (a 'lesson'). In order to ensure a smooth transition to the literacy hour and daily mathematics lesson during Year 1 (children aged five to six years), both are intended to be in place by the end of the reception year.

The curriculum guidance document stresses that the six areas are intended to help practitioners plan the learning environment, activities and experiences for children, and provide a framework for the early years' curriculum. However, this does not mean that young children's learning needs to be divided into separate and distinct areas, but rather that the document assists teachers in organising the curriculum. Thus, one 'unit' of experience may provide a child with opportunities to develop a number of competencies, skills and concepts across several areas of learning. For instance, creating a 'shop' area may help children to develop social skills, communicate their ideas to others, handle elementary money exchanges and use their experiences from shopping as a guide to appropriate behaviour when dealing with people. Thus, children can develop language, mathematical, physical, personal and social competencies through a single activity, though it is far from easy for a teacher to monitor progress and development in each area for every child when using this 'mixed economy' approach.

The early learning goals establish expectations that most children are likely to reach by the end of the Foundation Stage, but are not intended to provide a curriculum. The six areas (above) provide a structure for planning throughout the Foundation Stage, to be built on for future learning. By the end of the Foundation Stage, it is likely that some children will have exceeded the goals, whereas other children will be working towards some or all of them. Those who are still 'working towards' normally include younger children (summer born), those without early years' experience (such as nursery education), those with special educational needs and those learning English as an additional language (EAL).

The guidance identifies 'stepping stones' of progress towards the early learning goals and so helps practitioners to understand and interpret what the goals mean for young children throughout the Foundation Stage. The stepping stones identify the sorts of knowledge, skills, understanding and attitudes that children need if they are to achieve these early learning goals by the end of the Foundation Stage. Progression is shown by the use of yellow, then blue and then green bands that are not intended to be age-related goals, and the number of steps varies between and within areas of learning. In some cases the stepping stones relate to an individual aspect of an early learning goal, while in others a group of closely linked aspects are brought together.

Although the stepping stones are not age-related, it is anticipated that most three-year-old children in the Foundation Stage will be better described by the steps described through the yellow band, while the green band will usually reflect the attainment of five-year-old children. Although the stepping stones tend to be presented in a hierarchical order, not all children conform to this sequence of learning. For example, some children will attain confidence in some of the later stepping stones but struggle with some of the earlier ones. Again, some stepping stones will be achieved quickly, whereas others will take a lot longer. However, if all goes well, as children move from one stone to another, they should take with them what they have already learned and continue to practise, refine and use their previous learning.

Once children reach the reception class, the teacher in charge has a major responsibility in monitoring and assessing children's competence and progress. Completion of the full schedule is onerous. Many versions of this 'baseline assessment' have been employed.

The National Literacy Strategy

The National Literacy Strategy was launched in 1998 as part of the government's attempts to raise standards in schools (DfEE, 1998a). Basic literacy involves the ability to read and write, speak and listen; however, fuller details were included in this framework document and required that literate primary pupils should be able to:

- Read and write with confidence, fluency and understanding
- Use reading cues to monitor their reading and correct mistakes
- Use the phonic system to read accurately
- Use the spelling system to spell accurately
- Have fluent and legible handwriting
- Have interest in developing a fuller vocabulary
- Write using a range of genres
- Be familiar with narrative structures
- Use and understand non-fiction texts
- Plan, draft, revise and edit their own writing
- Use a suitable technical vocabulary to discuss their reading and writing
- Be interested in books and evaluate their content
- Develop powers of imagination, inventiveness and critical awareness through reading and writing.

(Fuller details can be found on pages 3–5 of the document)

The structure for teaching literacy focuses on reading and writing objectives linked to designated texts. Except in the case of reception age children, the objectives are sub-divided for each term. Key Stage 2 objectives assume that pupils will have attained a basic level of reading fluency, so that by Year 3 the majority of children should be able to:

- read simple narrative and information texts with confidence
- read aloud accurately and silently with understanding

Consolidation and development of these skills are expected to take place over Years 3 and 4 and beyond. Three 'strands' to literacy work are identified for all children:

- Word level: emphasising phonics, spelling and vocabulary
- Sentence level: emphasising grammar and punctuation
- Text level: emphasising comprehension and composition

Details about curriculum content are contained within the closely prescribed framework. Teachers are only given a small amount of flexibility in the way they plan and teach literacy as the structure of the literacy hour itself is tightly defined. Thus, the first 15 minutes should be spent on shared reading and writing with the whole class using the appropriate text; the second 15 minutes with the whole class examining phonics and spelling (at Key Stage 1) and spelling, vocabulary, grammar and punctuation (at Key Stage 2). The next 20 minutes is devoted to group and independent activities; teachers should organise the class in such a way that they can give close attention to one or two groups while other children work independently on reading and writing tasks. Finally, the remaining ten minutes requires the teacher to bring the whole class together for a plenary session in which reviewing, reflection and consolidation can take place.

It is obvious that the literacy hour does not allow much flexibility in terms of teaching approach. However, there are a number of factors to take into account when planning the lesson:

1 Time management is very important. The clock takes centre stage during the literacy hour!

2 The first half-hour or so spent teaching the whole class requires a lot of careful preparation so that the necessary text, sentence and word 'levels' can be addressed.

3 The pace of teaching must be sufficiently fast to engage the children's interest, while sufficiently measured to ensure that they have time to think about and absorb its content.

4 Verbal interaction with children should involve an opportunity for them to contribute to the lesson and not merely sit listening to the teacher.

5 Time must be allocated in planning the various differentiated tasks for the whole class during the 'group and independent work' phase.

6 Children work at differing speeds and it is important to ensure that the tasks allow every child to succeed, while offering more able (or faster) workers the opportunity to extend their understanding.

7 Gathering children together for the plenary phase is likely to be more successful if a few minutes' warning is given before they are told to complete their work.

8 Due to the tight schedule of the hour, unfinished and hurried work may become more common.

There are also some practical points to consider. If children come straight from an assembly, they may already have been sitting on a hard floor for quite a long time; further sitting still can mean that too much is being expected of their patience! Similarly, if children come in from the playground (especially on a windy day) they will take a few minutes to settle. It is often worth giving them a 'settling task' for a few minutes before asking them to come together for the opening phase of the literacy hour.

The Literacy Hour Framework is meant to introduce common practices and routines across the school in order that the quality of teaching and its impact upon pupils' achievements can be easily monitored. It does, however, require a considerable amount of effort on the part of teachers and pupils to maintain the approach from day to day. As such, it is important to avoid any sense of 'here we go again' but rather to use the time as a stimulating opportunity to interact with children and establish a sound basis for other curriculum work.

Activate your thinking!

Towards the end of the group time the children are still engrossed in their work. What factors would you take account of in deciding whether to allow them additional time or move to the next phase of the lesson?

Good practice

Never assume that the so-called 'independent' group can be fully independent. Spend extra time explaining the task to avoid a situation in which the children are struggling to cope. At the same time, always introduce a straightforward open-ended element to engage their interest, should they conclude the main activity sooner than anticipated.

It is worth noting that Hardman, Smith and Wall (2003) noted that during literacy lessons, even teachers that used a strongly interactive style tended to focus on question and answer that required low cognition and asked only a small number of genuinely challenging questions that caused pupils to think hard. Teachers were also inclined to accept brief answers from children instead of probing what they had said and encouraging them to think more deeply. The teachers who were willing to dwell on a topic of interest for a little longer generally elicited more thoughtful and extensive responses. Teachers of younger children were especially prone to accepting superficial answers and opportunities for sustained and extended dialogue were rare. For further information about questioning, see the section devoted to this subject in Chapter 5 and Moyles 2003.

The National Numeracy Strategy

The National Numeracy Strategy was implemented in September 1999 in an attempt to raise teachers' expectations and improve standards in mathematics (DfEE, 1999a). The National Numeracy Project defines numeracy as follows:

Numeracy means knowing about numbers and number operations. More than this, it requires an ability and inclination to solve numerical problems, including those involving money or measures. It also demands familiarity with the ways in which numerical information is gathered by counting and measuring, and is presented in graphs, charts and tables (DfEE, 1999a, page 6).

Every teacher has to teach maths daily for between 45 minutes and an hour and lessons should, ideally, incorporate the following elements:

- Regular oral and mental work
- Good quality questioning to the whole class
- A variety of whole-class teaching and group work
- Instruction, demonstration and explanation
- Formal and informal assessment of pupils' progress
- Identifying and correcting pupils' misconceptions

The Numeracy Strategy encourages teaching approaches which give more emphasis to oral and mental work before written methods are introduced. As calculation skills require that pupils must learn some things by heart, daily practice to reinforce their grasp of the facts is essential, supported by the use of correct vocabulary and notation. Numeracy should, wherever possible, be used in subject areas outside the immediate maths lesson.

Effective teaching involves using whole-class teaching as a means for pupils to respond to questions, ask their own questions, learn from one another and explain where they are unsure about mathematical concepts or techniques. Teachers must be ready to listen closely to what children are saying and offer comment which helps them think 'beyond' the immediate problem and consider the way that maths influences real-life situations.

Group work should be differentiated with respect to pupils' attainment, though creating too many groups may be counter-productive as classroom management becomes difficult due to the spread of demands upon the teacher's time. Paired work may be helpful, with activities such as number games where pupils can probe one another's thinking and interact purposefully. Individual work also has its place in teaching maths; however, too much individual work may lead to teachers spending too much time 'troubleshooting' and not enough time on teaching strategies for solving problems.

Finally, parents are important in promoting positive attitudes towards maths and supporting their children's learning of numeracy. As such, regular homework and close liaison between parents and schools is essential. Nevertheless, teachers and head teachers will have to bear in mind that some parents have a negative attitude to maths and others do not possess more than a basic level of understanding of the subject. Children from weak academic backgrounds may be further disadvantaged if parents respond negatively to a school's request for their help. Similarly, account needs to be taken of children with SEN and English as an additional language in determining the most effective teaching approaches.

Activate your thinking!

How much mental agility do the children require to respond to your questions? How much opportunity do you give them to ponder problems at length?

The use of ICT

We have, over recent years, seen a significant change in the status of Information and Communications Technology in primary schools, leading to a situation in which it is now considered to be one of the 'core' areas of the curriculum, alongside English, mathematics and science. The Government has also shown itself to be committed to supporting the development of ICT in education. The White Paper *Excellence in School*, for example, stated that 'We are determined to create a society where, within ten years, information and communications technology (ICT) has permeated every aspect of education' (DfEE 1997). This support has taken the form of increased funding for equipment and the training of all teachers.

The Standards for the award of qualified teacher status state that Information and Communications Technology (ICT) has an important role to play in most aspects of teachers' work in schools: in teaching and learning for individuals, small groups and whole classes; and in planning, assessment, evaluation, administration and management. The Professional Standards for Qualified Teacher Status sets out two aspects of ICT competence which trainees can be expected to develop and demonstrate:

- How best to use ICT to teach the subject(s) they are trained to teach, and
- Their own ICT skills, which will allow them to, for example, complete pupils' records of progress, prepare resources for pupils and keep to a minimum their administrative tasks.

In each of these two aspects, trainees' expertise should be such that they can easily identify opportunities to use ICT and know how to do so confidently and independently (DfES/TTA 2002).

With respect to identifying opportunities, it should be stressed that the use of ICT must clearly support good practice in teaching the subject concerned. It can, for example, enable the teacher to respond to a pupil's piece of writing at different stages of the process due to the fact that the text could be saved and progressively modified over a period of time. Within the context of mathematics, a child can be encouraged to develop logical thinking from an activity which involves instructing a programmable robot (i.e. Roamer) to follow a particular path, and then to modify these instructions in the light of the robot's movement.

The second point is associated with a teacher's ability to use ICT in a way that supports their own professional role. Commonly, teachers download the latest guidance for aspects of teaching such as 'support for early years' from the OFSTED website, or using a wordprocessor to prepare a standardised template for lesson planning, or even attempting to find the desired teaching post on 'TES Jobs' (www.tesjobs.co.uk).

The National Curriculum for ICT

The statutory statement on the use of information and communication technology across the curriculum within the National Curriculum states that pupils should be given opportunities to apply and develop their ICT capability through the use of ICT tools to support their learning in all subjects with the exception of physical education at Key Stages 1 and 2 (DfEE/QCA 1999). The document goes on to say that pupils use ICT tools to find, explore, analyse, exchange and present information responsibly, creatively and with discrimination. They learn how to employ ICT to enable rapid access to ideas and experiences from a wide range of people, communities and cultures. Increased capability in the use of ICT promotes initiative and independent learning, with pupils being able to make informed judgements about when and where to use ICT to best effect.

Organisation of ICT resources

Schools will organise their ICT resources in different ways, according to the number of computers that they have and also the space that is available to house them. Decisions about organisation may also be influenced by a teacher's preferences with regard to teaching and learning style. Many schools will have one or more computer suites which could be used to accommodate large groups or even a whole class of children such that they can all work at the computers at the same time. The suite will often consist of a room that can either be booked in advance by the teacher or will be timetabled for each class throughout the week. Some teachers will continue to have one or more computers in their own classroom, enabling the children to make use of it throughout the day.

Over recent years an increasing number of schools are purchasing *interactive whiteboards* for use in the classroom. These have proved to be particularly effective in whole-class teaching situations; for example, as part of a literacy or numeracy lesson. Another way that schools have chosen to deploy their ICT resources is set up clusters of computers in, for example, the library or other open-access areas around the building. A much more flexible solution to the problem of providing access to ICT for the pupils is to employ portable computers, that can be moved to wherever the children happen to be working, which may be outside the classroom (or even outside the school).

Management of self

Enthusiasm in teaching is important and can sometimes compensate for other shortcomings. However, as noted in Chapter 2, even the greatest enthusiasm fades in the fierce glare of regular classroom commitments and other school responsibilities, which drain and enervate. All too easily, the early gush of commitment to the job can be replaced by the heaviness of fatigue, so it is important to keep things in perspective and take note of the fact that:

- Teachers are only one of the children's educators
- Children suffer if teachers work so hard that they become exhausted
- Every teacher has poor lessons from time to time
- Mistakes are inevitable and should be viewed constructively rather than as a cause for despair.

Teaching is both exhilarating and tiring. Exhilarating because of the engagement in an exciting and stimulating process; tiring because of the constant expenditure of effort to ensure that the children are learning and on-task. The personal satisfaction gained as a result of a good lesson can keep a teacher fresh and in good spirits long after it is finished. Tiredness, on the other hand, can lead to listlessness and a distorted sense of priorities. Minor problems expand and fill the horizon. A tutor's constructive advice feels like a major reprimand. A lively group of children comes across as an untamed rabble!

In addition, sensible pacing throughout each lesson and pausing from time to time to enable body and mind to relax are essential for combating fatigue. It is possible to retain a relaxed yet purposeful approach during lessons if you:

- Feel in control of the situation
- Provide appropriate learning opportunities for the children
- Do not attempt to achieve too much in a single lesson
- Ensure that the children work as hard as you!

If every lesson is spent hauling the class along, like a mule pulling a cart through a swamp, then it is little wonder that teachers tire quickly. If they flit from one child to another in an effort to respond to everyone's questions, behaviour and demands, they will soon feel exhausted and dispirited. If they spend most of the lesson on direct teaching, leaving themselves little time to recover between sessions, their energy level will drop rapidly. Good teachers do not exhibit manic behaviour but pace themselves in such a way that over the weeks and months of the term they can maintain the consistency necessary for effectiveness. Teachers should not, therefore:

- Spend too much time talking during a session
- Rush around doing things for the children that they can do for themselves
- Feel guilty that they are not 'actively on task' for every moment of a session.

Teachers should make sure, however, that they:

- Leave opportunity for moving around the class to monitor and praise the children in their work
- Encourage children to be independent and try to resolve their own problems
- Step back from the flurry of activity and review the success of their classroom management.

Activate your thinking!

It is generally agreed that an on-task work rate of about 75 per cent is reasonable. How do the children and you compare with this figure? How do you know?

Management of self can be compared to an aeroplane pilot who sometimes has to grip the controls and steer the plane in a predetermined flightpath, sometimes has to manoeuvre and change course if the conditions demand it and sometimes puts the plane on automatic pilot to chat with crew and passengers. For the pilot, different amounts of concentration are required at different stages of the journey. The take-off and landing present the most hazardous and stressful stages, whereas the main part of the journey allows for moments of relaxation and flexibility. There would be a sharp decrease in air travel if passengers believed that the pilot was continuously under pressure! Similarly, those teachers who never use the 'auto-pilot' during a session have either failed to plan their lessons appropriately or fear that if they take their hands off the controls for two minutes the enterprise will crash.

Unless teachers find some time for stepping back and gaining an overall impression of the children's progress and the direction of the lesson, they will be swept along from start to finish and feel more tired than the children by the end of it. Unfortunately, some teachers feel guilty about separating themselves from the main action for a time, either because they think that they will be failing in their job or because they fear disruptive behaviour. These concerns are understandable but unnecessary since:

- The well organised lesson does not require constant teacher intervention and interaction with pupils. It should be possible to stand still for a few moments and scan the class without the lesson falling apart
- Stepping back actually enhances the teacher's ability to monitor and assess the situation and take appropriate action or make suitable responses.

Activate your thinking!

Who is most tired at the end of the session, you or the children?

Good practice

Find a way to isolate yourself from the class for a minute or two each lesson whenever possible by standing at a particular spot in the room with your arms folded to observe what is happening without being disturbed. If you let the children know what you are doing they will soon stop bothering you because they know this is your 'time-out'.

Case study

A group of six Year 2 children, mixed ability and academically weak, were working with a trainee teacher, Mia, in an art area adjacent to the main classroom. The area had two tables, a sink, a workbench and various science and technology resources. Mia planned to introduce the lesson by reference to previous work and explain what the children were to do. She was going to instruct them to pour lukewarm water into glass bottles and wrap them in different materials (secured with elastic bands) to insulate them. The children's task would then be to measure the temperature immediately and then after a ten-minute interval. Mia hoped that in doing so they would come to realise that the temperature loss was different depending on the material used and thereby reinforce the concept of insulation.

During the ten-minute 'cooling time' interval, Mia decided to engage the children in a series of questions and answers so that they would not become restless. After that time she would let them measure the water temperature a second time, feel the outside of the bottle and make statements about the insulation properties of the materials. Finally, she thought that it would be a good idea for the children to share their experiences in a plenary, in which she would record their answers on a large sheet of paper under three main headings: *What we did/What happened/What this means*.

The problems

The lesson idea was sound and the practical work had the potential to take learning forward and engage the children's enthusiastic participation. However, by the end of the session Mia was weary, frustrated and a bit depressed about the children's fractious behaviour and way the lesson had deteriorated. The reasons for this disappointing outcome can be explained as follows.

First, Mia did not clarify the significance of the current work for the children or explain what she hoped they would learn. Consequently, it seemed to the children as if they were being taken on a 'mystery tour' rather than having a reasonably clear idea about their ultimate destination. Second, there were a variety of organisational and management problems that Mia had failed to foresee:

■ The bottles were made of glass and potentially hazardous.

■ Water spilt over the table and soaked some of the photocopied sheets.

■ The scissors were not sharp enough to cut the material properly, which meant that the children became reliant on adult help and the process was slowed.

■ The thermometers were too closely calibrated and difficult for children to read.

■ Children held the thermometers in the water so that they touched the bottom of the bottle, thereby giving a false reading.

■ The slowness of the wrapping meant that considerable temperature losses occurred before the insulation material could be placed around the bottle.

■ Children fiddled with the bottles and fabrics during the question-and-answer time, annoying the trainee and souring the atmosphere.

■ The process of writing down children's responses onto the sheet of paper was ponderous for the teacher and difficult for them to read due to her hurried scrawl.

Most worryingly, Mia had not grasped the basic scientific principle for herself. When the children felt the warmth coming through to the outside of the bottles, they ignored the data from the temperature measurements (though in fact they were generally inaccurate) and assumed that the warmest bottle was the best insulated when, in fact, it was the other way around. Far from explaining the true situation, Mia brightly confirmed their comments and commended them for getting things correct!

Activate your thinking!

How could some or all of these problems have been avoided?

Possible lesson modifications

As well as taking a few moments to tell the children why they were about to perform the experiment and giving them opportunities to ask questions, clarify their concerns, chat to a friend or offer suggestions, Mia could have taken a number of simple steps to ensure that the organisation and management of the lesson was more effective. Thus:

- Use plastic bottles instead of glass.
- Use funnels for pouring the water.
- Pre-cut the material.
- Use larger calibration thermometers.
- Train the children to hold the thermometers correctly before commencing the practical work.
- Place bottles out of reach on the shelf while the question-and-answer session takes place.
- Give more time to explaining the insulation concept.
- Supply children with activity sheets with boxes to tick or colour as a means of self-recording.

Comment

As a lot of time was spent coping with practicalities, not enough time was left to give a sufficiently rigorous explanation about the key concepts. The lesson was highly teacher-directed, which meant that the children did not have the opportunity to explore ideas or modify the proceedings. A more successful outcome could have been gained by thinking more carefully in advance about the organisational implications. In the prevailing circumstances, there was little sense of enthusiasm among the children.

Standards

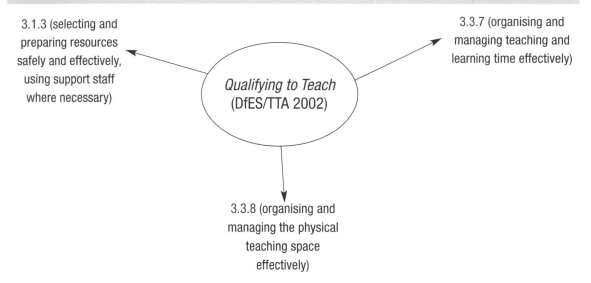

3.1.3 (selecting and preparing resources safely and effectively, using support staff where necessary)

Qualifying to Teach (DfES/TTA 2002)

3.3.7 (organising and managing teaching and learning time effectively)

3.3.8 (organising and managing the physical teaching space effectively)

Further reading

Drake, J. (2003) *Organising Play in the Early Years*, London: David Fulton.
Full of interesting ideas and activities that provide plenty of useful material for teachers of younger children.

Hayes, D. (2003) *Planning, Teaching and Class Management in Primary Schools*, London: David Fulton.
The book covers the relevant standards and offers strategies for their practical application and successful attainment.

Assessment, Recording and Reporting

Introduction

In this chapter, we explore the many facets of the assessment process, ways in which information about children can be recorded and some techniques for reporting to parents and colleagues. An exploration of formative and summative assessment, the importance of monitoring and intervention, and the factors influencing a teacher's judgement about children's work form the balance of the chapter.

ASSESSMENT

Forms of assessment

The close relationship between effective planning, monitoring of progress and assessment that informs further planning has been a theme throughout this book. The importance of clarifying learning objectives and appropriately differentiating work to take account of children of varying abilities has been placed firmly at the heart of the teaching and learning process. In particular, any assessment of children's progress has to be considered within the teaching programme as a whole, for pupil progress is not only an indicator of children's ability, but of the appropriateness of the curriculum provision and the skill of the teacher to motivate and inspire. Assessment should not be viewed in isolation but as part of a broader picture which is built up over time by teachers' evaluation of pupils' progress and, where appropriate, results from formal tests. The teacher's role in the process is crucial as children are observed daily and a picture of their understanding and attainment is acquired through regular verbal and social interaction in the classroom setting. As Stierer *et al.*, (1993) rightly comment:

> . . . the assessment of young children can only be valid and authentic when it is achieved through the gradual building up of a picture of the child based upon evidence collected over time in a range of everyday contexts (page 9).

Lloyd and Beard (1995) argue that assessment opportunities exist whenever children are working alone, in a group, on problem-solving activities, in fantasy play and in the playground, as well as in the structured classroom environment. Drummond (1993, 2003) similarly argues that assessment involves far more than pragmatic procedural conformity or a means of social control. Rather, assessment makes 'moral and philosophical demands on our thinking...The practice of effective assessment requires a thorough understanding and acceptance of the concept of rights, responsibility and power, lying at the heart of our work as teachers' (page 11). Drummond offers numerous examples from classroom practice to unravel the complexity of children's learning. She insists that whatever the external requirements of product-focused assessment, teachers must be aware of the sense of personal failure that assessments can engender. Drummond suggests that all educators are alert to three fundamental questions in respect of learning: (1) What is there to see? (2) How best can we understand what we see? (3) How can we put our understanding to good use? However, as explored in Chapter 4, it is often a challenge for teachers to know what children know! Indeed, the notion that a teacher can look into the head of each and every child to ascertain precisely what the child understands about every aspect of every subject is clearly impossible. And even if it *were* possible to do so, devising a programme of work and teaching approach to fully respond to all the vagaries of children's knowledge and understanding would make equally impossible demands of practitioners. In reality, assessment helps teachers to understand better where children are placed with regard to key concepts and the acquisition of facts. It is only the children who can make sense of things and establish meaning for themselves. Assessment, therefore, is a process to assist teachers in facilitating learning but not a guarantee of it.

Assessment takes many different forms, some of which are carried out formally in response to specific criteria and others that are rooted in regular classroom interactions. However, with regard to assessment criteria, it is important to focus on concepts and skills, and not on superficial factors. For instance, a design and technology experiment that involves children creating a wheeled vehicle to ascertain (say) factors influencing movement down a slope, assessment criteria should relate to the conceptual principles underpinning the lesson rather than the ability to handle materials. Thus, criteria might include (a) understanding that there is a causal relationship between incline and speed, (b) the ability to make comparisons between the performances of varied types of moving object, and so forth. The criteria that focus on learning are different in kind, and more important, than those of a functional nature, such as being able to construct a moving object or use materials appropriately. Assessment has a number of implications for teaching:

All assessments should help teachers plan more effectively

Assessment is of little value in its own right unless teachers use the results to modify their practice, teaching approach and curriculum content. The quality of children's learning, their ability to co-operate and collaborate, and the continuity of experience all contribute to the evidence upon which teachers can base amendments to the teaching programme.

Assessments can have important consequences for a child's future

If assessments are used as a basis for decisions about competence, allocation to groups and (in some cases) future school placement, there needs to be confirmatory evidence which can be used for verification. Some schools maintain records that consist of photocopied samples of children's work taken (say) once per term to illustrate the sort of progress that they are making over time.

Assessments have implications for the school and its staff

The results of national assessments (SATs) are used as a measure of a school's effectiveness. A lot of time is spent by teachers of Year 2 and Year 6 children in preparing them for the end-of-key-stage tests. The results of the KS2 tests are collated and published.

For all teachers, assessment involves a great deal of informal data gathered throughout the day as pupils work with set tasks. This informal assessment is carried out by listening to what children say, watching the mistakes they make, reflecting on the reasons for errors and misconceptions and asking questions to clarify the extent of their understanding. Interestingly, in their study of effective primary teaching Gipps *et al.* (1999) found that 'Over half the teachers explained that they used listening as an assessment technique' (page 81). In doing so, teachers have to recognise that children's mistakes can be due to misunderstanding about what is required rather than the inability to grasp the concept. A poorly produced piece of work may say more about motivation, misunderstanding or uncertainty about the task than a lack of conceptual understanding.

Teachers often find it helpful to use *elicitation* techniques to gain a clearer picture about the things that children know, understand and have experienced. In addition to information gleaned through discussion and question-and-answer, three elicitation methods are helpful:

1 Divide the children into pairs or small groups with a blank sheet of paper and ask them to write down as many words associated with the topic that they can think of. Groups of younger children require direct adult assistance with the task.

2 As in 1 above but give the children a number of key words or phrases (five, say) to use as starting points for a 'bike wheel' diagram, with spokes from the centre and other associated words written at the end of each spoke.

3 As in 2 above but incorporating pictures, diagrams and other visual representations.

Following this opportunity to record their ideas, the information on the sheets can be shared with the rest of the class and, perhaps, placed around the room on temporary display.

Assessment based on the Foundation Stage curriculum helps teachers to develop a richer and more diverse perspective on the attributes that children should be encouraged to develop, using the following ten headings:

1 Personal, social and emotional wellbeing of children.

2 Attitude and disposition to learning.

3 Social skills.

4 Attention skills and persistence.

5 Language and communication skills.

6 Reading and writing skills.

7   Mathematical ability.

8   Knowledge and understanding of the world.

9   Physical development.

10 Creative development.

When considering the development of 'the whole child' these Foundation Stage assessment points remind us that while academic prowess is important, educational progress involves the heart and mind, as well as the head. There are some key qualities (such as creativity) which, though they defy quantitative measurement, are nevertheless prized attributes if children are to attain their potential and eventually become thinking, responsible adults.

Taking account of circumstances

Carrying out effective assessment for every child in the class is a demanding and difficult skill and requires teachers to be alert and closely engaged with children's understanding of the work. Wragg (1997) reminds us that in the classroom environment, where so much is happening so quickly, 'teachers have to think on their feet and are denied the luxury of hours of reflection over each of their pedagogical choices' so that 'assessment has to be carried out on the move' (page 5). Accurate assessments therefore require a combination of these rapid skills during lessons (for immediate purposes) and creating a composite picture over the longer term. Every decision about the quality of children's work also needs to be made with reference to a number of factors, including:

- The child's age
- The child's work habits
- The child's past accomplishments
- The learning climate
- The quality of the teaching.

The child's age

Assessment approaches varies according to the age of the child. Older primary school pupils tend to produce a great deal of written and other 'visual' forms of work which can be used for assessment purposes. However, since younger pupils produce relatively little written output, teachers have to rely more on their observations of children and the things that they say about their work. Thus, 'the younger the child, the less tangible the evidence of learning and the more the teacher has to rely on observation and discussion' (EYCG 1998, page 26).

The child's work habits

Children may be slow workers or deep thinkers. They may struggle with particular aspects of the work. There will be gaps in their knowledge. Some children hesitate to tackle unfamiliar or demanding tasks; others relish the challenge. Many children operate more effectively when working with a partner. These factors should be taken into account when work is assessed. A slow worker may produce a high quality final product if allowed extra time. A faster worker may be capable of a better end product if the first attempt is treated as a draft. Children working in pairs may accomplish more if together or (perhaps) separated. With the advent of lessons in which specific time allocation for different phases is considered to be critical, there is less flexibility to allow for such individual differences. You are sometimes faced with a dilemma about what might have been produced by a child under different circumstances.

The child's past accomplishments

As teachers get to know children better, they begin to assess their achievements and potential more accurately. A child may have made considerable strides to accomplish something which, for other more capable children, would be unacceptable. Over time, it becomes evident whether children are progressing satisfactorily in respect of past achievements or whether they are lazy, indifferent or unmotivated. Although formal assessments such as national tests and tasks may provide a grade or figure, they do not take account of these distinctive factors. Although it is part of your responsibility to help children to develop less secure areas of their knowledge and understanding, it is patently obvious that expectations must be reasonable and informed by earlier achievements.

The learning climate

Lessons take place under varying circumstances: some enjoy undisturbed tranquillity; others endure the loud noises from local building work. Some lessons take place within the regular routine of daily lessons; others are wedged between swimming and the end of the day. Some lessons are uninterrupted; others stop and start as children go out for music lessons, extra tuition and so forth. The quality of resources can also affect achievement, particularly for experiential tasks in which practical investigations form the heart of the lesson. Similarly, the behaviour of peers and numbers of pupils in the room can all have an effect on learning outcomes. Teachers need to be wise when selecting work that is 'typical' of a child's ability to ensure that adverse contextual factors did not appreciably influence the outcome.

The quality of teaching

Teachers sometimes blame a child for underachieving or producing a poor piece of work when they bear some of the responsibility. If an explanation of the task is poor, expectations are not clarified or organisation is clumsy, it should be no surprise if the results are disappointing.

Formative assessment

The type of assessment that is ongoing and helps children to improve the quality of their work is referred to as *formative assessment* and is found in the warp and weave of classroom life

(Cullingford 1997b; Torrance and Pryor 1998). Good relationships and a relaxed atmosphere allow this to take place constructively and unthreateningly. The use of question-and-answer sessions, child–teacher dialogue and the teacher's professional judgement are all important elements of formative assessment. The teacher's informal records (both written and remembered) will be full of perceptive observations about individuals:

'Emma benefited from the extra help in spelling.'

'John still struggles to grasp the concept of area.'

'Ranjit is showing a talent for expressive painting.'

'Briony works well with her friend Eileen but seems lost when asked to work alone.'

'Ziad is a good reader but struggles at number work.'

'Darren seems to be tone deaf.'

And a thousand other insights that help to build up a picture of an individual child and guide future planning and appropriate work. These insights are not gained, of course, through detached observation and evaluation of children's work, but rather through active involvement in their learning. An integral element of this involvement is *monitoring* (close awareness of what children are doing and thinking about their work) and *intervening* (offering direct and indirect support to children while they are engaged in work). Unless you sit with your eyes and ears closed during a lesson, it is impossible to avoid monitoring progress! Children will normally let a teacher know if they have concerns or questions about tasks, but it is also important to develop the skill of scanning the class to pick up clues about the level of adult support that is needed. As explained in earlier chapters, the relationship between monitoring and intervening is not an exact science. Sometimes you may be aware that a child is struggling but decide to delay your intervention to allow opportunity for the child to think and engage with the problem. On other occasions you may decide to be highly specific and tell the child precisely what must be done. These judgements are difficult ones and do not form the heart of this present chapter. Suffice it to say that the formative assessment of children's progress provides numerous insights into at least five things:

(a)   The clarity of the task (your responsibility).

(b)   The child's conceptual grasp of the task.

(c)   The child's willingness to persevere with the task.

(d)   The child's self-confidence.

(e)   The extent of the child's ultimate success in accomplishing the task.

Unless (a) is clear, everything else will be distorted. If (b) the child lacks understanding, it may be that you have assumed too much or failed to explain adequately. If (c) the child is unwilling to persevere, it may signal a poor attitude or a weak aptitude towards learning. If (d) the child lacks self-confidence, you have a major part to play in helping to build self-esteem using confirming strategies. If the end result is disappointing, points (a) to (d) need to be reviewed.

As you become more familiar with the class and the evidence accumulates, these general observations can be sharpened:

'Emma can now learn a list of words and get them correct in a spelling test but cannot use them successfully in a piece of open written work.'

'John understands that units of measurement are needed to measure area but cannot understand why using smaller units produces a larger total.'

'Ranjit has an excellent sense of perspective but lacks experience of mixing paints.'

'Briony has a good brain but is afraid of making a mistake.'

'Ziad can read aloud accurately but without any great understanding.'

'Darren is fine in the lower ranges but gets lost as the notes rise.'

It is not difficult to see that formative assessments are of little value unless action is taken to remedy a situation or encourage greater achievement. The process may be considered as comprising five stages:

Stage 1: A general impression is gained from children's work and comments.

Stage 2: Over time, a more exact judgement is made of the child's aptitude and ability.

Stage 3: Action is taken to improve or enhance the situation.

Stage 4: A further 'fine-grained' assessment is made on the basis of the revised work programme.

Stage 5: Individual needs are more adequately catered for, especially children with particular learning difficulties.

Two important things need to be understood. First, the best formative assessments are also *diagnostic*; that is, not merely descriptive but providing evidence to assist in the formulation of appropriate teaching and learning strategies. Second, there is a limit to the amount of informal formative assessment that a teacher can record or remember. A system has to be established whereby the evidence from children's work and their responses to questions and so forth can be confirmed and, in some cases, quantified.

By how much has Emma's spelling improved?

Does John have similar difficulty with other aspects of measurement?

Can Ranjit transfer his skills to drawing and planning in DT?

What is Briony capable of achieving under ideal conditions?

Would Ziad benefit from focusing on specific aspects of textual interpretation?

Is Darren's problem one of confidence or competence or physical limitation?

Answers to these detailed questions allow teachers to modify work for an individual child or group of children in order to improve their chances of grasping the skills and concepts in the area of weakness or enhancing their experience in areas of strength. The process of formative assessment should constitute part of the overall framework of planning, practice and recording.

- *Planning for teaching and learning*: based on the school's agreed curriculum programme.
- *Teacher assessment*: daily observation and professional judgements based on the quality of work that children are producing.
- *Modified practice*: adjustment of work patterns on the basis of the formative assessment.
- *Evaluative assessment*: focused judgements with reference to National Curriculum documents.

- *Recorded findings*: using recording sheets.
- *Reporting findings*: to parents and colleagues, in person or in writing.

Despite the helpful information accrued through assessment, it is important to be reminded that the simplistic notion of a procedure whereby teachers introduce a topic, sets tasks, assess children's progress and adjust their teaching accordingly is an idealised version of the reality. Ultimately, children must make sense of learning for themselves, aided by informed adults and peers.

Monitoring

As referred to in the previous section, monitoring progress is an essential skill for every teacher to develop and is concerned with two aspects of classroom life: effective learning and effective discipline. The two elements are often closely related; well-behaved and motivated children have a much better chance of doing well than restless, bored ones! The following five factors need to be considered as part of the ongoing process of assessing pupils' progress through monitoring:

The clarity of the task

Whether there are specific areas of the work causing concern to one or more pupils which need the teacher's attention.

The task demands

Whether the demands made by the task are enthusing and motivating pupils.

The availability and distribution of resources

Whether every pupil is receiving a fair share of resources and gaining access to the equipment.

The level of co-operation/collaboration

Whether children are working together responsibly.

The standard of work

Whether pupils' achievements match their potential.

Teacher assessment of pupil attainment (as opposed to formal testing) relies largely upon monitoring their progress during the lesson and examining the results of their endeavours by looking at their written and recorded work. Monitoring progress during the lesson requires a number of sophisticated skills including the following:

Seeing what needs to be seen

Monitoring demands focused and deliberate observation of a given situation.

Drawing the correct conclusions about what is seen

For instance, whether particular forms of pupil behaviour contribute to or detract from effective learning.

Deciding what action should be taken

That is, determining the appropriate form of intervention.

Considering that this process has to take place spontaneously on numerous occasions during a session, it is hardly surprising that inexperienced teachers sometimes find it difficult to be aware of what is happening throughout the classroom. Before teachers make decisions about suitable intervention strategies, they have to synthesise factors that arise from the monitoring process and make a number of judgements as a consequence. For instance:

General class order

Are pupils concentrating satisfactorily on their work? Is the noise level too high? Are groups collaborating or chattering? Is the movement around the room purposeful?

The behaviour of individuals

Is the child sufficiently compliant, bearing in mind his or her previous history? How many minor infringements should be ignored (if any)? How often should verbal reprimands be used? (See also Chapter 8.)

Health and safety

Are the pupils' actions potentially dangerous? What is 'reasonable risk'? How long should the situation be left? Will pupils' common sense prevail?

During monitoring of pupils' work during the lesson, a teacher inevitably confirms the acceptability of children's effort and progress. Every time you tick a page, express pleasure in a child's response or commend an approach, you are providing a confirmation of its validity. Indeed, offering immediate endorsement of a child's work provides valuable incentive and/is preferable to the familiar and rather uninspiring process of: work is set/children do the work/the work is handed in/the teacher assesses the work/the work is handed back. The appropriateness of your responses based on the above considerations, will not only influence the learning climate but will determine how and when you intervene.

Intervention

Children need adult and peer support in their endeavour to master new skills and concepts. Teacher intervention can be required for any one of at least five reasons:

- The teacher's poor initial lesson introduction, resourcing or organisation means that further explanation is required
- Poor matching between child/group and task leading to confusion or uncertainty
- The child's lack of confidence (as opposed to ability) leading to tentativeness

- The child's lack of ability leading to not knowing how to do the task
- The child's lack of concentration leading to the need for regular reminders.

In every teaching-and-learning situation, a variety of intervention skills and judgements are required:

Knowing when to intervene

Part of knowing when to intervene is discerning when to leave things alone. Experienced teachers seem to develop an aptitude for spotting those events, comments and behaviours that require immediate attention, those that can be left for a time and those which are best ignored. It is important to weigh up the situation, remain calm and avoid saying too much before the child has had time to speak and the facts become clear. Once the position has been clarified, appropriate action can follow, though its precise nature has to be determined 'on the spot'.

Allowing time for pupils' self-correction

Sometimes it is useful to allow time for the pupil to self-correct rather than rushing in immediately, particularly if the lesson purpose is principally about allowing pupils to grapple with difficulties rather than providing immediate solutions. Children need to be taught self-sufficiency rather than unintentionally promoting their over-reliance on a teacher, but there is little point in leaving a child to flounder for too long without offering help. (See later in this section.)

Knowing how to say what has to be said

Two teachers monitor children's work and offer suggestions for improvement: the first teacher depresses the pupil by being heavily critical; the second brings about the desired change by the use of carefully chosen words, precise guidance and suitable target setting. It is obvious which of the two approaches is going to bring about enhanced learning.

Unless the occasion is a formal test in which assistance is not permitted, every teacher has to balance the importance of offering encouragement and guidance to children with intervening to such an extent that the child loses ownership of the task. Many children are happy to be told instead of putting their minds to the problem. Consequently, a pattern of behaviour emerges:

1 Child engages with task

2 Child encounters difficulty

3 Child asks for assistance and advice

4 Teacher obliges

However, it is useful to introduce a 'delayed intervention' by employing phrases such as 'Have a try for yourself first and I'll come back in a moment if you are still stuck' or 'Ask a friend first, then ask an adult'. You can also use a three steps procedure that children must always follow, namely: (1) Think for yourself (2) Ask a classmate (3) Ask an adult. Consequently, the behaviour pattern is gradually changed, as follows:

1 Child engages with task

2 Child encounters difficulty

3 Child thinks about solutions for one minute

4 Child seeks advice from a friend

5 Child seeks advice from an adult

A lot depends on the nature of the lesson as to how flexibly the steps need to be followed; for instance you may want the children to work independently. However, the principle of children learning to think for themselves before seeking help allows you to evaluate children's ability to solve problems, rather than their ability to prise information from the teacher! Much formative assessment is based upon this interplay between intervention and giving children time and freedom to explore, evaluate, experiment, argue and so forth.

Assessments must, therefore, take into account the extent of teacher intervention and perhaps, peer involvement, in assessing work. Teachers have to weigh the benefits of co-operation and shared learning experiences with the possible disadvantage that one child may do most of the thinking and planning, while the other coasts.

Teachers also have to make allowances for particular times of the day and circumstances in judging how and when to intervene. Experienced teachers allow children time to settle after a 'wet' playtime rather than raise tension by being unduly assertive and may be more lenient with the work standards of a pupil who has come to school burdened with emotional cares than with a pupil who is being unnecessarily casual. Over time, all teachers tend to fall into particular patterns of monitoring and intervention that will have consequences in promoting sound learning and discipline. As a result, it is essential to think carefully whether the intervention strategies were the most effective ones in the circumstances or whether different actions might have resulted in more successful learning outcomes. Making such judgements comes as a result of time spent engaged in active classroom teaching, reflection on children's responses and evaluation of work quality.

Activate your thinking!

Consider the truth of the following statement: Every intervention is preceded by an assessment based on careful monitoring of a child's progress.

Good practice

Categorise the types of active intervention you commonly use under the following headings: (a) those that result from a child's question (b) those that result from your awareness of a problem (c) those that enhance work that is already of good quality.

Summative assessment

By contrast with ongoing formative assessments, those that take place at the end of a definable period of time such as the end of a day or half term or year or at the conclusion of a Key Stage are referred to as *summative*. The outcomes from summative assessments are intended to confirm the teacher's opinion of what children have learned and what progress has been made. Summative assessment is more systematic than formative assessment and may take the form of a written or verbal test carried out under specified conditions or a series of small tasks with which children have to engage in order to show their level of competence. The most significant type of summative assessment is through the national tasks and tests that relate to the core subjects of the National Curriculum, the results of which must be made available to the parents of each child. Some schools provide parents with the teacher's assessment of the child's progress in all the curriculum subjects once a year. Reports on art, music and PE only refer to end of Key Stage descriptions rather than the level descriptions used for the other non-core subjects. A summative assessment is not required for religious education. The use of ICT is now firmly established in schools, and pupils' ability needs to be monitored closely and their progress noted in reports to parents. ICT is sometimes referred to as the 'fourth core subject' to highlight its significance.

Summative assessments also have to take account of short-term target setting (see later in this chapter) whereby pupils are given specific learning targets to achieve by a given time. Although the targets do not form part of the formal assessment process, they help teachers to keep close track of pupil achievement. Through target setting, summative and formative assessment become two sides of the same coin: the formative element influences children's progress that is ultimately identified through the summative assessment. In turn, the summative element provides information for teachers to become more alert to the suitability of their formative assessment, and so on.

The process of assessment and recording and reporting children's progress is a crucial element of the teacher's work. A number of booklets have been produced by the Qualifications and Curriculum Authority (QCA) to help teachers understand the requirements of national testing; these are essential reading for a fuller understanding of the assessment process.

Feedback to children

One of the principal ways in which a positive learning environment can be achieved is through effective and sensitive feedback to children about the quality of their work. It is essential to ensure that marking work not only provides information for the teacher but for pupils, offering useful data to them about their work and progress. Sometimes the feedback will be verbal and sometimes in the form of a grade, mark, smiley face or another symbol, remembering that the child who has persevered to achieve something worthwhile deserves the same level of commendation as the more capable pupil. Clarke (2001) suggests that teachers carry out as much marking as possible with children present, rather than marking away from the child, though this is not easy in practice. It is also important for teachers to avoid falling into the 'yes, but' habit, whereby children never receive unconditional praise because the imperfections of the work are highlighted at the same time as the approval. Although it is part of your role to help children improve their work, this should not be done at the expense of them feeling that absolutely *nothing* will ever satisfy their finicky teacher! The following principles will help to ensure that feedback is beneficial:

1 Mark as much as possible with the child present and celebrate achievement spontaneously.

2 Consider the *effort* made as well as the outcome, being careful not to foster excessive competitiveness.

3 Take account of circumstances in making judgements. For example:

   ■ The difficulty of the work

   ■ The time available

   ■ Whether the child was trying to be innovative

4 Avoid the impression that the only reason the children are doing the work is to please the teacher!

5 Keep your eye on the long-term intentions for children's attitude to learning:

   ■ Enthusiastic and motivated

   ■ Self-sufficient and independent

   ■ Confident at his/her own level

Activate your thinking!

Black and Wiliam (1998) suggest that part of the teacher's role is to raise children's self-esteem by promoting a culture of success and encouraging children to tackle problems without fearing the consequences of failure. How do you rate yourself in this regard?

The need for accurate assessment also places a responsibility upon teachers to ensure that they use the most appropriate descriptors. For instance, when describing a child's work, teachers frequently make use of a general term such as 'good'. In doing so, they can be making a number of different statements:

■ It is good compared with the last piece of similar work the child completed

■ It is good compared with other children's work in the group or class

■ It is good because the child has made a considerable effort to do well, despite the relatively poor quality of the end result

■ It is good compared with other children of the same age in neighbouring schools (far more difficult to ascertain)

A similar list can be made about why the work is described as 'poor'. Even if a piece of work is judged as poor, teachers have then to determine what should be done about it. Simply telling children that their work is poor or giving them a low mark is probably only confirming what they already know, so teachers need to employ strategies to assist children to do better next time or to improve their current piece of work. This process may involve speaking to an individual, asking for the attention of the group or providing more direct teaching to the whole class in the form of explanations, demonstrations or exposition. A number of individuals may not have grasped what the teacher intended them to do and may need a few minutes of intensive tuition before they can respond adequately. The task may expect too much of the children and to redress the mismatch between task and ability, remedial work or a modification to what is required may be needed before further progress is possible.

Positive remarks about a child's progress may be useful as a means of encouragement but unhelpful in diagnosis. A 'Good, well done' indicates the teacher's pleasure but may have limited value for ensuring that the child has thoroughly grasped the intended concept, skill or knowledge. A 'Good, well done, I can see that you have really tried hard' indicates that the teacher is pleased with the effort made despite the outcome. However, a 'Good, well done in these particular ways' is better still. The distinction between the different expressions is significant for children who may subconsciously perceive that the only way to earn favour with the teacher is to 'do good work'. More open relationships result in a fuller discourse and pave the way for more focused attention on specific areas of work. Most children try hard for most of the time, but it is worth reminding yourself that everyone, including adults, has off-days.

Activate your thinking!

Whatever form assessment takes, three factors are always relevant:

- Where a child 'started from' before trying to assess progress
- Ensuring the form of measurement of ability is valid
- The close link between assessment, planning and record-keeping.

Good practice

As you give feedback, put yourself in the children's place and imagine the impact of your words upon their determination to do better and to their self-esteem.

Assessments and learning objectives

It is important in assessing children's progress to bear in mind both the lesson objectives and continuity in learning, expressed through building conceptual understanding in a systematic (though not inflexible) way. Many tasks and activities involve several stages before completion. For example, a painting may require time spent on colour mixing, a backwash, use of different paint textures and addition of fine detail that may not be achievable in the space of a single session owing to practical factors. Similarly, a drama production normally involves preparation through role-play, improvisation and rehearsals prior to the final performance. In English, draft versions of a piece of writing usually contain mis-spellings and grammatical errors that need to be corrected before the final version is produced. It would be unreasonable to treat these early stages as if they were the completed task and base judgements upon them, though teachers pick up many clues by observing how a child approaches the work. The establishment of clear learning objectives and time spent explaining the nature of the tasks to the children is essential. Children may panic and rush to complete a piece of work for fear that time constraints make such haste necessary, when a more considered and thorough job would have been possible had you made the position clearer.

For instance, consider how planning a number of maths lessons on naming and using common coinage with reception age children might link with assessment criteria. The teacher may design a series of sessions consisting of four broad phases:

Phase 1: Understanding the use of pennies to pay for goods up to the value of 5p.
Phase 2: Understanding the use of pennies to pay for goods up to the value of 10p.
Phase 3: Establishing the exchange relationship between 1p, 2p and 10p coins.
Phase 4: Establishing the exchange relationship between 1p, 2p, 5p and 10p coins.

Of course, each phase will not necessarily correspond to a single lesson. The concepts associated with each phase may have to be revised and rehearsed a number of times before learning is secure. The problem for a teacher is to determine when such learning has taken place. Using assessment criteria provides a means by which this can be undertaken. In the above example, each set of objectives is accompanied by a corresponding set of criteria that are used to assess the children's progress. Thus:

Phase 1 assessment criteria
The children can:

■ Identify and name pennies
■ Count out the coins up to 5p
■ Exchange the coins for items costing up to 5p.

Phase 2 assessment criteria
The children can:

■ Count out the pennies up to 10p
■ Count the cost of buying more than one item up to 10p.

Phase 3 assessment criteria
The children can:

■ Identify and name the 2p coin
■ Exchange pennies for 2p coins

- Count the amounts of money using 1p and 2p coins up to a maximum of 10p.

Phase 4 assessment criteria
The children can:

- Identify and name 5p coins
- Exchange 1p and 2p coins for 5p coins
- Exchange 1p, 2p and 5p coins for one or more items costing up to 10p.

There may be disagreement about the ordering of the criteria and the way that they are arranged, but the principle of linking lesson objectives and the assessment of pupil attainment across a period of time is one which often underpins planning. Although children do not learn in the smooth, uninterrupted fashion that the above criteria may suggest, the principle of assessments which relate to learning objectives is valid for all subject areas. Keeping track of children's progress requires careful judgement about the evidence to use in forming an opinion about children's progress. The issue of recording pupil attainment is addressed later in the chapter.

Target setting

In recent years, the need to identify and reach targets has become rooted in work at every level of society. Schools are no exception. Wyse (2001) refers to the complexity of setting targets and subsequent assessment, notably the amount of interaction time with pupils that was required to plan future targets in literacy. He suggests that for the process to be purposeful, 'high levels of skills and understanding were required to be coupled with the ability to develop strategies to improve management of the process' (page 16). From his study of final year trainee teachers, Wyse noted the following (paraphrased and amended):

- Accurate target setting has to be based on a clear understanding of previous development and attainment
- It is important to recognise that children reach the same targets at different rates
- Targets should not be too numerous or difficult
- Frequent reference to targets is necessary, supported by maintaining target sheets, cards or notices for each child
- Targets need to be discussed orally to support understanding and to assess progress
- It is important to identify the nature of what the target is related to (level descriptions, SAT, Framework for Teaching, etc.)
- A lot of marking can be replaced by oral discussion with children
- Specific marking is more productive than making general summary comments
- Formative assessment (feedback and intervention during lessons) is particularly useful for the purpose of setting and monitoring targets

- Self-assessment is a useful tool to enhance pupil participation
- Extra adult support is often necessary to enhance target setting
- Unachievable targets are demotivating for children and result in slower progress

Clarke (2001) suggests that there are three broad types of targets:

- Quantitative targets using numerical data (such as a percentage of children to reach a particular pass rate)
- Qualitative targets based principally on written evidence (such as children's ability to spell certain words correctly in different contexts)
- Non-recorded targets based on children's self-evaluation of their progress (such as those resulting from informal conversations between teacher and taught)

The principles of target setting (based on those suggested by Clarke, page 86) are that targets should be at three levels: school, class and child. They must be realistic, manageable and challenging and based on an analysis of data from children's achievements, including regular summative assessments. Targets should be expressed in appropriate language that children can understand, and shared with children (in the short-term) and with parents (in the long-term). Children should participate in establishing and meeting targets, which should be regularly reviewed. It is important that targets are supported and met by effective teaching, learning and assessment, and not allowed to become free-standing entities, detached from the regular classwork and homework. Target setting has, therefore, become significant for every teacher and is important at three levels:

(a) Immediate targets for individual children in different subject areas.

(b) Longer-term targets for children over (say) half a term.

(c) Targets for year groups of children in national tests.

Immediate targets for individual children

These targets are based upon children's ongoing classroom work. As teachers evaluate pupils' progress, particular aspects of their work are identified as needing special attention and improvement. Recognition of pupils' achievements inevitably involves seeing how the present work can be improved or built upon. Older pupils can take some responsibility for monitoring their own progress and establishing reasonable targets; younger ones will need the strong support of teachers to identify specific ways in which improvements can be made. With or without active teacher involvement, target setting for individual children needs to take place with respect to the following:

- Target setting must be specific. Broad targets such as 'I must get better at reading' are inadequate. Instead a target such as 'I must learn to pause at full stops when reading out loud' or 'I must select non-fiction books for personal reading' should be identified. Similarly, in maths there is little point in setting a target such as 'I must learn my multiplication tables' but rather 'I must use my calculator to check my work, not to carry out the calculation' or 'I must work out multiplications without adding up all the numbers'. Target setting can also include specific aspects of improving presentation of work, learning to work as a member of a group and mastering techniques.

■ Target setting must be realistic. Learning does not follow clearly defined pathways. It is gradual and, in some cases, wholly unpredictable. If targets are too ambitious, children will lose heart. If they are undemanding, children will not take them seriously. Learning will not necessarily come more quickly simply because targets have been set. Nevertheless, a sensible target can act as a prompt or encouragement for children to focus their energies constructively.

■ Target setting must take account of time factors. Most concepts and skills cannot be mastered overnight; it takes a lot of trial and error, perseverance and determination before understanding comes and abilities are honed. Although it is easy to monitor the setting of a few spellings to be learned at home, targets which involve a lot of library research (for instance) will take longer to achieve than those which can be done on the spot.

■ Target setting must be manageable. There is little point in having a system that is so unwieldy that it cannot be managed. Sophisticated systems are fine in theory but usually crumble on the sharp edge of reality. Manageable strategies include giving children small 'Targets' notebooks to write down their targets (or, where appropriate, have them written by the teacher). Some teachers use a system of marking work in different coloured pens or markers to indicate that the area of work requires improvement or needs to be more thoroughly mastered. Whatever system is adopted, it is important to minimise the workload and not distract from the main purpose of promoting successful learning by creating a lot of additional paperwork.

Longer-term targets for individual children

Most schools encourage the children to 'look ahead' and discuss with the teacher and/or their classmates the things that they are keen to improve and attain over (say) the next half-term. It is impossible and undesirable for children to become submerged in minutiae, such that they become obsessed by the need to 'hit' a large number of disparate targets, but a sensible discussion about key learning needs can help to focus attention on desirable outcomes. For instance, a child may be struggling in changing from printing letters to a cursive script and require guidance, constant practice and opportunities to use the skill in extended writing. Again, a child may be perplexed by the concept of division of whole numbers in mathematics, necessitating a considerable amount of concentration and wrestling with the principles that support the operation before understanding comes.

By contrast to the more immediate targets that can be achieved through pupils' self-motivation and resoluteness, longer-term targets necessitate a need for expert advice and support from an informed adult. In other words, the mere agreement about a target serves limited purpose unless there is a strategy to help the child achieve it.

The achievement of a target can be problematic, as even the most carefully defined outcomes are subject to personal opinion and interpretation. For example, it is difficult to determine whether a child is writing more creatively or is able to participate more constructively in a discussion than was previously the case. Nevertheless, it is important to review targets periodically and help children to take some ownership of their learning instead of relying wholly on an adult's direction and approval.

Targets for year groups of children

National tests have become increasingly important for all schools as a failure to improve year upon year can bring about additional inspections or intervention by the DfES. The establishment of targets has created a considerable amount of activity in schools and local education authorities as they have responded to the considerable challenge in raising standards of literacy and numeracy. Part of the process of reaching and maintaining these standards involves a process known as Agreement Trialling, in which teachers responsible for children of the same age in a district (or, in the case of large schools, within the school) meet to consider their assessments of work to ensure that there is comparability. The agreement trials are time-consuming but, as Gipps and Clarke (1998) discovered from their extensive survey, 'it is the only way within the present system that any form of consistency will be achieved' (page 14).

On the other hand, it is possible that pupils may be burdened with the weight of teacher expectations, especially if they fail to achieve at least level 2 (at Key Stage 1) or at least level 4 (at Key Stage 2) in Standard Assessment Tests (SATs). Schools are being encouraged to give 'booster classes' to underachieving pupils at Key Stage 2 which, though they may have a positive impact upon attainment, could be deleterious to children's self-esteem and confidence if they perceive themselves to be failures. It is therefore essential for teachers to keep target setting in proportion and not allow it to completely dominate the educational agenda. Many schools use end-of-year (non-statutory) tests to monitor pupil progress and identify weaknesses. A few schools test children every half term. With the advent of 'value-added' league tables that rely on the *progress* that children have made from the previously established benchmark, even schools with a large number of children attaining level 4 in the end-of-key-stage tests are being obliged to aim for an increase in the number attaining level 5.

Targets also play a significant role in teacher appraisal, adding to their significance for practitioners at all levels of experience. Not only do teachers have to take increasing responsibility for their own development by setting themselves professional targets, the attainment of the children in their classes is a key factor in determining their suitability for advancement. While it is reasonable to expect teachers to deliver on standards, there is an increasing understanding on the part of policy-makers that the one-size-fits-all philosophy pervading the education system has to be more sensitive to local factors.

Limitations of targets

Setting targets depends on teachers being clear about what children know and planning accordingly. However, there are strict limits on how detailed these insights can be. While it is relatively simple to ascertain whether children possess certain forms of knowledge, such as being able to recite the alphabet, count to 20 or know historical dates, it is almost impossible to be discern precisely what every child understands about (say) human behaviour or the morality of historical events. These limitations have two consequences. First, it is tempting to concentrate exclusively on aspects of knowledge that are measurable. Second, the concept of matching teaching to 'gaps in children's knowledge' is something of a fallacy. Setting targets is a useful strategy for maintaining a well-controlled teaching system but to be truly effective it must also acknowledge that not everything worth knowing falls neatly into the teach/assess/amend teaching formula. Teachers are understandably reluctant to improve test results for the sole purpose of complying with political ambitions or advancing their own career prospects.

Assessing collaborative activities

Assessment of individual children is more difficult when children are involved in collaborative work. Although enhancing skills in collaborating is a valuable dimension of learning, it can also mask the progress in learning made by individuals. The sight of children explaining to and assisting one another is rightly viewed as worthwhile by most teachers; however, this is different from one child acting as a surrogate teacher and continually intervening in another child's work. For example, if four groups of children are engaged in doing the same task, there will be different levels of interpretation and outcome depending upon the ability and expertise within the group. The teacher will need to be aware of the group's potential and previous learning when determining what constitutes a satisfactory learning outcome, as reflected in the quality of the group's recording of findings or presentations.

From Figure 7.1 Assessment of groups through outcome we can see that the least able group (A) may follow the procedures without deviating from the teacher's instructions. Group B may follow the procedures but interpret them more imaginatively. Group C may amend the procedures significantly and introduce their own ideas and modifications. Group D (the most able) may reinterpret the task and develop a wholly innovative approach that answers different questions and involves other pathways from those envisaged by the teacher. Although teachers will expect all children to reach their potential and make the best contribution possible, they will also take into account the children's potential. That is, Group A will be commended for accurately following the set procedure while Group D's accomplishments will be assessed using a different set of criteria. If, on the other hand, Group C operated only at the level expected from Group A, then the task was too tedious, the group were under-performing or the teacher's original expectations were misconceived. Differentiating through outcome provides the teacher with a means of acknowledging a group's particular contribution and effort without directly comparing group with group. A less able group may achieve a lot within the limits of their capability and the teacher's expectations.

Confirmation of progress in learning will rely upon the individual's contribution to the group effort as perceived by the teacher, subsequent work in the same area of learning, ability to explain things coherently and the quality of the write-up or other representation of the work such as diagrams, maps, pictures or models.

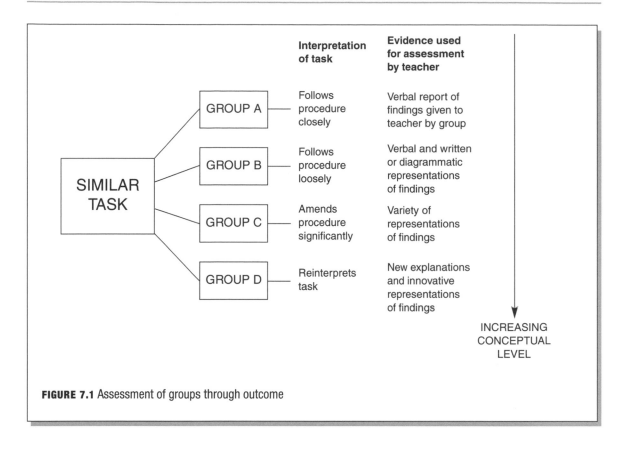

FIGURE 7.1 Assessment of groups through outcome

Sometimes a teacher's assessment will be based on factors other than the final work outcome. For instance, willingness to co-operate, creative thought, enthusiasm or commitment to completing the task are important assessments which relate more closely to social behaviour, personal growth and attitude than to measurable academic performance.

Activate your thinking!

As it is not possible for one teacher to know about each child's work and progress in detail for every curriculum area, judgements have to be based largely upon the outcome of the group's combined efforts.

Good practice

Select a 'key' child from each group each week for careful observation and assessment. Choose a new target child from each group every week until you have worked your way through each one.

Assessing children for whom English is an additional language

Standards for qualified teacher status include the following requirement:

> Trainees are able to support and identify the levels of attainment of those pupils who are learning English as an additional language, with the help of an experienced teacher where appropriate. Trainees can begin to analyse the language demands and learning activities in order to provide cognitive challenge as well as language support (S3.3.5, S3.2.5)

In particular there is a need to assess pupils' competence in English through their ability to comprehend through listening, speaking, reading and writing. Pupils' responsiveness when hearing English spoken can be assessed with reference to the 'extended scale for listening' (QCA 2000). Their ability to speak and use spoken English can be assessed with reference to the 'extended scale for speaking'. Their familiarity with the conventions of print and understanding written English can be assessed with reference to the 'extended scale for reading'. Their ability to write for different purposes can be assessed with reference to the 'extended scale for writing'. Broadly, it should be possible to make judgements for listening, speaking, reading and writing using the descriptions below. Thus:

Listening

You can distinguish between children who respond to spoken English in specific circumstances (e.g. a regular instruction such as 'please sit down'), those who can understand what is said but do not respond, and those children who can talk to others as a result of their understanding.

Speaking

You can distinguish between children who are able to say a few words, those who can sustain a conversation, and those who can modify their speech according to context and circumstances.

Reading

You can distinguish between children who are able to grasp basic written conventions those who can read with support, and those who can read with a large degree of independence.

Writing

You can distinguish between children who are able to write English letters and their name, those who can use letter patterns, and those who can write recognisable letters, words and phrases.

Formal assessment of English as an additional language are described with reference to a scale consisting of four stages for those who have yet to reach National Curriculum attainment target 1, namely:

- Step 1 ... *for the least competent users*
- Step 2
- Level 1, 'threshold'
- Level 1, 'secure'

Characteristics of each stage are described closely in QCA (2000), pages 12–15. The scale for speaking and listening is separately listed for the four stages but combined for level 2 and above. There are separate scales for reading and for writing. As with all assessments, however, the purpose of placing a child at a particular stage is not for the sake of completing a record sheet and satisfying external requirements, but to assist the child's learning. Subsequent planning of an appropriate curriculum programme for children with EAL will depend upon a variety of factors, not least whether there are other children in the class with the same first language and the availability of a teaching assistant. It is also important to take account of the disorientation that a child experiences when suddenly thrust into a confusing new situation, with unfamiliar language, cultural norms and procedures. Every new child takes time to adjust to the pattern of working, and this problem is magnified for a child who speaks little or no English. Your assessment record might consist of a summary paragraph about the child's abilities in speaking and listening, samples of written work as evidence for writing, and regular reading records for progress in reading. Assessment profiles of this kind should allow you to trace the child's curriculum experience in school and provide diagnostic information that allows you to discuss the child's progress with other staff and parents.

Activate your thinking!

The assessment of children's work can tell teachers as much about the effectiveness of their own teaching as it does about the child's learning.

Good practice

Use assessment as a forum for celebrating success.

RECORDING AND REPORTING

Forms of records

The emphasis throughout this book has been upon the inter-relationship between planning, assessment, record-keeping and reporting children's progress to parents both informally and formally. Few practitioners enjoy keeping records, but they are a necessary part of professional responsibility. Following any block of teaching and learning, a teacher is faced with a number of questions:

- How much did the children learn from the lesson or lessons?
- What evidence is there of group and individual progress?
- How will this affect future plans?

- How will the evidence be recorded?

Although teachers hold a lot of information about children in their heads, there is a need to keep written records that assist with the twin requirements of planning future work and reporting to parents. The difficulty for teachers is deciding what to record and what to omit. It is no exaggeration to claim that teachers could spend more time recording than teaching if they attempted to write down everything.

The precise forms of records that are maintained depend upon their purpose. Records take a variety of forms and are kept for a number of different purposes, including:

Organisational planning

This type of record is based on curriculum coverage. For example, noting which group has covered which topic and modifying the content of future lesson plans as a result.

Strategy for managing

This type of record is purely functional and acts as a reminder for teachers and assistants about the children's level of engagement with work. For example, checking who has read to the teacher during the week, noting who has used the computer.

Information relating to National Curriculum demands

This type of record offers evidence of children's progress that helps to inform formalised teacher assessments. For example, evidence for end-of-key-stage assessment.

Information for parents

This type of record is a summary of key facts for easy transmission to a third party. For example, informal notes in preparation for parents' evening.

Recognition of children's efforts

This type of record consists of representative samples of children's work for inclusion in a Record of Achievement folder, class books, wall displays.

The most immediate records for teachers to maintain are those that show areas of work covered (curriculum coverage) and those that show children's progress (individual records). It is important to distinguish between the two types of records for, as noted earlier, mere completion of a task or activity does not necessarily show the extent of understanding or mastery, as the following makes clear:

Curriculum coverage

Records of curriculum coverage take many forms. The best are straightforward to use and easy to modify. A rigid, over-detailed format is time-consuming, rarely justifies the effort and should not be confused with the detail required for end of Key Stage national tests and tasks. Many schools plan in half-termly blocks in which the main topic, theme or subject is identified and National Curriculum, NLS and NNS links established. A weekly overview is then drawn up by staff teams that teach the same age group or by individual teachers; lesson planning emerges from this common structure. The subsequent records of curriculum coverage reflect the nature of the planning and are likely to take one of two forms: records that state curriculum coverage based primarily on Programmes of Study (PoS); and records based primarily on concepts, skills and knowledge.

Much depends on the way in which a particular school organises its learning programme: the more subject-centred the programme, the more likely that PoS predominates; the more process-centred or thematic the programme, the more likely that concepts and skills are emphasised. Two simple examples of proformas are shown in Figure 7.3 Record of activities for the whole class and Figure 7.2 Curriculum continuity planning sheet.

Record of activities for the whole class

Figure 7.2 can be used when the activities (or tasks) are appropriate to the whole class. For example, the children might all be doing some observational drawing. The record sheet will help the teacher to see who has completed the task and who has not. The names of the children are written in the left hand column. The activity is written in the skewed box near the top of the page. The appropriate box is ticked or shaded when the child has completed the activity or task. A simpler version with fewer names can be adopted to record the work of a single group. If several groups are involved with different curriculum areas, the need for maintaining careful records is even greater.

A curriculum continuity planning sheet

Figure 7.2 Curriculum continuity planning sheet indicates the sort of record that can easily be made of coverage in core subjects and provides an overview of the planning process. The numbers on the left hand side refer to the weeks of the topic, theme or project. A note of the specific teaching area covered or the National Curriculum reference can be made in the subject columns. The sheet can be modified in imaginative and useful ways; a similar format can be used for other subjects.

> ### Good practice
>
> It is useful for new teachers to see samples of previous end-of-year reports from across the age range spectrum as a means of identifying the overall curriculum and school learning priorities.

Individual progress

Since it is not possible to assess a child's thought processes directly, teachers have to collect evidence relating to the product of those thought processes. The most usual product is a piece of written work, but observations help the teacher by providing information from ongoing interactions while the child is working (Cavendish and Underwood 1997, page 91).

Term:_____

Curriculum area ──────────▶

Progression (e.g. weekly)

	Mathematics	English	Science
ONE			
TWO			
THREE			
FOUR			
FIVE			

FIGURE 7.2 Curriculum continuity planning sheet

TOPIC/THEME

Names of
children   Activities

FIGURE 7.3 Record of activities (for the whole class)

Records of activities covered with a group or class are important but do not tell us anything about the assessment of individual pupil progress. Use of National Curriculum documents such as the PoS assist in planning and monitoring curriculum coverage but are less helpful for charting individual progress. Ideally, it is desirable to plan every intended learning outcome for each child, monitor progress, assess the extent of the learning and record it in a manageable form. In practice, this is impossible unless the class is exceptionally small. Teachers may suffer agonies of conscience over the fact that their files are not full of pages of information plotting the progress of every child in every aspect of learning in every subject area, but such self-recrimination is unnecessary. We have seen that learning is rarely smooth and uninterrupted but that in the ongoing process of formative assessment, most children can be deemed to have a broad grasp of the intended outcome if they complete the set work to the teacher's satisfaction. Use of benchmark assessment practice places more emphasis upon work outcomes than is necessarily desirable. However, if it is accompanied by careful monitoring of the ongoing work, then individual notes about a child can focus on the perceived difficulties (and, by inference, ways to tackle them) rather than endlessly listing the things that the child knows and understands. Records can then be used diagnostically to improve future teaching and learning rather than as a descriptive list. It is important to remember that this is for the purpose of record-keeping and provides a workable system rather than an unattainable ideal. Thus:

Records of work covered by groups of children

It is often easier to record the tasks and activities completed by groups of children than by individuals. However, this information does not tell a teacher how well children coped with the tasks and activities or which children struggled and which prospered.

Records of satisfactory work completion

They provide a suitable yardstick and are within the capability of busy teachers.

Records of every individual's progress in detail

Careful records have to be kept for core subjects, especially in the areas of literacy and numeracy. Information can be gained from in-class tests, information from completed exercises and verbal contributions. However, it is not necessary or sensible to maintain detailed records for all children of every step they take in their learning. The only essential records are those that teachers need (a) for the purposes of modifying their lessons to make them more relevant and appropriately differentiated; and (b) for reporting to parents.

Activate your thinking!

The more information children are given about what they are meant to achieve, the more they can be involved in monitoring their own progress.

Good practice

In maintaining records, assume that children *can* do it and understand it, unless it is obvious that they cannot!

As a first step in assessing and recording individual's progress during tasks and activities that you have allocated, it is helpful to use a 'Goldilocks and the Three Bears' approach in subdividing the children. A small number of children may struggle because the content of lessons is 'too hot'. A small number may sail through because the content is 'too cold'. The majority will cope comfortably because the content is just the right temperature. By placing children in one of the three categories, it soon becomes obvious where the problems lie and what sort of help is needed. For example:

Too hot: Malichaba, Esmie, Tallis.
Too cold: Damien, Chris, Becks, Amanda.
Just right: The rest of the class!

Consequently, pupils in the 'too hot' category require less demanding curriculum content; those in the 'too cold' category need more demanding work. The process is more manageable and representative of true ability if records show the extent of individual progress across a series of lessons rather than a single one. Although this unsophisticated approach cannot be used for formal records, it is useful as a memory aid for busy teachers.

In an attempt to balance reality with aspiration, some schools have more sophisticated records relating to the core subjects only, one sheet per child. These usually contain details about the content and learning relating to particular attainment targets in a subject; these are ticked or blocked according to an agreed system and kept with the child's records, sometimes together with a sample of work for evidence. Schools will often have an agreed marking policy to support the monitoring process so that there is consistency across and within year groups. As a trainee teacher, you may have to use an existing school record system or complete sample records on proformas supplied by the Faculty/College. Typically, inexperienced trainees are asked to identify a small number of children and track their progress; more experienced trainees, especially those in their final placement, should be looking ahead to the time when they will have responsibility for a full class of children.

Activate your thinking!

After three weeks with your class, a parent comes into the room and approaches you. 'Hello', she smiles, 'I'm Delia's mum. I wondered how she was getting on in her work.' Where would you begin? What would you say?

Good practice

Consider how you would explain the way in which you record children's progress to an interested friend who does not work in education.

Case study: Sample reports for parents

Earlier in the chapter, it was emphasised that records of children's progress and attainment serve two principal purposes. First, so that you have access to data that may influence your lesson planning; second, to provide information in formal records for other audiences (parents, colleagues). The two reports below are genuine, though some details have been altered to ensure anonymity. As a trainee teacher, you will not be required to write such a report, but as soon as you qualify and take responsibility for your own class, you will be! In studying the examples, bear in mind that the body of the text is generated by computer software but that the teacher still needs to know individual children well enough to provide specific insights into their progress. No report can say everything about a child, so a selection of key issues and learning outcomes is inevitable. Making this selection provides one of the key challenges for a teacher, who may be writing up to 30 reports for infants (reception/KS1) and even more for juniors (KS2). Note also that the new responsibilities of TAs may include the administration (but not the writing) of reports, though how this works in practice will depend upon school circumstances.

1. Saleha, Foundation Stage

Personal, Social and Emotional Development: Saleha has been eager to learn and is confident about speaking in a whole-class situation. She has improved in learning to wait her turn to speak. Saleha has become more independent but still needs reassurance from adults at times. She enjoys looking after visitors and is very caring towards children that are hurt or upset.

Communication, Language and Literacy: Our class work has covered a variety of traditional tales, modern fiction books and humorous poems. We have used illustrations to help us predict stories and used initial letters to help us work out unfamiliar words. Saleha enjoyed writing notes to the imaginary creatures in the garden and has been involved in preparing and presenting short plays in front of the other children. Saleha's reading is progressing very well and she can read a wide range of words appropriate to her age. Her writing has also developed well and she takes a pride in being neat. Saleha is now listening more carefully to adults and is working much better as a member of a group. She loves to hear stories, songs, music, rhymes and poems. Saleha's literacy work has developed well and I am extremely pleased with her overall progress. She is now ready to tackle the greater demands of Year 1 work.

Mathematical Development: Key objectives for this year have been to become familiar with numbers from one to ten, using them in songs and rhymes, counting situations and simple quizzes. We have also introduced the numbers 11 to 20. Saleha handled 1p, 2p and 5p coins. She used and described basic 2D and 3D shapes and also used non-standard but uniform units (such as hands, feet, bricks) to estimate and measure lengths, masses and capacities. Saleha continues to learn quickly and has exceeded the minimum expectations for the year.

Knowledge and Understanding of the World: The reception group took part in a 'forces and motion' science topic by bringing in wheeled vehicles and observing the result of pushing and pulling them along. We also had races between toy cars and discussed why some toy vehicles are faster than others are. During our 'sounds and hearing' topic the children described sounds that they heard around them, both in the school building and grounds. We observed what happens when we move away from the source of a sound. Saleha took part in these sessions and was very interested all that happened. In the ICT suite, she learned mouse control and became familiar with a range of computer programs. She also used a 'floor turtle' to estimate distances. In RE, Saleha listened with interest to stories and was willing to discuss what they meant.

Creative Development: Saleha has represented her creative ideas in a variety of ways and has grown in confidence. She has worked happily on group projects, such as building large models that are later played with, and individual projects when she did painting and collage. Saleha has learned to use a range of tools and materials, and particularly likes colouring on her own. She recognises that instruments can be played in a variety of ways and has developed group pieces based on moods and places.

Physical Development: Saleha has become more independent and now responds well to instructions. Her co-ordination continues to improve and she is becoming more spatially aware. Saleha has had PE lessons using the climbing apparatus and is learning to move carefully around others and handle small equipment. She especially likes PE outside, when we play whole-class games and team sports.

Personal Comments: Saleha is enthusiastic about all that we do in school. She picks up new ideas very quickly and has made excellent progress overall. I am sure that she will do well in Year 1.

Head Teacher's Comments: Saleha's good humour and determination to do well, even when she has been a little uncertain, has been delightful to see. Well done, Saleha!

Targets for Next Year: Saleha must build on her good progress this year and continue enjoying learning.

2. Marshall, Year 3

Visits
Autumn Term: Museum, local Priory, Woodland walk
Spring Term: Cathedral
Summer Term: Local Mosque, local Christian Centre

ENGLISH
Reading curriculum:

- Range of fiction genre, including play scripts and poetry
- Library skills and use of the Dewey system
- Research skills, scanning, skimming, note-taking
- Phonics and spelling

Writing curriculum:

- Writing for a variety of purposes (creative, narrative, persuasive, research, expressive, instructional)
- Sentence grammar and punctuation

Reading: Marshall has made good overall progress. His expression is developing well and he is noticing punctuation in the text. He is able to talk about his reading and make inferences from the text. Marshall receives extra literacy support and is able to apply skills learnt to his own reading. He has begun to scan text to find information.

Writing: Marshall has made steady progress. He has lovely ideas for story-writing and is remembering to use adjectives to create a picture for the reader. His enthusiasm to write sometimes means that Marshall misses out words and forgets to use punctuation, making it difficult to follow the story plot. He can use a simple dictionary but does not always check his spellings. In handwriting, Marshall still needs to make tall and short letters more clearly distinguishable. He can join up his letters but does not always do so.

Speaking and Listening: Marshall is able to listen and ask questions to help his understanding. He has an intermittent stammer that can cause him difficulty in expressing himself.

Next Steps in English: Marshall needs to make inferences from the text when reading. In writing, he needs to check his work more carefully to make sure that sentences make sense. He needs to think more carefully before speaking.

MATHEMATICS
Mini-topic curriculum:

- 2D and 3D Shape
- Symmetry
- Weight and length as forms of measurement
- Data-handling
- Angles and movement
- Volume and capacity
- Time

Marshall has worked hard and made steady progress. At the start of the year he found mental/oral subtraction problems difficult but is now much more confident. He is able to find the inverse for addition and subtraction sentences and is being encouraged to use more than one strategy to solve problems.

Next Steps in mathematics: Marshall needs to look carefully at a number sequence to find pattern and use this to predict the next number.

SCIENCE
Curriculum:

- Shadows and reflections

- Earth in Space
- Materials and their uses
- Changing materials
- Teeth and healthy eating
- Living things and their environment
- Green plants as organisms

Marshall is able to talk about the properties of materials and sort them into groups according to their properties. He can describe differences between living and non-living things and has begun to think about factors that cause change.

Next Steps in science: To plan a fair investigation where only one factor will change, other factors remaining constant.

HISTORY
Curriculum:

- Romans as an in-depth study
- Anglo-Saxons (outline study)
- Vikings (outline study)

Marshall thoroughly enjoyed the visit to see the Roman exhibits at the museum and the old Roman wall. His hands-on experience brought history to life for him. He has developed a growing awareness of chronology and can give some reasons why people leave their homelands and settle in another country.

GEOGRAPHY
Curriculum:

- Locality studies: the local woodland walk
- Settlements: the country of Zambia
- Mapping skills and co-ordinates

Marshall can compare different localities, noticing similarities and differences in land use and physical features such as valleys and wooded areas. He is aware of how some land use has changed and can make suggestions as to how it might be improved.

ART:
Curriculum:

- Colour-mixing and combinations
- Powder paints portraits
- Observational drawings of plants and flowers
- Batik flowers and weavings

Marshall has worked hard to create texture in his artwork with paints, drawings and textiles.

Following the educational visit, he produced a weaving that reflects the colours and feelings of the landscape. He includes a lot of fine detail in his drawings.

MUSIC
Curriculum:

- Structure and pitch
- Duration and dynamics
- Timbre and texture
- Listening and appraising
- Composing own music

Marshall is now able to recognise notes of differing pitch (high, low, the same). He has created repeated sound patterns and has begun to work with others to fit patterns together. He has also started to understand that layering sounds creates musical texture.

PHYSICAL EDUCATION
Curriculum:

- Games–sending and receiving ball-skills, racket-skills, team games
- Gym–pathways and levels using floor and apparatus
- Dance–linking movements, responding to narratives, rhythm and tempo

Marshall shows good control when planning a sequence of actions, both on the floor and on benches. In games he has learned the skills of attack and defence, as well as developing accurate overarm and underarm throws.

RELIGIOUS EDUCATION
Curriculum:

- Exploring what is meant by faith and the difference it can make to people's lives
- The place of worship and prayer
- Signs and symbols
- The significance of Christmas and Easter
- Basics of Christianity and Islam

Marshall is able to think about his own experiences, commitments and values, and contrast them with those of other people. He can explain how some aspects of religious belief are practised. He can retell the Easter story.

DESIGN TECHNOLOGY
Curriculum:

- Making permanent joins
- Investigating different temporary joins
- Making picture frames
- Moving toys

- Linkages and levers
- Problem-solving 3D construction challenges

Marshall knows how to join a range of different materials to create permanent and temporary fixtures. He can talk about the uses for different joins. He has used his skills to create a picture frame.

INFORMATION TECHNOLOGY
Curriculum:

- Word-processing and text handling
- Textease
- Graphics
- Data-handling
- Control and programming using Roamer
- Creating and sending emails

Marshall has used computer software to recreate part of an artist's picture and used the full range of tools to create texture. He has used a simulation program, involving mathematical problems and logical thinking. He has input data for data-handling and used word-processing. Marshall has some understanding of the function and purpose of emails.

PERSONAL, SOCIAL, CITIZENSHIP AND HEALTH EDUCATION
Curriculum:

- Friends and relationships
- Healthy living
- Keeping safe

Marshall is now able to express his opinions and give reasons for doing so. With adult support, he is able to set termly targets for his development. He is also able to identify things he has achieved. Marshall understands why rules are needed and begun to exercise a level of responsibility in the classroom.

SUMMARY: Marshall has been a lovely member of the class. He has grown up a lot during the year and is taking more responsibility for his own learning. He still struggles to concentrate for any length of time and is sometimes easily distracted. Marshall tends to be careless with his work and needs to check more carefully before being satisfied. He loves to play with other children but does not have a close friend.

Attendance:

- Number of sessions attended since last September   292
- Total possible sessions since last September   308
- Percentage attendance   95%
- Number of unauthorised absences   0

End of key stage assessment

The following is an example of an End-of-Key-Stage 1 assessment:

	Teacher assessment	Task result	Test result
LITERACY			
■ Speaking and Listening	2	N/A	N/A
■ Reading	2	2A	2A
■ Writing	2	2B	N/A
NUMERACY	2	N/A	2
SCIENCE	2		

NOTE: *There are no tests or tasks in Science for KS1*

Level 1 and W (working towards Level 1) represent achievement below the nationally expected standard for most 7-year-olds. Level 2 is divided into three grades: 2A, 2B and 2C. Level 2B represents achievement at the nationally expected standard for most seven-year-olds. Levels 3 and 4+ represent achievement above the nationally expected standard for most seven-year-olds.

Activate your thinking!

Imagine you are the parent. How easily would you interpret the information provided?

Good practice

Formulate three key targets each for Saleha and Marshall in the core subjects.

Standards

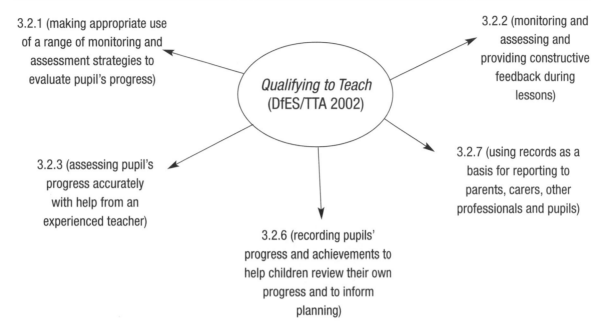

3.2.1 (making appropriate use of a range of monitoring and assessment strategies to evaluate pupil's progress)

3.2.2 (monitoring and assessing and providing constructive feedback during lessons)

Qualifying to Teach (DfES/TTA 2002)

3.2.3 (assessing pupil's progress accurately with help from an experienced teacher)

3.2.7 (using records as a basis for reporting to parents, carers, other professionals and pupils)

3.2.6 (recording pupils' progress and achievements to help children review their own progress and to inform planning)

Further reading

Briggs, M., Woodfield, A., Martin, C. and Swatton, P. (2003) *Assessment for Learning and Teaching in Primary Schools*, Exeter: Learning Matters.

Drummond, M. J. (2003) *Assessing Children's Learning*, London: David Fulton.
A smoothly written book with a balance of theoretical perspective and practical examples, written by an author with considerable experience in this field.

8

Behaviour Management

Introduction

Most children enjoy school, behave sensibly for the majority of the time and want to have a positive relationship with adults and other pupils. This chapter explores a range of issues associated with children's behaviour and the strategies available for ensuring that the teaching and learning process is not hindered by the struggle to maintain order. A variety of discipline strategies are offered for consideration but it is acknowledged that behind every settled classroom is a lot of hard work by the teacher in establishing and maintaining positive relationships, generating work that motivates the children and enforcing an agreed behaviour policy.

Creating a positive learning environment

It takes only a few minutes in a classroom to detect whether a teacher has managed to establish and maintain a positive learning environment. In the best-run classrooms, the children are lively but not silly, speak naturally to adults, treat one another kindly and want to do their best to succeed. Teachers use humour without losing control and children respond to instructions, and even to being chastened, without rancour or discord. Trainee teachers often say of such situations: 'That is how I want my own classroom to be.'

The terminology used for class control issues varies. The word 'behaviour' tends to be used with respect to the child's actions and 'control' and 'discipline' with respect to the teacher's actions. That is, the teacher attempts to influence the child's behaviour through effective discipline in the belief that this is the most effective way of exercising control. However, the imposition of external constraints have limited value in as much as children ultimately need to exercise self-control rather than have it imposed.

Furthermore, it is important to remember that behaviour does not simply encompass a child being good or naughty; it also includes other manifestations such as exhibiting shyness, withdrawal from mainstream activities and idleness. These, too, are behaviours commonly seen in classrooms with which teachers have to cope.

Teachers quickly discover that children's willingness to comply and conform to established norms of behaviour varies considerably. Some children do not have the strategies, willpower or grasp of conventions to know what 'behaving' means or the strategies to change it. As a result, the unacceptable behaviour continues and inexperienced teachers in particular may become increasingly exasperated, berating the child by fruitlessly repeating the demand to 'behave'. In addition, a small number of children understand the conventions but wilfully disregard them. Children therefore need to be provided with an enforceable rule framework, sensibly but consistently applied, within which they can gradually strengthen their own self-control. Dreikurs *et al.* (1998) stress the importance of helping children to take responsibility for their own actions. They cite an example of a boy who kept calling out in class. The teacher despaired of finding a solution until she asked the boy for his suggestions. He imposed a sanction on himself (loss of two minutes free time for each transgression) and the problem was cured within a week! Newell and Jeffery (2002, pages 43–8) emphasise that teachers should model good behaviour to children. Strategies include being prepared to say sorry, explain that teachers as well as children have rights, taking a keen interest in learning, demonstrating a strong sense of purpose in teaching and showing that even difficult behaviour can be overcome. Teachers have to take into account the age and experience of the children, as well as school behaviour policies, but the twin principles of consistency and fairness must apply whatever the circumstances.

Unacceptable behaviour

Unacceptable behaviour takes many forms. Some children constantly push the boundaries and their names are upon every teacher's lips. Some children cause trouble for certain teachers but act sensibly for others. Whereas children who actively resist conforming and often behave unreasonably may require special help and intervention policies, the majority can be dealt with using basic classroom rules and procedures. Learning to cope with the vagaries of children's behaviour is helped when teachers understand that unacceptable behaviour is sometimes due to an uncertainty in children's minds about what is acceptable. It is also important to recognise the difference between two types of inappropriate behaviour, namely, children who misbehave and children who fail to conform.

Children who misbehave often do so out of choice. They understand the rules but make a decision to disregard them; they are also aware of the likely consequences but hope that they won't get caught or are insufficiently impressed by the sanction to worry. Younger children are more likely to misbehave due to a lack of understanding of the rules and school conventions or confusion about expectations.

Some children fail to conform, either because they do not see the need to do so or lack the maturity to comply. In most cases, the situation can be remedied by patient, persistent explanation and use of peer pressure. Children new to school may simply lack awareness of what is required; older ones may be egocentric or come from a family/cultural background that fosters single-mindedness. Typically, the behaviour of non-conformists varies little inside and outside school. Such children seem puzzled when confronted by an insistent adult who explains to them that a particular action is not acceptable. Parents, when asked about their non-conformist children, will often sigh and admit that they cannot do anything much with them either! Children who fail to conform may be highly motivated or sluggish, popular or aloof, pleasant or miserable, but they have in common their persistent refusal or inability to act in a conventional manner. Non-conformists wander when they are meant to be seated, approach their work differently from others, insist on working alone instead of collaboratively and show an attitude towards the teacher which varies from disdain to wild enthusiasm. Repeated day after day the irregular behaviour can cause teachers to become irritated and frustrated.

It is a challenge to channel the energies of non-conformist children into productive activities. Teachers are keen to curb the unacceptable behaviour but fear that if they are too insistent the child concerned may suffer a loss of confidence or start to rebel and turn into a persistent offender. Regular calm explanations and consistent teacher direction help to regulate the situation but the children's inability to grasp conventions makes the process protracted.

Inappropriate behaviour of all types may not arise due to pupils' inability to understand what is expected of them but from a teacher's failure to gain pupils' respect due to a timid personality, mundane teaching approach or lacklustre content to lessons. In such cases, efforts to gain control are likely to fail. McPhillimy (1996) issues a warning about the need for teachers to examine the *cause* of problems rather than their symptoms:

> Misbehaviour in itself is therefore mainly a symptom of a problem rather than the problem itself. If the underlying problems are dealt with, then the symptom is likely to disappear (page 61).

Activate your thinking!

Consider the children in your class who exhibit inappropriate behaviour. Try to categorise as follows:

- Those who are regularly mischievous but generally harmless.
- Those who misbehave wilfully.
- Those who are non-conformists.

Consider how you might react to the same sort of inappropriate behaviour from a child in each of the categories.

Factors influencing behaviour

Terminology is important when considering issues of control and discipline. *Bad behaviour* involves making a judgement about someone's actions and intent. In school, the person evaluating the behaviour is usually the teacher and the one being judged, the pupil. Bad behaviour may be wilful (deliberate) or unintended. Similarly, all children (and adults, for that matter) are capable of *irresponsible* behaviour when, for a short period of time, common sense and rational thought seem to disappear. Such moments are different from the concept of indiscipline which occurs when children know what they should do but choose not to do it.

When teachers have to deal with unsatisfactory behaviour, it is a signal that something has already gone wrong, so it is important for them to give serious thought as to why it has happened and whether it can be prevented in the future. If a framework of rules is established early on, discussed with the children and frequently reviewed, it provides a yardstick against which to judge behaviour and determine sanctions (where appropriate). However, it is important to distinguish between 'order' in the classroom and an 'orderly' classroom. Order can be achieved by insisting that the children adhere to a rigid set of requirements of the 'do this but do not do that' type, reminiscent of military commands. Children have only to step slightly out of line to invoke a sanction, placing a considerable strain on the purposeful classroom environment that you are trying to achieve. Orderliness, on the other hand, stresses the fact that the classroom functions smoothly because everyone is clear about the boundaries, involved in reviewing them and invited to talk sensibly about infringements. In an orderly classroom, teachers and ATs are uncompromising about deliberate improper behaviour, but more concerned with achieving satisfactory outcomes than inflexibly applying sanctions. Punishments should be reserved for deliberate offending against the rules. Unintended infringements and silliness can normally be resolved through dialogue.

Adult–child relationships

We have already noted that the majority of pupils of all ages want to do well and please their teacher. Effective working relationships develop gradually through regular interaction between adult and child, relevant work and interesting lessons. Teachers who are harsh, unreasonable, condescending or insincere are inviting problems of indiscipline as children react offensively towards such attitudes or lose confidence and thereby underachieve. A positive classroom climate is assisted by being firm, fair and tolerant of genuine mistakes. Teachers who have a natural manner and develop a sincere approach to their teaching, aided by a cheerful disposition, are unlikely to suffer unduly from misbehaving pupils.

Developing a philosophy

Establishing and maintaining high standards of behaviour depend, in part, upon a teacher's philosophy of education. As noted elsewhere in this book, teachers will use teaching strategies and approaches which reflect their own beliefs about the ways that children learn best. Teachers who are willing to persevere in order to achieve their educational aims, yet who are ready to accept advice and modify their practices accordingly, are usually at ease with themselves about their work, and transmit this confidence to their pupils. Teachers that have no clear idea about the direction of their teaching, and meander from one extreme to another, are almost certain to produce an unstable learning environment.

Cementing the bond

Children react adversely against autocratic teachers, those who try to lord it over them and those who demand too much, too soon, without offering patient help and advice in the completion of tasks. It is essential for teachers to win pupils' co-operation and show that they like them, but in such a way that the separate adult and child identities are maintained. To win co-operation necessitates teachers taking a real interest in the children, listening to their comments and requests, and responding with positive suggestions, praise, encouragement and trust. All teachers have times when they struggle to make headway with their class; the bank of goodwill that is stored up during the 'plentiful' times needs to be there to draw on in the hard times.

True freedom

It should be evident that blatant contravention of rules has to be dealt with firmly, yet some inexperienced teachers seem to imagine that if things are ignored they will fade away naturally. However, offering pupils 'freedom in learning' is not the same as giving them 'freedom to behave in any way they choose'! Children need to know where the boundaries lie in terms of appropriate behaviour, including the way they address one another and the teacher, their application to the task in hand and the extent of their co-operation. The occasional unsettling incident in which children say, in effect, that they are free to do what they want, how they want, provides a stark reminder (if any were needed) that selfish behaviour leads to unhappiness and insecurity rather than any helpful form of freedom.

Emphasising the positive

Most unsatisfactory behaviour can be resolved without causing humiliation or loss of face to either child or adult. This is not the same as saying that children should get away with things, as pupils need to realise that every action has a consequence. Some children are unaware of the impact their behaviour has on others and it needs to be pointed out to them that they have responsibilities as well as rights. The majority of children respond positively to genuine praise and encouragement, and even the most mischievous tyke prefers specific guidance and the opportunity to master skills and to learn something new. Although class control and discipline require the application of appropriate techniques and strategies to curb inappropriate behaviour and ensure that potential troublemakers are kept in check, the most effective learning environment grows in the soil of high motivation and a desire to learn. Children will not want to misbehave if, in doing so, they reduce the thrill and adventure that happy learning experiences bring.

The teacher's role

Although it is not popular to say so, teachers can sometimes contribute to the causes of bad behaviour. Unfairness, impatience and poor lesson preparation can create the conditions for resentment and discontent to occur. The end result is a deterioration of the atmosphere, control problems and a negative impact on learning. Jacques (2000) comments that 'When faced with a difficult class, the tendency is for trainees and even experienced teachers to blame the children and attribute the bad behaviour to all sorts of factors' (page 122). Jacques emphasises the point that different circumstances simply mean that different discipline strategies have to be employed. While in the normal run-of-the-mill times, a teacher can rely on the existing good relationship that exists with pupils to allow simple tactics such as a shake of the head to diffuse the situation, on other occasions some tight control strategies have to be employed. Nevertheless, if children are regularly proving to be a headache, it is important to take a step back and consider reasons other than placing the blame *wholly* on them.

There are many ways in which poor behaviour may be, at least in part, a reflection of teacher failings; for example, it might come about through a lack of dialogue with the children that lead to misunderstandings, intolerance, inappropriate lessons, harsh sanctions or petty fault-finding. Conflict is not inevitable and can usually be avoided by following the advice offered elsewhere in this chapter and implementing appropriate strategies. By following the advice listed below, your classroom has a good chance of becoming the positive and industrious working environment you want it to be.

Stay calm and alert

Teachers have little chance of improving a situation of potential conflict if they lose their self-control. When problems appear to be developing, it is important to reassure pupils that things are in hand. This can be done by breathing deeply, speaking a little more slowly than usual, smiling gently when speaking and keeping wide-open eyes. Potentially difficult situations can often be defused if teachers simply refuse to be rattled by them.

Do not jump to conclusions

Situations are not always what they may seem. Taking time to discover the facts before making a judgement or accusation and issuing sanctions is essential in settling disputes. It is better to spend a little time sorting out a *real* problem than acting decisively in dealing with an imagined one! Pupils become exasperated and annoyed when teachers blunder in and make matters worse by jumping to unwarranted conclusions.

Concentrate on what children are saying

The only way for teachers to discover the truth is to listen carefully to what children have to say. Some teachers try to listen but due to the pressure of the moment do not properly hear what is being said. The most effective teacher–pupil relationships are built by teachers who listen to their pupils and hear their voices (Wise 2000).

Enter a constructive dialogue

Although children normally begin by defending their actions, accusing others or reacting angrily, it is important to introduce a positive element to the conversation as soon as possible. Skilled teachers ask distracting questions which focus attention away from the problem. Once the children become less animated and begin to speak in a natural tone, the main issues can usually be discussed without undue rancour.

Avoid banal questions

Some questions that teachers ask are not really questions at all, but rather a poor attempt to exercise control through using veiled threats. For example:

- What's the matter with you today?
- Do you want to stay in at playtime?
- Weren't you listening?
- Would you behave like that at home?

Such pointless questions are likely to irritate children and may invite ridicule and sarcasm from older pupils.

Demonstrate genuine caring

Although teachers care about their pupils, it probably does not occur to most pupils that this is so! Teachers have, therefore, to demonstrate a caring attitude through the way they address children, the interest they show in their welfare and the action they take to ensure that justice is done and that no child is disadvantaged. Caring is also shown by insisting that rules are followed and by giving vulnerable children a secure framework within which to develop good patterns of behaviour.

Facilitate agreement about the way ahead

In situations of potential conflict, it is possible for teachers to deal with the immediate circumstances but fail to offer pupils a strategy for the future. Once a satisfactory dialogue has been established, children must be given clearly defined steps to follow so that improvements can be monitored and approved, both by the teacher and the child.

Silly behaviour

Very few children are deviant, though some are regular rule-breakers and persistent offenders. Most unacceptable behaviour is due to silliness rather than deviance and takes a number of different forms:

- *Uncontrolled behaviour*: shouting out an answer to a question without permission.
- *Arrogant*: calling out a 'clever' remark.
- *Distractive*: showing off by doing something daring.
- *Detached*: deliberately working very slowly.
- *Spiteful*: teasing another child.
- *Insolent*: asking pointless questions.
- *Deceptive*: pretending not to understand.

These instances are common in some classrooms and are associated with inappropriate work, boredom or general lack of respect. They can signal that it is time to change content, terminate a teaching approach or re-evaluate lesson management. On such occasions it is important that teachers try to understand the behaviour and respond positively. Thus:

Uncontrolled behaviour: children who call out without permission lack self-discipline or do not understand the rules.

Arrogant behaviour: children who call out a silly remark may be signalling a lack of respect for the teacher or simply showing off to impress friends.

Distractive behaviour: children who show off are probably doing so because it is more enjoyable than concentrating on unstimulating work.

Detached behaviour: children who work very slowly may be showing that they are not prepared to engage with uninteresting or unduly demanding activities.

Spiteful behaviour: children who deliberately tease another child are enjoying the power that accompanies ridicule.

Insolent behaviour: children who ask pointless questions are wasting time but avoiding confrontation with the teacher by giving the appearance of interest.

Deceptive behaviour: children who pretend not to understand may be trying to undermine the teacher's authority and create a distraction from the main point of the lesson.

These and similar strategies are used by the small number of children who have decided that messing about is preferable to concentrating on the work; their actions are deliberate but not necessarily serious if attended to appropriately from an early stage. Although teachers rightly feel annoyed by the disruptions, they also act as a warning signal about the need to review the lesson's effectiveness and relevance. It is difficult to make every lesson stimulating and relevant for all children, but persistent boredom not only affects the quality of the children's work but influences their attitudes (Figure 8.1 The consequences of boredom).

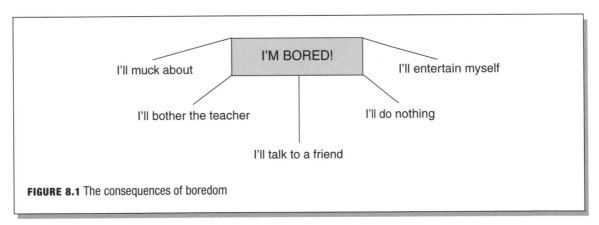

FIGURE 8.1 The consequences of boredom

Faced with silly behaviour, inexperienced teachers may be tempted to ignore it or hope that by sounding fierce they can minimise the disruption. In fact, ignoring the behaviour is rarely effective (though there are exceptions to this rule, see later) and may indicate to the class that the teacher is not in control of events. Similarly, severe comments often make matters worse in the long term and lead to teacher exhaustion and distress. The problem with harsh reactions is that they deal only with the symptoms and not the underlying causes such as boredom, bravado, inappropriate lessons, inadequate lesson management, and so on. Quite often, these underlying causes take time to diagnose and remedy, so a teacher may have to resort to *holding measures* as a temporary means of counteracting the silly behaviour. Examples of holding methods for each of the above categories of behaviour include the following set of reactions:

Uncontrolled behaviour: 'Olive, you forgot our count to three before you speak rule. Please remember in future.' (The response is merely a statement of fact and avoids attributing blame.)

Arrogant behaviour: 'John. Remember to put your hand up first and take your turn if you've anything to say.' (The response strengthens the teacher's authority, reminds everyone of the rules and avoids confrontation with John.)

Distractive behaviour: 'Please sit still on your chair, Rhoda, we don't want anyone injured, thank you.' (The response focuses upon Rhoda's welfare rather than her inappropriate behaviour.)

Detached behaviour: 'Are you finding this difficult, Ellie? Perhaps I can help you along a bit.' (The response allows the teacher to set short-term targets for Ellie.)

Spiteful behaviour: 'If you've got anything to say, Ben, say something kind; otherwise keep quiet. Let's see how helpful you can be for the remainder of the lesson; I'll ask you about it after everyone has gone out.' (The response indicates the teacher's displeasure, sets boundaries upon Ben's behaviour and offers him the chance to redeem himself.)

Insolent behaviour: 'Put your hand up if you think you know the answer to Gordon's question.' (The response focuses upon Gordon's 'ignorance' and allows other children to gain satisfaction from offering the correct answer. An ironic afterthought is also useful: 'It looks as if everybody knew the answer except you, Gordon! You will need to work harder if you want to keep up with the others.')

Deceptive behaviour: 'If you don't understand by now, Julie, you'd better stay behind after the lesson and I'll explain it to you then.' (The response calls Julie's bluff and puts the onus upon her to complete the work.)

Activate your thinking!

Poor behaviour will never improve of its own accord!

Good practice

Don't just remind the children of the agreed procedure; *rehearse* it with them.

These holding responses do not solve the underlying problem but do allow a teacher to continue the lesson without undue disruption, losing face or causing damage to relationships.

If the behaviour is repeated or is serious, the teacher will certainly want to see the child after the session and express disapproval in an uncharged atmosphere or in the presence of a senior teacher. Children who misbehave through silliness rather than deviance are corrected through a combination of firmness, fairness and attention to future lesson content and delivery. Teachers who rely on the holding strategy without looking more deeply into the situation are likely to experience a recurrence of the unwanted behaviour and further struggles to gain control.

Whenever possible, speak to a child directly after the session about the unacceptable behaviour. Make sure that other children nearby do not interrupt you. Tell the child how you feel. Express your disappointment. Ask for an explanation. Listen carefully to the reply. Don't patronise or ridicule. Stay calm and serious but speak naturally. Look the child in the eye and try to show that you are interested in what she or he has to say. If appropriate, ask the child what he or she suggests can be done to improve the situation. End the conversation positively and indicate that you are expecting something better in future. Over the next few sessions, do not pay the child unnatural attention but if possible find opportunity to commend work. Don't expect miracles. Keep things in proportion. React but don't over-react to silly behaviour.

> ### Good practice
>
> Try treating silly pupils with a greater level of seriousness than their behaviour deserves. Pretend that they are sensible children and trust them with some responsibility. Speak to them in a more 'grown-up' manner. Evaluate over a period of a few weeks whether the way you treat them affects the way they begin to behave.

Deviant behaviour

In contrast to silliness, deviant forms of behaviour can be intimidating to the teacher and threaten the wellbeing of the other children. Deviant behaviour is typified by one or more of the following: belligerent answering back, fierce anger, agitated protest and shouting, and refusal to do any work. Every school has a policy for dealing with this type of indiscipline and the agreed procedures have to be consistently followed if progress is to be made. If the child exhibits worrying traits of the sort described, it is likely that the head teacher is already well aware of the problem; however, you must still ensure that you keep senior staff informed about developments. In situations where there are repeated instances of wilful behaviour, write a brief note of each incident (what happened and when) for future reference.

Deviant behaviour in which pupils are wilfully disobedient or defiant is thankfully rare but can be unnerving for teachers who then agonise over ways in which they might contain a situation which will certainly not correct itself without intervention. While action is being taken with the assistance of more experienced colleagues, you will have to be sternly insistent and openly state to the child the things that will not be tolerated. Setting realistic and enforceable short-term goals is essential. Inducements to more acceptable behaviour have to be used within a strictly defined code, explained to the child and, if possible agreed verbally by him or her. More serious situations will involve the SENCO and, perhaps, parents. Progress is likely to be slow and in a tiny minority of cases you may only see marginal improvement. If the indiscipline becomes very serious and other children's learning is deemed to be suffering, the head teacher may decide to remove the child from the classroom or, in the most extreme cases, exclude him or her from school. Unfortunately, children who exhibit deviant behaviour often come from homes in which such behaviour is condoned or parents have been unable to deal with it themselves. Trainee teachers should never be, and rarely are, left to struggle unassisted with devious children.

Finally, it is important, though difficult to try and distinguish children who are behaving deviantly from those who are struggling with a diagnosable condition, such as attention deficit and hyperactivity disorder, ADHD (see, for example, Kewley 2001). Although there is still active debate about the concept of ADHD, the principle for every teacher should be to deal with the causes of the behaviour as well as the consequences.

Responding to unacceptable behaviour

Taking suitable action when faced with poor behaviour is one of the challenges that teachers face as they seek to establish a well controlled yet inspiring classroom environment. Tolerance of minor instances of unacceptable behaviour may be counter-productive if it leads to a worsening situation in the long run. On the other hand, early intervention can also be unhelpful if it disrupts the flow of a lesson, sours the atmosphere or creates unease among more timid children. Some trainee teachers regret that they were 'too soft' early on in their teaching and insufficiently firm in the opening encounters with a new class. Others employ unnecessarily heavy-handed tactics when a lighter touch would be enough, thereby causing ill-feeling and dismay among the children. There is always a danger of developing an impulsive response to every slight breach of the rules that result in stress for both teacher and children.

Circumstances need to be taken into account when deciding how to respond to misbehaviour. For instance, the child who is normally sensible but on one occasion excitedly throws a rubber across the room is unlikely to repeat the action if chastened; it would be foolish to over-react by using fierce remarks or invoking a sanction. On the other hand, a persistently troublesome child is unlikely to respond to a gentle approach or to sanctions that have been used repeatedly without effect. In this case, a much firmer response is required (in accordance with school policy). Similarly, common sense suggests that end-of-term bravado or wet playtime excitement induces unnatural behaviour and should be treated understandingly. At the other extreme, a single act of bullying needs to be dealt with firmly, regardless of the circumstances.

If teachers show agitation every time a child is perceived as behaving unacceptably, it is the child who is controlling the situation and not the teacher. Unless the boundaries of acceptable behaviour are clear, the action–reaction process continues, both teacher and child become edgy, and nothing is improved. During succeeding days, the pattern is repeated:

Step 1: Child behaves unacceptably > Teacher responds agitatedly

Step 2: Child repeats the behaviour > Teacher responds sternly

Step 3: Child repeats the behaviour once again > Teacher imposes sanction

And so on.

The problem with this action–reaction process is not only that the child is dictating the pattern of teacher response but that the causes of the unacceptable behaviour are not being addressed. In particular, a characteristic of effective behaviour management is that it *acts to prevent*, deter or reduce the undesirable actions, rather than remedying them once they have occurred. Understanding the distinction between 'prevention' and 'cure' is important for every practitioner. Poor behaviour is an indication of the behaviour management's failure.

Whether unacceptable behaviour is an occasional wilful act or a persistent trend, teachers understandably interpret it as a challenge or threat to their authority and a reflection upon their ability to cope. However, if these feelings result in a series of instinctive, defensive reactions, little is gained and the situation will probably worsen. Teachers rightly argue that 'something has to be done' but it is not merely a case of 'doing something' but of doing the right thing. In deciding upon the most appropriate strategy to use, a number of factors need to be considered:

A teacher may not recognise the message that the behaviour carries

Sometimes poor behaviour indicates that there is something wrong with the lesson, the teacher's attitude or the teaching approach. It is easy to blame the children or refer to a class as 'difficult' without examining other factors that may be contributing to the problem. Inappropriate work, over-reliance on a single teaching method or poor organisation can create or foster a restless climate.

There is often a difference between the teacher's and the children's perceptions

Although there are obvious instances of unacceptable behaviour, teachers may find themselves attaching far more significance to an act than was intended. Even wilful behaviour is not necessarily directed at the teacher but may be a consequence of youthful exuberance or high spirits. Learning to distinguish between silliness and wilfulness is a skill that every teacher needs to sharpen.

Children may be experiencing hardship outside school

Uncertainty or anguish about personal circumstances can make it impossible to behave rationally. Children, like all of us, react differently when home life or relationships are unsteady. Allowance needs to be made for irrational behaviour, provided some positive steps are then taken to remedy the situation if it continues, such as involvement of the head teacher, advice from the SENCO or notifying parents.

Responding to unacceptable behaviour is a challenge for every teacher. It requires patient, determined application, particularly in new situations. Strategies that appear to work with one group of pupils may be less successful with a different set of pupils, even in an almost identical situation. The challenges are particularly acute when starting to teach in a new school, where codes of conduct and accepted procedures are taken for granted by the existing staff and pupils but have yet to be learned by the new teacher. Trainee teachers on placement are, of course, regularly experiencing this impediment, but Neill and Caswell (1993) describe how this situation faces all new teachers, even experienced ones:

> Experienced teachers who move to a new school are sometimes surprised by the sudden need to put effort into controlling their classes. They are not always aware how much they previously relied on their thorough, but subliminal, knowledge of the formal and informal procedures of their old school and their reputation among the children (page 4).

Consequently, if you are a trainee teacher on placement, it is hardly surprising if the first few weeks with a new class prove to be challenging.

Activate your thinking!

Consider the extent to which pupils' behaviour patterns have been determined by: (a) their uncertainty about the rules; (b) their wilfulness; (c) your own lack of dynamism and resourcefulness.

One way or another it is essential that you do not exacerbate control and discipline problems by your ignorance of the way things are done in the school/classroom or pupils' expectations about what is required of them. If children sense that you are allowing them liberties that their other teachers forbid, they are likely to take advantage of you. The following offers a summary of key strategies.

Speak naturally

Shouting rarely works and damages the classroom climate as well as your voice. Developing a strong voice takes practice but is more effective than a shrill or strained one. Ideally, your voice should be natural and carry authority for, as Rogers (1998) puts it, 'the adult tongue is a powerful weapon' (page 223).

Distinguish between enthusiasm and disobedience

Some children get so absorbed in their work that they are reluctant to stop. Avoid being irritated; instead say something like 'I'm pleased that you are so keen on your work, Jack, but everyone is waiting for you'. Younger children's voices become high-pitched if they get carried away with enthusiasm for what they are doing. Persevere with gentle, personal (rather than public) reminders to individual children to speak normally. It is worth modelling the different voices to a child and encouraging him or her to practise using an appropriate tone with you.

Make your instructions direct and specific

A comment like: 'Douglas, please concentrate on what Rachel is saying' is preferable to 'Douglas, stop messing about with Wayne'. Again, it is better to say 'Put your pencils down after finishing the next sentence and look this way' than to say 'Everybody pay attention to me'. Many teachers give out too many general statements such as 'Settle down' or 'Get on with your work quietly' or the ubiquitous 'Sh-hh' rather than giving specific commands.

Relax your voice when asking for children's attention

If possible, lower the pitch rather than raising it. Give pupils time to respond. If they are slow in responding, use a technique such as 'fingers on lips' (or the agreed signal to pay attention) or say 'If the person next to you is not yet paying attention, please whisper in his ear that we are waiting'.

Decide when it is right to get angry

Some trainee teachers feel awkward about expressing anger. Instead, they hold their feelings in and pretend to be sweet and sugary with the children. Anger is neither right or wrong. It depends on the circumstances under which it is used. In the general run of classroom life, a teacher who frequently got angry would either be a nervous wreck or be terrorising the children! Anger should be expressed calmly but assertively through voice tone and body language. The best teachers do not have to raise their voices but have the ability to speak so directly and coldly that even the worst offender is stopped short.

Do not confuse anger with rage

Most adults can, if they wish, frighten children by their rage and temper. This is professionally unacceptable and may even be interpreted as bullying. If you feel yourself 'coming to the boil' it is better to stop the lesson and stare through the window for a few seconds, hands loosely at your side and breathing deeply. Slowing the voice, deepening the tone and moving a little closer to the children will convey your feelings and may save you from saying something in the heat of the moment that you later regret.

Commend appropriate behaviour

When pupils respond appropriately, thank them and continue immediately. Do not begin a speech to the effect that you are not prepared to be kept waiting like this in future, etc. When a class is settling or coming to order, commend the children who are doing well rather than spending all your time criticising the unco-operative types. When the class is settled you can spend a moment saying 'Well done. I was very pleased that so many of you tidied up so quickly. Thank you. A few of you were leaving it to the others. I've made a note of who you are and next time I shall expect you to make a special effort.'

Motivate pupils to secure best results

It is important to remind yourself of the cardinal truth that motivated children rarely misbehave. If pupils are under-stimulated, unclear about what is expected of them and get away with work of mediocre quality, then it is little wonder that their behaviour deteriorates and their respect for you diminishes. Make your classroom buzz with interest and be a place where children can learn about the world, themselves and one another.

First encounters

Throughout their student life, trainee teachers dream of the time when they will have their own classes, free from the constraints of fitting in with someone else's routines and preferences, and liberated from being assessed by class teachers, mentors and college tutors. In reality, to have your own class is both delightful and daunting: delightful because it is the culmination of years of study and provides the opportunity to exercise your own judgement; daunting because you quickly become aware of the enormous responsibility lying before you.

To paraphrase comments from many newly qualified teachers as they reflect upon their first day with a class: 'When you walk into that classroom, shut the door and look at the class of children in front of you, you suddenly realise that you are on your own. You don't know whether to cry from fear or elation!' This mixture of emotions that wells up when newly qualified teachers first face their class is a powerful one. Over the coming days and weeks, nervous teachers discover that they are not alone, that education is a joint endeavour involving colleagues, parents and numerous unseen members of the community. Nevertheless, those first few days are important in respect of maintaining and establishing order. More experienced teachers have the advantage of knowing the ropes and having had opportunities to establish their relationships and school-wide reputation; new teachers have not. More experienced teachers are described by the children in various ways:

'Miss Chapman's really nice.'

'Mr Howard plays his guitar and does singing with you.'

'Mrs Ballam brings in animals from home.'

'Mr Fielding'll *do* you if you muck about!'

And so on. After teaching for a few years, the reputation of teachers (for better or worse) goes before them and provides a platform for establishing a satisfactory learning environment. The new teacher and trainee teacher, entering the classroom for the first time, do not have this advantage, and need to work hard to ensure that things run smoothly. In doing so, a number of assumptions can be made:

- The children will be as excited and expectant as you are

- Many children will gradually test the boundaries of behaviour and note your reactions

- No matter how much planning is done, it will take time before things settle into a routine

- There will be some misunderstandings as the settling process takes place

- Relationships lie at the heart of a successful time in school.

Even experienced teachers find that it can take several weeks before the classroom rhythm becomes established with a new class. In particular, the first few days are crucial. Younger children require specific guidance about basic procedures; older ones need to know how the teacher's expectations and ideas differ from those of previous teachers. Even if new teachers feel insecure and uncertain about what to expect, they need to give a strong impression of decisiveness and confidence to convince the class that they are in control and intend to be taken seriously. As part of the settling procedures, certain times of the day and certain events provide opportunities for unacceptable behaviour. Teachers sometimes refer to these occasions as the 'sticky spots' and the following are typical:

The start of a session

This is an important phase of every lesson. Simple strategies such as counting down from five to one, encouraging children to chant a simple rhyme as they settle or subtracting the time you are kept waiting from their playtime assists a smooth start. Eventually you will want the children to settle without direction, though very young children may need guidance about where to sit. If the children have been sitting in assembly just beforehand, it is sensible to use a few stretching exercises or give them a minor desk-task (such as copying some spellings or drawing a diagram) before commencing the formal session.

After a wet playtime

Children will have been inside with little chance to expend their energy. The classroom may be hot and airless and the children restless. Consequently, except in the worst weather, it is worth opening the windows for a few minutes and (again) spending a short time in a simple but orderly whole-class activity. For example, using a 'do this, do that' game or write-draw five things that wriggle to move (or similar). Although the settling activity takes up a few minutes, it is preferable to making an attempt to begin the proper lesson with restless children who have little inclination to learn.

Moving out of the classroom

Children who tend to misbehave usually find some opportunity to do so when moving from place to place. Consistent routines and clearly rehearsed expectations will reduce the likelihood of thoughtless behaviour but the prankster or mischief-maker will sometimes take delight in disrupting proceedings by noise, detours and squabbles. Until the situation is under control, inexperienced teachers need to be firmly insistent and rigorous in approach. Later on, when things have settled, a more relaxed approach will be possible. Strategies such as standing at the front of the queue, facing the children, asking them to stand upright and still, and choosing who should go first and last all help to maintain an orderly atmosphere.

Special occasions

Children would not be children if they did not get excited during special occasions. Changes of routine, greater freedom of movement around the school, teacher activity and the arrival of visitors all combine to create an atmosphere in which conventional procedures fluctuate from normal. Even sensible children can exhibit a surprising side to their natures; passive children become active and active children become hyperactive. At such times, teachers need to remain exceptionally calm themselves; it is easy for adults to get caught up in the frenzy and worsen the situation by over-reacting. A cool, purposeful attitude and firmness mixed with under-standing can help to keep matters under control.

As with all aspects of school life, there is no substitute for thinking ahead. Most problems can be avoided through sensible preparation and recognising that there will always be situa-tions in which some children try to take advantage and others simply get carried away with excitement. Equally, a failure to come to grips with the sticky moments can jeopardise the rest of the teaching programme as bad habits spread to other areas of classroom life.

Strategies for improving classroom behaviour

Every teacher wants to have a well ordered classroom in which children are learning, teaching is taking place effectively and there is a sense of purpose and endeavour. No teacher wants to waste time in dealing with squabbles, confrontation or pettiness that result in an unsatisfactory lesson and a reduction in pupils' appetite for learning, even those with a positive attitude. Chapman (1995) summarises the position succinctly:

> If I cannot manage a class sufficiently well, the most invigorating and original lesson will fail. If I cannot control children using positive means wherever possible, then their self-esteem and motivation will be damaged (page 36).

We noted earlier in the chapter that there is no substitute for having effective working relationships with children, interesting and relevant work for them to do, and clarity of purpose. We have seen that the key to dealing successfully with misbehaviour is to try and prevent it from happening in the first place. Most experienced teachers seem to deal successfully with incidents as they occur but this instinctive response is due to years of coping with similar circumstances. The correct action comes so naturally that they rarely reflect on why they act as they do. However, it is worth remembering that every experienced teacher has worked hard to reach this point of competence and almost as hard to maintain it. There are no quick-fix solutions to gaining and maintaining control in the classroom.

Some trainee teachers may be deceived into thinking that if they could only discover the right strategy to use with children, then all their discipline problems would be solved. Consequently, a mythology grows up in which slogans are employed to reassure anxious students. Thus:

'Begin by being fierce and ease-off later'
'Let them know who is the boss'
'Don't smile for quite a while'
'Don't give them a moment to breathe'

And similar phrases that offer a distorted perspective about the realities of adult–child relationships. In fact, as noted earlier, the best teachers rarely need to employ such stern, and ultimately unsustainable, tactics. Nevertheless, it is useful to have an 'armoury' of strategies from which you can select as appropriate. For instance, you may normally be extremely affable but become angry if a child wilfully disobeys an instruction.

Helpful strategies include:

- Gazing hard at the transgressor and acknowledging the pupil's appropriate response
- Going across and speaking quietly but firmly to the individual concerned

- Signalling the child to come across to you and explaining your dissatisfaction

- Chivvying and gently chiding ('Come on Andrew, more work and less chatter please. I'll give you until half-past to finish')

- Giving a specific command to clarify work expectations ('Sam, I want you to have finished that page by ten o'clock please').

Unhelpful strategies include:

- Shouting (other than in cases of health and safety)

- Calling out an individual's name across the room in a fierce voice (as it distracts everyone else and draws attention to the transgressor)

- Using a pseudo-question as part of a generalised command to no one in particular such as 'Can everybody get on quietly please' (as this is usually obeyed by those who conform and ignored by those who do not)

- Using the same child's name in a non-specific rebuke such as 'Daniel, get on with your work' (Daniel needs to be given a clearer instruction).

However, it takes time and experience to know which approach to use on which occasion and with which child. Sometimes it is difficult to achieve a satisfactory balance and there is bound to be a time of adjustment with a new class.

Whatever strategy you use to improve pupils' behaviour, it is important to resist lapsing into an artificial pattern of responses in the hope of gaining popularity or creating a false climate of enthusiasm for learning. McPhillimy (1996) views the matter like this: 'Mechanical, calculated smiles and praise, as well as being morally repellent are very unlikely to be effective as a reward' (page 80).

To avoid the risk of confrontation, it is tempting to take the easy route and pander to the small number of disruptive children at the expense of the others. For instance, a teacher may decide not to tackle an adventurous lesson for fear that the unusual circumstances or increased opportunities for naughtiness will prove irresistible to the disrupters and the whole lesson purpose will be undermined. Instead, they opt for a heads-down, individual paper and pencil approach is adopted, resulting in a far less engaging teaching and learning environment. While a heads-down approach has advantages in reducing noise level and leaving the teacher available to monitor the classroom more easily, it is difficult to maintain such an approach without stagnation and alienating the children who wish to benefit from exciting opportunities. Any heads-down containing strategy must, like most control techniques, be used sparingly, for in the longer term the innovative and interesting lesson will provide the foundation for strengthening the bonds between teacher and children and enhancing the learning environment. It is axiomatic that the few do not dictate your agenda or unduly influence the teaching approach at the expense of the majority.

Body language

Body language can be a powerful strategy for maintaining effective discipline. Neill and Caswell (1993) claim that teachers' verbal communication strategies can account for up to 80 per cent of the impression they convey to pupils and have at least four important functions:

- Gaining pupils' attention
- Conveying the teacher's enthusiasm to the class
- Dealing with confrontations and other control issues
- Relating to individuals during lessons.

Neill and Caswell argue that non-verbal signals send messages to pupils which identify teachers' feelings (both positive and negative) and support their spoken word. Thus, as well as teachers preparing lessons thoroughly and developing effective speech, they also need to cultivate appropriate body language.

Positive body language should include the following:

- Good eye contact with children
- Affirmative nods (expressing interest and approval of child)
- Expressive and reassuring facial tones
- Open body position (indicating trust)
- Facing a child directly when speaking one-to-one
- Squatting or sitting at children's eye level when speaking one-to-one
- Smiling and laughing at genuinely humorous situations.

Less helpful body language includes:

- Poor eye contact
- Sighs and distracted facial movements, suggesting boredom or limited interest
- Stony-faced responses, indicating a lack of warmth
- Compressed body position, showing suspicion
- Side-on position when speaking to individuals, indicating adult superiority
- Scowling, accompanying loud verbal rebukes
- Maintaining a rigid stance when speaking one-to-one
- 'Never smile until Christmas' attitude.

However, 'less helpful' body language, if used occasionally, can be a powerful device for showing disapproval. If teachers are respected and liked by the children, such action can reinforce their authority. On the other hand, without children's respect, the use of negative body language can lead to a further breakdown in relationships.

Activate your thinking!

Read the accompanying extract from Canter (1998) about assertive discipline. Think especially about (a) principles that apply to every teaching situation (b) modifications to practice depending on the age and maturity of the child (c) the impact it might have on children exercising self-control.

'This [assertive discipline] approach is based on the idea that pupils and teachers have rights as well as responsibilities. Pupils need and respond to limits set by teachers, and teachers therefore should ensure those limits are established...A positive classroom atmosphere is established through meeting pupils' needs, planning and implementing classroom rules, teaching pupils how to behave appropriately, providing positive attention and engaging in productive dialogue with disruptive pupils. Teachers are described as assertive if they effectively communicate the behaviour required of their pupils and the actions by which they intend to achieve this behaviour. Appropriate actions must follow words, otherwise responses are non-assertive and therefore ineffective. Teachers must respond positively to pupils who display appropriate classroom behaviour, thus recognising their efforts to achieve the teachers' goals. It is important that teachers are sincere when recognising pupils' attempts to meet their expectations (page 44).'

Coping with insolent behaviour

It is unusual to encounter a lot of insolent behaviour in primary schools, although it would be foolish to imagine that it can never happen, even in the most settled circumstances. Despite following the strategies suggested earlier in the chapter, you may discover that you are faced with some difficult situations from time to time, especially if you are a trainee teacher working with a demanding group of older children. Interesting lessons of the type described elsewhere in this book go a long way towards moderating the worst excesses of insolent behaviour but if it does happen it is likely to emerge in one of the following forms.

Pupils ignore you

If you are addressing a large group or class and some pupils ignore what you are saying, it is reasonable to stop, wait and make a comment such as 'Please look this way and watch my lips'. It may be, of course, that the very children you are concerned about will not respond because they are not listening in the first place! In such a situation, it is sometimes helpful to put the person's name in front of the statement; thus: 'Patty, please look this way and watch my lips. Thank you.' If you are speaking to a small group of pupils and one or more begin to look around at their friends or stare away while you are speaking, it may be that you have not yet established your authority in the class or that the children are nervous about the close encounter with you or that they do not accept your authority. It is essential to remain unruffled, ask for their attention, and to say what needs to be said clearly and unambiguously (without threats). Whenever possible, end the conversation on a positive note, even if it's only: 'Do you understand what I have said to you?' and if they affirm it: 'Well done. Off you go.' If you feel that there are deeper issues at stake it is not worth trying to resolve them through a single conversation. However, you can begin the process of establishing your presence as a teacher by being clear, definite and showing that you won't stand any nonsense.

Pupils answer back

Children answer back for a variety of reasons. They may find what you say unsatisfactory or unhelpful or confusing. They may just want to show off in front of their friends. A small number of children answer back because they do not have the social skills to interact with an adult. You have to determine which of these reasons is the most likely. It is usually fairly plain when a child is showing off and a simple response such as: 'Please don't show off, Eric,' before continuing with what you were saying is surprisingly effective. If the behaviour continues, you must exert your authority quickly and calmly to prevent the situation getting out of hand. There are a number of possible approaches:

- Use an *indirect strategy* such as: 'Stephen, please sit up straight, keep your hands and tongue still, and look at me.' This approach has the advantage of diverting attention from the original behaviour but needs to be followed up at a later stage (perhaps after the class has gone) when you can warn the child that you will not tolerate such rudeness.

- Respond with a *sense of outrage*, such as saying quietly (in a cold tone of amazed incredulity): '*What* did you say?' If the child refuses to respond, then add: 'Don't let me hear you calling out in class like that again. If you want to say something put your hand up like everybody else' before continuing.

- *Align yourself with another teacher*, such as saying: 'Alexis, you would not speak to Mrs Archer like that, so please don't do it with me!' If the child persists or argues back then say to the rest of the children 'Please put your hand up if you know what Alexis should have done,' wait for correct responses, then remind Alexis that, as everybody else seems to know the rule, would she kindly learn to do the same.

- Use an *abrupt approach*, such as 'Stop! No. You know the rule, Chang, so please don't interrupt me or call out.' A palm held out towards the child adds weight to your comments. If possible (but not threateningly) take a pace or two forward and lean forward while speaking to emphasise the fact that the child is not going to 'hide' behind the space between you.

- Ask the child to *stand up and repeat the remark*. There are dangers attached to this strategy as the child may gain further publicity for the clever comment. If, however, the child declines, it is worth pretending to make light of the matter momentarily by saying in a gentle tone with a hint of menace: 'No, we would all love to hear what you said, then you can go and explain to Mrs Archer why you have been so rude'. If the child refuses to respond, carry on immediately with what you were saying before being interrupted, glancing sternly across at the child from time to time.

Whatever response seems appropriate, keep the lesson flowing but do not ignore rude or 'smart' remarks that other children have obviously heard, as if they had never been made. It also goes without saying that you should make quite sure that the child really *was* answering back and not merely struggling to find the right form of words. Clearly stated rules for class-room talk, understood by all the children, make your task of maintaining order much simpler.

Pupils treat your commands as optional

Very young children may not always realise that what an adult says, an adult means! They set their minds on doing something and the fact that you have told them to do something else seems to have little impact. In such cases, a lot of patient perseverance is required, taking into account that they may have come from a home, nursery or play-school situation where they could make many more of their own decisions and may therefore perceive a teacher's insistence as unreasonable. With the majority of children, loving firmness and persuasion (such as mentioning the exciting things that are possible *when* they have completed the task you have set them) usually does the trick. Older pupils may be more mischievous and pretend that they do not understand in the hope that the teacher will give up trying to explain. A group of children may decide not to obey what you have said, either because they do not want to do it or because they genuinely think that there is a better option. When children ignore your request, it is normally best to ask them what they are doing and why they are doing it. If they give a reasonable response, you may wish to allow them to carry on (at least for a time) while reminding them that in future they should consult you first before making decisions. If you are not happy that they should continue, ask them what they *ought* to be doing and do not let them off the hook until they tell you. You can then insist that they do what they are told. Pupils treat a teacher's instructions as optional for many reasons, not least that they have misunderstood what has been said to them; your clarity of speech and careful lesson management is therefore essential in minimising the risk.

Pupils respond with ribald comments

This normally applies to older primary pupils and happens for one of four reasons: (a) the children are over-excited and need to calm down before lesson progress can be made; (b) they have got away with it before and are trying their luck again; (c) they are bored and distracted by the lesson content or the teacher's lacklustre delivery; (d) they lack motivation generally and have become disaffected with school. Your response depends upon the reason for the behaviour:

- If the children are over-excited and calling out silly things you have a choice over whether to change course for a few minutes and give the whole class a straightforward task until they are more composed (during which time you can quietly single out the culprits and speak sternly to them).

- If they are trying their luck, use one of the tactics suggested above for when children call out.

- If they are bored, you need to increase the lesson's tempo, ask some interesting questions or get the class working on group activities fairly quickly.

- Disaffection has deeper roots and you cannot hope to solve the situation by yourself. It is worth noting, however, that Kinder *et al.* (1996) claimed that disaffection is normally the result of boredom, anger or even fear. They suggested that improvement will come gradually as lessons are made more relevant, teachers are perceived as fair, pupils are treated with respect rather than disdain and (in some cases) parents are involved in working out solutions. Such improvement does not take place overnight.

Warning signs need not spell disaster if appropriate action is taken quickly. This involves teachers in making the sort of instant responses described above but also, more importantly, examining their lesson content, delivery, organisation and management to see if negative pupil behaviour results from one or more weaknesses in these areas. Insolent behaviour is always unsettling, sometimes worrying and occasionally frightening for teachers. If handled badly it can result in confrontations and angry scenes. If handled correctly it is an opportunity to learn about effective classroom strategies for dealing with disruptive youngsters.

Activate your thinking!

Consider the truth of the statement: Insolent behaviour has its roots in disaffection.

Good practice

Aim to be friendly towards children but not friends.

Special cases

All children are special to their parents, friends and family. Somebody treasures even the children who cause a teacher anguish and frustration. Trainee teachers who imagine that the mother or father of the class troublemaker feel the same resentment as they do have a nasty shock in store. Although parents may acknowledge their son's or daughter's shortcomings, their love remains undiminished and they will quickly defend their offspring if they think that the teacher is unfairly critical.

All teachers experience children who cause particular problems through being unco-operative, unwilling or unsettled. A minority of unco-operative children resists offers of help, disturb others in the class and generally upset the classroom atmosphere. Particularly difficult children act as a distressing reminder that sometimes, despite a teacher's best efforts, there appears to be little that can be done in the short-term to remedy a situation. A child who struggles with academic work may react to his or her difficulties by behaving erratically. A disturbed child may be academically capable but fall behind due to having a poor attitude or personality defect. The reverse is also true: a child who begins to succeed will probably behave in a more settled manner; the child whose circumstances become more secure will begin to gain success in schoolwork. It is important to be aware of these links as the special needs of children are evaluated. By adopting a positive attitude, taking an interest in the children's out-of-school interests and enthusing about their achievements, you have more chance of eliciting the very best from them.

Older primary boys

Children at every stage present their own challenges and joys; as such, there is no 'easy' age group. Different teachers like working with different year groups and it is interesting to reflect upon the similarities and differences in emphasis between teachers of nursery, Key Stage 1 and Key Stage 2. In previous chapters, we saw how very young children find adjustment to school routines difficult; teachers of Key Stage 1 children spend a lot of time and effort encouraging good learning habits, independence and basic skills. Teachers of seven- to nine-year-olds cope with classes of very mixed ability, in which some children still display immature behaviour, while others press ahead and make heavy demands upon the teacher's resourcefulness. During the transition between Key Stages 1 and 2, dominant children emerge and children with learning difficulties are identified more readily. Some groups of older children provide particular challenges to a teacher's ability to maintain control and ingenuity, courage and determination are called for. Although all children exhibit inappropriate behaviour at times, it is often with the oldest children that control issues become sharply focused. They can be simultaneously a great delight and infuriatingly troublesome.

Older boys are often enthused by sport (especially football), swopping cards, displaying their latest fashion fads and showing off to the girls. These characteristics are not true of every older boy, of course, but even the most enthusiastic teacher can feel exhausted after handling their loud demands, excited responses, intensity of feelings and the rapid movement from protective comradeship to antagonistic dispute. The expression that 'boys will be boys' may invite criticisms of stereotyping but does indicate the impact that groups of older boys, who have been together in school since they were very small, can prove a handful (as well as a delight) for any teacher.

It is important to recognise that high spirits rather than wilfulness are at the heart of much banter and conceited behaviour exhibited by outgoing older boys. Things really matter to them and often lead to expressions of indignation and highly charged reactions as they attempt to justify their behaviour or criticise others. Although not every older boy behaves in this manner, many do, and with this in mind teachers must ensure three things:

That they are firm but not unreasonable

For instance, to punish an older boy who loves to play a sport by denying him the chance to do so because of his overzealous behaviour in a lesson can be counter-productive, resulting in grievance, frustration and resentment (though such a course of action may be necessary if the non-co-operation persists).

That they don't allow dominant boys to suppress or exclude less assertive children

Dominance should not be allowed to frighten other children or damage their self-esteem. The non-sporty boys sometimes have a difficult job to compete and find their place in the social hierarchy; it is the teacher's responsibility to ensure that they have opportunities to succeed and gain status in other ways.

That they make it clear that the high standards the boys set themselves in sporting activities are equally necessary in academic work

Some boys who throw themselves into outdoor activities are loath to apply the same rigour to their class work. It is useful to face this inconsistency openly with them and attempt to feed their enthusiasm into the academic rather than suppress their love of physical activities.

Older boys are an exhausting but exciting group to work with. If teachers can win their hearts by energy, fairness and enthusiasm they will secure undying loyalty and receive commitment and wholehearted zest for learning, but troughs as well as peaks should be expected.

Older primary girls

Most girls are enthusiastic about the work and determined to do well. However, a small number of mature older girls find it hard to feel part of a primary school culture and may express this by separating themselves from other children or showing disdain for academic work and sport. Girls normally mature earlier than boys and precocious older children may find that they are emotionally and physically advanced compared with their classmates. They have to cope with adolescence and rapid growth at a time when they are still in the primary school environment. This can be difficult for them to accept and can result in times of intensity, exaggerated behaviour and an explosion of boy-related imagery, conversation and action. It is important to remember that these girls are grappling with a rapid series of changes in their lives and bodies and need to be treated with courtesy and consistency.

It is sensible to avoid heavy-handed approaches that threaten to humiliate older girls, or being patronising to them. Younger male teachers, in particular, need to be discreet: although gentle teasing and pleasantries are part of the interactive process and can lead to a healthy relationship, men should think carefully about words and body language which may be misconstrued. Dominant older girls can also be bossy and occasionally unkind to their less mature peers and, in some cases, may try to lure passive girls into a closely knit group open only to those who will espouse their particular, closely defined attitudes. In dealing with older dominant girls, a number of factors need to be considered:

Those who mature early do not do so out of choice

It is easy for a teacher to resent their intrusion into the otherwise child-like environment. A tolerant understanding of the emotions at work is essential.

Mature older girls are still primary school pupils and come under the same general rules of conduct

Although sensible discretion needs to be exercised, it would be a mistake for teachers to allow any non-conformist behaviour to dominate classroom or school life.

chapter 8 Behaviour Management

Unkind words and vindictive attitudes from mature girls towards weaker children is as serious as physical bullying

It should be dealt with according to the school's agreed policy. For trainee teachers, unsure about how to cope with regular minor instances of gossip or unkindness, the best course of action is to seek advice from senior colleagues.

Firm control needs to be exercised over mature girls who endeavour to draw less mature, wide-eyed boys into silly or disruptive behaviour

The boys are often thankful to be saved!

Although some older girls can disturb a class through their casual approach and restless behaviour, they usually respond well to teachers who offer them the opportunity to behave maturely within clearly defined limits. Despite their unpredictable behaviour, they often prove to be among the most loyal and supportive class members during times of crisis. Maturity cuts both ways. On the one hand it may serve to upset and unsettle. On the other hand, it can produce remarkable examples of loyalty, sensitivity and enthusiasm to delight and encourage weary teachers.

Demoralised children

Occasionally teachers come across children who, for various reasons, seem to have given up on school (Lang, 1990; Varma, 1992; Makins, 1997). They may not be persistent troublemakers and may even plod along with the work, albeit unenthusiastically, but it is evident that they have lost heart and are simply passing the time as comfortably as possible. Typically, such children will be at the upper end of the school, though younger children can show the same attitude. Although the reasons (such as home circumstances) may lie outside the teacher's immediate control there are a number of positive things that are worth considering in order to help the children regain their zest for school and learning.

Find regular opportunities to interact on a one-to-one basis

In the busyness of the day it is difficult to find opportunities to interact on an individual basis with every pupil other than during formal sessions, such as question-and-answer, when the adult–child relationship is influenced by epistemology rather than empathy. However, a deliberate attempt to exchange a private word with key individuals each day helps to build understanding and convince the children that the teacher's interest in them goes beyond merely improving their academic results.

Avoid making a fuss

Unless they are displaying their disillusionment by wilful misbehaviour, children often shun the limelight and do not want to be the public centre of a teacher's attention. Attempts to grant them a form of 'celebrity status' by making an undue fuss of their endeavours will often backfire and cause them to become more inhibited. By giving individuals deliberate, regular

289

and low-key attention, teachers can enhance their feelings of self-worth and raise their self-esteem.

Take an interest in their out-of-school activities

Children who lack academic motivation will sometimes spark into life when a teacher shows an interest in their hobbies or pastimes. The occasional enquiry about how they are getting on in a sports tournament, competition or in collecting items of interest can sometimes initiate a trust in the teacher which increases the child's determination to succeed in school work, too.

Enthuse gently about their successes

Depressed or unmotivated children not only believe that they have failed in the past but convince themselves that they are incapable of improving their situation. Teachers can contribute to the confidence-building process by making specific comments about positive achievements. Although it takes time to convince demoralised children that they can succeed, they need help in being able to recognise where progress has been made and (like every other pupil) how to improve their existing achievements.

Request their assistance

Asking children who seem to have given up to assist another child or to take responsibility for a small but important task is a useful means of building self-esteem. Children who have become used to a cycle of failure and defeatism may take some persuading that they have the capability to undertake the task, but success breeds success.

Persevere

Confidence and self-belief are not developed overnight. However, teachers who are willing to persevere and establish an open, positive approach with pupils that celebrates modest achievements and offers specific support when progress is slow, will help children to rediscover their zest for learning.

One of the reasons that many people become teachers is because they enjoy working with and supporting children. Helping children who are finding life difficult to cope with is an excellent opportunity to gain that kind of fulfilment.

Good practice

Use the above strategies over a period of two weeks to evaluate the improvement in the attitude towards and aptitude for work of any disaffected children.

Confidence and judgement

Establishing and maintaining class discipline is a difficult and demanding task for every teacher, especially for trainee teachers and inexperienced practitioners. However, all teachers can improve the situation by ensuring that lessons are interesting and relevant, instructions are clear and specific and responses to unacceptable behaviour are appropriate. All teachers who successfully maintain order possess two essential qualities: *confidence* and *wise judgement*.

Confidence emerges gradually. It grows when you know what you are doing and why. It is a delicate flower and can easily be crushed by a poor lesson, an unthinking comment from a colleague or a seemingly intractable situation involving a recalcitrant pupil. Positive body language, firm but natural speech, and a strong, enthusiastic personality all contribute towards confidence-building. It is helpful to remember that you are a capable adult who possesses the knowledge and skills to teach effectively. Consequently, nothing (and certainly not a naughty child or unthinking adult) is going to deter you from achieving your goals. In addition, however, it is equally important to recognise that some discipline problems will be the result of your own inexperience; the passage of time, acting upon advice from others, and your own thoughtful deliberations will combine to improve the situation gradually.

Wise judgement is more difficult to define or recognise. Some teachers seem to possess an instinct for handling situations; many have to learn the hard way! However, the following ten-point strategy will help you to improve your success rate:

- Have a big 'presence' around the room (but not brash!).
- Practise your diction and speak at a speed which allows pupils time to absorb what you are saying.
- Keep up a reasonable pace to the lesson; vary your tone and communicate your enthusiasm through firm statements of approval.
- Avoid confrontation wherever possible, but if it is not possible make sure that the outcome leaves your authority and the pupil's self-esteem intact.
- Use good quality questions and show a keen interest in pupils' replies.
- Organise thoroughly and anticipate sticky spots.
- Do not introduce activities which might excite too much fervour until you are sure that you have sufficient class control.
- Concentrate on the act rather than the perpetrator.
- Think positive. Be positive.
- Convince yourself and your children that they have got a teacher in a million!

Activate your thinking!

How would you act wisely in the following circumstances?

1 How would you handle a situation in which the more assertive children were dominating the use of equipment during collaborative activities?
2 How might you react if Freda, aged nine, told you that she did not have to do what you say because you were 'only a student'?
3 What options would be open to you if the same two children were always last to be chosen for games' activities?

4 What would you do if you were told a racist joke by a child in the class?

5 The school governors are concerned to make sure that the books on the classroom shelves are suitable for children. What criteria for selection would you use?

6 How would you handle a situation in which Meena, aged eight, came to you in tears because no one wanted to play with her?

7 How might you respond if a child confided in you that his parents were divorcing?

8 What action might you take if some children in your class complained that an eight-year-old girl called Rosebud, who was new to the school had been swearing openly at other children? Would it make a difference if you knew that Rosebud was from a very unsettled background?

9 How would you react if a parent told you that she did not want her five-year-old daughter Suki sitting next to a particular child because the child smelled?

10 How would you respond if a parent told you that she did not want her ten-year old son, Ethan sitting by Brian because Brian was always asking him questions about the work?

Case study

It is Wednesday morning in a Year 4 class. Tim and Ali, firm friends, sit together pondering the work in front of them. The trainee teacher is still finding her feet and determined to clamp down on inappropriate behaviour.

Trainee: Okay, get on with your work.

Tim: (speaking to Ali) What are we meant to be doing?

Ali: I dunno. (Tim gazes around hoping to gain a clue from what the other children are doing.)

Tim: We're supposed to write something down about the things we saw on our walk, I think.

Ali: I dunno. I'm just gonna write something. It doesn't matter. (Ali begins to write studiously, bent over his paper, hoping that the trainee doesn't look too closely.)

Tim: I'll ask Angie. (He gets up and wanders over to Angie.)

Trainee: (crossly) Sit down Tim and get on.

Tim: I was just asking Angie something.

Angie: (a conscientious girl, anxious that she might be getting in trouble, glances nervously at the trainee) Go away, Tim. You're bothering me.

Trainee: (assuming that Tim is being troublesome) Sit...down...and...get on!

Tim: (slumps back into his seat, chin on hand) This is useless!

Fifteen minutes later Ali has written half a page of low level work but in bold handwriting. Tim has scrawled a few indecipherable words on the sheet and sits staring vacantly into space. The trainee is praising Angie and others for their efforts. Then she walks across to Ali and Tim.

Ali: (glancing up) Look, Miss, what I done!

Trainee: (without reading it closely but noticing the tidiness and length and relieved that he has made an effort) Well done, Ali, that's excellent! (turns to Tim, looks at his paper and scowls) What on earth do you call that? (Tim says nothing). Right! You can stay in at playtime and finish it off.

Tim: Tim: (urgently) But Miss, I've got to see Mr Ward about playing in the team and...

Trainee: You can forget about that. I'm sick of you messing about and not doing your work and if you say another word you can come with me and see Mr Pretiman! (Tim visibly shrinks; Ali glances across sympathetically; a few children in the corner snigger quietly).

The trainee's perception of the boys' behaviour was affected by her initial belief that Tim was causing trouble. From this point, the relationship between adult and child became tense. Dialogue was limited due to the trainee's unwillingness to ensure that Tim was clear about the task and to offer some ongoing 'scaffolding' to his learning through appropriate monitoring and intervention. Her failure to explain the task adequately and her apparent reluctance to attend to Tim's individual learning needs meant that at the end of the allotted time his progress was minimal and she felt obliged to invoke sanctions. The end result was an unhappy child and a strained trainee. Tim was far from being a model pupil, but the trainee made the situation worse by her ill-judged comments and hasty reactions.

Activate your thinking!

■ What are the prospects for settled relationships and effective teaching and learning if these conditions persist?

■ What is the trainee likely to say to Ali's and Tim's parents during the parent interviews?

■ Why were the boys unclear about the task in the first place?

Good practice

Examine your class list and sub-divide the children into three broad categories:

1 The majority who endeavour to work hard and do their best
2 The smaller number who will get away with things unless prevented
3 The minority who cause regular problems.

Reflect upon appropriate strategies for moving children from group 2 to group 1 and those in group 3 to group 2. Celebrate that there are so many names in the first group!

Standards

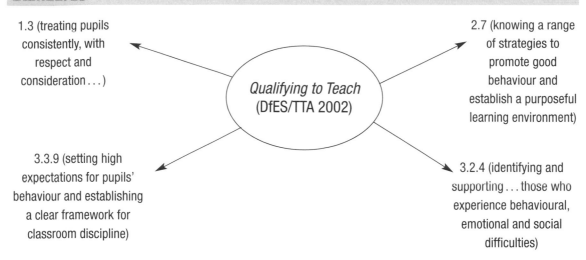

1.3 (treating pupils consistently, with respect and consideration . . .)

2.7 (knowing a range of strategies to promote good behaviour and establish a purposeful learning environment)

Qualifying to Teach (DfES/TTA 2002)

3.3.9 (setting high expectations for pupils' behaviour and establishing a clear framework for classroom discipline)

3.2.4 (identifying and supporting . . . those who experience behavioural, emotional and social difficulties)

Further reading

Porter, L. (2000) *Theory and Practice for Teachers*, Maidenhead: Open University Press.
The book provides a comprehensive overview of the major theories of behaviour, illustrated with numerous case studies. It covers the secondary as well as primary phase.

Tileston, D. W. (2004) *What Every Teacher Should Know About Classroom Management and Discipline*, Thousand Oaks, Cal: Corwin Press.
A book that is easy to dip in and out of. It has a strong US flavour in the way it is written but approaches issues from a different perspective.

CHAPTER

9

Inclusion and Special Educational Needs

Introduction

Over the past 20 years the education of children with Special Educational Needs (SEN) has assumed an increasingly high profile in schools. Once seen as a specialist area, it is now confirmed as the responsibility of every teacher. This chapter starts by reviewing background information about relevant legislation and giving a historical perspective on the subject. An understanding of the terms 'special educational needs' and 'inclusion' is explored, with reference to the Code of Practice. Finally, advice is offered about successfully dealing with SEN in the classroom, including writing an independent education plan (IEP) and working with other professionals.

Legislation

Until 1971 about 1 per cent of the population was deemed uneducable, and did not attend school at all. When this population became the responsibility of the Department of Education and Science (as it was then known), a committee was set up under Baroness Warnock to report on the education of 'handicapped' children (the 'Warnock Report'). The committee widened its brief, abandoning the notion of handicaps, establishing instead the notion of Special Educational Needs, and moving beyond the 2 per cent who were then educated in Special schools to an estimated 20 per cent of children who were likely to experience a type of SEN at some time in their school career. This larger group had formerly been referred to as 'remedial' or slow learners, and was educated in mainstream schools.

The report 'Children with Special Educational Needs' was published in 1978 and paved the way for the far-reaching legislation of the 1981 Education Act. The Act stated that, in principle, children with SEN should be educated alongside their non-disabled peers, that their resource needs should be safeguarded by a 'statement of need' that would be binding on the Local Education Authority, and abolished the former categories of handicap to replace them with a single notion of special educational need. However, a set of descriptive categories were still deemed necessary (e.g. moderate learning difficulties, hearing impaired etc.). The Act came into force on 1st April 1983 and the period since then can best be seen as the attempt by the teaching profession to move from a *segregated* form of provision to an *inclusive* one. To

295

understand the difficulties in so doing it is worth looking briefly at some of the historical background.

Historical background

The system we have inherited grew up piecemeal over a considerable period of time and has embedded in it periods of inertia and little thought given to appropriate forms of education for all children. Some countries, such as Italy and the Scandinavian countries were, for historical and geographical reasons, able to build education systems based on more inclusive assumptions. Britain, in 1983, already had a fully entrenched segregated system, and undoing the precedent is proving to be a difficult task. British teachers were used to a system that spared them from having to deal with the neediest pupils. Furthermore, there were specialist schools and a variety of specialist professionals who prided themselves on their ability to deal with the children's needs in specialised, separate accommodation, and it has been difficult for professionals to give up the status of being the experts in a certain field.

Barton and Tomlinson (1984) traces the changes in statutory categories for special provision. In 1886 there was statutory provision for those diagnosed as Idiots and Imbeciles. These seemingly insulting words were at the time clearly defined clinical categories, comprising those that we would now describe as having profound or severe learning difficulties. By the end of the century categories of schools for the blind and deaf had also been established. These again were intended to be special in terms of extra, rather than different. Schools were founded for the indigent blind, indigent meaning needy or impoverished; a stereotype of the 'blind beggar' is one such example. These institutions taught crafts and trades that would provide some sort of financial independence, and were seen as a philanthropic act, unavailable in the general school system. These institutions were normally founded by charitable or religious bodies, and went beyond what was available from the state. Similarly separate institutions were set up for the 'physically defective', again focused on trades. After the First World War came the development of separate schools and classes for the 'feeble minded', who were judged incapable of following the normal curriculum. The growth of educational psychology under Cyril Burt saw the widespread use of IQ tests to identify those in need of special education (an IQ of 70 or below being the cut off point).

Thus, a range of separate provision grew up in piecemeal fashion, seen at the time as appropriate and additional to the norm. When the 1944 Act secured universal free education, including secondary education, it was deemed necessary to extend this right to all 'educable handicapped children.' Consequently, until the 1981 Act, special educational provision was premised on categories of handicap, rather than educational need and access to a common school experience and curriculum. All sorts of problems emerged as educationists attempted to make the system work. These and many other issues led to the questioning of the various forms of provision and the categories and labels that were in use, and to focusing instead on the actual educational needs of actual children. This bold move engendered the current debate, including the use of language in labelling, and issues about segregation, integration and inclusion.

The language of special education

Prior to the 1981 Act labels were used to describe the features that led to educational difficulty, e.g. an educationally sub-normal child, a blind child. The Warnock Report sought to move away from this and focus on the needs of the child in the particular context of provision they found themselves in. As early as 1984 Lady Warnock herself admitted regret about coining the term 'special educational needs' and wondered how long it would be before the word 'special' accrued pejorative connotations. We can now see that in the intervening period the term has indeed come to function as a label for children, rather than focusing on their needs. In every staffroom it is possible to hear talk of 'SEN children' or 'statemented children', neither of which is accurate. A statement of special educational needs is about provision, and not about the child.

There is a considerable variability in the use of statements across the country. The possession of a statement says more about the *situation* the child is in than anything intrinsic to the child, yet labels that focus on the child are still in common use. As more and more money is devolved to schools the use of the statement will decline, and we will have to cast around for another label. One way and another, it is important to see children as individuals with different needs that change over time rather than members of a group, all assumed to have the same characteristics.

The problems attached to seeing pupils in terms of labels rather than as individuals are well documented. For instance, two groups of trainee teachers are shown the same piece of videotaped classroom activity. One group is asked to record what they saw without further guidance; the other group is told that some members of the class in the tape exhibit features of learning and behavioural difficulties. The first group sees only the normal classroom interaction, whereas the second group is able to identify a range of special needs, in line with its expectations. The study demonstrates that we tend to see what we believe or are told is present. It points up the danger of attaching negative labels to aspects of behaviour so that practitioners have preconceived ideas about what they will see, and subsequently confirm what they are led to believe is there.

Using language accurately and appropriately is something to which every teacher should aspire, and it is important to avoid unintentionally giving offence or being insulting by the inaccurate use of terms. This issue is given a thorough airing in Corbett's thought-provoking book, provocatively entitled: *Bad-Mouthing, The Language of Special Needs* (Corbett 1995). Basically the situation can be greatly improved if we remember three simple precepts:

1 Avoid language that is clearly insulting or inaccurate, e.g. mongol, spastic, cripple, wheel-chair-bound.

2 Avoid patronising euphemisms, e.g. vertically-challenged, differently-enabled etc, as these tend to deny a person's lived reality.

3 Use the preferred terminology of the group in question, e.g. Down's Syndrome, Deaf etc. This usage will change over time, but it is a real sign of respect when talking to children and their families that you have bothered to adopt non-offensive terminology.

Most of the categories of learning difficulties listed earlier are typically of low incidence. For instance, you may never teach a child with Down (or Down's) Syndrome or Autistic Spectrum Disorder. However, it is important for you to develop an inclusive philosophy, being willing to support a range of learning difficulties where necessary, and knowing where to go for additional knowledge and support at the appropriate time. The Code of Practice gives useful outlines, there is a plethora of practical guides available (see the David Fulton catalogue for numerous examples) and the internet is a wonderful source of information if used with discrimination. All teachers, however, need to be aware of the common condition known as 'glue ear'. Many young children experience heavy catarrh, which leads to an intermittent hearing loss that can have an effect on language development. The condition passes as the child grows older, but the gaps in learning remain, and the effects on further development are cumulative and need to be addressed. Decongestants and the fitting of grommets (by means of a small operation) can alleviate the symptoms and allow the child full access to language, especially at the vital stage when sound symbol correspondence is being achieved. Nevertheless, you should be on the lookout for children suffering intermittent hearing loss, urge parents to take medical action and ensure that the child, who may appear distant or confused, is able to understand the teaching that he or she is experiencing, especially in the field of language development.

Activate your thinking!

What labels have you heard used to describe children with SEN? Consider whether labels tell us more about those using them, rather than those they purport to describe.

Segregation, integration or inclusive education?

Segregation

Perhaps the major determinant of our success in educating children with SEN is our view about what should be done, and whereabouts it should come in the schooling process. The ideology behind segregation is that we are only responsible for children of 'normal' abilities and that specialist teachers should take the residue elsewhere, so we should resist changing our practice along inclusive lines. The term segregation not only applies to separate special schools, but also to segregation in mainstream schools, by special classes for the least able, groups permanently composed on ability lines, and withdrawal from class for 'extra help' on an ongoing basis. Recently, there has been a less visible form of segregation, when a classroom assistant is attached to one child and sits with him/her, accentuating the child's difference and progressively disempowering the child's opportunity to become an independent learner. There are, and have been shown to be, all sorts of practical problems with this sort of segregated education, which can be summarised thus:

- Because a group of children share some difficulties, it does not follow that they require the same kind of education provision.

- Children that are separated have limited access to a model of 'normal' classroom behaviour.

- When children are extracted from class they are falling further behind in the regular class work.

- The work they do under segregated conditions may not be related to the curriculum or the skills they need to access it; rather, it may be practice in basics unrelated to the curriculum or an excessive concentration on the use of worksheets.

- There is a lot of evidence to support the principle that children learn most effectively in group interaction, so the efficacy of 'one to one instruction' is questionable.

All children have varying abilities in different areas, so even if they benefit from individual instruction in one area it does not mean that they should be excluded from wider class and social activities. Even where children value separate treatment, there are stigmas attached to being seen as different by other members of the class. The practice of removal gives strong messages to the child about their perceived low standing, and damages their self-esteem and self-efficacy. Because of the above factors and the staffing costs involved, there has been a move towards more integrative and inclusive practices.

Activate your thinking!

Try to imagine what it must feel like to be treated differently from most other children.

Integration

Integration is the name given to the process whereby the formerly excluded were to be brought back into regular schooling, either moving from special to mainstream schooling, or by adopting class or group-based activities rather than individual 'remediation'. Through the 1980s 'integration' was the watchword, despite concerns as serious conceptual difficulties began to emerge. Pupils were to be integrated, or re-integrated, but the nature of the receiving school system remained immune to change. In other words, the basic assumptions behind the curriculum, assessment methods and teaching remained unaltered, the task was seen as fitting the child to the provision, not vice versa. As the school system had not been designed on the principles of inclusive assumptions, i.e. that it should be open to all members of the community, the practices it had developed over the period marked by segregation were not based on the widest needs in the community. The buildings were certainly inaccessible to anyone with problems with mobility, the curriculum was not necessarily relevant to all, and the practices of grading made it inevitable that a certain percentage of children would experience failure and the stigma that went with it. It was probably optimistic to believe that the ills of segregation could be alleviated by easing a few more disabled people into a system that was not designed with them in mind. From this point, educational policy started to move towards the principle of an inclusive system to meet all needs, though in some cases the practices that were used for integration have continued, and merely changed their name to inclusion!

Activate your thinking!

In what ways does integration benefit the mainstream population?

Inclusive education

Inclusive Education is best understood as an aim, aspiration or even a philosophy, rather than as a set of techniques that can be applied to a situation. It is a state that we move towards and a notion that regulates our efforts. Consequently, the school community is charged with offering education to all members of the community that it serves by modifying the way that all those involved work so that all needs are considered. Practices that tend to exclude would need to be eliminated in favour of more inclusive practices. Moving in an inclusive direction entails a problem-solving exercise on behalf of all those involved. For an account of a move towards a more inclusive ethos see the account of just such a problem-solving approach applied to the development of an inclusive school (Thomas 1998). For the current statutory position about inclusion issues, see the DfES document, *Inclusive Schooling* (DfES 2001a).

The role of the teacher in addressing Special Educational Needs

The duties of schools and teachers are clearly laid out in the Code of Practice and the Special Needs and Disability Act. (For access to this documents and updates on government publications visit the DfES website http://www.dfes.gov.uk/sen/). All schools should have copies of these documents, as well as the 'Toolkit', a set of practical pamphlets on implementing the Code of Practice. Personal copies can be ordered direct from the DfES.

The Code outlines the framework for identifying, assessing and making provision for children's special educational needs, though the actual assessment and teaching measures used are left for individual teachers and schools to develop. The Code sets out the framework clearly (see below) and should be consulted by all teachers. Whenever you work in a school it is essential to be aware of the identity and role of the Special Educational Needs Co-ordinator (SENCO) and of others, including the governors who have statutory roles in the schools SEN policy (see sections 1.39, 4.15, 5.30, and 6.32 of the Code for information on roles and responsibilities).

The Code sets out a graduated approach to identification, assessment and provision. It makes clear that the Code is only concerned with interventions that are additional to or different from those provided as part of the school's usual differentiated curriculum and strategies. This principle underlines very firmly that schools should already be catering to a wide range of educational need through differentiation. Specifically focused and planned teaching will help to prevent difficulties in learning from arising, and flexible teaching and assessment strategies help all pupils to have access to the curriculum. Despite teachers' best efforts, however, it is likely that some children will experience difficulties that require extra or different kinds of support for learning. The Code describes two stages at which this more focused assessment and provision operate, these are known as School Action and School Action Plus.

At the level of *School Action*, the teacher decides that the child may need further support to help their progress, following consultation with parents. The SENCO is then involved, and short-term support from outside agencies may be involved (see section on working with other professionals later). Information about the child's academic progress is gathered, and evidence collected about the interventions that have been previously tried. The information is recorded on the child's individual record, and an Individual Education Plan (IEP) is produced laying out the plans for the next stage of the pupil's education.

School Action Plus involves a request for help from external services, and will normally follow a decision made by the SENCO and colleagues, in consultation with parents, after the evidence from a review of the IEP indicates that there is a need to consult specialists. A range of specialists may be approached, depending on the nature of the need, and a new IEP produced. As the IEP is reviewed and monitored, the school may request a statutory assessment from the Local Education Authority if the pupil has demonstrated a significant cause for concern. This assessment process may lead to a formal statement of special educational needs that will specify the additional support required or, in some cases, a move to specialist provision from outside the school. At this stage it is necessary to define more specifically the nature of the child's special need. The suggested categories are:

Cognition and Learning Needs

- Specific Learning Difficulty (SpLD)
- Moderate Learning Difficulty (MLD)
- Severe Learning Difficulty (SLD)
- Profound and Multiple Learning Difficulty (PMLD)

Behaviour, Emotional and Social Development Needs
- Behaviour, Emotional and Social Difficulty (BESD)

Communication and Interaction Needs

- Speech, Language and Communication Needs (SLCN)
- Autistic Spectrum Disorder (ASD)

Sensory and/or Physical Needs

- Visual Impairment (VI)
- Hearing Impairment (HI)
- Multi-Sensory Impairment (MSI)
- Physical Disability (PD)

Other (OTH)
Chapter Seven of the Code of Practice goes into more detail on these categories and the resultant needs of the children.

Assessment

There was a time when specialist teachers were equipped with a battery of tests and associated remedial programmes. These were designed to identify and 'remediate' weaknesses in child's abilities through the diagnostic/remedial approach. The emphasis has now changed to looking at all children in terms of access to the curriculum, which is already assumed to be differentiated for a range of needs, and open to the schools normal assessment procedures.

Importantly, teachers now look for strengths as well as weaknesses, pay attention to learning styles, monitor and celebrate progress, however slow in coming. They search for alternative learning strategies that are appropriate for the child, rather than trying to 'fix' the child's perceived shortcomings. If the general assessment policy is adequate, then good practice renders the information that teacher's require in order to assess the pupil's needs. Subsequently, assessment linked to pupils' learning needs is used to generate individual learning targets for each child. The process is monitored and feeds back into a review of those targets for all pupils, which provides a sound basis for the more fine grained assessment needed to support a range of specific needs (see Figure 9.1, Teaching, assessment, targets and individual needs).

GOOD PRACTICE provides assessment information
ASSESSMENT INFORMATION generates learning targets
LEARNING TARGETS are monitored
MONITORING provides finer-grained assessment information
FINER-GRAINED ASSESSMENTS facilitates support for a range of particular learning needs

FIGURE 9.1 Teaching, assessment, targets and individual needs

Assessments aim to facilitate the matching of educational experience to the pupil's needs (see Chapter 7). For children with special needs, therefore, teachers should monitor closely the interventions that have been tried, learning from them. Particular notice should be taken of what works, as a picture of the pupil's favoured learning styles and areas of particular difficulty is slowly constructed. Many children learn best through a visual or a kinaesthetic ('touching') mode, so teachers need first to be assessing the preferred learning style of the pupil, then to devise strategies which capitalise on their strengths. In this way they gradually find ways to enhance their abilities in modes that they find more difficult.

> ## Good practice
>
> As far as possible, assessment should be part of the normal classroom experience. Children with a history of failure are more likely to be put off and under-perform if they are aware that they are being tested and treated differently from everyone else.

Targets and the Individual Education Plan

The Individual Education Plan is an important tool in meeting a child's learning needs. The form of the paperwork varies from one local authority or school to another, but contains the following information:

- The short-term targets set out for the child
- The teaching strategies to be used
- The provision to be put in place
- When the plan is to be reviewed
- Success and or/exit criteria
- Outcomes that are recorded when the IEP is reviewed

(Based on DfES 2001b)

The IEP should only record that which is additional to or different from the school's differentiated curriculum plan for all children. It should be crisply written and focus on three or four individual targets, chosen from those relating to the key areas of communication, literacy, mathematics and behaviour and social skills that match the child's needs. Crucially, the IEP must be discussed with the child and the parents. As with all learning, the more the child is involved in understanding and monitoring his own targets, the likelier it is that they will be reached.

It is important to realise that while the targets are individual in that they relate to a child's specific needs, this fact does not imply that they involve only individual, solitary tasks. Many effective targets outline strategies for including the pupil in collaborative or whole-class activities where this has been a problem in the past.

At this stage it is not necessary to categorise the pupil's special need, but to concentrate on their particular learning needs, realised as workable targets. These should be as precise as possible. For example, if phonic awareness has been identified as a target then the particular elements that the child has to concentrate on must be capable of being defined, and the variety of ways in which the content can be addressed. Similarly, if concentrating on spelling is identified as a target, the range of strategies and experiences that will be worked on must be specified. There is little point in giving spellings for a test without offering advice about how to go about learning them. When vague language is used to define targets, such as 'improve spelling' or 'behave appropriately', there is little clue as to what the child should actually do and it is extremely difficult to show that progress is being made.

There is very good reason for restricting the number of targets to three or four. Remember how disheartening it is to have a page of work returned with corrections in red all over it. It is too easy for teachers to give the message that the child is a failure at this aspect of learning, and despair about how to address all their weaknesses at once. Many children are tempted to give up. If, however, children's attention is directed to specific, achievable targets, they learn to succeed and become more optimistic about their future chances of success. It is vital to enhance our pupils' self-efficacy beliefs, i.e. whether they think they are capable of achieving, for this is the key to motivation. Too many children expend great energy, and no little ingenuity, in avoiding tasks because the fear of failure is too great. The secret is for you to engage them in progressively demanding experiences that they feel that they can succeed in, given appropriate support, and engender a history of achievement, rather than failure.

Teaching approaches

Teaching children with SEN should be seen as a subset of good teaching for all, not as a different kind of practice. It is helpful to remember that everyone finds difficulty in learning certain things at some level, but we can all make progress when the conditions are favourable and supportive. It is helpful to be reminded that by the time children start school they have already shown themselves to be expert at learning, having absorbed more in their first five years than they will ever learn again. Furthermore, they will continue to learn things that are important and useful to them outside their school education. It is therefore more positive to view the child as a teaching challenge or opportunity rather than as someone with a 'learning difficulty'.

Flexibility is a key factor in teaching. If a child is finding difficulty in learning then it is wise to try a different approach, rather than repeating the same teaching more slowly (like a tourist attempting to order food in a foreign restaurant). Keys to flexibility include:

- A focus on oral work
- Sustained meaningful talk through discussion
- Use of group and peer support
- Encouragement of 'multiple literacies' (a range of varied sources) in providing evidence of learning
- A concentration on the processes of learning in different subjects as well as the recording of knowledge.

Most importantly it is always necessary to try to discern what meaning children are trying to make or express, rather than discounting their efforts as incorrect understandings. Pupils' miscues can be very revealing and provide a starting point for building on their ideas rather than demolishing them and starting again. For instance, when setting out subtraction sums such as 45 – 27 then some children always subtract the smaller from the larger number and will come up with the answer as 22 (by subtracting the smaller digits from the larger ones, 4 – 2 and

7 – 5). The children concerned are clearly capable of subtracting digits, but have either misunderstood the algorithm or have not developed a sense of place value. The perceptive teacher sees the incorrect answer as an opportunity to explore the child's lack of full understanding and not simply as something wrong that must be done again. Some seemingly bizarre answers or contributions in class discussion often make perfect sense if you are willing to explore the meaning that the child is intending and identify gaps in knowledge or conceptual understanding that can be used as a basis for the next stage in the pupil's learning. Too often, however, a teacher already has the correct response in mind, and quickly moves on to a child who is more likely to give the approved answer, thereby overlooking the opportunity that the original misconception has provided.

The importance of oral work for children with special educational needs in a group or paired context cannot be overstated. McNamara and Moreton (2001) give a very useful rationale, and many examples of good practice, arguing that the best way to learn something is to have to teach it. For example, how many teachers knew much about the Aztecs before they had to plan lessons about them? Peer tuition and support are therefore very important tools. Whenever possible, you should provide the children with the experience of being 'the expert' in at least one small area of the curriculum, as this is a powerfully affirming experience for a child used to being labelled a 'slow learner'.

Recording

Children do not become disenchanted with school because they find the curriculum uninteresting, but because they are daunted by the demand to write everything down, when writing for them is a slow, exacting process. Of course teachers must help every child to be more literate, but not at the expense of engagement with the curriculum and loss of motivation. There are many ways to evidence learning other than by individual children recording outcomes in written form unaided. For example, evidence of children's learning can be revealed through oral presentations, drawing, singing, drama, by contributing to group posters or presentations, or by having another child doing the writing task. (See also the use of story explored by Leicester and Johnson 2004.) With writing especially, it is important to remember that it is something activated in the mind. The process of physically writing things down, or scribing, is a separate (though related) activity. Thus, many famous authors have exciting ideas in their heads and choose to use audio technology and secretarial services, rather than writing manually to express what they want to say. Similarly, pupils with special educational needs can be encouraged to be writers if someone else assists with the act of writing. Drafting and editing conferences (where an adult or more capable pupil discusses with the individual ways to improve and enhance what has been accomplished so far) can be used to help the child shape and refine the writing, while gradually giving him or her more responsibility for the surface features as well as content.

Maintaining the integrity and complexity of the subject matter is also important. It is depressing to witness children with SEN effectively being excluded from the curriculum subjects by being given repetitive, low level tasks that do not engage the mind in the distinctive processes of the subject. For instance, investigative science is an area of the curriculum that fascinates children and they enjoy the chance to observe, categorise, hypothesise and experiment. None of these processes necessarily involve writing, though recording in some form is an important element of the process. Yet children with SEN are often denied involvement in these exciting opportunities, and are offered instead simplified worksheets, filling in gaps so that vocabulary can be learnt and similar tedious tasks. In such cases, they are really only receiving extra English tuition with the main subject providing the backdrop. The same issue can be applied to other subjects such as history and geography, where the pupil needs first to be engaged with the processes of the subject. Attention can then be given to refining their recording skills. However, you should avoid subjecting children to a plethora of worksheets (for instance) before they are offered the opportunity to do anything interesting; neither should they be sent off just to 'draw a picture of it' while their peers are engaged in genuine problem solving activity.

Activate your thinking!

Consider the truth of the statement: Children with special educational needs require stimulation, not stagnation.

Good practice

Implement a 'no worksheet' day in which you promote creativity instead of conformity.

Working with other professionals

In supporting children with special educational needs you will inevitably work with a range of other professionals. Learning to work co-operatively, and take and give direction appropriately are essential skills that need to be developed. The key colleague is the SENCO, who will usually be the link person to other professionals, so it is vital that you talk to the SENCO about the additional help for children and practitioners that is available. The educational psychologist also plays a major role in supporting teachers and children, and might co-ordinate the work of other professionals. Most local authorities have a range of specialist or advisory teachers that are available for help and advice. These include specialists in teaching the hearing impaired, visually impaired and other areas of learning difficulty, behaviour support teams, a range of para-professionals such as speech therapists and physiotherapists, social workers, educational welfare officers, and medical services. More and more multi-agency work is being encouraged, so it is very important to be aware of the range of services in your own area. Trainee teachers are unlikely to have direct dealings with these service providers, but it is worth being alert to their existence and ways in which they are able to help you.

You will also work increasingly with learning support assistants in your own classroom (now subsumed under the general role, Teaching Assistants). Working as a team and improving the learning environment for all children, rather than sitting an adult alongside the 'problem child' to keep him or her occupied, needs careful planning and liaison with the support staff. Outside the professional domain you will also work with parents (perhaps in as well as out of school time) and members of the community who volunteer their services. Recruiting and managing these sources of additional support has to be fully thought out and integrated into a school-wide plan. If you are new to the school it is essential to find out how the system operates. It is important to be clear about what support you wish parents to give. Parents' evenings are a useful occasion to make suggestions about helpful and unhelpful methods of supporting a child, perhaps by inviting them to produce a home-made video. See Chapter 3 for more information about working with other adults.

It is possible and desirable for all teachers to develop their teaching so that it is more accessible and inclusive. Perhaps the pupils who find the greatest difficulty in learning can be teachers' best critics, indicating where they need to be clearer or more flexible. If you make learning easier for those experiencing the greatest difficulty, you will improve it for all the children in your class.

Case study

Vijay, aged nine years, had a troublesome speech impediment. Owing to a jaw deformity, he spoke slowly and occasionally slurred his words. Worse still, his poor muscle tone would sometimes result in traces of saliva trickling from one side of his mouth. As a result, Vijay experienced severe embarrassment that affected his self-esteem and confidence. The teacher tried hard to include Vijay, encourage him in his work and involve him in whole-class activities, but he remained subdued and deliberately curbed a lot of his natural spontaneity and enthusiasm. After several discussions with parents and with advice from the SENCO, they agreed that to raise Vijay's self-esteem, they would offer him a responsible and privileged task as one of the six school librarians. This post gave him some genuine responsibility that did not require too much speaking but allowed him to interact with a wider range of children. The teacher also mastered and began to use some simple sign language with the whole class from which Vijay (especially) gained considerable benefit. The strategy also had the unexpected consequence of reducing noise levels generally. Finally, during choir practice, a TA noticed that Vijay had quite a good voice and his singing did not appear to be affected significantly by his impediment. The teacher gently encouraged Vijay to take a supporting role in the school concert, which was very successful. At a subsequent meeting with Vijay's parents to discuss his progress, they commented that he had never been happier at school.

Standards

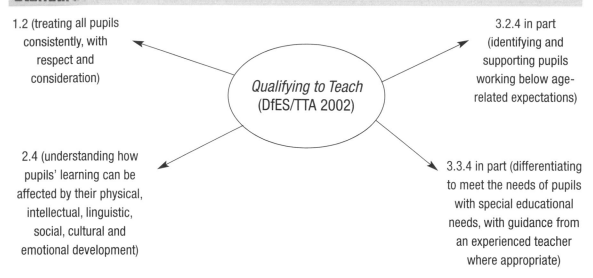

1.2 (treating all pupils consistently, with respect and consideration)

3.2.4 in part (identifying and supporting pupils working below age-related expectations)

Qualifying to Teach (DfES/TTA 2002)

2.4 (understanding how pupils' learning can be affected by their physical, intellectual, linguistic, social, cultural and emotional development)

3.3.4 in part (differentiating to meet the needs of pupils with special educational needs, with guidance from an experienced teacher where appropriate)

Further reading

Carpenter, B., Ashdown, R. and Bovair, K. (eds) (1996) *Enabling access: Effective teaching and learning for pupils with learning difficulties*, London: David Fulton.
Deals with the implications for different curriculum areas and contains good practical suggestions.

Cheminais, R. (2001) *Developing Inclusive School Practice: A practical guide*, London: David Fulton.
Another easy-to follow guide, clearly presented and imaginatively structured.

Cheminais, R. and Gains, C. (2000) *Special Educational Needs for Newly Qualified and Student Teachers*, London: David Fulton
A step-by-step guide through the main issues, offering sound practical advice, especially for assessment.

10

The Induction Year

Introduction

All newly qualified teachers are required to serve an induction year (DfEE 1999b), which was introduced to provide a solid basis for professional and career development. At its best, induction helps new teachers to show their potential, make rapid progress in becoming effective practitioners and make an impact on the school's overall development and progress. This chapter contains advice about achieving these goals.

Background

You saw the job advertised and made your application. When the governors received the application form, they probably knew nothing about you, so the form was initially their only source of evidence. They were persuaded that you were someone worth considering further, so they followed up one or more of your referees. Eventually they decided to put you on a 'short list' and invite you for a more formal interview (though the degree of formality varies considerably from school to school). The head teacher and staff were asking four basic questions about the candidates:

- Can this person handle a class from top to bottom? That is, can this person do the teaching and give the children a good deal?
- Will this person fit into our staff? (Is s/he reasonable, pleasant, honest, sympathetic etc?)
- How will parents react to this person? (Is s/he approachable, a good communicator, understanding etc?)
- Will this person help to raise standards of academic achievement, especially in core subjects?

They saw from your initial application that you were someone who might fit the bill. You were invited to look around the school and sensibly kept a low profile while staying alert and picking up clues about the school's priorities. Before the formal interview, you may have written down some likely questions that the panel might ask you and recorded your answers on to a tape. You were horrified how hesitant you sounded (everyone is the same) but it gave you time to think through and clarify your beliefs beforehand.

During interview the panel expected you to be passionate about your desire to teach in *their* school (not just any old school). Your letter of application was further scrutinised, your references studied closely, and your response to a series of probing questions satisfied them that you were the person for the job. Perhaps you were asked questions such as:

- How will you organise for learning in literacy to differentiate for the ability range?
- How will you organise your room?
- What sort of things will you do to promote creativity?
- Can you describe for us the sorts of contributions that you can make to the school's work in your specialist curriculum area?
- How will you ensure that every child reaches his or her potential?
- What sort of things would you do to promote an effective working relationship with parents?
- How will you know that you are succeeding in raising standards?

You were not confident with every answer and did not try to pretend that you knew if you were uncertain. You did your best to be honest, upbeat, cheery but not unnatural, relaxed but alert. You listened carefully to the questions and thought briefly before you responded. You were positive, but tempered it by stressing that you wanted to continue learning and do well. You did not raise dilemmas or problematic issues. Finally, despite your nerves and uncertainty about some of the tougher questions put to you, a combination of your personality and responses convinced the head and governors that you were the best person for the job. Congratulations! Now the fun begins!

Activate your thinking!

How would you respond to the following interview questions?

Professional requirements
What sort of learning climate will you promote and how will you go about it?

Teaching and learning
How will you go about setting high, but not unreasonable, expectations for the full range of ability?

Adult relationships
- How will you employ the skills of a 0.5 teaching assistant?
- What practical steps will you take to involve parents in learning?

Self-development
How will you know if you are succeeding as a teacher?

Preparation and planning
How will you organise your literacy lessons?

Purposeful teaching
What strategies might you use to motivate children who find learning difficult?

Special needs
How do you envisage an 'inclusion' policy operating in your classroom?

Organising and managing
Teachers are busy people. How will you prioritise your time and workload?

Behaviour and discipline
Describe the way that you will ensure that children are well-disciplined without being crushed in spirit?

Extended professionalism
Tell us something about the duties of a teacher other than teaching.

Assessment
How will you use assessment to improve teaching and learning?

Equal opportunities
What steps will you take to ensure that all children have a fair chance?

Requirements

The most recent set of Induction Standards came into force on 1 September 2003 to ensure that NQTs are able to:

- Benefit from and contribute to the sharing of effective practice
- Widen their vision
- Experience opportunities for subject specialism and classroom-focused development
- Contribute to the workforce reform agenda
- Begin developing leadership qualities

The induction year can be served in any maintained school, with certain exceptions:

- Pupil referral units.
- Secure training-centres.
- Schools requiring special measures, unless one of Her Majesty's Inspectors certifies in writing that the school is suitable for providing induction.
- Independent schools that do not meet specified criteria.
- Further Education Colleges, unless a sixth-form college.
- Independent nursery schools and other early years' settings that do not meet the criteria described in the section on independent schools above.

■ British Schools abroad, apart from those described in the section on independent schools above.

Fuller details of all the above conditions may be obtained from the website: www.teachernet.gov.uk

If you are interested in working in an independent school, it is essential to check that the school is approved by the DfEE to run an induction programme.

During the induction year, NQTs are entitled to receive support from the head teacher and staff, and must reach clearly defined standards in their classroom practice and wider professional conduct as staff members (Cole, 1999; 2002). Normally, NQTs will start their induction year as soon as they leave training college and commence their first permanent teaching post. Those who only manage to acquire a temporary post lasting less than one year can build up to a total of one year in different schools. For instance, an NQT might find employment in three separate schools, each lasting one term, or work for two terms in one school and a term in a second school. In unusual circumstances such as lengthy sick leave or maternity leave, the induction process can be extended beyond the one year until the equivalent amount of time has been served.

If an NQT has been absent from work for 30 school days or more during the induction period, the induction period is extended by the aggregate total of absences. For example, if they are absent for a total of 35 days, the extension will be for 35 days. If a female NQT has a break in the induction which includes statutory maternity leave, she may choose whether or not to have the induction extended by the equivalent of the part of her absence which was statutory maternity leave. A final decision is normally made by the NQT when she returns to work and has given the matter careful thought, but any such request cannot be denied by school governors. However, if an NQT chooses not to extend her induction period following an absence of maternity leave she is still assessed on the same basis as any other NQT.

As part of teachers' continued professional development, each is allocated a fellow staff member to be a mentor (induction tutor) who will help the NQT to negotiate his/her first year. The induction tutor offers advice about many aspects of school life, such as time management, handling paperwork, dealing with troublesome children, relating to parents and maintaining a reasonable work/leisure balance. By the end of their induction year, all new teachers must have demonstrated their mastery of the Qualified Teacher Status (QTS) standards on a consistent and sustained basis, while teaching continuously in a school, with the direct and personal responsibility and accountability for pupil performance that accompanies it. They must also have shown that they have built on, and progressed beyond, the QTS standards (DfES/TTA 2002) in key areas such as managing pupil behaviour and contributing to pupils' learning, and to the planning and achievement of their school's performance targets.

NOTE: This document applies to teachers in England. The Welsh Office has published a separate set of proposals.

Conditions

The Teaching and Higher Education Act 1998 introduced arrangements to provide all NQTs with a bridge from initial teacher training to effective professional practice. Information available from the DfES website describes how the induction programme 'is intended to provide well-targeted monitoring and support, within the context of a reduced timetable, and to help embed an ethos of continuing professional development (CPD) and career development during an NQT's first year of teaching. This in turn helps them to give of their best to pupils.'

NQTs will not normally be expected to endure excessive demands by (say) having to take a very large class or a group of particularly difficult pupils. They should only teach for only about 90 per cent of the time to give them opportunity to gain wider experience by working alongside a colleague, visiting other successful schools and attending courses.

The induction tutor may be a senior teacher (in a larger school) and the deputy head or experienced teacher (in a smaller school). The mentor will encourage an NQT to contribute to curriculum working parties, act as a guide in visiting other local schools (including a special school) to enhance the NQT's knowledge and experience of education, and facilitate working with the SENCO. Establishing and maintaining contact with other new teachers in the area is essential, as it is easy for NQTs to become isolated in their first post and imagine that they are the only teacher in the world struggling with discipline and keeping pace with the relentless demands that teaching sometimes imposes. As Cockburn (1996) realistically acknowledges:

> Whether you are an experienced teacher or new to the profession, starting a new job is often an exhilarating, challenging and daunting experience rolled into one (page 27).

Part of your development as a teacher is learning to work with and alongside colleagues, accept majority decisions and strive to work within the agreed guidelines and policies. You will not agree with everything that is taking place when you arrive at the school or all the subsequent decisions. Some aspects of school life will irritate you. Some colleagues will disappoint you. Some procedures will appear unnecessary or irksome. Although you are entitled to ask for explanations about why things are done in certain ways, it is important to understand that every new teacher has to learn to fit in to the school situation as it exists. This is not to say that with your influence certain aspects may not change or be modified over time, but the best forms of change come slowly and, however convinced you may be that you know best, it is wise to listen, watch and wait before passing judgement. Your contributions to debate will be valued and respected if you express them with humility and a genuine willingness to learn.

As a qualified teacher you are expected to contribute towards the whole school endeavour and make an effort to lend your expertise to improving standards of learning, behaviour and social awareness. Just as happy children work more enthusiastically, so a contented staff will achieve more than a miserable one. You may not believe that you have much to offer your colleagues as a newly qualified person, but this is untrue. Other teachers and ancillary staff, while anxious that you settle in quickly and do well in your job, also hope that you will play your part in being an effective team member. Head teachers want teachers that helps to raise morale, work well with colleagues and provide a positive role model.

Succeeding in your induction year

You will have worked very hard to gain QTS and been looking forward with excited anticipation to the day when you have responsibility for your own class. In the light of all the effort you have made to reach this point, the induction year may give the appearance of being yet another hurdle. However, it is important to view the year as part of the support mechanism available to new teachers, without which you would be less equipped to deal with the rigours of teaching. The induction year standards are not dissimilar to those for qualified teacher status. You need to be able to demonstrate your competence in planning, teaching, class management, monitoring, assessing, recording and reporting. You must, of course, take account of the needs of individual children and ensure that all children are included (see Chapter 9). There are also expectations with respect to deploying and working with other adults (including parents), implementing school policies (such as dealing with bullying and racial harassment) and taking responsibility for your professional development (see Tickle 2000).

Success in the induction year is much less a case of whether or not you will pass (as almost everyone does) but of how much progress you make as a teacher during that time. If you end the year feeling more confident about the job and your ability to thrive, then the year has been a success. Remember that the induction year is only the first of many years that you will spend as a teacher (Bubb 2004), so see your progress in the longer term, rather than 'surviving' to the end of next summer term!

Positive attitudes

Active and enthusiastic collaboration is at the heart of effective schools, so make it your aim to get on well with everyone in school, including non-teaching staff, and maintain a positive attitude towards life. You do not have to go around the school with a permanent grin on your face, of course! A pleasant smile and responsive manner is quite sufficient to convince those around you that you are worth all the effort they expend on your behalf. Similarly, the respect that you display towards other adults working in the school will help to seal your reputation as a person of integrity. Positive attitudes are contagious; they not only affect the quality of interpersonal relationships with colleagues but upon the classroom teaching-and-learning environment.

Effective schools are places where teamwork and staff loyalty are embedded into the fabric of the place. Being a teacher, like most other jobs, is as much about corporate endeavour and teamwork as the technical ability to teach. Once you enter a school, you have a responsibility to a range of different groups: children, parents, governors, members of the community and your colleagues. Even if you are a novice teacher, you must still demonstrate a willingness to support other teachers and trainee teachers in their efforts to improve their practice and contribute to the children's education. Genuine comments to staff expressing your appreciation for their help and the way that you value their guidance will greatly encourage them. Similarly, the caring way in which you react to colleagues, especially when they need someone to talk to about important issues, will create enormous goodwill and strong feelings of camaraderie which are essential for effective teamwork. Commitment to fellow workers goes beyond sitting and listening while they sound off their complaints; it involves being willing to act for your colleagues in practical and active ways whenever possible.

Getting on well with the head teacher

You will probably have quite a lot of contact with the head teacher during your early days in school as a qualified teacher. Most head teachers make a special point of nursing new members of staff through their first few weeks in the job rather than leaving it all to the induction tutor. Others believe that it is better to stay at a distance and allow new teachers to make their mistakes in private. Although head teachers tend to be extremely busy at the start of term and may seem a bit distracted, you should not misinterpret this as unfriendliness. Over time, you will discover that heads are under a lot of pressure to achieve high standards of education in the school, though many of their struggles take place behind closed doors. Head teachers have spent many years in school and cannot be fooled by a jaunty remark and artificial smile, but they appreciate teachers and other adults who have the courtesy and maturity to make good eye contact and speak out clearly. If you ever apply for a post in another school, you will need to put the head teacher as one of your referees. Head teachers talk to one another regularly and if you have impressed one head teacher, there is a strong chance that your reputation will reach the ears of other local head teachers. You can be sure that whether or not the head is personable, you are rarely off his or her mind when you first arrive in school!

Activate your thinking!

How true are the following? (a) I am displaying a willing, enthusiastic approach to the job (b) I am doing my best to value those around me (c) I am making the best of those things that irritate me.

Contributing expertise

Every teacher has some special skill or ability that may be useful for the common good and benefit colleagues and children. Learning to learn from one another is something that every school has recognised as important. NQTs are sometimes appointed on the understanding that they will try to contribute curriculum strengths as a co-ordinator, leader or curriculum manager throughout the school. However, this is difficult even for experienced teachers and places heavy demands upon an already busy practitioner (Webb 1994; Farmery 2004). There is always so much to do and think about that finding the time and opportunity to work alongside colleagues, advise them about possibilities for developing a curriculum area or taking their class as a subject specialist is difficult. All schools have a development programme in which subjects and topics are examined systematically, giving the teachers responsible for that area the opportunity to share and to exercise leadership during the discussions. In some cases, the teacher concerned may be asked to provide a draft policy statement, guidelines or a review of the existing situation. Extra responsibility for curriculum development or an aspect of learning (such as assessment and recording) has to be fitted alongside other teaching duties. Few schools have the resources to give teachers the time to pursue these responsibilities during the school day, though with the restructuring of the workforce it may be possible to free some time through use of experienced TAs.

As part of team membership, teachers have to attend staff meetings. Full staff meetings are normally held once a week, though additional team planning meetings and age-phase meetings are commonplace. Attendance at meetings can become burdensome and all teachers have to make allowance for the time and energy they consume. When decisions have to be made, some schools make them on a strictly democratic basis in which a vote is taken; others use curriculum leaders and senior staff to draw up papers for discussion and present suggestions about future programme modifications. These are subsequently discussed and revised until a suitable format is agreed across the staff. In a small number of schools, the curriculum leader and the head teacher determine the strategies beforehand; these are presented to the staff for implementation rather than acceptance, modification or rejection. In such cases, debate is concerned with the detail rather than the substance of the issue. Most teachers welcome clearly presented ideas that will help their teaching and supervisory responsibilities but are suspicious of innovations which they perceive as reducing their autonomy. Finally, all head teachers are subject to Government demands and requirements. Local Education Authorities also put pressure on schools to adjust what are perceived as weaker areas. A coming inspection sends shivers down the spine of every practitioner and school governor, and numerous preparation meetings are held beforehand.

From time to time, the school governors decide that the school's budget allows them to give teachers an extra allowance for their contribution as curriculum leaders. Additional increments are offered to the teacher directly or, more usually, the post is advertised internally and any member of staff can apply. The requirements of the post may vary: 'language co-ordinator' or 'assessment at Key Stage 1' or 'curriculum leader in science'.

Although certain teachers have formal responsibilities for areas of school life, there are a number of teachers in every school who, by dint of personality, length of service at the school or experience are the 'unofficial leaders' of the staffroom. To the newcomer, unofficial leaders may not appear initially to be influential but behind the scenes they are affecting the course of staff opinion and attitudes towards options and decisions. Some NQTs may find themselves benefiting greatly from their informal advice and counsel.

Older, experienced teachers can offer leadership through their calm presence during turbulent times. Younger staff can lead through their infectious enthusiasm, willingness to embrace change and introduction of new ideas. The secret of effective informal leadership is to support the official leadership wholeheartedly, while using every opportunity to encourage others, empathise with the downhearted, sympathise with the broken-hearted and provide practical support and advice to colleagues in need. The best informal leaders do not seek adulation or power for its own sake; instead, they gain satisfaction from being positively influential and genuinely admired by staff and parents.

Activate your thinking!

What percentage of your time do you spend throughout a week on classroom teaching, other supervisory duties, attendance at meetings and general preparation and maintenance tasks? Consider whether you should make adjustments.

Good practice

Establish a network of friends, supporters and other new teachers for encouragement, sharing problems and celebrating successes.

Growth and development

During your induction year you will need to secure and enhance the competencies that you acquired during your training. It is worth bearing in mind that however well you performed as a trainee teacher, there will always be areas of your teaching requiring close attention. Even some of the basic skills, such as class control, can prove difficult during your first post. It takes time to settle in and find your feet, so you will have to persevere and use every strategy at your disposal to avoid feeling overwhelmed. You will also need to take account of the standards in the professional codes for the General Teaching Councils in England, Wales and Scotland. Thus, the GTC for England refers to young people as pupils, teacher colleagues, other professionals, parents and carers, school in context and learning and development. Wales GTC includes details relating to teaching and learning, pupils, colleagues, parents/guardians, other professionals, and professional development. Scotland GTC (by far the longest established of the three) focuses on expertise, collegiality, equal opportunities, responsibility, legal framework, responding to individual needs, professional relationships and professional integrity. (See Arthur *et al.* 2004.) As you increase in confidence and find your way through the initial challenges, allow the following principles to act as a guide:

- Learn to trust your own judgement
- Share your concerns and joys with colleagues and friends
- Pace yourself so that you don't attempt too much, too soon
- Use every possible resource available, including published material such as textbooks
- Take proper rest and holidays.

The head teacher is obliged to commit resources towards helping you to develop your competence by releasing you from class teaching on occasions, giving you time to work alongside more experienced teachers in the school from time to time, and attend organised training sessions at nearby professional development centres. Your Career Entry and Development Profile (CEDP) will provide a useful starting point for future career development and should be used alongside the issues arising from the regular review meetings with your mentor to shape and refine your skills. For instance, your CEDP may show that you have had little opportunity to master aspects of ICT or gained limited experience of teaching PE while you were a trainee teacher. Whatever the specific area for enhancement, you will be encouraged to learn from other colleagues with more expertise and attend appropriate courses to extend your knowledge. Do not be embarrassed that you have areas which require further development, as even qualified teachers need to update and refine their knowledge and understanding, regardless of the years they have been teaching.

Whatever your particular subject expertise may be, you need to concentrate on the following aspects of your role during the induction year, and persevere with those aspects that you find difficult. The following list, based on guidelines for the induction of new teachers (DfES 2001c) offers a useful means of monitoring your progress:

Classroom order

Securing good classroom order by establishing effective relationships with pupils and clarifying with your pupils what you are, and are not, prepared to tolerate.

Lesson planning

Planning lessons thoroughly, but with awareness that teaching is not an exact science. That is, to be willing to deviate from the plan if, during teaching, it becomes clear that a different approach is called for.

Target setting

Monitoring pupils' progress and setting appropriate learning targets for groups of children or individuals. For instance, a group of children may need more opportunity to work co-operatively. An individual may be set specific time limits to complete work or given a longer-term goal such as mastering a family of spellings or learning how to access information sources.

Assessment

Assessing pupils against tests and targets. Taking account of pupils' previous achievements from reports, notes and conversations with other teachers and (in some cases) parents, and talking to the children themselves.

Individual differences

Identifying and supporting low achievers, either through appropriate tasks, support from peers through collaborative activities, or help from a teaching assistant.

Special educational needs: Working in conjunction with the SENCO for pupils who provide exceptional challenges. Parents are involved from an early stage.

Classroom climate

Helping to create socially responsible attitudes among pupils by encouraging co-operation and collaboration rather than animosity and selfish forms of competition. Incorporating ethnic and cultural diversity in your teaching. Valuing every child as a unique and special individual.

Home–school

Taking every opportunity through formal and informal liaison with parents to express your enthusiasm for their children's progress and communicating your pleasure (and occasional concerns) by word of mouth and letter (see Chapter 3). This is particularly important for new school entrants in the Foundation Stage of their education.

Other adults

Ensuring that ancillaries are clear about their role and your expectations of them. It is worth remembering that assistants now have the opportunity to gain formal qualifications and regularly update their skills. Experienced TAs may sometimes be capable of supervising a class during your absence.

Staff membership

As noted earlier, playing your part as a team member by offering support and encouragement to those with whom you work. Implementing school policies as fully as possible, and informing senior staff where you experience difficulties in so doing.

Wider role: Contributing to extra-curricular activities where appropriate. Helping to maintain and enhance the school's reputation in the community by your positive attitude, creative teaching and personable manner.

If the list looks daunting, remember that you have already demonstrated your capability during pre-service training and have a whole year to improve weaker areas. Some requirements will naturally fall into place; others will need perseverance over a period of time. Mistakes and occasional instances of poor judgement are inevitable; try to take it in your stride and not become dispirited if things go wrong. The induction year may well prove to be the most demanding, worthwhile and exciting time of your life so far.

Making the transition

It takes time to adjust from being a student to being a 'real' teacher. Newcomers have to adjust quickly to a new community, getting to know people, routines and facts, appreciating the ethos of the school and understanding protocol. Breaking into the professional circle can be forbidding and requires a subtle blend of tact and assertion. You have been a trainee teacher for at least a year, possibly three or four years, and suddenly, like a chrysalis turning into a butterfly, you grow your wings and become a fully-fledged teacher. If you don't feel like one and wonder if it can really be true, don't be alarmed. Most NQTs wonder how they are ever going to survive and if they have got what it takes to make a success of the job. It is not uncommon to experience a sharp decline in confidence following the end of your training course and, though you wonder at yourself for feeling this way, to half-wish that you could be a student again with all the protection it afforded. When you were training, the children in your teaching experience schools sometimes asked you the same question at the start of every new placement: 'Are you a real teacher?' and you hardly knew what to say. You probably ended up by sounding a little indignant and replying that *of course* you were a real teacher (but not feeling like one at all). You longed for the day when you could answer the question honestly, but now that the day has arrived you still find yourself wondering if it is true.

And other anxieties may begin to emerge: What if you are asked by a parent if this is your first class? What if colleagues begin to probe your subject knowledge, classroom management expertise and understanding of assessment and reporting procedures? In fact, what if someone begins to expose all the sorts of things that troubled you as a student, but that you successfully concealed from the tutor? In short, what if you are found out? Panic may set in as you realise that you know absolutely *nothing* about teaching, you don't know why on earth it ever occurred to you to be a teacher, and you wonder why you didn't take your friend's advice and do a different job. 'Too late now!' you lament.

If you are feeling this way, you can be reassured that although some parents may ask if this is your first class, and colleagues will chat about aspects of school life and how to cope with it, they rarely do so with ill intent. In fact, parents often like their children to have new teachers in the belief that they will introduce fresh ideas and sparkle to the teaching and learning environment. Many colleagues are hoping to get some useful suggestions from you to use in their own lessons. The arrival of this talented young star is eagerly awaited, so make sure you don't do or say too much at the start that reveals your insecurities and damages your image!

To a certain extent, the nervous tension that rises from the pit of your stomach towards the end of the holiday period will be a feature throughout your career. If you ask experienced teachers about the few days leading up to the start of a new term, they will confess that it is a miserable time as doubts about their own ability to cope with the demands of the job surface, and uncertainty hangs over them like a damp fog. Once they are back in school and the new term begins, the tension evaporates in the fever pitch of meeting the children, organising lessons, relating to colleagues and parents, re-establishing their credentials as a teacher to be reckoned with, and reminding themselves that they have not, after all, lost their ability to thrive and prosper in teaching. So don't be surprised if you have similar sorts of worries before the start of every term and equally powerful feelings of reassurance once you have begun.

New challenges

Being a qualified teacher carries many advantages over being a trainee teacher. For a start, you will not have a tutor observing your lessons, though you will not be spared this ordeal entirely as there will be occasions when a senior colleague comes to watch you teach. However, you will be able to discuss issues on an equal footing rather than feeling at the mercy of the college assessment system. Second, in the earlier stages of the school year there will be far fewer forms to complete, though as the year unfolds there will be a lot of recording and report-writing to do. Third, there will not be any need to write screeds of self-analysis about how you might have improved your lesson or what went wrong during the session (although it is worth keeping a diary about important issues that emerge throughout the year). The most notable advantage about leaving student days behind is being able to relish the freedom you gain from knowing that you are no longer dealing with somebody else's class and will not, after a period of some weeks, have to hand the children over to the class teacher again and trudge wearily back to college for more lectures.

Gradually, however, other aspects of the job will emerge that you may or may not be expecting. The rest of this chapter is designed to assist you anticipate some of those challenges, deal with them effectively and play your part in providing the sort of education that you would want for your own children, were they in your class.

Doing your best

You want to do well in your new job, of course, but beware of trying to do everything at once. It is true that you are to some extent under scrutiny, but most teachers are too busy with their own affairs to worry about what you are getting up to. It is important to recognise that you will tire very quickly during the first term, so it is essential to pace yourself and not to develop a whirlwind mentality, flitting from one thing to another like a performer keeping plates spinning on the end of a dozen canes. You will want to be determined but not frantic; conscientious but not a perfectionist; idealistic but also keeping your feet firmly anchored to the ground. Contrary to how it might be expressed in the media and by some politicians, the future educational success of the kingdom does not rest solely at your feet! You are neither responsible for every bit of learning that children experience nor the only contributor to the aspirations of every parent. You have an important role in ensuring that your class makes good progress in learning, and there would be something strange about teachers who were not interested in ensuring that their pupils attained the highest standards, but you are not the only interested party or influential factor. Some children are motivated by caring and thoughtful parents; others are not. Some children have material advantages that benefit their progress; others lack the basics. Some children are emotionally secure; others are vulnerable and frightened. As the teacher, you have to provide the best education for them that it is reasonable to expect, but you are not a miracle worker and should not attempt to be so.

The truth about being a teacher is that even if you worked 24 hours a day and performed heroic deeds, it would not satisfy all the demands that are made of you. Regardless of the time you arrive at school and leave for home; despite the countless hours you commit to preparation, marking and sorting out individual needs, it will never be enough. It may sound trite, but the old adage that you can only do your best applies to teaching as much as to any other job. Some teachers allow the job to dominate their lives and seem to spend every waking hour in tasks associated with it. Although it can be difficult to stop yourself from becoming obsessed with your new role, it is important to resist the relentless demands that might be made of you by the many different people associated with the school. Like the waves of the sea, additional work and commitments will keep rolling up to your feet, and though you may sometimes feel like King Canute in trying to repel the tide, it is worth persevering to develop a lifestyle that allows for recreation and separation from the job's requirements. This will not be easy. Most NQTs acknowledge that the first year is difficult, demanding, stimulating and a bit scary; yours will not be any different. The advice contained within this book should help you to keep things under control. One thing is for sure: if you don't look after yourself, nobody else will.

Another important thing to remember is that although you are new and feel vulnerable, the children and parents see you as 'the teacher' (albeit young looking, perhaps) and do not distinguish you from any other teacher in the school. So you do not have to prove yourself in the same way as when you were a student. You can move into the realms of super-teacher and being the focus for hero-worship when you have got a few years of teaching under your belt. Concentrate on your classroom work, make an effort to be a supportive colleague and a good team member, and don't use your inexperience as an excuse for a poor quality performance.

Health issues

Illness is an unfortunate fact of life. Trainee teachers and qualified teachers alike are prone to succumb to it at some time or another. As a student, it was possible to miss a couple of lectures if you felt ill or, if it was during a teaching experience, to grit your teeth and struggle on for a couple of weeks until the end of the placement. As a qualified teacher the battle to retain good health is complicated by two facts. Firstly, that the daily contact with children increases the likelihood that you will pick up infections. Secondly, that as you are now the responsible person for your class, you will be reluctant to take time off and disadvantage the children. You may also be anxious lest your absence is perceived by colleagues or the head teacher as a sign of weakness. Worries about comments such as 'They don't make them like they used to' and 'The slightest little thing and these new teachers take a day off' may unduly influence what you decide to do and tempt you to struggle in when you should have stayed at home. There is little point in crawling in to school when you should be resting in bed.

It is important that you protect your health to minimise the possibility of picking up every nasty bug that is floating around the school, so it is essential to do regular exercise and maintain a balanced lifestyle. On the other hand, even the fittest person suffers from ill health occasionally, so you should not view time off work as a crime. In fact, if you go in to school when you are unwell, you may cause one of four unpleasant effects:

1 You are unable to teach properly, so the children do not learn much.
2 The illness tends to make you less tolerant and more grumpy than usual, thereby damaging your relationship with the class.
3 Others may catch your germs, causing more staff and child absences.
4 You further damage your health by working when you should be resting.

In short, if you are unfit for work you should not agonise about it, but accept the fact and let the school know as soon as possible. If you feel unwell during the previous evening, inform the head or deputy straight away; tell them that you are coming down with something and will probably need to take time off. If, by the following morning, you have made a miraculous recovery, inform them immediately to prevent any unnecessary arrangements being made. The chances are that if you feel really unwell in the evening, you will not have recovered sufficiently by the next day.

If possible, try to indicate how long you expect to be off work. This helps the head teacher to plan whether there is a need for substitute teachers or, if necessary, whether to farm out groups of children from your class to other teachers. If it is not possible to say how long you expect to be off school, keep the secretary/administrator or head teacher informed of your progress.

Activate your thinking!

Teachers who take care of themselves are in a better condition to take care of the children in their care!

When you do return to work, it will be assumed that you are fit and well. Do not expect much sympathy or any allowance for the fact that you are still struggling. This is not callousness, but simply a reflection of the fact that it is not normally practical to nurse along a half-fit colleague; either you are well enough to do the job or you are not. If you go in to school when you should still be off sick, you can antagonise other staff who will probably perceive your courage as foolhardiness.

Dealing with your emotions

One of the unexpected elements of being a teacher is the emotional strain it brings. All NQTs know that the job will be demanding and consume a lot of time and energy. They may be less prepared for the inner turmoil which can sometimes threaten to undermine the good work they are doing. Common questions that can disturb and upset you include:

- Did I do/say the right thing when I dealt with the incident?
- Will the child be encouraged or upset after I spoke to him about his attitude?
- How will parents react when they hear that I kept their daughter in during break-time to finish her work?
- Is the child all right after sustaining that small bump on the head?
- Am I coping with my responsibilities or are people secretly saying that I'm not up to the job?
- Did I speak out of turn during the staff meeting when I expressed my frustration with the present arrangement?
- How will I cope with all the demands and expectations that are being placed upon me?
- Can I ever hope to motivate that difficult child?

There are no easy ways to deal with emotional pressures, but it is important to remind yourself regularly that you have been appointed on merit. Other candidates applied for the job, but only you were successful. Nevertheless, you have to accept that in the rush and tumble of school life you will make minor errors of judgement. These occasions do not, however, spell the end of your teaching career! In trying to maintain a sensible perspective on events, it may be helpful to remember that every NQT has had to tread the same path as you have. Some new teachers have had a smooth passage; others have struggled. It may be the case that those who have had fewer problems were the less ambitious teachers, preferring to 'play safe' and maintain a strictly controlled environment based on closely regulated lessons and rigidly enforced behaviour management. More ambitious new teachers may encounter more problems initially because they want to 'light a fire' and passion for learning in children through creative teaching and innovative activities. As a result, children become more animated, noisier and self-confident, with the discipline challenges that such behaviour evokes.

Resist the tendency to confuse your inexperience with incompetence. The former is true of every new teacher, whereas the latter is rarely true of *any* teacher. Try to focus your attention on your positive attributes and successes and, if problems begin to emerge, seek advice earlier rather than later. In addition to the induction tutor, it can also be useful to confide in a friendly, older colleague who understands what you are going through and will help you to be more objective in your view of your progress.

Most teachers encourage children to keep a profile of their achievements but fail to do the same for themselves! Your emotional stability is likely to ebb and flow throughout the term. Fatigue, over-commitment and a defensive attitude all conspire to drain your energy, reduce your confidence and open you to fears and doubts which would not normally bother you. Give your emotions as much attention as you do to every other part of your mind and body.

Checklist

At the end of your first term as an NQT, divide the following list into three groups: those things you are doing well; those you are doing satisfactorily; and those you are doing badly. It is likely that nearly all will fall into the first two categories.

- I am taking an interest in the welfare of individual pupils.
- I am preparing my lessons thoroughly.
- I am taking account of differences in pupils' ability.
- I am teaching consistently.
- I am maintaining an industrious classroom climate.
- I am getting on with my colleagues.
- I am making contact with parents.
- I am keeping up with my marking.

- I am setting suitable homework tasks.

- I am keeping my room in reasonable order.

- I am attending the required staff and team meetings.

- I am motivating and inspiring the children.

Activate your thinking!

During your induction year you should take account of the following targets:

By the end of term 1: to consistently meet the standards for QTS and begin to meet the induction year standards.

By the end of term 2: to make good progress towards meeting the induction year standards.

By the end of term 3: to meet fully the requirements for the satisfactory completion of the induction period.

(For fuller details, see DfEE 1999b, section 56)

Case study

When Carmen was appointed to a post in a large infant school as a teacher for reception-aged children, a teacher who was just completing his induction year gave her the following advice. First, he suggested that it was useful to sort out certain details before the term began:

- The names, ages, dates of birth and any major details of children's ability and aptitude.

- Reports and records, school policies, schemes of work, long-term plans.

- Special needs children and their support.

- Samples of children's previous work.

- The names of other teachers, assistants, caretaker, cleaners, etc.

- The School Prospectus.

- Staff handouts on health and safety (including fire alarm procedures).

- The person you can contact during the holiday for help/advice.

- Timetables, school starting and finishing times, breaks, lunch times.

- Procedures for attendance registers and dinner registers.

- Times of assemblies and if/when your class may be involved (though don't volunteer too quickly).

- Regular weekly meetings and events, such as staff meetings, team meetings.

- Important dates during the first term that you need to know in advance, such as Parents' Evenings, staff training days.

- The system for setting and monitoring homework.
- The school's dress code, including expectations for PE and games.
- How tea and coffee are provided; how to pay for it; whether you need your own cup!
- Whether you will be required to do any additional duties, such as bus duty.

He also recommended:

- Put names on drawers and pegs, and make sure resources are clearly labelled.
- Plan the furniture layout, including the siting of computers to suit your way of working (you're in charge now!).
- Check that you have sufficient stock for the first couple of weeks, including paper of various kinds, exercise books, paper, pencils, markers, chalk, scissors...
- Set up a book display and have some tried and tested storybooks for reading to the class.
- Make a simple, bold but interesting display, perhaps including some artefacts with a few questions.
- Check the whereabouts of the equipment for PE and games. If possible, make an inventory.
- Have paper cut to a variety of sizes, ready at hand.
- Have a good supply of easy-to-do work sheets and handouts to give you a breathing space during the first few intensive days.

Within the first week...

- Establish your ground rules immediately but don't expect miracles. Learn to persevere.
- Explain to the children your expectations about behaviour and standards of work and regularly remind them.
- Be firm about things like the need to share, your dislike of bullying and your insistence on a harmonious working environment.
- Establish a clear system for leaving and entering the classroom.
- Make sure that you have some informal contact with parents at the start and end of the day.
- Ensure that all your children achieve success in some aspect of their work as early as possible.
- Praise and commend genuine effort at every opportunity.

Be realistic...

- Do not to try to 'make a big impression'. Be yourself. Don't get exhausted. Work steadily.
- You may get the feeling that you are being watched. You are! Use it to show what you are made of.

- Parents will be asking what you are like. What will the children say?

- Sort out your priorities. Fabulous lessons can wait for a while until you have settled and established your routines.

- Don't be too upset when you make mistakes. The person who has never made a mistake has never made anything!

- However successful you were on final TP, the first half-term of your first post is likely to be quite demanding. Try to stay cheerful but don't be afraid to seek advice if you are struggling.

The common experience of new teachers is that sorting out the classroom often takes much longer than expected. Although colleagues are as helpful as possible, everyone is so busy at the start of the term that they cannot spare much time to help. Even if you are not able to fulfil all of the above action points, things fall into place very quickly once the term begins. The more that is in place beforehand, however, the easier the start to the new term becomes.

Further reading

Holmes, E. (2003) *The Newly Qualified Teacher's Handbook*, London: Kogan Page.
The book provides an extensive treatment of the issues, packed full of information.

Working Within the Law

Introduction

This chapter examines how common law and statute law affect the work of teachers. It aims to provide a background understanding of selective matters that arise in classrooms, schools and the learning environment. This is important since you will have to uphold the law in the teaching profession on a daily basis. It assumes that you do not have background knowledge of law, and therefore, the chapter avoids using technical language or addressing complex legal issues.

Background

Education is one of the most regulated sectors of public life, as more legislation is passed in education than in any other sector and the last 20 years have witnessed an explosion of regulation (Ford *et al.* 1999). Other non-education legislation also has important implications for teachers, even though it was not framed with schools in mind; for example, The Children Act 1989. At the same time, the period has witnessed an increase in litigation, as a result of growth of consumerism. Common law and statute law impose a wide range of duties and obligations on individual teachers. Some of the important Circulars and Codes of Practice will be referred to later in this chapter. Circulars, while not being legally binding, are interpretations of the law. They provide guidance and set out recommended practice. Some Codes of Practice, however, have statutory force. If, as a teacher, you are prosecuted for a breach of the relevant law and it is proved that you did not comply with the relevant provisions of the statutory Code, you will need to show that you followed the law in some other reasonable way or a court will find you at fault. The law of education derives from two main sources:

- Acts of Parliament supported by provisions set out in Statutory Instruments and Orders, these are referred to as statutory sources and take precedence over other laws.

- Common Law, these are decisions of judges in individual cases which are sometimes, but not always interpretations of statute law. Decisions in these cases are reached by considering precedents, and the legal reasoning used to decide a case in a higher court will bind all lower courts when dealing with the same issue.

In recent years the influence of the European Union has become significant as the European Convention on Human Rights and various European Directives have been incorporated into UK law. Since the introduction of devolution there are a growing number of differences between the English and Welsh education systems. This separation is likely to increase further. Teachers should be aware that legislation is frequently amended and new regulations and orders introduced. As a teacher, you have a professional responsibility to keep up to date with the way in which laws and Codes of Practice impact upon your classroom and teaching. See for example, Ruff (2002).

Teachers' conditions of employment

Teachers employed by LEAs and governing bodies in England and Wales are employed under statutory conditions of employment. The School Teachers Pay and Conditions Act 1991 was repealed and largely re-enacted in the Education Act 2002. A major change, however, related to the provision for the Secretary of State to bypass the School Teachers' Review Body and make an order on pay and conditions in certain circumstances, thereby introducing a degree of flexibility into the conditions. The STRB is an independent body which makes recommendations to the Government on the pay and conditions of employment of teachers in England and Wales. The STRB annual School Teachers Pay and Conditions Document deals with pay, professional duties and working time arrangements. The document is not comprehensive and does not deal with a wide range of important employment matters, such as issues relating to maternity/paternity leave, sickness, disciplinary procedures etc. These matters are found elsewhere in other national and local agreements. It is a basic duty of teachers to observe the list of general professional duties spelt out in the Conditions Document, which sets out the terms of the contract of employment. The duties which are stated in the contract are termed *express* terms, since they are explicitly stated in writing. If you refuse to undertake any of the listed duties you could be in breach of contract and face disciplinary action.

Within the contract it expressly states that it is the duty of a teacher to comply with the reasonable direction of the head teacher. Similarly, a teacher must perform such duties as may be assigned to him or her in accordance with reasonable directions. So, unless the teacher can show that what he/she is directed or required to do is unreasonable, he/she should accept it. In addition, teachers will be subject to other contract terms which are set out in a letter of appointment from the board of governors. Express terms here will include the point on the salary spine, special duties attached to the post and date of commencement. These individual contracts cannot contain any duties or terms which are inconsistent with the statutory documents. Job descriptions do not have legal force, but they can be used in cases of dispute to clarify the parameters of the post.

The current Conditions do not contractually require teachers to administer medicine or supervise pupils taking it. Nor do the conditions include the provision of first aid. Teachers can, however, volunteer to administer medication or become a first-aider. If you agree to take on this responsibility you should insist on proper training and guidance. You should also ensure that you are properly indemnified by the Local Education Authority against any liability for damages or other compensation. Teachers have a common law duty of care to act as a reasonably prudent parent and this might in extreme circumstances extend to administering medicine or taking action in an emergency, such as using a drug injector (an epipen) following an anaphyllatic reaction. The Children Act 1989 provides that a person who does not have a parental responsibility, but has care of the child to act *in loco parentis* should do what is reasonable in all circumstances for the purpose of safeguarding the health and safety of a pupil. This would exceptionally allow teachers to give consent to necessary emergency treatment in the absence of parental consent.

New workload agreements between the Government, local education authorities and teaching unions mean that there are new clauses in the 2003 Document. Remodelling of the teacher's contract is ongoing; further details about the role of adults in school can be found in Chapter 3. Since September 2003 teachers' contracts state that teachers should not be routinely required to undertake certain clerical or administrative tasks, such as bulk photocopying or collecting money from pupils or parents, and that these tasks will be transferred to support staff. Teachers with management responsibilities must be allocated reasonable time within the school day to discharge them. Teachers should be aware, however, that they may be asked to carry out a routine task, particularly if support staff is not available. The head teacher must act reasonably in making a request of this nature. New clauses scheduled for future years promise teachers a reasonable work–life balance and limit the amount of time teachers can be asked to spend covering for absent colleagues. Guaranteed preparation, planning and assessment time will also be incorporated into the teachers' contract.

There are other contractual terms called implied terms, which are not expressly stated since they are felt to be obvious to the parties to the contract. For example, teachers also have an implied duty to behave in a professional manner, not to steal or act dishonestly, to be co-operative and reasonable in carrying out their duties and not wilfully to obstruct the employer. Employers have an implied duty to provide a safe workplace and pay the agreed salary.

Activate your thinking!

Are you clear about your rights and responsibilities as a trainee teacher or NQT?

General Teaching Councils

The Teaching and Higher Education Act (England and Wales) 1998 established General Teaching Councils. The newly established General Teaching Councils (GTC) for England and Wales are modelled on the Teaching Council for Scotland which has been in existence since 1965. GTCs are statutory, self-regulating professional bodies for teachers. 'They seek to raise the standard of teaching by maintaining and promoting the highest standards of professional practice and conduct in the interests of teachers, pupils and the general public' (GTC website, www.gtce.org.uk).

It is a legal requirement for teachers with Qualified Teacher Status to be registered with the respective GTC. Trainee teachers and overseas teachers qualify for provisional registration. One of the functions of the GTC is to investigate and hear cases against registered teachers through its disciplinary committees. Such cases occur, for example, where it is alleged that the teacher is guilty of unacceptable professional conduct, serious professional incompetence, or where a teacher has been convicted of a relevant offence, which raises questions about his/her fitness to be a registered teacher, except where the case involves the safety and welfare of children. These latter cases are referred to the Secretary of State. Other misconduct cases are referred to the GTC. Professional incompetence cases are referred to the GTC by the employers. The disciplinary committees have to consider whether any action should be taken to that teacher's registration. The GTC has a range of disciplinary powers ranging from removing a teacher's name from the register, suspension, insisting that the teacher should meet specified conditions in order to maintain registration, or issuing a reprimand. A recent example from England featured a primary school teacher who repeatedly failed to hand in curriculum planning and evaluation files to the principal for monitoring. The teacher was reprimanded by the GTC. A mathematics teacher, who was found guilty of gross professional misconduct for swearing at pupils and undermining colleagues, was struck off the register for two years, and a former deputy head of a primary school has been banned from teaching pupils under 13 because of the way he treated pupils with special educational needs. The teacher in question failed to provide equal opportunities to pupils, especially those with special educational needs, and called them names. Only one teacher so far has been permanently removed from the register.

Teachers need to be aware that even though they may not have been convicted of a civil or criminal offence in a court of law, their behaviour in classrooms, schools or on school sponsored activities and in private life may constitute unprofessional conduct or incompetence which indicates unfitness of character to be a registered teacher. For example, an infant school head teacher who made false travel claims and forged the signature of the chair of governors was found by the GTC for England to have been guilty of 'unacceptable professional conduct'.

School discipline

Schools are under a legal obligation to maintain good order and discipline among the pupils. All schools operate a behaviour/disciplinary policy that sets out the rules and regulations, and punishments which are applied within the school. Provided the rules and sanctions are reasonable, applied in a non-discriminatory manner and publicised to pupils, parents and staff, they will be held to be lawful. The European Court of Human Rights has stated that school discipline is not a breach of the European Convention on Human Rights. Problems can, however, arise for teachers in applying the rules. The area of school discipline has given rise to considerable litigation. Traditionally, schools dealt with matters of fighting, bullying and school security internally, but in some areas this situation is changing, and schools are now more likely to call for the police to deal with violent pupils than to put pupils and teachers at risk.

Corporal punishment

The intentional use of force as a form of punishment was abolished in all maintained schools as a result of the Education (No. 2) Act 1986, section 47. Abolition of corporal punishment in independent schools came about as a result of the Education Act 1996 section 548, substituted by the Schools Standards Framework Act 1998, section 131, and came into operation in September 1999. Teachers and other school staff are not entitled, irrespective of parental consent, to administer physical chastisement to any child in the United Kingdom. Any teacher who administers corporal punishment would be in breach of his/her contract of employment. Corporal punishment would also be a breach of the Human Rights Act 1998, Article 3.

Corporal punishment includes not only the use of the cane, strap or slipper but also other forms of physical force such as slapping, rough handling, e.g. holding pupils in a headlock, shaking, pinching, prodding, pulling pupils' hair, pushing, tying pupils up, taping their mouths, or throwing missiles at, or towards, pupils.

Any teacher using physical force against pupils may be liable to a civil action for 'battery' and could also face disciplinary action from the employing authority and/or the board of governors. The case would also be referred to the GTC. Battery is defined as the application of physical force, either through direct physical contact or through some weapon or missile. For example, there was an action where a teacher was charged with battery after spilling orange juice over a ten-year-old pupil on a school trip. The pupil's mother alleged that the teacher had deliberately spilt the orange juice over the child. If the use of physical punishment is severe and the pupil suffers actual bodily harm a criminal action could be instituted against the teacher. For example, a teacher was found guilty of common assault in 2001 after pushing a nine-year-old pupil against a wall, banging his head and prodding him. She was ordered to pay £100 compensation to the pupil and carry out 140 hours community service (reduced to a two-year conditional discharge on appeal). She will not be permitted to work again as a teacher.

Pupil restraint

Common law, however, does recognise that under certain circumstances, members of a school staff are permitted to commit a 'battery' and use reasonable force. This application of force will not be treated as corporal punishment. These powers were often misunderstood so the Education Act 1996 section 550A, inserted by Education Act 1997 section 4, set out to clarify the position. The legislation gives explicit powers to schools and teachers to use reasonable force to prevent pupils committing any offence, causing a personal injury, or engaging in any behaviour prejudicial to the maintenance of good order and discipline.

Circular 10/98 (DfEE 1998d) gives examples of the circumstances in which physical intervention might be appropriate and discusses the meaning of 'reasonable force'. The Circular explains what types of force might be justified, e.g. blocking a pupil's path, and those which are inadvisable, e.g. holding a pupil round the neck or twisting limbs. It explains that there is no legal definition of 'reasonable force', so it is not possible to set out comprehensively when it is reasonable to use force, or the degree of force that may be reasonably used. It will always depend on all the circumstances of the case. There are two relevant considerations here:

- The use of force can be regarded as reasonable only if the circumstances of the particular incident warrant it. The use of any degree of force is unlawful if the particular circumstances do not warrant the use of physical force. Therefore physical force could not be justified to prevent a pupil from committing a trivial misdemeanour, or in a situation that clearly could be resolved without force.

- The degree of force employed must be in proportion to the circumstances of the incident and the seriousness of the behaviour or the consequences it is intended to prevent. Any force used should always be the minimum needed to achieve the desired result.

Whether it is reasonable to use force, and the degree of force that could reasonably be employed, might also depend on the age, understanding and sex of the pupil (and any physical disability he/she may have). When restraining a pupil a teacher should refrain from using threatening language.

Good practice

If you encounter a disturbing situation, remain calm, address those concerned by name, ascertain the facts and don't jump to conclusions. If the perpetrators refuse to co-operate or respond to reason, seek assistance from a colleague.

It is important that when reasonable force has been used by a teacher that the incident is recorded. A short factual account of the incident should include the following information:

- Name(s) of the pupil(s) involved, and when and where the incident took place
- Names of any witnesses
- Why the use of force was thought to be necessary
- Details of how the incident unfolded, the steps taken to defuse the situation, the degree of force used and how was it applied
- The pupil's response, and the outcome of the incident
- Details of any injuries suffered by the pupils and/or any property damaged.

The case of a primary head teacher, who was initially fined and sentenced to a three-month suspended sentence after slapping a ten-year-old boy who pushed her, illustrated the difficulties which can arise in interpreting section 550A, particularly where pupils with behavioural difficulties are involved. After successfully appealing the conviction she was suspended by her board of governors and became subject to an investigation by the police, the Crown Prosecution Service and the County Council. It was eventually concluded that there was no 'credible evidence' against her. She returned to work after 18 months suspension. Teachers need to take special care in the area of pupil restraint since they could be convicted on the basis of uncorroborated evidence.

Detention

The right of teachers to impose detention as a disciplinary sanction has been upheld by the courts since 1908. Unreasonable detention could however lead to a civil action for false imprisonment. This situation arose in 1980 in the case of *Terrington* v. *Lancashire County Council*, when Mr Terrington claimed damages for the false imprisonment of his son, who had been detained by the teacher along with the rest of the class for ten minutes after the end of school. The judge held that it was reasonable to detain a class for ten minutes as a disciplinary sanction but warned that such a punishment should not be indiscriminate, since one is then punishing innocent pupils as well as guilty ones. Teachers need to avoid the use of blanket detentions where whole classes are punished.

The judge further stated that had the father withdrawn his permission from the school regarding the use of detention as a form of punishment, the claim for false imprisonment would have been successful. The judgment introduced an element of doubt regarding detention as a sanction. The Education Act 1996, however, states that detention is not unlawful even without parental consent if the following conditions are met: the principal must have made known within the school and to parents that detention after school hours is a disciplinary option; the detention must be reasonable and parents must be given at least 24 hours' written notice that the detention is to take place.

Section 550 B (4) states that the following issues should be taken into account if a detention is reasonable: whether the detention constitutes a proportionate punishment in the circumstances of the case: and whether there are any special circumstances which should be taken into account including, in particular, the pupil's age, any special educational needs he may have, any religious requirement affecting him, and the provision of travel arrangements.

The question arises as to whether detaining pupils infringes Article 5 of the Human Rights Act 1998 – the right to liberty and security. It is considered unlikely that detaining (pupils) at lunchtime or after school on one-off occasions as a consequence of their misbehaviour is likely to fall foul of Article 5 (Whitbourn 2003). A 15-year-old pupil in Scotland mounted a legal action for compensation after repeatedly serving detention for a series of allegedly 'trivial' incidents.

Confiscation

Teachers need to check that the sanction is clearly spelt out in the school's policies and procedures. Common law permits teachers to confiscate private property, such as mobile phones, cigarettes or jewellery. The confiscated items should not be retained by the teacher, since that would amount to theft, but should be returned at the earliest suitable opportunity, unless there is a policy which permits retention, e.g. flick knives as offensive weapons would not be returned. Dangerous items, such as weapons, illegal drugs and obscene materials should be handed to the head teacher. Care should be taken not to destroy the items or make personal use of them. It is not considered that confiscation infringes a child's human rights nor is it a breach of UK law. For example, the law permits staff to take temporary possession of suspect substances for the purpose of protecting the health and safety of the pupil.

Searches and seizures

Teachers are permitted to search a pupil's desk or locker, but not a school bag, if they have reasonable cause to believe that it may contain unlawful items. If pupils are suspected of concealing illegal items on their person, they should be asked to empty their pockets voluntarily, but they are not obliged to do so. Physical searches should not be conducted by the teacher. A body search without consent would be regarded as an assault/battery. Random searches are inadvisable since they could contravene the right to privacy in the Human Rights Act 1998. Teachers should not attempt to disarm pupils brandishing offensive weapons, such as knives. The police should be called to deal with such pupils. Under the Offensive Weapons Act 1996, it is illegal to carry an offensive weapon on or around school premises without good reason.

Bullying

Teachers have a duty of care towards pupils and have to take reasonable steps to prevent pupils from being bullied, otherwise there could be a claim for negligence. It is now possible that two clauses of the Human Rights Act, the right to an education, Article 2 of the First Protocol and/or the right to be free from degrading treatment, Article 3, could be attached to the negligence action thereby making the teacher's task more onerous. Teachers need to be aware that bullying can take many forms, ranging from verbal insults or racist remarks, to physical actions such as hitting, or indirect manifestations, such as spreading rumours. Teachers need to be aware of their school's anti-bullying policies and procedures. Sanctions for serious and persistent bullying can include exclusion. See Chapter 1 for further details about dealing with bullying in school.

Permanent/fixed period exclusions

Exclusion of pupils from school is a very serious matter, and sizeable numbers of primary age pupils find themselves being excluded. Nearly 1500 primary pupils were excluded in England in 2001. Exclusions are instigated following serious breaches of a school's discipline policy. Exclusions can be either fixed term or permanent. Fixed term exclusions of a pupil must not add up to more than 45 days in any one year. Only the head teacher or acting head can exclude a pupil. The offences for which exclusion can be implemented include:

- Serious actual or threatened violence against another pupil (including bullying) or a member of staff
- Sexual abuse or assault
- Supplying an illegal drug

- Carrying an offensive weapon
- Persistent and defiant misbehaviour including bullying (which would include racist or homophobic bullying or repeated possession and/or use of an illegal drug on school premises).

Exclusion should not be used for:

- Minor incidents such as not doing homework
- Poor academic performance
- Lateness or truancy
- Breaching school uniform policy including hairstyles and wearing jewellery, except where the policy has been wilfully and defiantly flouted
- Breaching a home–school agreement
- Punishing pupils for the behaviour of parents, e.g. where parents have not attended a meeting.

Before a decision to exclude is taken, the head has to consider all the relevant facts and evidence, and take into account the school's policy on equal opportunities and decide to what extent the pupil is culpable. Also, a decision has to be reached whether the sanction is proportionate to the offence committed, and whether the incident in question might have been caused by racial or sexual harassment.

The DfES publication, *Improving behaviour and attendance: guidance on exclusions for schools and pupil referral units* (DfES 2003d) explains the law and what is expected of the various bodies when pupils are excluded. In an important House of Lords judgment (February 2003) the Law Lords ruled that teachers were entitled under trade dispute laws to refuse to teach violent pupils who were legally entitled to be in school. Teachers need to ensure that other forms of punishment do not constitute inhuman and degrading treatment as this would be a breach of Article 3 of the Human Rights Act 1998. Care should be taken to ensure that pupils are not humiliated in front of other pupils, for example, putting a dunce's hat on a pupil, as this could give rise to an infringement of the child's human rights.

Activate your thinking!

The fact that children have rights does not necessarily make what they are doing or saying right!

Equal Opportunities Policy

Circular 10/99, *Social Inclusion: Pupil Support* (DfEE 1999c) states that parents and pupils should know that schools have equal opportunities policies and are committed to equality of opportunity irrespective of gender, race or disability. This statement is necessary, or schools could not meet their obligations under the wide range of anti-discrimination legislation, e.g. Sex Discrimination Act 1975. Teachers have to ensure that all policies, procedures and resources are monitored to ensure that they do not discriminate against any of the identifiable groups. The duties under anti-discrimination legislation are wide and breaches of the laws can result in civil action.

Sex Discrimination Act 1975

The Sex Discrimination Act (SDA) 1975 prohibits discrimination on the grounds of gender and applies to men and women, boys and girls. While it is permissible to have single sex schools, there must be no discrimination against either boys or girls within schools. The Act recognises both direct and indirect discrimination. Direct discrimination is always unlawful and arises when a person is treated less favourably than others because of their gender. Indirect discrimination may or may not be unlawful. It arises when a requirement is applied equally across the sexes, but is such that the percentage of one gender that can meet it is considerably less than the percentage of the other gender. The SDA forbids discrimination as regards access to benefits, facilities and services, though it does contain exceptions which permit single sex sport, on the grounds that there are physical differences between the sexes, based on physique and strength.

Teachers need to guard against stereotyping men or women as regards employment in lessons, or boys or girls in relation to their roles. For example, mixed activities should be offered as the norm, and boys and girls should equally participate in tasks around the school. It may not be unlawful to have single-sex groups within a mixed-school provided it does not give the pupils in these groups an unfair advantage or disadvantage over pupils in other groups.

The issue of school uniform has led to legal challenges under the SDA. School uniform rules must ensure that one gender is not treated less favourably than the other. So it would be unlawful to allow boys to wear what they wish while insisting that girls follow a particular dress code. Problems arise, however, when schools have a uniform policy based on sex, in trying to determine whether the different rules mean less favourable treatment for one gender. For example, it has been argued that forbidding girls to wear trousers is discriminatory and forces them into accepting a stereotypical role.

Race Relations (Amendment) Act 2000

The Act amended the 1976 Race Relations Act. The latter set out to make racial discrimination unlawful, while the 2000 Act tries to ensure that discrimination is eliminated. The Act has introduced a new general duty on LEAs to eliminate unlawful racial discrimination, and to promote equality of opportunity and good relations between persons of different racial groups. This applies among other things to discipline and exclusions. The Commission for Racial Equality has produced a *Code of Practice on the Duty to Promote Race Equality* and a non-statutory guide *The Duty to Promote Race Equality: A Guide for Schools*. See also Chapter 2. Schools have to be sensitive to the needs of different races and religions and these needs have to be accommodated within the uniform policy. It would not be appropriate to discipline a pupil from a particular racial or religious group because of non-compliance with the school uniform policy.

Teachers have a very important role to play in challenging stereotypical views on race. In particular the vexed issue of the high exclusion rate for boys of Afro-Caribbean origin prompts the Code to consider whether incidents of bad behaviour are caused by racial harassment. The Code suggests that teachers need to ensure that they avoid any risk of stereotyping and that they are alert to cultural differences in manner and demeanour. They are advised to take care in selecting resources and to present a balanced perspective on different cultures and races. By creating an open climate in classrooms, teachers should avoid making any pupil feel guilty or embarrassed. It is recommended in the Code of Practice that they should aim to value diversity. This legislation also requires schools to have a formal racial discrimination policy that promotes multiculturalism and monitors racist incidents. All incidents of racist behaviour should be recorded and referred to senior management. In the case of serious incidents this should be done at the earliest possible opportunity.

Special Educational Needs and Disability Discrimination Act 2001

The Act strengthens the rights of pupils with special educational needs and disabilities to be educated in mainstream schools. The definition of disability under the Act covers pupils with physical, sensory, intellectual or mental impairments. The overall aim of the Disability Discrimination legislation is to ensure that disabled pupils are not treated less favourably than non-disabled pupils and are not disadvantaged in any aspect of school life. Under the Act it is unlawful to discriminate against any disabled pupil by excluding him/her from the school. The Disability Rights Commission has published a Code of Practice which explains schools' duties to disabled pupils. All pupils should have equal access to the curriculum and national strategies, to school trips and the full range of sporting, recreational and social experiences. It is unlawful to discriminate, without justification, against any pupil because of a disability. For example, a county court awarded £3000 to a pupil who was not permitted to go on a school trip because of diabetes. Further issues relating to special educational needs are addressed in Chapter 9.

Medicines

A controversial point relates to the administration of medicines. Clearly pupils requiring medication are put at a disadvantage if this provision is not available in schools. Further guidance on this issue is provided in Circular 14/96 – *Supporting pupils with medical needs in schools* (DfEE 1996) which points out that where pupils have medical needs, the school may have to make provision to safeguard their health and safety.

The Children Act 1989

The welfare of the child is the paramount consideration of the Act. Under the Act it is the child who has the rights rather than the parent. The Act introduced the concept of 'abuse' (see also

Sage 1993). The word, however, is not defined in the legislation. The Social Services recognise four categories of abuse. They are:

- physical
- sexual
- emotional
- neglect

Teachers have a legal duty to report immediately any suspicions of physical or sexual abuse to the teacher designated for child protection; it is their responsibility to pass these concerns on to the social services. Teachers have no duty to investigate cases of suspected abuse. If a pupil tells you he/she has been abused you should listen very carefully, try to write down his/her own words, and if possible avoid interrupting him/her. Care should be taken to frame any queries openly, and to avoid leading the pupil in any way. You must not give any undertaking of confidentiality to the pupil. A written, dated record should be made as soon as practicable.

If criminal charges are instituted against the abuser, teachers can be called to give evidence in court. Those giving evidence may be cross-examined and should take care to focus on what the pupil said, using his/her own words and the circumstances of the incident. Paradoxically, since the introduction of the legislation there has been a significant increase in the number of allegations of 'abuse' made against teachers by pupils or parents. Many allegations against teachers have proved to be false, malicious, or misplaced but, unfortunately, in a small number of cases the allegations have been justified. Government figures for 2002, for instance, show that 960 allegations of abuse were made against teachers, mostly involving physical abuse, yet only 30 resulted in a criminal conviction. Major difficulties and problems occur when a teacher has been accused of abuse. Some teachers' lives and careers have been destroyed as the result of abuse allegations. Specific guidance on teachers and child protection, and on teachers facing allegations of abuse is found in DfEE Circular 10/95 *Protecting children from abuse: The role of the education service* (DfEE 1995).

As a result of the Act teachers are very wary of touching pupils in case they are accused of abuse. Teachers should not instigate any physical contact with pupils. There will be occasions when physical contact is unavoidable and necessary. Physical contact may be necessary to demonstrate instructional techniques in class, in sport or in first aid. Touching may also be appropriate if a pupil is in distress and needs comforting. Care should be taken to avoid any displays of affection, such as hugging. Where a pupil instigates contact by hugging the teacher, the response should be reasonable, for example, a comforting hand on the shoulder.

Good practice

Avoid situations where you are alone with a child.

Sex education

Under the Education Act 1996 maintained schools are required to have a written sex education policy. Primary schools, however, are not legally obliged to provide sex education. The DfES recommends that all primary schools should operate a sex and relationship education programme. This programme should be located within the PHSE framework. The objective of the programme is to support pupils through their physical, emotional and moral development. The content of the programme should be concerned with the changes in the body brought about by puberty and how a baby is conceived and born, as set out in KS1 and KS2 of the National Science Curriculum. See also DfES 2000, *Sex and relationship Education Guidance*.

Pastoral care and negligence

All teachers have a legal duty to take reasonable care of pupils who are in their charge. In this respect teachers have to exercise an *in loco parentis* role. This is especially the case in relation to younger pupils. It would be an act of negligence, not to carry out this duty properly, if failure to supervise reasonably leads to a pupil injury/death. In a legal action for negligence the claimant would have to prove on the balance of probabilities that the pupil injury or death resulted from the teacher being in breach of the duty of care. The court would examine the full circumstances of the accident. Thus:

- The ages and capabilities of the pupils being supervised, the appropriateness of the activity, what dangers or hazards were foreseen by the teacher?
- What equipment or apparatus was used?
- Was supervision active or passive?
- What instructions were given to the pupils?
- Did instruction conform to normal and accepted practice?
- Were LEA or school policies followed?
- Where was the teacher located when the injury took place?
- Did the pupil receive immediate attention following the accident?

The court would then try to ascertain the reasonableness of the teacher's actions, and determine whether the injury could have been avoided. If the injury could not have been avoided, the action for negligence and compensation will be unsuccessful.

In a landmark decision (September 2003) a teacher was jailed for one year following the death of a ten-year-old boy on a field trip. The teacher was found guilty of manslaughter which required proof of conduct comprising a breach of the duty of care owed to the deceased that was both the substantive cause of death and was so grossly negligent that it merited criminal sanctions. The DfES has stated that this is the first time a teacher has been jailed for negligence.

Courts accept that teachers cannot do the impossible, and protect pupils from every possible danger every minute of the school day. Schools and teachers are therefore not automatically to blame in the event of every pupil injury. For example, a pupil absconded from school and ran out into a busy road and was badly injured by a vehicle. The parents sued for negligence on the grounds that supervision had been inadequate. The court, however, turned down the claim saying that the school and teachers had done everything reasonably possible under the circumstances, but the pupil was determined to surmount the safeguards.

Fulfilling the duty of care cannot be left to chance and teachers need to think ahead and plan accordingly. They should conduct risk assessments within their classrooms to identify any possible hazards and do everything that is reasonably practicable to minimise risks. If an accident does occur in your classroom, or is reported to you, ensure that you record full details of it in the school accident book.

Activate your thinking!

If a child is injured or in distress, do you know the procedures? If not, why not?

Good practice

Check with the host teacher and teaching assistant whether there are children who have any covert susceptibilities.

Health and safety/risk assessments

Under the Health and Safety at Work Act 1974 and subsequent legislation the head teacher carries the ultimate responsibility for ensuring that day-to-day health and safety complies with school policies and with statutory legal requirements, such as conducting risk assessments. The implementation of *risk assessment* procedures is a legal requirement of the Management of Health and Safety at Work Regulations 1999. The task of risk assessment can be delegated to other staff to carry out in their classrooms or curriculum areas.

School trips

The question of risk assessment is a central concern for teachers who organise school trips. Conducting risk assessments for trips involves more rigorous planning than school-based activities, since more hazards are likely to be encountered, particularly if the trip involves a residential stay. The risk assessment would need to be appropriate to the nature of the trip. Schools have to do what is 'reasonably practicable' to avoid risks. Concerns about the safety of pupils on school trips has led the Government to publish a series of materials which supplement the DfES's own publication entitled , *Health and Safety on Educational Visits* (DfEE 1998b). Risk management procedures have been strengthened by appointing a named member of staff to undertake the role of educational visits co-ordinator. This person will deal with specific concerns such as completing risk assessment forms and seeing they are approved by the board of governors and the LEA. In the smaller primary schools this person is likely to be the head teacher.

Failure to observe the Management Regulations can result in the Health and Safety Executive (HSE) seeking to impose fines or imprisonment through the courts. A breach of any of the main statutory duties constitutes a criminal offence which can be punished by a fine in the courts. Normally the HSE will take action against the employer. However, in some circumstances where a teacher failed to carry out the school's health and safety policy, the HSE may take action against the teacher as well as the employer. Additionally, the failure to conduct adequate or reasonable risk assessments for school trips will be a significant factor in civil and criminal cases where teachers are charged with negligence following an injury or death. For further details about the practical arrangements for school visits, see Chapter 3.

Knowledge is liberty

The intention of this chapter has been to heighten awareness of important matters and, hopefully, to reduce the possibility of legal entanglements or litigation. Knowledge of basic legal rights and responsibilities may help allay any fears or misgivings you encounter about the legal position of teachers. The law acts as a safety net for pupils and teachers alike, offering both a protective framework in which they can carry out their daily tasks with confidence and security.

Standards

1.2 (treating pupils consistently, with respect and consideration) ← *Qualifying to Teach (DfES/TTA 2002)* → 1.8 (aware of, and work within, the statutory frameworks relating to teachers' responsibilities)

Further reading

Lowe, C. (1999) *Pupils, Their Education and the Law: A Casebook Approach*, Birmingham: The Questions Publishing Company Ltd.
This book offers a concise guide to the essential concepts of education law as it relates to pupils and their schooling. The author uses relevant cases to show how the law has been interpreted.

Raymond, C. (ed) (1999) *Safety Across the Curriculum*, London: Falmer Press.
This book helps teachers fulfil their responsibility for the management of safe practice in selected areas of the primary school. It focuses on key aspects of teachers' legal and professional responsibilities in curriculum areas involving a degree of risk.

Conclusion: The Way Ahead

Professional learning

Although you are rightly concerned with the successful completion of your training course and acquisition of QTS, your development does not stop there, as there is always more professional learning to do. The induction year means that you will have to continue extending your expertise throughout the first year of teaching, but your future progress will depend upon your enthusiasm, commitment and ambition. After the initial settling period is over, it is surprisingly easy to lapse into a self-satisfied mode and imagine that somehow you have 'arrived' in teaching. In fact, the best teachers are those who are never fully satisfied with their performance and consider themselves to be life-long achievers (Glover and Law 1996). Teachers who grow complacent are in danger of atrophying, depending too heavily on past experiences and growing stale without realising it. It is actually possible to get *worse* at teaching as well as better at it!

Once qualified, you will probably find that all your attention is focused on your classroom teaching and learning to prosper as a member of the staff team. There are publications to consult that summarise recent education research findings, but many teachers admit that they never read a journal unless they are taking an advanced course or degree. This is understandable but regrettable. There are a number of publications specifically designed to help busy teachers keep abreast of key findings and it is worth consulting one with summaries of findings from a broad range of education interests rather than those issued by the Government.

In addition to ensuring that their staff have good teaching skills, enjoy a good working relationship with children and a knowledge of the curriculum, head teachers and governors value particular characteristics in their teachers. See how you shape up as someone who is willing to:

- Continue learning and persevering
- Assume a fair share of the responsibilities
- Take a positive approach to the job
- Relate well to colleagues, ancillary staff and parents
- See the funny side of life
- Contribute positively to the full breadth of school life
- Encourage others whenever a suitable opportunity arises.

Heads and governors are not well disposed towards teachers who think they know it all, who constantly complain, put minimal effort into their work and walk around with a glum face as if the world owed them a living. They will celebrate the positive difference that you make to the atmosphere of the staffroom and school by your presence.

Relish the joys of teaching

Regardless of the difficulties and challenges that your first year of teaching brings, it is good to remind yourself that this is the way that you want to spend your life. It is probably true to say that with the exception of parents, teachers are the most influential figures for most pupils, and the effect of their teaching will far outlive the whims of Government, policy-makers and educationists.

You will not always succeed. Some days you will feel, and will be, uninspiring. On other days your most carefully laid plans will fall apart at the seams. Despite the occasional setback, however, there are many privileges in being in the job, not least the thought that the impact of your words, actions and ideas will play a significant part in shaping and developing young lives. Nothing can take that entitlement and responsibility away from you.

Activate your thinking!

Think of ways to bring joy into the classroom. Smile and laugh at children's innocent antics and remarks. Be willing to dance, sing, cheer, celebrate, empathise and love. Look for ways to make even mundane learning interesting. Think of the thousands of children you will influence as a teacher. Never lose sight of your calling.

Good practice

Write down this list of statements. Pin them up somewhere. Read and inwardly digest them each day!

- I contribute to the development of good relationships in the school.
- I have a reputation for being a pleasant, warm and caring person.
- Children in my class are making good progress with me.
- I keep events in proportion and do not become too intense or too indifferent.
- The school would be a poorer place without me.

Now start believing it!

Reference

Brighouse, T. and Woods, D. (2004) *The Joy of Teaching*, London: RoutledgeFalmer. *The title says it all!*

References

Adams, J. C. (2002) *Local Delivery of a National Agenda: Citizenship, rights and the changing role of school governors in England and Wales*, Hertfordshire: University of Hertfordshire.

Advisory Centre for Education (2001) *Governors' Handbook*, 5th edn, London: ACE.

Alderson, P. (1999) *Young Children's Rights: Beliefs, principles and practice*, London: Save the Children/Jessica Kingsley.

Alexander, R. (1997) *Policy and Practice in Primary Education*, 2nd edn, London: Routledge.

Arthur, J., Davison, J. and Lewis, M. (2004) *Professional Values and Practice: Achieving the Standards for QTS*, London: RoutledgeFalmer.

Ayers, H. (1996) *Assessing Individual Needs: A practical approach*, London: David Fulton.

Balding, J. (1996) *Bully Off: Young people that fear going to school*, Exeter: Schools Health Education Unit, Exeter University.

Balshaw, M.H. (1999) *Help in the Classroom*, 2nd edn. London: David Fulton.

Barton, L. and Tomlinson, S. (1984) 'The politics of integration in England', in Barton, L. and Tomlinson, S. (eds) *Special Education and Social Interests*, London: Crook Helm.

Beane, A. L. (1999) *Bully Free Classroom*, Minnesota: Free Spirit Publishing.

Beardsley, G. and Harnett, P. (1998) *Exploring Play in the Primary Classroom*, London: David Fulton Publications.

Bearne, E. (1996) *Differentiation and Diversity in the Primary School*, London: Routledge.

Beveridge, S. (2004) *Children, Families and Schools: Developing partnerships for inclusive education*, London: RoutledgeFalmer.

Biott, C. and Easen, P. (1994) *Collaborative Learning in Staffrooms and Classrooms*, London: David Fulton.

Black, P. and Wiliam, D. (1998) *Inside the Black Box: Raising standards through classroom assessment*, London: King's College School of Education.

Brandling, R. (1982) *A Year in the Primary School*, London: Ward Lock.

Brooker, L. (2002) *Starting School: Young children learning cultures*, Maidenhead: Open University Press.

Brown, B. (1998) *Unlearning Discrimination in the Early Years*, Stoke-on-Trent: Trentham Books.

Brown, E. (1999) *Loss, Change and Grief: An educational perspective*, London: David Fulton.

Brown, M. and Ralph, S. (1994) *Managing Stress in Schools*, Plymouth: Northcote House.

Bruce, T. (2001) *Learning through Play*, London: Hodder & Stoughton.

Bubb, S. (2004) *The Insider's Guide to Early Professional Development*, London: RoutledgeFalmer.

Byre, B. (1993) *Coping with Bullying at School*, London: Cassell.

Canter, L. (1998) 'The assertive discipline approach', in Ayers, H. and Gray, F (eds) *Classroom Management*, London: David Fulton.

Carlyle, D. and Woods, P. (2002) *Emotions of Teacher Stress*, Stoke-on-Trent: Trentham Books.

Carter, J. (2002) *Just Imagine: Creative ideas for creative writing*, London: David Fulton.

Cavendish, S. and Underwood, J. (1997) 'Keeping track: observing, assessing and recording in the learning relationship', in Kitson, N. and Merry, R. (eds) *Teaching in the Primary School*, London: Routledge.

Chapman, R. (1995) 'New to teaching', in Bell, J. (ed) *Teachers Talk About Teaching*, Maidenhead: Open University Press.

Charlton, T. (1996) 'Listening to pupils in classrooms and schools', in Davie, R. and. Galloway, D. (eds) *Listening to Children in Education*, London: David Fulton.

Charlton, T., Jones, K. and Flores-Hole, H. (1996) 'The effects of teacher behaviour upon pupil behaviour', in Charlton, T. Jones, K. and Cummings, M. (eds) *Pupil Needs and Classroom Practices*, Cheltenham: Park Published Papers.

Clark, C.M. (1995) *Thoughtful Teaching*, London: Cassell.

Clarke, S. (2001) *Unlocking Formative Assessment*, London: Hodder & Stoughton.

Clegg, D. and Billington, S. (1997) *Leading Primary Schools: The pleasure, pain and principles of being a primary head teacher*, Maidenhead: Open University Press.

Cockburn, A.D. (1996) *Teaching Under Pressure*, London: Falmer Press.

Cole, M. (ed) (1999) *Professional Issues for Teachers and Student Teachers*, London: David Fulton.

Cole, M. (ed) (2002) *Professional Issues for Teachers and Student Teachers*, 2nd edn, London: David Fulton.

Collins, M. (2001) *Because We're Worth It: Enhancing self-esteem in young children*, Bristol: Lucky Duck Publishing.

Commission for Racial Equality (2002) *A Guide for Schools*, London: CRE.

Cooper, H., Hegarty, P. and Simco, N. (1996) *Display in the Classroom: Principles, practice and learning theory*, London: David Fulton.

Corbett J. (1995) *Bad-Mouthing: The language of special needs*, London: Falmer Press.

Corrie, C. (2003) *Becoming Emotionally Intelligent*, Stafford: Network Educational Press.

Cotton, T. (1998) *Thinking About Teaching*, London: Hodder & Stoughton.

Cox, S. and Heames, R. (1999) *Managing the Pressures in Teaching*, London: Hodder & Stoughton.

Crozier, W.R. (2003) 'Shyness in the classroom'. Paper presented at the BERA Annual Conference, Edinburgh, September 2003.

Cullingford, C. (1991) *The Inner World of the School*, London: Holt.

Cullingford, C. (1997a) 'Assessment, evaluation and the effective school', in Cullingford C. (ed.) *Assessment Versus Evaluation*, London: Cassell.

Cullingford, C. (ed) (1997b) *Assessment Versus Evaluation*, London: Cassell.

Curry, M. and Bromfield, C. (1998) *Circle Time In-Service Training Manual*, Tamworth: NASEN.

Day, C. (2004) *A Passion for Teaching*, London: RoutledgeFalmer.

Dean, G. (1998) *Challenging the More Able Language User*, London: NACE/David Fulton Publications.

Dean, J. (1992) *Organising Learning in the Primary School Classroom*, London: Routledge.

Dean, J. (2001) *The Effective School Governor*, London: RoutledgeFalmer.

Denton, C. and Postlethwaite, K. (1985) *Able Children: Identifying them in the classroom*, Berkshire: NFER-Nelson.

Department for Education and Employment (1995) Circular 10/95 *Protecting children from abuse: the role of the education service*, Sudbury: DfEE Publications.

Department for Education and Employment (1996) Circular 14/96 *Supporting pupils with medical needs in schools*, Sudbury: DfEE Publications.

Department for Education and Employment (1997) *Excellence in Schools*. London: Stationery Office.

Department for Education and Employment (1998a) *The Literacy Strategy*, Sudbury: DfEE Publications.

Department for Education and Employment (1998b) *Health and Safety on Educational Visits*, Sudbury: DfEE Publications

Department for Education and Employment (1998c) *Homework: Guidelines for primary and secondary schools*, London: Crown Copyright.

Department for Education and Employment (1998d) Circular 10/98 *Section 550A of the Education Act 1996: The use of force to control or restrain pupils*, Sudbury: DfEE Publications.

Department for Education and Employment (1999a) *The Numeracy Strategy*, Sudbury: DfEE Publications.

Department for Education and Employment (1999b) *The Induction Period for Newly Qualified Teachers*, Sudbury: DfEE Publications

Department for Education and Employment (1999c) Circular 10/99 *Social Inclusion: Pupil support*, Sudbury: DfEE Publications.

Department for Education and Employment/Qualifications and Curriculum Authority (1999) *The National Curriculum: Handbook for primary teachers in England Key stages 1 and 2*, London: DfEE/QCA.

Department for Education and Skills (2000) *Sex and Relationship Education Guidance*, Sudbury: DfES Publications.

Department for Education and Skills (2001a) *Inclusive Schooling*, Sudbury: DfES Publications.

Department for Education and Skills (2001b) *Individual Education Plans*, Sudbury: DfES Publications.

Department for Education and Skills (2001c) *The Induction Standards*, London: DfES Publications.

Department for Education and Skills (2002a) *Special Educational Needs Code of Practice*, Annesley: DfES Publications.

Department for Education and Skills (2002b) *Time for Standards: Reforming the school workforce*, London: Crown Copyright.

Department for Education and Skills (2003a) *Excellence and Enjoyment: A strategy for primary schools*, London: Crown Copyright.

Department for Education and Skills (2003b) *Aiming High: Raising the achievements of minority ethnic pupils*, London: Crown Copyright.

Department for Education and Skills (2003c) *Raising Standards and Tackling Workload: A national agreement*, London: Crown Copyright.

Department for Education and Skills (2003d) *Improving Behaviour and Attendance: Guidance on exclusions for schools and pupil referral units*, Sudbury, DfES Publications.

Department for Education and Skills/Teacher Training Agency (2002), *Qualifying to Teach: Professional Standards for Qualified Teacher Status and Requirements for Initial Teacher Training*, London: TTA.

Desforges, C. (1995) 'Teaching for order and control' in Desforges, C. (ed) *An Introduction to Teaching*, Oxford: Blackwell.

Desforges, C. and Abouchaar, A. (2003) *The impact of parental involvement, parental support and family education on pupil achievement and adjustment: a literature review*, Research Report 433 for the DfES, London: Queen's Printer copyright. (www.dfes.gov.uk/research/data)

Dickinson, C. (1996) *Effective Learning Activities*, Stafford: Network Educational Press.

Dillon, J.T. (1994) *Using Discussion in Classrooms*, Maidenhead: Open University Press.

Doust, S. and Doust, R. (2001) *Governor's Handbook: A comprehensive guide to the duties and responsibilities of school governors in England and Wales*, London: Advisory Centre for Education.

Drake, J. (2003) *Organising Play in the Early Years*, London: David Fulton.

Dreikurs, R., Grunwald, B.B. and Pepper, F.C. (1998) *Maintaining Sanity in the Classroom*, London: Taylor and Francis.

Drummond, M.J. (1993) *Assessing Children's Learning*, London: David Fulton.

Drummond, M.J. (2003) *Assessing Children's Learning* (2nd edn), London: David Fulton.

Drummond, M.J. and Pollard, A. (1998) *Exploring Play in the Primary Classroom*, London: David Fulton.

Duffy, B. (1998) *Supporting Creativity and Imagination in the Early Years*, Maidenhead: Open University Press.

Early Years Curriculum Group (1998) *Interpreting the National Curriculum at Key Stage 1*, Maidenhead: Open University Press.

Epstein, D., Elwood, J., Hey, V. and Maw, J. (1998) *Failing Boys? Issues in Gender and Achievement*, Maidenhead: Open University Press.

Eyre, D. and McClure, L. (ed) (2001) *Curriculum Provision for the Gifted and Talented in the Primary School*, London: David Fulton/NACE.

Farmery, C. (2004) *Successful Subject Co-ordination*, London: Continuum.

Fell, G. (1994) 'You're only a dinner lady! A case study of the SALVE lunchtime organiser project' in Blatchford, P. and Sharp, S. (ed) *Breaktime and the School*, London: Routledge.

Fisher, J. (ed) (2002) *The Foundations of Learning*, Maidenhead: Open University Press.

Fisher, R. (1995) *Teaching Children to Learn*, Cheltenham: Stanley Thornes.

Fitzgerald, D. (2004) *Parent Partnerships in the Early Years*, London: Continuum.

Ford, J., Hughes, M. and Ruebain, D. (1999) *Education Law and Practice*, London: Legal Action Group.

Fox, G. (1998) *A Handbook for Learning Support Assistants*, London: David Fulton.

Fried, R. (1995) *The Passionate Teacher: A practical guide*, Boston: Beacon Press.

Gardner, H. (1985) *Frames of Mind: The theory of multiple intelligences*, New York: Basic Books.

Garrick, R. (2004) *Outdoor Play in the Early Years*, London: Continuum.

Gilbert, I. (2002) *Essential Motivation in the Classroom*, London: RoutledgeFalmer.

Gill, V. (1998) *The Ten Commandments of Good Teaching*, California: Corwin Press/Sage Publications.

Gipps, C. and Clarke, S. (1998) *Monitoring Consistency in Teacher Assessment and the Impact of SCAA's Guidance Materials at Key Stages 1, 2 and 3 (Final Report)*, London: QCA.

Gipps, C., Mc Callum, B. and Hargreaves, E. (1999) *What Makes a Good Primary School Teacher?* London: RoutledgeFalmer.

Glover, D. and Law, S. (1996) *Managing Professional Development*, London: Kogan Page.

Goldthorpe, M. (1998) *Effective IEPs Through Circle Time*, Wisbech: Learning Development Aids.

Goleman, D. (1995) *Emotional Intelligence*. New York: Bantam.

Grainger, T. (2003) 'Creative teachers and the language arts', *Education 3–13*, 31 (1), pp. 43–7.

Greenwood, C. (2004) *Understanding the Needs of Parents: Guidelines for effective collaboration with parents of children with SEN*, London: David Fulton.

Griffiths, N. (1998) *A Corner to Learn*, Cheltenham: Stanley Thornes.

Hallgarten, J. (2000) *Parents Exist, OK? Issues and visions for parent–school relationships*, London: IPPR.

Hardman, F., Smith, F. and Wall, K. (2003) 'Interactive whole class teaching in the National Literacy Strategy', *Cambridge Journal of Education*, 33 (2), pp. 197–215.

Harlen, W. (2000) *The Teaching of Science in Primary Schools*, 3rd edn, London: David Fulton.

Hart, S. (2000) *Thinking Through Teaching*, London: David Fulton.

Hastings, N. and Wood, K.C. (2002) *Reorganising Primary Classroom Learning*, Maidenhead: Open University Press.

Hayes, D. (1998) *Effective Verbal Communication*, London: Hodder & Stoughton.

Hayes, D. (2002) 'Prospering on school placement', *Primary Practice*, 32 (Autumn) pp. 32–4.

Heeks, P. and Kinwell, M. (1997) *Learning Support for Special Educational Needs*, London: Taylor Graham Publishers.

Henry, M. (1996) *Young Children, Parents and Professionals*, London: Routledge.

Heyda, P.A. (2002) *The Primary Teacher's Survival Guide*, Portsmouth, NH: Heinemann.

Hicks, D. (2001) *Citizenship for the Future: A practical classroom guide*, Godalming: World Wildlife Fund.

Houghton, D. and McColgan, M. (1995) *Working With Children*, London: Collins Educational.

Howe, M.J.A. (1990) *Sense and Nonsense About Hothouse Children*, Leicester: BPS Books.

Hughes, M. (1997) 'Other adults in the classroom', in Craig, I. (ed) *Managing Primary Classrooms*, London: Pitman.

Hughes, M., Wikeley, F. and Nash, T. (1994) *Parents and Their Children's Schools*, London: Blackwell.

Hymer, B. and Michel, D. (2002) *Gifted and Talented Learners*, London: NACE/David Fulton.

Jackson, M. (1987) 'Making sense of school' in Pollard, A. (ed) *Children and Their Primary Schools: a New Perspective*, Lewes: Falmer Press.

Jackson, M. (1993) *Creative Display and Environment*, London: Hodder & Stoughton.

Jacques, K. (2000) 'Managing challenging behaviour', in Jacques, K. and Hyland, R. (eds) *Professional*

Studies: Primary Phase, Exeter: Learning Matters.

James, F. and Brownsword, K. (1994) *A Positive Approach*, Twickenham: Belair Publications.

Jeffrey, B. and Woods, P. (2003) *The Creative School*, London: RoutledgeFalmer.

Johnson, G., Hill, B. and Tunstall, P. (1992) *Primary Records of Achievement*, London: Hodder & Stoughton.

Johnston, J. (2002) 'Teaching and learning in the early years', in Johnston, J., Chater, D. and Bell, D. (eds) *Teaching the Primary Curriculum*, Maidenhead: Open University.

Jones, R. and Wyse, D. (2004) *Creativity in the Primary Curriculum*, London: David Fulton.

Jowett, S. and Baginsky, M. (1991) *Building Bridges: Parental involvement in schools*, Windsor: NFER/Nelson.

Kalliala, M. (2004) *Play Culture in the Changing World*, Maidenhead: Open University Press.

Katz, L.G. (1995) *How Can We Strengthen Children's Self-Esteem?* Illinois: ERIC Clearinghouse on Elementary and Early Childhood Education (www.kidsource.com)

Katz, L.G. and Chard, S.C. (2000) *Engaging Children's Minds: The project approach*, 2nd edn, Stamford, Connecticut: Alex Publishers.

Kerry, T. (1998) *Questioning and Explaining in Classrooms*, London: Hodder & Stoughton.

Kewley, G.D. (2001) *Attention Deficit Hyperactivity Disorder*, London: David Fulton.

Kidwell, V. (2004) *Homework*, London: Continuum.

Kinder, K., Wakefield, A. and Wilkin, A. (1996) *Talking Back: Pupils' Views on Disaffection*, Slough: NFER.

Kissock, C. and Iyortsuun, P. (1982) *A Guide to Questioning*, Basingstoke: Macmillan.

Koshy, V. (2000) *Mathematics for Primary Teachers*, London: Routledge.

Kreider, H. (2000) *The National Network of Partnership Schools: A model for family-school-community partnerships*, University of Harvard, Harvard Family Research Project.

Kutnick, P. (1994) 'Use and effectiveness of groups in classrooms: towards a pedagogy', in Kutnick, P. and Rogers, C. (ed) *Groups in Schools*, London: Cassell.

Lampard, L. (1994) 'Children as researchers' in Frith, P. and Mahoney, P. (ed) *Promoting Quality and Equality in Schools: Empowering teachers through change*, London: David Fulton.

Lang, P. (1990) 'Responding to disaffection: talking about pastoral care in the primary school', in Docking, J. (ed) *Education and Alienation in the Junior School*, London: Falmer Press.

Lawrence, D. (1997) *Enhancing Self-Esteem in the Classroom*, 2nd edn, London: Paul Chapman.

Lawson, S. (1994) *Helping Children Cope With Bullying*, London: Sheldon Press.

Leicester, M. and Johnson, G. (2004) *Stories for Inclusive Schools: Developing young pupils' skills in assembly and in the classroom*, London: RoutledgeFalmer.

Lindon, J. (1997) *Working With Young Children*, 3rd edn, London: Hodder & Stoughton.

Lloyd, C. and Beard, J. (1995) *Managing Classroom Collaboration*, London: Cassell.

Lloyd, G. (ed) (2004) *Problem Girls*, London: RoutledgeFalmer.

MacGilchrist, B. (2003) 'Primary learners of the future', *Education 3–13*, 31 (3), pp. 58–65.

MacGrath, M. (2000) *The Art of Peaceful Teaching*, London: David Fulton.

McEwan, E.K. (1998) *How to Deal With Parents Who Are Angry, Troubled, Afraid or Just Plain Crazy*, Thousand Oaks, Cal.: Corwin Press.

McNamara, S. (1997) 'Children with special educational needs' in Kitson, N. and Merry, R. (eds), *Teaching in the Primary School*, London: Routledge.

McNamara, S. and Moreton, G. (2001) *Changing Behaviour*, London: David Fulton.

McNess, E., Broadfoot, P. and Osborn, M. (2003) 'Is the effective compromising the affective?' *British Educational Research Journal*, 29 (2), pp. 243–57.

McPhillimy, B. (1996) *Controlling Your Class*, Chichester: John Wiley.

Makins, V. (1997) *The Invisible Children: Nipping failure in the bud*, London: David Fulton.

Manning-Morton, J. and Thorp, M. (2003) *Times for Play*, Maidenhead: Open University Press.

Maynard, T. (2001) 'The trainee teacher and the school community of practice', *Cambridge Journal of Education*, 31 (1), pp. 39–52.

Mills, J. and Mills, R.W. (1995) *Primary School People: Getting to know your colleagues*, London: Routledge.

Morgan, N. and Saxton, J. (1991) *Teaching Questioning and Learning*, London: Routledge.

Morrison, K. (2001) 'Jurgen Habermas', in Palmer, J. A. (ed) *Fifty Modern Thinkers from Piaget to the Present*, London: RoutledgeFalmer.

Mosley, J. and Grogan, R. (2002) 'Quality Circle Time for Teachers', *Primary Practice*, 32 (Autumn) pp. 4–8.

Moyles, J. (ed) (2003) *Interactive Teaching in the Primary School*, Maidenhead: Open University Press.

National Primary Centre (NPC)/Oxfordshire County Council (1993) *Year 6 Teachers and More Able Pupils*, Oxford: NPC.

Neill, S. and Caswell, C. (1993) *Body Language for Competent Teachers*, London: Routledge.

Newell, S. and Jeffery, D. (2002) *Behaviour Management in the Classroom: A transactional analysis approach*, London: David Fulton.

Nias, D.J. (1989) *Primary Teachers Talking: A Study of Teachers at Work*, London: Routledge

Nias, D.J. (1997) 'Would schools improve if teachers cared less?' *Education 3–13*, 25 (3), pp. 11–22.

Nias, D.J., Southworth, G.W. and Yeomans, R. (1989) *Staff Relationships in the Primary School: a study of school cultures*, London: Cassell.

OFSTED (1993) *Achieving Good Behaviour in Schools*, London: HMSO Publications.

OFSTED (1998) *The Annual Report of Her Majesty's Chief Inspector of Schools*, London: The Stationery OFfice.

OFSTED (2003a) *Yes He Can: Schools where boys write well*, HMI 505, London: Crown Copyright.

OFSTED (2003b) *Expecting the Unexpected: Developing creativity in primary and secondary schools*, HMI 1612, London: Crown Copyright

O'Hara, M. (2004) *Teaching 3–8* (2nd edn). London: Continuum.

Olweus, D. (1993) *Bullying at School*, Oxford: Blackwell.

Orr, R. (2003) *My Right to Play*, Maidenhead: Open University Press.

Papworth, M. (2003) *Every Minute Counts*, London: Continuum.

Pollard, A. and Filer, A. (1996) *The Social World of Children's Learning*, London: Cassell.

Pye, J. (1987) *Invisible Children: Who Are the Real Losers at School?* Oxford: Oxford University Press.

Qualifications and Curriculum Authority (2000) *A Language in Common*, Sudbury: QCA Publications.

Qualifications and Curriculum Authority (2001) *Curriculum Guidance for the Foundation Stage*, Sudbury: QCA Publications.

Quinn, V. (1997) *Critical Thinking in Young Minds*, London: David Fulton.

Ransom, S. (1993) 'From an entitlement to an empowerment curriculum' in Barber, M and Graham, D. *Sense, Nonsense and the National Curriculum*, London: Falmer Press.

Rigby, K. (2001) *Stop the Bullying*, London: Jessica Kingsley Publishing.

Roffey, S. and O'Reirdan, T. (2003) *Plans for Better Behaviour in the Primary School*, London: David Fulton.

Rogers, B. (1998) *You Know the Fair Rule*, 2nd edn, London: Pitman Publishing.

Ruff, A.R. (2002) *Education Law: text cases and materials*, London: Butterworths.

Sage, G. (1993) *Child Abuse and the Children Act*, London: ATL Publications.

Salo, U. (2002) 'What a teacher! Students write about teachers', BERA Conference, September 2002, Exeter, England.

Sarason, S.B. (1999) *Teaching as a Performing Art*, New York: Teachers College Press.

School Teachers' Review Body (2003) *School Teachers' Pay and Conditions Document 2003*, London: The Stationery Office.

Sedgwick, F. (1989) *Here Comes the Assembly Man: A year in the life of a primary school*, Lewes: Falmer Press.

Sharman, C., Cross, W. and Vennis, D. (2000) *Observing Children: A practical guide*, London: Cassell.

Sharp, S., Thompson, D. and Arora, T. (2002) *Bullying*, London: RoutledgeFalmer.

Silcock, P. and Brundrett, M. (2002) *Achieving Competence, Success and Excellence in Teaching*, London: RoutledgeFalmer.

Skelton, C. (2001) *Schooling the Boys: Masculinities and primary education*, Maidenhead: Open University Press.

Smart, J. (1995) *Educational Visits*, Leamington Spa: Campion Communications.

Smith, J. and Lynch, J. (eds) (2005) *The Primary School Year*, London: RoutledgeFalmer.

Smith, P.K. (1994) 'Play and the uses of play', in Moyles, J. (ed) *The Excellence Of Play*, Maidenhead: Open University Press.

Sotto, E. (1994) *When Teaching Becomes Learning*, London: Routledge.

Spear, M., Gould, K. and Lee, B. (2000) *Who Would be a Teacher?* Slough: NFER.

Stacey, M. (1991) *Parents and Teachers Together: Partnership in primary and nursery education*, Maidenhead: Open University Press.

Stern, J. (2003) *Involving Parents*, London: Continuum.

Stierer, B., Devereux, J., Gifford, S., Laycock, E. and Yerbury, J. (1993) *Profiling, Recording and Observing: A resource pack for the Early Years*, London: Routledge.

Suschitzky, W. and Chapman, J. (1998) *Valued Children, Informed Teaching*, Maidenhead: Open University Press.

Thody, A. and Bowden, D. (2004) *Teacher's Guide to Self-Management*, London: Continuum.

Thomas, G. (1998) *The making of the Inclusive School*, London: Routledge.

Tickle, L. (2000) *Teacher Induction: The way ahead*, Maidenhead: Open University Press.

Tizard, B. and Hughes, M. (1984) *Young Children Learning: Talking and thinking at home and at school*, London: Fontana.

Tizard, B., Blatchford, P., Burke, J., Farquhar, C. and Plewis, I. (1988) *Young Children at School in the Inner City*, London: Erlbaum.

Torrance, H. and Pryor, J. (1998) *Investigating Formative Assessment*, Maidenhead: Open University Press.

Turner-Bisset, R. (2003) 'On the carpet: changing primary teacher contexts', *Education 3–13*, 31 (3), pp. 4–10.

University of Southampton (2002) Website http://www.pgce.soton.ac.uk/it/cm/questioning, accessed November 2003.

Varma, V.P. (1992) *The Secret Life of Vulnerable Children*, London: Routledge.

Varma, V.P. (ed) (1993) *Coping With Unhappy Children*, London: Cassell.

Varnava, G. (2002) *How to Stop Bullying: Towards a non-violent school*, London: David Fulton.

Vincent, C. (2000) *Including Parents? Education, citizenship and parental agency*, Maidenhead: Open University Press.

Walker, D.F. and Soltis, J.F. (1992) *Curriculum and Aims*, New York: Teachers College Press.

Waters, M. (1996) *Managing Your Primary Classroom*, London: Collins.

Watkinson, A. (2003a) *The Essential Guide for Competent Teaching Assistants*, London: David Fulton.

Watkinson, A. (2003b) *The Essential Guide for Experienced Teaching Assistants*, London: David Fulton.

Webb, R. (ed) (1994) *Cross-Curricular Primary Practice*, London: Falmer Press.

Wenham, M. (1995) 'Developing thinking and skills in the arts', in Moyles, J. (ed) *Beginning Teaching: Beginning Learning*, Maidenhead: Open University Press.

West, J. (1996) *Child-Centred Play Therapy*, 2nd edn, London: Arnold.

Whitbourn, S. (2003) *Education and the Human Rights Act*, Slough: EMIE/NFER.

Williams, J. and Ryan, J. (2000) 'National testing and the improvement of classroom teaching: Can they co-exist?' *British Educational Research Journal*, 26 (1), pp. 49–73.

Wise, S. (2000) *Listen to Me! The voices of pupils with emotional and behavioural difficulties*, Bristol: Lucky Duck Publishing.

Wolfendale, S. and Bastiani, J. (eds) (2000) *The Contribution of Parents to School Effectiveness*, London: David Fulton.

Woods, P. (1997) *Restructuring Schools, Reconstructing Teachers: Responding to change in the primary school*,

Maidenhead: Open University Press.

Woods, P. and Carlyle, D. (2002) 'Teacher identities under stress: The emotions of separation and renewal', *International Studies in Sociology of Education*, 12 (2), pp. 169–89.

Wragg, E.C. (1997) *Assessment and Learning*, London: Routledge.

Wragg, E.C. and Brown, G. (1993) *Explaining*, London: Routledge.

Wyse, D. (2001) 'Promising yourself to do better? Target-setting and literacy', *Education 3–13*, 29 (2), pp. 13–18.

Yelland, N. (ed) (1998) *Gender in Early Childhood*, London: Routledge.

Electronic sources

BBC Learning: http://www.bbc.co.uk/learning/index.shtml

BECTa: (British Educational Communications and Technology Agency): http://www.becta.org.uk

Curriculum Online (DfES): http://www.curriculumonline.gov.uk

General Teaching Council for England: www.gtce.org.uk

General Teaching Council for Scotland: www.gtcs.org.uk

General Teaching Council for Wales: www.gtcw.org.uk

Grid Club: http://www.gridclub.com

ICT Advice (Becta): http://www.ictadvice.org.uk

ICTeachers (resources for teachers): http://www.icteachers.co.uk

ICT in Schools (DfES): http://www.dfes.gov.uk/ictinschools

Inclusion: Supporting Individual Learning Needs (NGfL): http://inclusion.ngfl.gov.uk/

Infant Explorer (Kent LEA literacy website): http://www.naturegrid.org.uk/infant/

National Curriculum in Action: www.ncaction.org.uk/

National Curriculum Online: http://www.nc.uk.net/

NGfL (National Grid for Learning): http://ngfl.gov.uk

QCA (Qualifications and Curriculum Authority) includes links to Schemes of Work: http://www.qca.org.uk

Standards Site (DfES, includes links to QCA Schemes of Work): www.standards.dfes.gov.uk

Teacher Resource Exchange: www.tre.ngfl.gov.uk

TeacherNet: www.teachernet.gov.uk

The Schools Communication Unit of the DfES operate the electronic TeacherNet site. This resource helps teachers obtain relevant information quickly and easily. It is an indispensable site for obtaining information on educational topics.

Trainee-teacher.co.uk: www.trainee-teacher.co.uk/

TTA (Teacher Training Agency): http://www.canteach.gov.uk/

TTA QTS Skills Tests – ICT

http://www.tta.gov.uk/training/skillstests/ict/index.htm

TTA QTS Skills Tests – ICT (interactive practice material)

http://www.tta.gov.uk/training/skillstests/ict/practice/index.htm.

Teaching Ideas for Primary Teachers:

http://www.teachingideas.co.uk

TEEM (Teachers Evaluating Educational Multimedia): http://www.teem.org.uk

TES (Times Educational Supplement): http://www.tes.co.uk

TES Jobs http://www.tesjobs.co.uk/

UK Online (Government services and information online) http://www.ukonline.gov.uk

Virtual Teacher Centre (VTC): http://vtc.ngfl.gov.uk

Index